Writing Well

NINTH EDITION

Donald Hall
Sven Birkerts

with Foreword by
Sven Birkerts

PEARSON
Longman

New York • San Francisco • Boston
London • Toronto • Sydney • Tokyo • Singapore • Madrid
Mexico City • Munich • Paris • Cape Town • Hong Kong • Montreal

For Gerry McCauley

Acquisitions Editor: Lauren A. Finn
Senior Marketing Manager: Sandra McGuire
Production Manager: Bob Ginsberg
Project Coordination and Electronic Page Makeup: Tom Conville Publishing Services, LLC
Cover Designer/Manager: Wendy Ann Fredericks
Cover Photo: © Micheline Pelletier/Corbis Sygma
Senior Manufacturing Buyer: Alfred C. Dorsey
Printer and Binder: RR Donnelley & Sons Company, Crawfordsville
Cover Printer: Phoenix Color Corporation

Visit us at www.ablongman.com

ISBN 0-321-43901-5

1 2 3 4 5 6 7 8 9 10—DOH—09 08 07 06

Contents

Foreword

The title says a great deal. *Writing Well*—the three simple syllables and that strong participial thrust. Active and direct, they reflect the main ideal of American, if not English-language, prose. Who would seriously contest that clear rigor, or deny that Donald Hall, the book's originating author, is himself an exponent of those very virtues? Which is to say: Is there any reason for his more recently arrived coauthor to be shilling on behalf of the self-evident?

Alas, it seems there is. As enduring as the primary virtues are, they are also context-bound, and what might seem to be their self-evident character is continually contested in the shifting field of the culture. Simply and broadly stated, we live in an era when powerful forces are changing how we behave, think, and how we communicate with each other. Just consider: when Donald Hall first published *Writing Well* more than three decades ago, the personal computer was just a gleam in the technophile's eye. The earth was still flat and writing was still a business of paper and pen, typewriters and correcting tape. Nor had the academy begun to experience the onslaught of theory, that vast and baffling array of *ism*s that undermined so many of our basic assumptions about expression. Many other things were different as well, but these two elements are especially relevant to the teaching and practice of writing. Before taking them up further, though, we need to look back for a moment at the book's beginnings.

Donald Hall established himself decades ago as one of our most esteemed poets, essayists, and men of letters, and *Writing Well* was written to present this writer's inside understanding of the dynamics—the ways and means—of expression. To "get" the book, we have to know a few things about Hall's literary background. For instance, that he came of age in the heyday of the modernist movement, reacting to its traumatized and often fragmented view of the contemporary predicament with his own clear-eyed and tempered lyricism. His writing sought to affirm the meaning and continuity of subjective experience and the ongoing viability of tradition. But his was no knee-jerk reaction, for he also engaged modernism deeply, learning from its brilliant practitioners and—importantly—compiling what have become the definitive craft interviews with giants like Ezra Pound, T. S. Eliot, and Marianne Moore. In each he prized their intelligence, scope, and linguistic inventiveness.

When Hall came to put together his book on writing, his practitioner's view of the art, he naturally drew on his own sensibility, his voluminous reading, his years of working in multiple genres, and his literary ideals as tested by his encounters with modernism. The result was a wide-ranging, witty, supremely informative, and inspirational text, shaped at every turn by his hands-on sense of craft. Hall is a native New Englander, and *Writing Well* is in many ways a New Englander's book—turning a skeptical eye to ornament, rhetoric, and inflated expression, it honors the materiality of language, the virtue of plainspoken clarity, and the uses of informed craft. Basically, Hall believes that the principles of effective expression can be identified and mastered, and that the procedures of good writing can be taught. "Writing well" need not be wishful thinking.

Hall's text was enormously successful, especially in its early editions—this was a voice, an approach, that people had been waiting for—and several generations of its beneficiaries are out there putting its many wisdoms into practice. But as I suggested, certain large-scale developments have put pressure on our writing culture and made it necessary to revisit the founding premises of the book. This means looking more closely at the transformations wrought in recent decades by the rise of academic theory, and, in my view more important, the full-blown emergence and implementation of digital technology.

From the late 1970s to, say, the late 1990s, all areas of academia witnessed the explosion of postmodern theory. Emerging in the wake of the social unrest of the late 1960s and the counter-culture, theory ventured a deep suspicion of authority, of hierarchies, of hard and fast divisions between disciplines of thought; it waged a full-out war on formerly "stable" intellectual assumptions. All disciplines were deconstructed, their premises shown to be unfounded. Discourse was seen to be first, "semiotic," later "constructed," the product of the exchange of arbitrary signs. Intentionality was questioned, as was any reference to any larger explanatory "master narratives." Not surprisingly, the assumptions of clear writing were undermined—"destabilized"—at every turn. There was, according to the theoreticians, no natural utterance. Every assertion concealed bias, masked different kinds of power and ambition.

Theory had two major consequences, at least where writing is concerned. First, it cast doubt on the whole enterprise of sense-making, surrounding all former convictions with cloud layers of uncertainty, and making all assertion—the core impulse of much expository prose—seem misguided. Like some dreary weather system, it hung on and hung on.

The second influence was more immediate. Theory injected abstraction, jargon, and orders of complex qualification into writing. And if the main effects were felt in academe, the general proliferation of "hegemonies," "discourses," and "gendered nouns" seemed to sap all writing of its original vigor and decisiveness.

The undermining effect of theory has been seconded by the other major development of our time, our more or less wholesale conversion to electronic communications, a transformation so all-embracing that those of us who came of age before computers are hard put to remember how we did things "before." But we can feel the differences, in writing as in daily living. We've all read the articles and editorials deploring soundbyte mentality and the deleterious effects of E-mail diction on contemporary prose expression. But there is also the way our increasingly screen-oriented lifestyles are changing both what and how we read, and by and large pulling us away from more nuanced literary prose in favor of a streamlined (some would say "dumbed-down") idiom. I see no sign that things will ever revert to their pre-electronic status quo. Where writing is concerned, we are for better or worse living in a new dispensation.

Where does this leave *Writing Well*—or any other writing text for that matter? What kind of writing do we now practice and what do we who teach offer as our aims? Do we hurry to fit our pedagogy to usages we hear in our electronic info-sphere, or do we draw a line and pledge ourselves to a richer, more complex, more "experienced" paradigm. If we believe that our expressions condition our ways of being as much as our ways of being condition our expressions, then the answer is obvious. We continue to espouse the ideal of writing well.

First in our own practice, but then inevitably as teachers and textwriters, Don Hall and I look to ideals of vigor and accuracy, but also to suppleness and nuance. We consider written prose to be an instrument with broad expressive range allowing the writer to convey information and embody thought; to persuade and seduce, and also to map the full spectrum of our feelings. Hall long ago took this as his founding assumption. He understood, as any writer will, that the comprehension, the mastery, of the craft moves outward, from love of the materials—words—to fascination with the uses they can be put to: in sentences, paragraphs, and ever-larger expressive units. And indeed, *Writing Well* was conceived concentrically, as an expanding field of awareness, reach and application growing as the core elements of expression were integrated. The pedagogy is loose, supple, leaving room at every turn for other panoramas, but the overall effect—the feeling—is nonetheless one of expansion.

Every writing text conceals a bias—this much we know from theory. Ours in *Writing Well* is toward a love of materials and a love of making. Seen in the right light, there is nothing more fascinating—and useful—to contemplate than the sense-making operation. How words can be weighed, hefted, and aligned to meet the needs of expression—and how there is beauty in the process. Writing this, I see how much the love of the art informs every stage of the book's presentation, from the general reflections to the close-focus "how to" discussions, to the examples and questions. To love something is to believe in—to wish for—its continuation. Don and I both believe that what is honest, well-made, and from the heart survives all chaos of relativism. Writing is bound so closely to who we are that its principles remain constant. We have tried to honor these principles as practitioners as well as teachers.

Sven Birkerts

Prefaces to the Ninth Edition

D.H.:

Thirty years ago I daydreamed about writing a textbook for composition. The premise was simple, and it remains the premise of *Writing Well* as Sven Birkerts and I prepare this ninth edition. This book intends not only to recommend good writing but to exemplify it.

When I began teaching at the University of Michigan, composition teachers were required to employ a textbook that began: "Master all aspects of the essentials of effective communication as an aid to clarity in the thought process of expository writing." Well, it wasn't quite *that* bad. But many composition texts still prescribe correct prose in language stiff, drab, passive, shallow, boring, and trite. How can anyone learn good style by reading revolting language? We learn by observing actions, not by memorizing advice. "Do as I say, not as I do" fails in child rearing as it does in composition teaching. A textbook that speaks of "effective communication" resembles a father who screams at his son: "DON'T RAISE YOUR VOICE!"

In *Writing Well* we mean to teach correctness, good style, and originality together. There's no point in teaching original expression without also teaching the conventions that permit a reader to understand the writer's intention. Good writing connects one human being to another.

There is a naivety, common among young people, that finds revision insincere, as if the first attempt at expression were always the truest or best. We need invention and we need revision. As we put it elsewhere: "Writing is acquiring material and it is also ordering and cutting that material. The writer must be a paradoxical combination of opposites, the big spender and the miser." In the process of writing, these two qualities sometimes come in sequence: invention followed by revision. More often, in the real moment of composition, the writer goes back and forth between revision and creation so rapidly that it is hard to tell the one from the other.

We need to combine these opposites in order to connect with the reader—with our audience, which is at the heart of everything. Teaching a vigorous and combative class of composition, we meet the defense of the cliché: "But it's *exactly* what I mean!" The answer to this defense brings audience in. If the purpose of writing is to make a passage from writer to reader, the narcissistic defense—". . . what *I* mean . . ." —is irrelevant. As with bad mechanics, bad style obscures. The trouble with trite expressions, passives, dead metaphors, vague intensives, jargon, and modish words is that these stylistic errors block the way from writer to reader.

Writing Well begins with a chapter that introduces values and methods, using for example largely essays of personal reminiscence. The second chapter speaks of reading, and reader response, sketching the relationship between language and audience. The third chapter presents ideas of process, the practicalities of essay writing, and tells the life story of one composition.

In its crucial center, *Writing Well* goes from small to large—from words to sentences to paragraphs. Most readers find "Words" the best part of *Writing Well*. Although the word is at the center of this book, and at the center of all notions of style, in the real classroom it is necessary to teach everything at once—structure, thought, paragraphing, originality, diction, clarity. Teachers must follow the order of instruction that they prefer. Whatever order teachers follow, the word will govern its center.

S.B.:

To follow up on Donald Hall's observations: In the beginning was the word, and we're still at it. Working on revisions for this ninth edition, I was struck more than once by an incongruous thought. How do we account for the fact that approaches to the teaching of writing—and hence textbooks—seem to change with every academic year while the ideals of good writing remain more or less constant? Is it that we still don't know how to teach the arts of self-expression and sense-making, or are textbook publishers caught up in the same cycle of planned obsolescence that feeds the market for so many big-ticket items? Is there any way in which this edition is superior to its eight predecessors? Superior? No, I would not go that far. But I will say that various changes—some minor, some more significant— have given the text the equivalent of a good aerobic workout.

With every work, not least a textbook about writing, there are places—introductions, transitions, examples and exercises—that the writer cannot read over without feeling the desire to meddle, to rephrase. From the first edition to the ninth, *Writing Well* has gone through its modifications. We have changed things in the interest of freshness, in the interest of clarity, and here and there on a whim—because it feels good to change the sound of a sentence. Doing this, we try to amuse ourselves. But we also have in mind the many devoted users of the book—they are owed some new examples and turns of phrase.

Then there are the changes that are made to reflect changes in the larger world. Since Donald Hall first conceived of *Writing Well,* our cultural life has been transformed by the computer revolution. Reading and writing now take place in a very different context, a fact that some may deplore but no one can refuse to recognize. The pedagogy of this text has tried to reflect the changes where it must (in new modes of research and documentation) but it has also continued to fight a rear-guard action. That millions of users now type telegraphic bullets to one another on the Internet does not mean that prose style must become telegraphic. Quite the contrary: The more new technologies and their habits of use put pressure on certain ideals of expressive writing—like complexity and nuance—the more zealous a book like this must be about keeping those ideals alive. In other words: Don't expect a special revised Internet Edition of *Writing Well* anytime soon.

The biggest single change in this edition is a new chapter on Writing Research (Chapter 8). The computer has changed a great deal about the way in which research is carried out. The procedures of documentation have naturally followed suit. The new chapter, which discusses the various aspects of writing research, also follows one student through all phases of a research project, from initial conception to the gathering of information, and from the organization of perspectives to the final presentation.

But while the modes of searching for and harvesting materials have been entirely transformed, the core imperatives of the writing remain the same. The reader looks for clarity, precision, a command of perspectives and scales of importance, and—always—grace in verbal presentation. I am tempted to offer the tired maxim: *The more things change, the more they stay the same.* But the vigilant editor in me refuses: It is just too obvious.

ACKNOWLEDGMENTS

People from whom we derive our ideas of style are the writers whose work we love. We quote many of these writers here, so that they may speak in their own voices and need not depend on the articulation of admirers. We do not quote them all. We owe our senses of style, as well as some ideas about it, especially to modern writers we grew up reading and imitating: Ernest Hemingway, Ezra Pound, Marianne Moore, George Orwell, Gertrude Stein, James Joyce.

In earlier editions of *Writing Well,* Donald Hall benefited from the help of many people. Because their help persists in this edition, we mention them again. At Little, Brown, first publisher of this volume, many people helped in the earlier editions: Margaret Zusky, Rab Bertelsen, Jan B. Welch, Dale Anderson, Elizabeth Philipps, Donna McCormick, and David W. Lynch.

Lawrence Russ and Rosemary Yaco helped Donald Hall in Ann Arbor. Some of the teachers whose suggestions informed earlier editions were Donald Butler, Terrence Collins, Steven V. Daniels, H. Ramsey Fowler, Neita Gleiker, Federick Goff, Richard Larson, Thomas Lux, Russell J. Meyer, Marcia Stubbs, M. Elisabeth Susman, Barbara Wicks, and Peter T. Zoller. Fifth edition helpers included Sally Crisp, Mark Halperin, Carol Hayes, Celeste Martin, Alan McKenzie, and Barry Weller. In the fourth, fifth, and sixth editions, the editorial assistance of Linda Howe was extraordinary. Traveling around the country, Donald Hall profited from many conversations with teachers of freshman English and with directors of writing programs; particularly important were visits to Ball State University, Oakland University in Michigan, the University of Wisconsin at Stevens Point, the University of Vermont, Syracuse University, Orange Coast College, Macon Junior College, the University of Pittsburgh at Bradford, the C. W. Post Campus of Long Island University, the University of Wisconsin at Eau Claire, Jamestown Community College, Behrend College, Mercer College, the University of Utah, Lynchburg College, and the Poynter Institute. It is impossible to list the names of everyone who helped, but here are a few: Thomas Carnacelli, Peter De Blois, William Hiss, Frederick Bromberger, Joann Mercer, Diana Anderson, Charles Berger, Muriel Allingham-Dale, Doug Carlson, Lynn Matson, Lawrence Mobley, Margaret Woodworth, Richard Lindner, John Coates, Joseph Trimmer, Susan Bartels, Mary Jane Dickerson, Sally Ronsheim; and Sandra Donaldson and Celia B. Diamond who spoke by letter. With the sixth edition we noted the help of Lisa Ede of Oregon State University and David Skwire of Cuyahoga County Community College.

We have profited from many suggestions we have received from Thomas Adler, Linda Albright, Robert Aldridge, Nell Altizer, Nancy G. Anderson, Maureen Andrews, David Baker, Barry Bakorsky, Anna M. Barnes, Richard Bausch, J. Charles Berger. William W. Betts, Jr., Dorothee Bowie, Margaret Brady, May Brown, Carl Brucker, Ingrid Brunner, Nancy Bunge, Edward Byrne, Harriet Carr, Fern Chertkow, T. L. Clark, Jerry Coffey, Steve Connolly, Mary Copeland, Edward Corbett, Gary Culbert, Paul Dameen, David Dawson, Miriam Dow, Helen Dunn, Oliver Durand, Anne Elam, Mary J. Elkins, Thomas Elliott, Richard Fine, Gala Fitzgerald, William T. French, Michele Giannusa, Peggy Gledhill, Robert M. Gorrell, Barbara Griffin, Richard Grounds, Norman Hane, Joan C. Haug, David R. Hauser, Joyce Hicks, Kathryn Holmes, D. Howard, M. Huyser, Walter Isle, Thomas Johnson, Paul Kameem, Sighle Kennedy, Sharon King, Opal A. Lanett, Jim Ledford, Karen B. LeFerre, Merrill Lewis, Sherry McGuire, Alan T. McKenzie, Peter W. Mackinlay, Lynne McMahon, Ann Maioroff, Andrew Makarushtra, Silvine Marbury, Doreen Maronde, Timothy Materer, Celest A. Martin, Michael Martin, Paul F. Michelson, Sr., Jean Michaupt, Patricia Moody, Jim Moore, C. R. Moyer, Fred Muramunco, Helen Naugle, Kenneth Newman, Richard O'Keefe, Steven O'Neill, Janice Philbin, Adele Pittendrigh, George Pittman, Martha Rainbolt, Kate

Reavley, Kenneth Requa, Elizabeth G. Richards, Chris Rideout, Florence Roberts, Judy Rogers, Monroe Roth, Sherod Santos, Charlotte W. Sargeant, Ted Schaefer, Michael Sexon, Susan Simpson, Harriet Susskind Spiegle, Sandra Stancey, Diane Stege, J. Stege, Pamela Stith, Margaret A. Strom, Sharon Stuut, Kathleen Sullivan, J. C. Taylor, George J. Thompson, Charles L. Tilgham, Darlene Unrue, Linda Venis, Lucien A. Waddell, Ricki Wadsworth, Nancy Walker, Martha S. Waller, James Watt, Richard Widmayer, Diane Williams, Louis Williams, Thomas Wilson, and George Wymer.

Students who mail in completed questionnaires help us to revise this text for future students. From the second edition through the sixth, Donald Hall was helped by Clayton Hudnall of the University of Hartford. In all editions, Donald Hall must acknowledge his debt to the late Richard Beal, of Boston University, who supplied strengths in the areas of his own weaknesses, who was tireless and good-natured and relentless and kind. Mike Moran of the University of Georgia has helped us, and from the University of Rhode Island Robert Schwegler contributed mightily to the changes made in the sixth edition and in the seventh. Other invaluable helpers to the seventh edition include James Peterson, Alan Jacobs, Joanne Charbonneau, Ralph Latham, Sarah Gallagher, Ed Silva, Richard Johnson, John Pahl, Carol Long, Kelly Dobyns, Tony Magistrale. Special thanks to Richard Marius, Nancy Sommers, Pat Hoy, Gordon Harvey, Jonathan Aaron, Sue Lonoff, Norm Katz, William Corbett, and the rest of the Expository Writing Department at Harvard. For the eighth edition, Sven Birkerts also thanks Carol Arber at Harvard's Lamont Library.

The authors would also like to thank these reviewers who helped shape the eighth edition: Richard Newhauser, Trinity University; Peter Johnson, Providence College; Eric Sonstroem, Indiana University at Bloomington; Kathleen A. O'Fallon, Butler University; Steve Connelly, Indiana State University; Tayo Olafioye, Mesa College, San Diego; Margaret Posey, Nebraska Indian Community College; Mark Hoyer, University of California, Davis; Wendy Bishop, Florida State University; John Ruszkiewicz, University of Texas at Austin. A special debt of gratitude to Janice R. Walker, University of South Florida, for her help on the ninth edition.

Donald Hall
Sven Birkerts

1

Introduction: Writing, and Writing Well

WRITING TO MAKE CONTACT

The uses and pleasures of writing, like those of speech, are very nearly endless. They encompass a grand spectrum, from the most basic information-giving functions to the most creative sorts of expression. We write recommendations, progress reports, and personal letters; we may also, if so moved, write travelogues, espionage novels, or philosophical reflections. Different as these uses are, they share in common the fact that they are communications: They are words arranged for a purpose. And depending on how well they are arranged, they communicate more or less effectively. The faith of this book is not only that effective use of language—writing well—is essential at every level of human endeavor, but also that it is something that can be learned.

Writing, again like speech, uses language as its medium, and for this reason it is closely bound to thought—indeed, to identity itself. How we think—so it is often said—is how we are. The words we put on a page reflect how we think at a primary level. The business executive who cannot set down a simple string of thoughts is likely to have difficulty with certain speaking contexts as well. Conversely, a graceful, lucid style will be interpreted by most people as testifying to the clarity of the writer's thinking process.

But this does not mean that anyone is condemned to be inarticulate. On the contrary, by learning to pay attention to language, and by practicing and absorbing certain basic elements of expressive technique, nearly anyone can improve not only the effectiveness of the words on the page but also the thinking process that puts them there. Writing and thought *are* inextricably bound. Without clear thinking there can be no clear writing. Writing well means thinking well.

The link between writing and thought is not, however, as straight-forward as we might suppose. For usually we do not think, then write. The thinking takes place, some of it, in the act of writing. We may write in order to discover what it is we think; or we may write to hone our most basic notions, to find for them subtlety and shape. That is, we think in the act of finding words—accepting some and rejecting others. Our thought is incomplete until we find a language and a shape by which we can transmit it to others. An essay reflects the contour of our thought; its sentences develop thought and carry it across to others. We write well when our prose style gives pleasure while it performs its other—its reflective or descriptive or informative—tasks. Part of the basic pleasure that writing produces comes from the creation of an understanding in the mind of another.

Here is one student's impromptu opening for an in-class writing exercise on the subject of college roommates:

> I walked in the first day and I couldn't believe what I'm looking at. A mess. No, worse than that, a disaster. And sitting in the middle of it all was this funny-looking guy.

The writer is clearly at the rough pencil-sketch level of expression. We sense what he is trying to communicate, but only approximately. The sentences feel sloppy—slangy and fragmentary. The lack of images leaves us with but the most general impression. Reading, we wonder: "Walked in *where?*" "First day of *what?*" "What sort of mess—open luggage, broken eggs?" and "What makes this individual 'funny looking'?"

When the student took up this subject again later in the term, he had begun to work toward a more vivid and communicative style:

> Walking into a new home for the first time can be unsettling under any circumstances, but that September afternoon when I opened the door to Cromwell 121, I almost turned right around and fled. I thought that I had mis-remembered the number, that this was the storage room. There were boxes piled from floor to ceiling all along the back wall. There were, in front of me, skis, shoes, sweaters, books, computer parts, spools of wire, CDs, the remains of a pizza, and who knows what else. On the windowsill, in a cage, something brown was sleeping. And underneath the cage, cross-legged on the bed, sat one of the tallest human beings I had ever seen.

This writer has made enormous strides. He has put some thought into creating a scene; he has generated suspense. And no less important, he has included details, the kind a reader needs. The writer has, this time around, imagined for himself a reader, someone to whom he wants to communicate his impressions. A more skillful writer could do more, could linger on the ingredients of the mess to create a more humorous or outrageous impression. But then, nearly all writing can be refined and improved. Only the real masters defy the would-be editor.

The point here is basic, but essential: When we write, we make a contract: *my words are addressed to the outside world; I construct sentences in order to
reach someone else.*

THE IDEA OF AN AUDIENCE

In writing and revising, writers face a thousand choices that they resolve by *the idea of an audience.* It helps to pinpoint an audience in the mind,
as we write, the way a lecturer may pick out one face to address, as if everything were intended for the one face only. Sitting at a desk alone, with no
listening face to remind us, we need imagination to sustain the idea of an
audience. In other contexts we constantly imagine audiences: walking
alone, or driving, most of us daydream encounters and conversations; we
invent speech and counterspeech; we imagine contact and communication.
For that matter, think about how we talk on the telephone. Even though
our listener may be a thousand miles away, and even though we communicate for ear contact alone, using only variations of pitch, volume, and
rhythm to get our point across, we still tend to *gesture* as if we had the person in front of us. We gesture, smile, frown, raise eyebrows, and make faces.
On-line chat discussions sometimes allow the writer to use gestures and facial expressions as well, using programmed verbs and typographical features
that may even simulate tone of voice. We do these things not because we
forget that our friend cannot see us but because we communicate more
thoroughly when we imagine complete contact. *The idea of an audience generates contact.*

When we write words on a page we cannot raise and lower the volume
of our speech or make faces, but by keeping the idea of an audience steadily
in the forefront of our minds, we use the gestural resources of language to
make contact with another person across the space of our difference.

HONEST AND DISHONEST EXPRESSION

An idea of an audience implies that we have something to say to
someone else—and that it is something worth saying. Alas, much human
language seems to serve the purpose not of making contact or revealing
but of concealing or of providing the appearance of communication instead of the real thing. We are all aware of honest and dishonest expression.
We have grown up on the false laughter of television, the fake enthusiasm
of advertising, and the lying assertions of politicians. If some falsity has not
entered our prose, we are made of aluminum.

We can be false in a thousand ways. We do it by telling outright lies
and we do it by keeping silent. But in these instances we understand our
own falsity. When we fool *ourselves* we are in more trouble. We fool ourselves with words that can mean almost anything. How much have we said
when we call someone *liberal?* We fool ourselves when we avoid blame by

leaving *I* out of the sentence, as when we knock over a lamp and claim, "The lamp was knocked over" or "The lamp fell," as if it acted by itself. We also fool ourselves by using clichés, trite expressions that have become meaningless substitutes for feeling and thought:

> a vital part of our future   bottom line
> made it what it is today   name of the game

Clichés are little cinder blocks of crushed and reprocessed experience. When we use them in writing, we violate our agreement to construct sentences in order to reach someone else. Clichés are familiar and comfortable; they seem to mean something. Indeed, when they were first coined, as phrases or figures of speech, they were often memorable expressions. But excessive usage has drained the life from them. We hear the familiarity but the original force of meaning is lost. When I tell you that the *bottom line* is the *name of the game* and *just what the doctor ordered,* I am telling you very little.

Every profession—medicine, law, theater, business—has its own clichés. We call the clichés that belong to a profession its *jargon.* One set of clichés appears especially at graduations, from primary school through graduate school:

> the future belongs to you.
> the challenge of new . . .
> in today's world . . .
> responsibility, good citizenship, service to the community . . .

The university, in fact, is a great source of jargon. Here are two paragraphs from a letter addressed by a newly elected college president to his faculty.

> Dear Members of the State College Community:
>
> I am deeply honored and challenged by the opportunity to join State College as its seventh president. The hospitality and spontaneous warmth of everyone we have met has made both Barbara and me feel very welcome. We look forward to making State our home as quickly as we can arrange an orderly transition from our current responsibilities.
>
> State College is rich in tradition: it is an institution with a past, and, more importantly, it is a college with a future. Building on its heritage, and maximizing its resources, State College can continue to achieve distinction by providing educational opportunities for young men and women.

This is the language we expect from officials—from politicians and bureaucrats, from the presidents of colleges and the presidents of corporations. It says nothing, and it says it with maximum pomposity. Every phrase is trite, and the phrases are stuck together with mortar like *is* and *and* and *with.* The edifice is reprocessed garbage:

> deeply honored
> challenged by the opportunity

> spontaneous warmth
> making . . . our home
> orderly transition
> current responsibilities
> rich in tradition
> building on its heritage
> maximizing its resources
> achieve distinction
> providing educational opportunities

One should mention as well the trite and meaningless contrast between the past, as in *heritage*—a word as hokey as *home*—and *a college* with *a future*. The contrast says nothing. Unless the collegiate doors are closing tomorrow, of course it has *a future*.

In the college president's letter, the smoothness of the masonry is exceptional, but the passage is almost without content. If we call the paragraphs insincere, it is because they express only conventional notions, not anybody's own ideas or feelings. Of course the author did not *intend* insincerity, nor did he feel that he was lying.

Sincerity has everything to do with the reasons for writing well. Peter Elbow says:

> I warn against defining sincerity, as telling true things about oneself. It is more accurate to define it functionally as the sound of a writer's voice or self on paper—a general sound of authenticity in words. The point is that self-revelation . . . is an easy route in our culture and therefore can be used as an evasion: it can be functionally insincere even if substantially true and intimate. To be precise, *sincerity is the absence of "noise" or static—the ability or courage not to hide the real message.*

The static is the distance between what the words say and what we sense lies behind them. The person with a pose of sincerity fixes us with his eyes, saying, "I am going to be wholly honest with you. I am a bastard. I cheat on my girlfriend and I steal my roommate's toothpaste." The real message has designs on us: "Love me, I'm so *honest.*"

The distance between the meaning (the apparently stated) and the expression (the really implied) ruins the statement and prevents real communication between people. The one exception might be the *ironic* statement, where the speaker trusts that her listener will feel the distance and pick up her point all the more acutely. A mother walking into the war zone of her daughter's bedroom might say: "This is lovely. I see that you heard what I asked you to do this morning." Most children will pick up the meaning behind the expression.

Sincerity is *functional* (Elbow's word) if we believe it, if we hear the voice of a real person speaking forth in the prose—whether of speech or of the written word. We must speak in a voice that sounds natural to reach the ears of other people. But finding this natural voice is not easy; the natural voice is usually not the spontaneous voice, for when we write without examining our words we often speak words that are trite and ordinary or even institutional. Writing well requires self-criticism, hard thinking, and analysis. It is worth it. Socrates made the commitment: the life that is unexamined is not worth living.

PLAGIARISM

We have been talking about the kind of dishonesty in writing that anyone can slide into without meaning to. But there is also the deliberate dishonesty of plagiarism, which we should speak of early in our approach to writing: stealing someone else's good writing is not an acceptable form of writing well.

Plagiarism is stealing the words or ideas of others and presenting them as our own. It is like cheating on tests; it is trying to steal a better grade. Obviously plagiarism is self-defeating because we cannot learn if we use somebody else's accomplishments as a substitute for our own endeavors.

It is also wrong.

Now I call it deliberate dishonesty and it is usually just that: the plagiarist props open a book beside the typewriter and copies word for word. However, some people come to college unsure of what plagiarism is. The ease with which computer files can be downloaded and copied has further confused many people. We are so accustomed to hearing and using other people's words that we forget where the lines are drawn. The matter is simple. The written word is a form of private property—and the use of that property without proper acknowledgment (or, in some cases, permission) is theft. In our society theft is punished. Every year, it seems, we read of cases of high-ranking politicians or scholars losing their positions and suffering embarrassment because they plagiarized.

When we consult any written source, on any subject we write about, we should take a note of that source (book, encyclopedia, magazine, newspaper, radio program, television show, electronic file) and list this source when we hand in our paper. (See pages 261–265 on documentation). If we quote from a source, we should use quotation marks *and* identify the source. But also, *if we use an idea—or sequence of ideas—from a source, even though we put it in our own words, we must always give the source of the idea.* If we take these precautions, no one can ever accuse us of plagiarism.

NEVER REPEAT ANYBODY ELSE'S IDEAS OR WORDS WITHOUT ACKNOWLEDGMENT.

EXAMINING THE WORDS

Writing well can be a starting point for all thinking. Self-examination finds what we have inside us that is our own. Understanding the self gives us a certain objectivity; it allows us to move outside the self, to read, to analyze, to define, and thus to make contact outside the self, with others. Self-examination, which may sound like an egotistical thing, can actually lead to the opposite. Self-examination can provide the basis for moving outside the self; looking inward is the basis for looking outward; writing is a social act that begins in privacy.

Of course we are stuffed with clichés—we have been exposed to them all our lives—but clichés are not "our own." We have swallowed everything that has ever happened to us: we dropped the bottle to the floor at the age of eight weeks and cried for the lack of it; the telephone did not ring last week, and we cried for the lack of it; the toy shines under the tree, the toy rusts behind the garage; the smell of bacon, the smell of roses, the smell of kittens and the litter in their box; the flowers and the beer cans emerging from the snow. Everything that ever happened to us remains on file in our heads. As a professor at MIT put it: the human brain is a big computer made of meat. The one difference is that we cannot call everything up just by punching a key. Large portions of what we have stored will only come back if the memory is somehow activated.

If the brain is a computer, we are all engaged in learning how to operate it. For the college president quoted above, the task of writing was simple: he was programmed to write that kind of prose; he pushed the right keys and his brain computer turned out preassembled units of academic jargon. But let us suppose that we are interested in something genuine, the voice without static, the utterance in which expression and meaning are the same. We must learn new ways to use the accumulation of words, sense impressions, and ideas that we keep on disk in the brain. Our words must not make rows of identical houses like the subdivision prose of cliché. "New" is fresh, genuine, ourselves, our own experience. Making it new, we make contact with the reader.

Freshness is not, however, the inevitable result of spontaneity. Writing freely, without pausing for correction, is a good way to practice writing, to learn to flow, and to uncover hitherto unsuspected material. It can be important to develop a sense of freedom in writing. But then there is the second half of genuine expression, the half that applies the mapmaker's more objective examination to the new country that has been explored. Examination and analysis, leading to revision, allow the writer to communicate with other human beings. Revising the map, we think of the reader; we revise to make contact with the reader. The idea of an audience must govern us. Writing well is a social act.

REVISING THE MAP

Almost all writers, almost all the time, need to revise. We need to revise because spontaneity is never adequate. Writing that is merely emotional release for the writer becomes emotional chaos for the reader. Even when we write as quickly as our hand can move, we slide into emotional falsity, into cliché or other static that prevents contact. We make leaps by private association that leave our prose unclear to others. We often omit steps in thinking or use a step that we later recognize as bad logic. Sometimes we overexplain the obvious. Or we include irrelevant detail. First drafts remain first drafts. They are the material that we must shape, a marble block that the critical brain chisels into form. We must shape this material in order to pass it from mind to mind; we shape our material into a form that allows other people to receive it. This shaping often requires us, in revising, to reorganize whole paragraphs, both the order of sentences and the sentences themselves. We must drop sentences and clauses that do not belong; we must expand or supply others necessary to a paragraph's development. Often we must revise the order of paragraphs; often we must write new paragraphs to provide coherent and orderly progress.

Good writing is an intricate interweaving of inspiration and discipline. We may need one strand more than the other. Most of us continually need to remember both sides of writing: *we must invent, and we must revise.* In these double acts, invention and revision, we are inventing and revising not just our prose style but our knowledge of ourselves and of the people around us. Like an artist going over a hastily drawn contour, we revise to get closer to the true perception. When Confucius recommended, "Make it new," he meant that we should keep faith with ourselves by responding honestly—and thus, freshly—to the world around us.

THEMES AND REVISIONS

On the first day of class the instructor asked the students to write for twenty minutes on "How I Came to College." Here is an impromptu theme by Nina Chan:

> My family has always valued education above everything else. One of the reasons they came to America from China was because they saw this as a land of opportunity for education. Their dream was to have their children attend the college of their choice and make a contribution to society. My parents and my uncle (we are a close family) worked very hard to make this dream a reality. My uncle paid for my violin studies for many years, and when he heard that I had been accepted into college he said, "I feel as if my own daughter had gotten that letter." Now that I'm here I'm terribly afraid to disappoint the people who wish so much for me. I can't fail them. When I attended a dorm seminar the other night on "pressure," I knew just what the counselor was talking about. Still, I had to wonder as I listened to him speak—is it pressure or is it just love? Or are the two sometimes the same?

Nina's in-class theme shows us a writer on the verge of finding her subject. The passage begins with sentiments from the cliché bin. Nina is expressing herself in the language of application forms, stringing together one trite phrase after another: "land of opportunity for education," "college of their choice," "Make a contribution to society," and so on. It is not clear whether Nina writes clichés because she thinks her teacher wants to hear them or because she believes that these phrases actually express her situation. She does not yet understand that the cliché is an obstacle to communication, a language device favored by those who have nothing to say or else would conceal the truth. The reader encountering a phrase like "contribution to society" absorbs it as automatically and unreflectingly as it was produced.

Midway through her theme, however, Nina approaches genuine expression. When she writes that her uncle said, "I feel as if my own daughter had gotten that letter," we begin to feel the emotional bonds that hold this family together. And when Nina admits to her fear of failure, we sense that she is closer to letting us know what her college experience has been like. Her mention of the dorm seminar solidifies the impression. The last two sentences allow us to understand her dilemma clearly. By including the detail about the dorm seminar she begins to persuade her reader. The anecdote suggests the pressure she is under. Showing makes contact; telling avoids it.

Later in the term, after her teacher discussed various strategies for introducing and developing personal narratives—and after a big change in her life—Nina decided to turn the subject of her impromptu theme into an essay. This time she began with the episode of the dorm seminar and went on to tell the *real* story of her college experience.

To Be (Myself) or Not to Be
Nina Chan

Sometime during the second week of college, I saw a sign posted by the dining hall: "STRESSED ABOUT SCHOOL?" The notice advertised an open seminar to be held that very evening in the Common Room of my dorm. The speaker was a psychologist who worked as the head counselor over in the Administration Building.

The fact that I attended says something about my state of mind. Classes had barely begun and I was already a walking disaster. I was having trouble sleeping, I was doing way too much snacking, and at least twice a day I broke down and cried for no reason. For no reason—ha!

I went to the seminar and started to take notes. The counselor was funny and tried to make everyone feel that being stressed was normal. I laughed along for a while, but then my mind started to drift. I see it now as one of those movie sequences: the voice was droning on in the background, but I was focusing on images from my memory. I was looking at scenes of family life.

What did I see? I saw my family—my mother and my two brothers and I—sitting at the dinner table waiting for my father to come home from his job. I saw my brothers poking each other and my mother saying (in Chinese), "Be respectful. Your father will want to see you behaving." And just as silence was restored my father walked in, smiling, tired, kissing us all before he changed for dinner and his night duties at his brother's restaurant.

I saw, or rather *heard,* my parents and uncle talking about me. They were sitting together in the living room and I was outside the door, eavesdropping. "I'll pay for two years," said my Uncle Lu, "and if her teacher thinks she has a real chance for the top, we will talk again."

And then I saw the ten years swirled together into a single picture. I was all ages at once, and short and tall. The one thing that stayed the same was the violin. It perched on my shoulder and I worked the bow. Practicing, practicing, practicing. In that one picture were the endless hours, the missed parties, all the frustrations and breakdowns. But there were also the good things: the times I got the Mozart piece right, the excitement I felt as I trained for my debut concert, the prizes I won. Those prizes put my extracurriculars over the top and helped me get into college—the first member of our family ever to get this far.

But then, just like in a movie, the images faded and I found myself back on a sofa in the Common Room. I felt more tears coming. I tried to listen to the counselor, to distract myself. He was saying, "You can't be all things to all people. You have to figure out, 'What is important for *me?*'"

That was what did it for me. I tiptoed out the door and ran up the stairs to my room. It was a good thing that my two roommates were out; I didn't want to talk to anyone. I had something to figure out. How was I going to tell my family that I did not want to be a violinist?

Everything around me mocked my situation. There was the music stand with the Prokofiev concerto, and there was my case on top of the bureau. I felt that I would go crazy if I had to pick that instrument up one more time and face those notes. But how could I stop? What would I say when my father called, as he did every Sunday, and asked, "How is the practicing?" Which would be worse, I wondered: not practicing or lying? My father would say: lying. But how would he feel if I told him the terrible truth, that I knew deep down that I was not cut out to be a concert violinist; that I had met some real musicians here and had realized right away that I did not burn to play in the same way they did? He would be shocked, depressed. He would remind me of the huge sacrifices that my Uncle Lu had made, how the whole family waited for me to become a famous violinist. He would say I was selfish, putting myself before the family. Could I tell him what the counselor had said, that you can't be all things to all people?

I have never known such pain as I felt that week. I called in sick for practice and missed half of my classes. I lay in bed under a mountain of covers and tried to ignore my roommates. When they were out I cried. There were moments when I thought I was losing my mind.

Then it was Sunday. The phone rang, as always, at 10:30. My family is nothing if not predictable. Or so I thought. After greeting everyone, I asked to talk to my father alone. He must have sensed that something was wrong because he was patient and spoke softly. This surprised me. I took a breath and said—it was the longest sentence I had ever spoken—that I wanted to give up the violin. Then I waited. Silence. I thought my head was going to burst. And then I heard my father's voice—almost a whisper. "Is that all?" he said. I nodded, before I remembered I was on the phone. "Yes." Another silence. And then, almost as if he was smiling, he said: "Set the violin aside, Nina. Don't get yourself worried. You are in college and you have important work to do."

I almost fell off the bed. But he was serious. He told me how he had been wondering when I would tell him. He had noticed for a long time that I was not as excited about my playing. "You have a long life in front of you," he said. And that was all. But as I held the phone and dabbed at my face with tissue, I realized something. I realized that love goes both ways. I had been so upset because I loved my parents and didn't want them to suffer. But they also loved me, and if love is anything, it is not wanting the other person to feel pain.

I think about these things a great deal now—every time I look inside my closet and see my brown violin case packed away in the corner.

Nina's essay, written only two months after her in-class theme, shows that she has made great progress in understanding the principles of good writing. To begin with, she has broken through the cliché barrier. Nina's essay tells of a real experience by using a writing voice that is her own. The reader realizes right away that the writer is not relying on formulaic expressions and secondhand sentiments. Nina is making an effort to tell the truth about her experiences and feelings, and we are won over to her cause.

But sincerity and naturalness are not enough by themselves. For an essay like this to work we must also be engaged by the narrative. All the honest declaration in the world is useless if the prose meanders pointlessly from place to place. Nina avoids this meandering through her use of a number of sound narrative strategies. For one thing, she elects to begin her reflective account with action—seeing the sign for the dorm seminar— thus leading the reader in immediately. To use the parlance of the Hollywood producer, she "cuts right to the chase."

The Hollywood connection is apt, for Nina has also found a way to dramatize her dilemma by depicting it through cinematic descriptions. Not only does the device allow her to organize what might otherwise seem random flashbacks, but also she establishes strong reader identification. We all know how movie flashbacks work, and we are interested to see how this author will adapt them for her own purposes.

Finally, Nina uses suspense, the most reliable of all narrative techniques. She sets the reader up, conveying her fear of her father's reaction to her news. We feel tense as we read toward the final scene. And then, when Nina has us poised ("Then I waited. Silence."), she hits us with the shock of reversal ("'Is that all?' he said.") We finish the essay feeling that we have been taken through an emotional cycle: There is a satisfying sense of closure.

Not only did Nina find a dramatic structure for her presentation, but also she used good detail. From the mention of the "sign posted by the dining hall" to the final image of the "brown violin case," the reader is able to picture what Nina is writing about. She has followed the cardinal wisdom: Showing makes contact; telling avoids it.

Nina's essay was the product of hard work. She wrote several versions before finding an approach that seemed right to her, and then she spent several hours revising. There were many breakthroughs along the way; each taught her something about the writer's craft. The most important recognition, however, was voice. To write the essay she wanted—needed—to write, Nina had to keep faith with her own perceptions and her own mode of expression.

EXAMPLES FROM PRINT

Nina Chan's original essay was impromptu, and the revision printed here came two months later. People who spend their whole lives writing often take longer still and struggle with the same enemies, disunity and evasion. Habitual writers differ from beginners in many ways. For one thing, they know that they are likely to fail at first. Some writers know that they may be weak in details; to succeed they must struggle to generate more of them. Others know that they often generate too many details and lose clarity of organization; to succeed they must pare words and organize. Whatever their problems, professionals learn to be patient. They expect writing to be hard work. They struggle with the same materials as beginners do and strive for a voice that makes contact with others.

People who write well begin by reading well. Reading good prose with close attention, we can acquire the manners that make the good writing we admire. We learn by immersion. The process can be compared to learning a foreign language by living with a family that speaks it. We pick up all kinds of information unconsciously—information that is often available to us when we want to produce certain effects in our own writing. Of course there is reading and reading: different uses of language condition us in different ways.

By way of introduction, take this opening passage from Robert A. Caro's biography of Lyndon Johnson. Notice how the author launches a work that will span not only a long and active political life but a tumultuous century as well:

> On the day he was born, he would say, his white-haired grandfather leaped onto his big black stallion and thundered across the Texas Hill Country, reining in at every farm to shout: "A United States Senator was born this morning!" Nobody in the Hill Country remembers that ride or that shout, but they do remember the baby's relatives saying something else about him, something which to them was more signif-

icant. An old aunt, Kate Bunton Keale, said it first, bending over the cradle, and as soon as she said it, everyone saw it was true, and repeated it: "He has the Bunton strain." And to understand Lyndon Johnson it is necessary to understand the Bunton strain and to understand what happened to it when it was mixed with the Johnson strain—and, most important, to understand what the Hill Country did to those who possessed it.

Robert A. Caro, *The Years of Lyndon Johnson: The Path to Power*

What might appear at first glance to be just a colorful bit of anecdote is in fact a highly strategic announcement of the biographer's theme, and it merits a closer inspection. The first sentence alone compresses a wealth of suggestion. The terms are mythic and are rendered as such. The "white-haired grandfather" is said to have "leaped" onto his "big black stallion" and "thundered"—we think of Paul Revere's legendary ride. And the contrast between the old man's white hair and the stallion's black is nothing if not dramatic. Moreover, we are instantly placed in a time and a geographical setting. This is "Texas Hill Country" and it is the era before the car and the telephone are in use. But the most important element of that sentence, the one we nearly overlook in reading, is the phrase "he would say"—"he" being Johnson himself. At a stroke we have learned how he liked to regard his own origins.

No less significant, however, are the opening words of the following sentence: "Nobody in the Hill Country remembers that ride . . ." The suggestion, of course, is that Johnson may have had a fondness for exaggeration, if not, in certain instances, outright invention. Such a suggestion has to carry weight when the biography is of one of our country's presidents.

The rest of the paragraph develops an equally important set of notions. For one thing, it introduces the idea of family characteristics and proposes the importance of the "Bunton" strain. At the same time, it creates suspense, planting in the reader's mind a pair of questions. One: What *was* the Bunton strain? And two: What was it about the Texas Hill Country that so affected the people who lived there? Answers to both questions will go a long way toward helping us understand the life and actions of this self-styled legend.

A closer look, then, shows us just how deftly Caro uses dramatic suggestion, detail, contrast, and suspense, and how deceptive this plainspoken anecdotal presentation in fact is.

Or take another paragraph, from fiction this time. One of the great prose stylists in American literature is Ernest Hemingway, who worked carefully on rhythm and sound. When he began writing as a young man, he studied style and practiced and revised, to learn the way to his own voice. He believed that the sounds of the words and subtle changes in the pacing of sentences helped to make the sense, or meaning, more vivid. A short story called "In Another Country," about some wounded soldiers in a hospital in Italy during World War I, opens with this paragraph:

> In the fall the war was always there, but we did not go to it any more. It was cold in the fall in Milan and the dark came very early. Then the electric lights came on, and it was pleasant along the streets looking in the windows. There was much game hanging outside the shops, and the snow powdered on the fur of the foxes and the wind blew their tails. The deer hung stiff and heavy and empty, and small birds blew in the wind and the wind turned their feathers. It was a cold fall and the wind came down from the mountains.

Such a simple style! And if we try to imitate it, we are likely to lace one shoe to the other. Reading it, we may notice that the grammar is simple, yet the length of sentence and clause—the units of rhythm—varies continually. We have to listen, to pay attention. The vocabulary is also simple—*the fall, cold,* and *wind* repeated, *wind* four times in the last three lines—yet expressive. The effect of the whole is hypnotic or dreamy, almost like a child's story; the war is around us, but *we* are not in it. Then the paragraph ends with the corpses of animals, described in loving detail. Look at the word *pleasant;* normally, we might find this word too general and want to ask *how,* exactly, did you feel? But here, in the emotions of the paragraph, the vagueness is an accurate understatement; it embodies the emotional restraint in this removal from war, the tentative acceptance that *we* are alive, unlike the animals outside the shops and the unmentioned combatants among whom *we* used to count ourselves. Though we don't generally think about how these effects are achieved as we react, we nonetheless pick them up. The more we read successful prose, the more likely we are to absorb the different ways that authors give their expression vigor and precision.

DISORGANIZED WRITING, POMPOUS WRITING

For a perverse sort of fun, let us rewrite the Hemingway passage in a couple of bad versions. We can call this exercise *downwriting,* turning something good into something bad. This practice can be instructive as we learn how to write. Mostly, we will try to improve bad writing; but sometimes we will imagine how we might have flubbed the opportunity for good writing that someone else took advantage of.

First, a parody (an imitation of a style, for the sake of mockery: a kind of downwriting) of the disorganized writing that most of us start with:

> September through December, in the fall, at any rate, the war still went on, but we ourselves weren't doing the fighting by this time. It got chilly then in the Italian city of Milan. It started to get dark earlier in the day. When it got dark they turned on the lights. It was nice to look in the windows of stores. There were a lot of dead wild animals outside of the stores. When it snowed it snowed on the animals' fur too. There was a lot of wind and it blew the animals' fur and it even blew the little ones around. It was really cold because the wind was coming down from the mountains, which were cold.

Actually, this parody is better than the prose most of us write at first because the writer observes real things. Most bad writing omits anything that might be interesting and expressive. The whole paragraph might be reduced to

> It was fall in Milan, Italy, one year during World War I. It got colder and the days got shorter.

But the short version omits all feeling. In the real paragraph, details of image and action carry the scene to the reader. You cannot reduce *War and Peace* to a telegram.

Or we could try it in Pompous Institutional Moderne, the language of the bureaucrat:

> During the autumn, the hostilities continued to ensue, but we personally no longer engaged in them. The daily temperature declined in Milan as the autumn continued, and the hours of daylight gradually contracted. When darkness ensued, lights were illuminated. It was altogether agreeable to promenade and investigate the contents of shop windows. There was considerable unrationed meat available at this particular time, by reason of the prevalence of slaughtered wild animals. Precipitation in the form of snow, as the months progressed, accumulated on the fur of these slaughtered beasts, and the cold breeze that accompanied the snow caused the tails of the animals to wave. Venison was at the present time available, as was small fowl. The extreme cold of this autumn is attributable to the fact that the prevailing winds came from the direction of the mountains, which because of their elevation and the snow which had already accumulated thereon, were lower in terms of temperature than the temperature which normally prevailed in the city.

This last writer, if he or she existed, might be elected chairperson of the Senior Class Gift Committee but would never by such language make contact with another human being. We learn to write well, if we learn, for good reason. If we write with the chaos of the first parody or with the pomposity of the second, we are in trouble in our heads and our hearts, not just in our writing. If we learn to write well, we will sharpen our wits on the one hand and limber up our imagination on the other—both together, or neither at all.

LEARNING TO WRITE WELL

How then do we learn to write well? The whole of this book tries to answer the question. But here at the outset let us mention three things that are essential. First, we can learn to read well, training ourselves to be vigilant and responsive. Reading helps writing by cultivating the verbal intelligence; it helps slowly, but it keeps on helping. Not only do we learn by example, absorbing the sound of good prose, the techniques, but we may also find ourselves acquiring the critical reflex. After reading a passage that strikes us in some particular way, we can pause to assess just how the writer achieved his effects. Was it through some vivid use of language, or some deft bit of narrative strategy? How did the writer use details to create a scene, or verbs to shape the presentation of an action? See the next chapter for more about reading.

Second, we can make it our practice to study writing—much as we might study any other subject. For good writing is not a mystery (though great writing is), and stylists are usually made, not born. We can learn the basic rules that govern prose writing, studying sentence structure, syntax, figures of speech, and the principles of persuasion and argumentation.

Third, and most important, we can write and rewrite and rewrite. It is axiomatic that we learn a good deal more by rewriting one passage five times than by writing five new passages and simply moving on. Rewriting is what allows us to see our prose as a made thing and to try out ways to make it better. Because rewriting our own work is so helpful, we must have writing to rewrite. We can start, possibly, by keeping a notebook or a journal. We can also look back to old papers and essays we have written for other classes. In these pages we may find a good deal of raw material to practice upon. Just like all professional writers, we must learn not to regard what we have put on the page as inviolable. Looking back without illusions develops the critical sense, which then becomes yet another path leading forward.

This rewriting process requires a great deal of attention. The writer spends more time listening, often, than she does putting words on a page. Listen to the sounds of words in combination, to their rhythms, and to the nuances of sense. *Is this what I am after?* For this reason, it may be advisable to work at rewriting with paper and pencil rather than at the computer. Rapid keystrokes and painless deletions often leave a writer satisfied with work that is merely competent.

Daily Writing

While we are learning to write, it is essential to write every day. Writing constantly will ease the work of writing and will give us a collection of words in which to look for ideas to develop and for sentences to revise.

Writing is a skill, like an athletic skill, which comes more naturally to some people than to others but which improves with practice for everyone. Practice is a necessity. Maybe the best method is to write daily dated entries in a notebook. This notebook sounds like a journal, but for most people a journal is like a diary and records merely the day's events:

> Had pancakes for breakfast. 9 o'clock boring . . .

Little entries that set out our daily schedule do not help us. Better are memories, whole anecdotes, ideas, and queries. Or it may help to concentrate on the world outside the self. Try describing some common object as accurately as you can—as if no one had ever seen it before. Ask yourself what details a painter's eye might select.

Doing daily writing means writing a page or two a day, every day, seven days a week, working rapidly and without trying to impose a direction on it, without conscious control or focus. Nor should a daily entry be continuous, necessarily. Some days one has apparently unrelated flashes of thought or memory. Some days one seems to have no ideas at all. On such a day, you may let your hand flow over the page with disconnected words and phrases.

Daily writing helps fluency, ease, and supply, but it gives us no practice in making shapes directed toward a reader: our work toward an audience, and our work on organization, will derive from social occasions like classes and conferences and from imagining social encounters. But in the meantime, daily writing will improve the fluency that we will later use for contact with others.

The novelist F. Scott Fitzgerald kept a notebook in which he recorded situations, observations, jokes, and anything else. Notice the sharpness of his details and images. The writer is never off-duty.

> Family quarrels are bitter things. They don't go according to any rules. They're not like aches or wounds, they're more like splits in the skin that won't heal because there's not enough material.
>
> Jules had dark circles under his eyes. Yesterday he had closed out the greatest problem of his life by settling with his ex-wife for two hundred thousand dollars. He had married too young, and the former slavey from the Quebec slums had taken to drugs upon her failure to rise with him. Yesterday, in the presence of lawyers, her final gesture had been to smash his finger with the base of a telephone.
>
> Run like an old athlete.

Daily writing can loosen minds. Our minds are made stiff, not by intellect, but by ready-made formulas of thought, by clichés both of phrase and of organization. These are restrictions we can do without. An economics student wrote this entry one day:

> Blue clouds in Arizona. I was hitchhiking last August, at the edge of the desert waiting for a ride that would take me across state. A little tree, a little shade. Sun so hot it melted turtles. Blue clouds of Arizona. Because there were no clouds at all, just blue glaring and turning white toward the sun. Like an egg only a lot brighter and hotter. Got a ride with a truck driver. "Never went to college myself. The war came along and then I had kids, you know. My daughter's at State." Jiggle. Oil. Hot. We had cheeseburgers in an airconditioned diner and I never felt so good in my whole life as when that ice-air hit me. Then the heat outside. Walking into the oven. [cliché]

There is no point to his story, or maybe no story. No one said he had to make a point. All he had to do was write a page. He was practicing. But along the way he found the powerful descriptive phrase "just blue glaring and turning white toward the sun." Fitzgerald might have been happy to hit upon such language.

Beginning a notebook of daily writing, almost everyone is shy and stiff, as if this private writing were a public performance. One student began her notebook:

> I am not "an emotionalist," if such a word exists. I feel as if I'm taking a step forward in saying that I tend not to be sincere in my writing. From this point forward I shall try to do so. I feel that I'm honest with myself, but when I know that others will read my work I unconsciously become dishonest as I write.
>
> If I were to write a short essay on any topic and hand it to a person to read, I wouldn't stay in the same room while the person read my work. Whether this is because of shyness or embarrassment, or both, I don't know.

Two months later, her prose was less self-conscious and more relaxed, and she seemed to enjoy herself more.

> They try to give something special every week. When I read eggrolls listed on the menu, I thought, great, my favorite thing in the world. But to my dismay, I was shocked at what the Stockwell Cafeteria had done. How could they destroy *my* eggrolls? I bit into one of them and I noticed *black,* inside my eggroll. Shortly later, I discover that *raisons* had been planted in the eggrolls! Raisons! How could they! It seemed that they just sat around saying, "What can we put in the eggrolls to make them terrible? We can't lose our image!" Of all the stupid things. That's enough to start a new war with China!

Nobody leaned over her shoulder, drew a red circle around "raisons," and wrote "raisins" in the margin. The student felt the freedom to find a natural—and believable—sound for her experience. Over the term her writing improved, perhaps because she wrote ninety-two pages of daily writing; her spelling stayed about the same.

Everybody who starts daily writing at first fears running out of material. Really, we have enough memory packed away, by age eighteen, to keep us writing until we are seventy. We gradually discover tricks that keep the pages coming. We should stop writing while we still have something to say; it is even wise to make an arbitrary rule: stop at the bottom of a full page, even in the middle of a sentence, and write nothing more until the next day. The next day, you will not have to sit and wait for the words to start.

Many students find that they work best with large categories of reminiscence, writing many pages—weeks of daily writing—on one general subject: my six best friends and their families, fishing trips with my mother, Christmas vacation, jobs I have had, my teachers in grammar school, pets, relatives, the Little League, 4-H clubs, fights with my brother, learning how to repair my ten-speed bike, my favorite meals, and my favorite jokes (one student remembered forty pages of jokes!). Some students interested in science and technology try to write about science in a language that nonscientists can understand—a difficult and useful kind of writing.

I talked with another freshman yesterday who made the same old mistake. Arguing about science and history, and what you could know for sure, he told me that some physicist had discovered that even in science you don't know anything for certain. And I tried to tell him about Heisenberg's uncertainty principle, but it's hard to explain it when people don't know some mathematics. Heisenberg showed that it's impossible to measure, accurately and at the same time, both the momentum and the location of a subatomic particle. This indeterminacy is totally insignificant with big things like baseballs and spaceships, but with an electron or a neutron, for instance, Heisenberg proved that knowledge of simultaneous momentum and position is impossible.

Giving a clear formulation to a difficult concept like this one brings a satisfying sense of mental order.

Daily writing is a means and not an end, however. Daily writing without an audience must prepare us to write for an audience. Our fluency is the tool by which we search out the shape of our thought, to reach out and connect with the reader. Unity, clarity, and the discipline of the sentence and paragraph—all are necessary to move the message from the writer to the reader. Once we have found an idea or an image or a secret lode of language, then we must learn to shape and control in order to communicate.

We need to learn all about language—choosing words; inventing metaphors, phrases, clauses, and sentences; and constructing paragraphs—before we can establish control over our writing. Of course we must try to make whole shapes, like the revision by Nina Chan, from the very beginning, even before we have learned that there are names for the things we are doing. It makes sense to look at what happens when we write an essay, and in Chapter 3 we will investigate the process of writing and look into suggestions for stimulating that process. But first, we must take a look at the more general problems of language and communication. We know that reading and writing are twins. If we investigate what happens when we read, it will help us to understand what should happen when we write.

EXERCISES

1. Write a page in a notebook, every day, for the rest of the term. Bring your notebook to conferences for your instructor to inspect, but not to correct. Bring it to class, if your instructor asks you to, with a page or a paragraph marked to read aloud. Discuss in class the problems and rewards of daily writing, giving one another suggestions for subjects.

2. Write a brief impromptu essay on the events of your first few days in college. You might write about motives and ideas like Nina Chan, or write a narrative like Ron Rector (see Exercise 12). Work to find unity and focus that will hold your essay together. Use specific details, examples, and anecdotes. Consider the students in your class as your audience.

3. Describe a common object (a lawnmower, a toaster) or action (sewing, shooting baskets) as if you are the first person to have seen it. Pretend, if you want, that you don't know the purpose of the thing or activity.

4. Find a paragraph of description or narration by a stylistically conscious writer like Fitzgerald or Hemingway. See if you can find how the author uses various sentence and clause lengths to add to his meaning. Find an image or descriptive detail that seems fresh to you and try to figure out how the author has achieved this effect. Try writing your conclusions in a short paragraph.

5. Take this same paragraph and *downwrite* it (see pages 14–15) to achieve one of these failures: disorganization, emptiness, or pomposity.

6. We discover ourselves by the language we use. Write a dialogue, or a conversation, in which two people reveal their characters by their language. Consider not only what words they use but also how they use them.

7. Analyze the language of the following essay. You might try entering it into a word processing program and running it through a style checker if you have access to one to help analyze sentence length, word complexity, and readability. Try revising the first paragraph.

My Big Moment

In my humble opinion, after all is said and done, opportunities for people to show what they are made of are conspicuous by their absence at this university. Because of this sad truth, the day I gave my report stuck out like a sore thumb. It was a red letter day. I had spent the entire year at college burning the midnight oil and leading a precarious existence earning my tuition working for a professor who was a veritable mine of information. I was very much interested in the finer things of life. My hopes to do things that would make me stand out from the crowd were usually doomed to disappointment. As I wended my way from class to class each day, and then to the job where I put my nose to the grindstone, I often thought that the events in my life at which I could point with pride were few and far between. But today would be different.

Today I, a rank outsider, would be the center of attention. People would realize that I was smart as a whip. They would listen with bated breath. At ten o'clock I stood as scared as a rabbit before the class. Although I was hungry as a bear because I had not eaten breakfast, I was calm and collected. I stood before them and I told the unvarnished truth about Man's mistreatment of Mother Nature. I explained that the powers that be must sit up and take notice of the fast and furious pace of pollution, and that there was a crying need for immediate action. I viewed with alarm the future of society when the purity of the very air we breathe hangs in the balance. When I concluded my few remarks, there was thunderous applause. I could tell I had hit the nail on the head. I was tired but happy. I had hit one out of the ball park.

8. Earlier you were asked to *downwrite* a passage. *Upwrite* these sentences. Use your imagination if you need to supply details.

> **a.** The car parked in front of the house was an ugly monster.
> **b.** We visited the Radio Shack. It was fun. The man talked a lot. He told us all sorts of things.
> **c.** Swimming lots of lengths in a pool is good for toning muscles but you get tired of the chlorine and I don't like the fact that they are always out of towels at the Y.

9. In *The Atlantic,* a writer criticized certain schools. In one paragraph, he wrote:

> In such places students are taught clichés. In one college a test consisted of stories with blank spaces to be filled with adjectives, the "correct" answers arcane or phony words used by *Time* magazine during the era of Henry Luce (but no longer used even by *Time*). In another college the blanks to be filled were the most hackneyed phrases, so that fires were always "raging," heavy rains always "torrential downpours" and recriminations always "bitter."
>
> > Ben H. Bagdikian, "Woodstein U.: Notes on the Mass Production and Questionable Education of Journalists"

Write a short paragraph in which you leave blanks for parts of clichés—usually an adjective or an adverb. Read it aloud in class to see if other students can fill in the "correct" clichés.

10. Here is another "How I Came to College" impromptu. (a) Criticize it for language and for structure. (b) Edit it. Rearrange and rewrite. Avoid clichés. Keep your audience in mind at all times. Be prepared to read the revised version out loud.

> I looked for work waitressing or anything last summer. Not finding anything school seemed like the best thing. Besides my family wants me to go. Learn a trade or skill I guess. So thats how come I am sitting here writing this!
>
> My girlfriend had already gotten in here and so she told me how to do it. I sign up and they tell me what I had to do. Just before I started classes I got the job I was looking for! But my father says you go to school. That's life.
>
> I can't tell yet how I like it or not. But I had a hard time getting here every morning because I don't have a car and, my

mother doesn't drive and my father needs it except on Thursdays. My girlfriend has a car, she drives me here MWF. Tuesday I take buses for one hour or so.

11. Here is a better example. (a) What makes it better? (b) In what ways could this student learn to improve her writing? Pay attention to mechanics, to focus, and to word choice. Pay attention to the author's idea of audience and think how it might be improved.

> All my life I have known that I would, some day, go off to school. By the end of my senior year in High School I knew where and when I'd be leaving and spent the summer getting used to the idea. But getting used to the idea was all I did—I did not begin to think or worry about what college was really going to be like. I did not spend hours contemplating the importance of "going off into the big wide world." I did not even speculate what things would be like, what if I hated my roommate, what if the work was too hard, what if I'm unhappy. I did not think about specifics, I had told myself that I would have time to get psyched the week before I left.
>
> But a week before the day I had planned to leave, before I had prepared myself I got a phone call from my father. He had to give a lecture at a convention on the west coast in five days. For him to make it we had to leave that day and he would drop me off in Michigan on his way to California. I had one hour to pack. One hour to collect all my belongings and somehow fit them into a car that looked like it could not hold half the things I wanted to take. It happened so fast I did not have time to think, I did not even have time to say goodby to my mother who was out shopping. We left in a hurry leaving behind many things I had forgotten to pack and a small note to my mother that simply said good-bye.
>
> If I had more time I'm sure my goodbye to my mother and friends would have been a long, emotional scene. Driving through my town I had no time to look at my Elementary School, my High School, the house of my best friend and get sentimental. It was pouring and concentrating on the driving was all I could do.
>
> The eleven hour drive also left no time for thought. I drove most of the way so that my father could prepare his speech. Every so often he would read parts to me to try them out. Our talk consisted of whether injection-lasers was a hyphenated word or not. (I still don't know.)
>
> Then I was here, in the dorm, with my roommate, in my classes. It seemed as if I had been here all my life and the trauma of leaving home was over. I did not even have time to think about it until later and then I could not even remember how it felt to leave home.

12. Here is an impromptu theme followed by a revision made late in the term. Compare the two essays. Correct the first version. What has the student learned? What is good about the revision? Can you find places in the revision where the writer could make further improvements? Pick one section in the revision and try to improve upon it.

> I almost didn't make it to college. When I was a junior in high school my parents split up. I lived with my mom who was, understandably, depressed a lot of the time. I guess I fell in with a bad crowd for a while. Knowing my mom would be working on Friday night—she had to take a job—I would head over to Brad's house. It usually got pretty wild there. Other guys would come by and bring beer. I got drunk quite a few times and my grades were really hurting. I had always been good at math and science, but all of a sudden I was pulling C's on my tests and I even got a note from my biology teacher.
>
> Luckily my mom got wind of the problem. She talked to her boss and got her schedule changed. Then she and I had a long talk and I admitted to her that I had let some things slip. "It's hard," she said. "But it's not ever going to get easier." She told me that I would be punishing myself in ways I couldn't even imagine if I didn't go to college.
>
> I got the message. I knew enough guys who hadn't gone on to school, who stayed around and work grind jobs. I knew I wouldn't be happy pumping gas or icing donuts. And the fact of the matter is that I didn't even like beer that much. So I opened my books again and studied for my finals, and if I didn't ace them the way I might have, I did well enough. I got into school so that I could take a course like this and tell my story.

The Narrow Escape
Ron Rector

When I was sixteen, a junior in high school, my parents got divorced. Life had been hard for a few years—arguments and slamming doors—and we had all seen it coming. But even if you see something coming, it usually looks different when it finally arrives.

At first I think I felt relief. After my dad moved out, things seemed remarkably calm. Mom worked extra hours at her job and spent a lot of time talking with her sisters. I did my odd jobs, kept up with my homework, and tried to look cheerful when I walked into the kitchen. For a while it worked.

But then the reality of mom's extra working hours began to sink in. "You're going to be on your own more," she had told me, and she was right. I hadn't known before how lonesome a house could feel. Now that mom wasn't around much I began to miss dad more. Then I would think of how things had been before all the fighting started and I'd really get depressed. All of a sudden homework didn't seem interesting or relevant.

It was during this time that I started hanging around with Brad and his friends. Brad's parents were divorced, too, but he seemed to have a pretty good attitude about things. When his mother went to work, he threw parties—wild, loud, fun parties. Brad's house was the place to show up at on Friday nights. There was beer and wine and music, and occasionally a police cruiser would shine its lights up and down the lawn.

The parties were one thing. I had my share of bad mornings—and I'm not particularly proud about that. But what was worse, really, was what happened to my school life. I had always done so well in math and science—I'd never gotten anything lower than a B+ on any test. But suddenly things started slipping. And then one day Mr. Wallace paused by my desk after he handed back my Biology exam. It was like he was searching my face for something. I had pulled a C-.

There were a number of things that combined to pull me around. For one thing, I don't like drinking that much and my body was really objecting to the pace. For another, I was getting bored. Brad is a nice guy, but the level of conversation with him and his friends never got very high. But the real clincher was coming home one night from Brad's and seeing my mother just sitting in the kitchen. She had just gotten home herself and she had her stocking feet up on a chair. She looked so *tired,* so utterly exhausted. I was about to say something like, "Mom, why are you doing this?" but then I realized. She was doing it for me. And when I realized that, I walked over and patted her head. I made a promise that I was going to be worthy of that tiredness. I was going to give her back something.

2

Reading, and Reading Well

"Because," said the writing instructor to his new class of freshmen, clearing his throat a few times to compel attention, "because we're going to be reading a variety of things in this class, and talking about what we read, I want to start off this morning with a short listening exercise." He paused long enough to see that he had captured their interest. "Now, I may be dating myself just a bit, but never mind. Do any of you remember a pop singer named 'Madonna'?" There were a few snickers, a general sense of name recognition. "Good. Then let me read a paragraph out loud to you. All you have to do is to listen carefully." Opening a book, he read:

> Originally I came, not to review Madonna, but to interview her. Now, when you are circling around a star of this magnitude—stacked like a package tourist above her fogbound airport—you never negotiate with the star herself. You negotiate with her people or, in best postmodern style, with her people's people: her agent's agent, her assistant's secretary's assistant's secretary. The messages come back in a remote and cautious cipher. At first it looked as though Madonna had singled me out as someone she was especially keen to see. (Truman Capote, I remembered, gave the same impression, an impression gravely qualified towards the end of the interview when he abruptly addressed me as "Tony.") A few days later Madonna apparently decided that, on the contrary, she didn't want to see me at all. The reason she seemed to be giving was this: I was too famous. Madonna (I wanted to tell her), don't say another word. I completely understand.

> From Martin Amis, *Visiting Mrs. Nabokov and Other Excursions.*
> Published in 1993 by Harmony Books, a division of Crown.
> Originally published in the United Kingdom by Jonathan Cape
> Limited in 1993. (Essay originally appeared in the *Observer,* 1992.)

"This," the instructor said, "is by a writer named Martin Amis, from a newspaper essay entitled "Madonna."

"I've never heard of him," said Carly Benz, "*is* he famous?"

"He's quite well known in England. He is the son of Kingsley Amis, who was a famous novelist."

"I've never heard of him, either," Carly shrugged.

"So, *is* he famous?" Tom Sleigh jumped into the discussion. "Because if he isn't you can read the whole thing as kidding, but if he really is—"

"Well, even if he is famous," said Lucy Broido, "he's not going to be as famous as Madonna. So you *have* to figure he's kidding. Being ironic, I mean."

"When you say 'kidding'—"

"Kidding as in poking fun," interjected Ben, "not kidding as in hurting feelings."

Carly was waving her hand back and forth. "I totally disagree. The whole thing about this guy is that he *hates* the way famous people act. He wants to stick it to Madonna and everyone like her. All this stuff about 'assistant's secretary'—he can't stand that he was being disregarded."

Allen Mattis shook his head. "You're wrong. He could care less. He's getting off a few clever remarks for a newspaper column and getting paid good money for it. Besides, he is sort of famous himself."

The discussion continued in this vein for a few more minutes, with some division over whether Amis was being lighthearted or bitter. The instructor was asked to read the paragraph again, but the reading resolved nothing. The instructor held back his own observations. He had been hoping for some split in views, for he had wanted to begin a discussion on reading by making it clear to everyone that interpretation is nearly always a complex and subjective activity. The obvious lack of unanimity in the class decided him: He would spend the upcoming sessions emphasizing the importance of attentive reading. He wanted his students to understand what they were doing when they worked through a particular passage. They would see for themselves how closely reading and writing are connected.

THE READING PROCESS

There is no writing well without reading well. The two activities are intimately connected; they are like sound and echo, body and shadow. For both take place in and through language. Where there is no language there is no thought. (Try having a wordless thought—it's impossible.) When we write we express our thoughts and experiences in language; at best, we arrange our words in logical order on the page. When we read we unravel those strings of words, turning them into an inner stream of thought, sensation, and emotion. Reading is the process of writing in reverse, and writing is the mirror image of reading. The mirror, if we stay with the analogy, is language itself.

This sounds mysterious, and in a way it is: we are, far more than we generally realize, creatures of language. Even in our most private moments we accompany ourselves with an inner sound track of thoughts, memories, and fantasies, and all of these, to some degree, require words. We may not hear our thoughts distinctly, the sound may be a vague murmur, but the fundamental connection is nonetheless there. It is by way of words and their meanings that we compose the sense of our lives.

Reading, we know, is a relatively recent human innovation, coming after millennia of spoken exchange. And the first readers knew nothing of the silent eye motion that we are accustomed to—they vocalized every mark. Indeed, Saint Augustine (345–430) remarks somewhere in his writings on the curious sight of a man reading without moving his lips.

We live in an age of information, where quick, silent scanning is the order of the day. A recent E-mail discussion on-line centered on the way that electronic technology may be changing our reading habits, as more and more of us become accustomed to quickly scanning through electronic messages. It may be hard for us to conceive what patient labor was needed to work through the pages of a text. But in fact all of us practice something similar at times. If a work is difficult, or if it has a particular verbal richness, we automatically change out of our rapid-scan habits. We move our eyes slowly and we listen. It is at these moments that we can most truly say that we are *reading* a piece of writing.

When we read this way—slowly, attentively—we translate the black markings of words into sounds. We speak those sounds internally and we try to hear them clearly. Though reading begins with the back and forth movement of the eyes, it only fully takes place when both inner voice and inner ear are engaged. Moving our eyes and listening, we absorb. Ideally, we structure the information and ideas into the clearest possible form so that we can follow and understand.

But we do more than just absorb: we also think our own thoughts and experience our own associations and responses to the words in front of us. These thoughts and associations weave like an ivy vine around the sense of what the other person is saying. For example, the first sentence of an essay by Caroline Bird entitled "College Is a Waste of Time and Money" reads: "A great majority of our nine million college students are not in school because they want to be or because they want to learn." When we read a sentence like this, we first do our best to grasp the logic of the assertion; we absorb and structure the basic information. We understand that a *majority* of college students are *not* in school because they *want* to be.

But even with a sentence this simple, we are probably doing other, more complex things. First, we very likely hear the structure of the whole: it is a negative assertion, telling us what is *not*. We therefore tend to grasp it as a part of an upcoming argument. Our experience as readers and listeners—we have all heard a thousand speeches—tells us that the negative will probably be followed by a positive. Our logical sense creates an expectation: if the majority of students are not in school because they want to be, *then* they must be there because. . . .

But logical expectation makes up only part of our total response. We may also accompany our reading with rapid-fire thoughts and associations like these: *nine million, that's not so many . . . out of . . . what is the population, 250 million? . . . a majority: 5 million, 6? . . . how do they know these things? . . . it's true, though, for some . . . Rick, Sandy . . . True for me? No, it's not that simple, more than just wanting to learn . . . .* Obviously this is a slow-motion study of a process that takes place very quickly, and obviously individual responses differ a great deal. But the point does not change: when we read we *absorb,* we *structure,* and at some level, we *respond.*

READING IS WRITING AND WRITING IS READING

When we read, we perform the same acts of organization and association that we perform when we write; we make choices. Reading a sentence like Caroline Bird's, we sound it out to ourselves. If we are Caroline Bird, writing, we do a similar thing: before the words take their place on the page as part of an argument or essay, they pass through the inner ear as if spoken. Some writers contend that the hearing and writing happen at the same moment and are virtually indistinguishable. In any case, try it for yourself: compose a sentence on paper without hearing it. It's impossible. Before, or as, we write we hear our words and test them for sense: we read.

There is another sense in which there is no writing well without reading well. Reading—the experience and memory of reading—is what gives us the backup for writing. When we read we absorb and store information. But we also absorb and store various structuring possibilities. This learning generally happens unconsciously; we are not aware of many of the things we learn. The same thing happens when we listen to other people talk. We experience and preserve the different ways of making sense, and we draw upon these ways incessantly when we write. If we *didn't* have these different options in our memory banks, we would be hard put to write anything more than the simplest building-block kinds of sentences: "John is thin."

When an experienced reader sits down to write, she has countless patterns in her memory. If "John is thin" does not satisfy her, she changes it. Memory might suggest an analogy—"John is as thin as a greyhound"— or a qualification: "Though he wears loose clothing to conceal it, John is quite thin." Every time a writer makes a decision about expression, it is with an awareness of the possibilities. Different patterns have different effects. The more we read—and the better we read—the larger a store we will have to turn to.

Reading as Detection/Reading as Construction

Reading, like thinking, is an extraordinarily complicated operation, and theoreticians write thick books to tell us why. Outwardly it's simple enough. We move our eyes from left to right and down the page, and maybe we mouth the sounds at times—either to clarify the sense or to add to our enjoyment (certain stories and poems beg to be read aloud). The more complex part of reading happens inside, behind the eyes. Here, as a sample, are the first few sentences from an essay by Mary Hood, "Why Stop?":

> There is an essential human ichor of awe, an instinct for reverence, a gracious sap which rises in us seasonally and flowers into devotions and wreaths. "Than longen folk to goon pilgrimages." Goon indeed. Every sap has its sucker. SEE THE CONTINENTAL DIVIDE IN ACTION, the billboard in the Rockies invites. The parking lot is not empty.

The odds are that a quick first reading of this passage will yield more confusion than sense. *Ichor* is an uncommon word; we might need the dictionary to learn that it means "an ethereal fluid supposed to flow in the veins of the gods." The quotation of the second sentence may be obscure as well: it is drawn from the Middle English of Chaucer's *The Canterbury Tales,* and in modern English would read, "Then the folk long to go on pilgrimages."

But Mary Hood is a clever writer with a love of wordplay, and even after we understand the references, our minds must shuttle back and forth to weave a coherent meaning. Before we can make any headway, of course, we have to recognize the tone. Hood is looking to have fun; she is leading up to her subject—the lure of unusual roadside attractions—with witty double meanings. We must be attentive, or we risk missing the humor.

Notice how Hood sets us up for surprise. We have read the fancy (some might say precious or overwritten) first sentence and the intimidating quotation from Chaucer. Quite possibly we prepare ourselves for a long stretch of high-minded prose. Suddenly we encounter "Goon indeed." Hood forces us to do a double take; she thwarts our expectations. Is she playing a game with us? She seems to be reading the Middle English spelling *goon*—for *go on*—as if it were the slang word for someone stupid or inept. Before we can decide how to interpret this new possibility we need more information. We read on.

Every sap has its sucker. Now it seems more likely that Hood has been setting us up, feeding us the lofty prose of the first two sentences in order to pull the rug out from under us. The word *sap* obviously refers back to *a gracious sap* in the first sentence, but the associations of that word and *sucker* suggest that she was just waiting to ambush us. The puns are flying in all directions. The statement literally means that every different sap has a creature that will feed on it. But a *sap-sucker* is also a bird known for extracting sap from trees with its beak. And a *sucker* is also a slang word for a fool; and a *sap,* too, is a sucker, a fool, possibly a *goon.*

We have read only four sentences, two of them fragment-length, and already we have performed complex mental feats, reading for subtleties of tone, juggling the connotations of words, and cross-checking references from one line to the next. Who will deny that reading can be every bit as demanding as mathematics or chess? As readers (and, implicitly, as writers) we should be aware of this complexity, the better to give our fullest concentration.

We should also keep in mind, with this passage as with many others, that our responses will differ greatly depending on our associations, our store of background information, and even our tolerance for wordplay. A reader familiar with the Chaucerian reference will applaud Hood's cleverness more readily than one who has never heard of Chaucer. One person might laugh at the multiple pun of the *sap/sucker* line—another might, so to speak, gag.

PHILOSOPHIES AND POLITICS

The possibilities for diverse responses among readers are probably greatest with literary works like poems, stories, and novels; poets and fiction writers are more likely to make use of ambiguity and to exercise the more suggestive properties of language. A straightforward description or analysis in a history textbook will probably generate more agreement than dissension, at least about *what* is said. However, we should not assume that any act of reading is simple or that any two readers will ever completely agree about the meaning of a passage.

Our backgrounds and our personal associations to words are not the only things that color our responses to the words on the page. Our political and philosophical beliefs—and biases—influence us enormously. Also, we tend to be unconscious of them, which makes them hard to detect when we revise. Consider this sentence: "Ann is a model wife and homemaker." Your grandmother might read these words without flinching, nodding approval. A veteran of the woman's movement, on the other hand, might feel her blood start to boil. Our politics are by no means limited to Republican or Democrat. All choices and thoughts are conditioned by our beliefs—beliefs, for instance, about human equality, environment, economics. . . .

Words do not exist neutrally, except perhaps on the dictionary page. They occur in context; they pass from speaker to listener, from writer to intended audience. If we read the sentence "Harry comes for a large family," we probably respond to the word *family* as we would to any simple noun used in an informational context. But if we read "Harry believes in family values," *family* has become a loaded word. It calls to mind the rhetoric of election speeches and it implies a range of meanings charged with strong emotional associations. To be a proponent of "family values" is, in our present social climate, to be politically conservative. If Harry is for family values, it most likely means that he opposes abortion and gay rights. We could compile a list of similarly loaded words, words like *motherhood, ecology, nuclear, communist, choice, technology.*

The programmed data links of computer hypertext make some of these associations obvious to the reader. In a hypertext, words like *family values* can become paths to other texts, texts that may define the words, explain the author's point of view, or present conflicting points of view by other authors. But, as active readers, we make these associations whether or not the author intends them or makes them explicit.

READING TONE

We have seen that words do not exist neutrally, that we all draw constantly on our unique experience and our often unconscious beliefs as we read and listen; we interpret everything according to who we are. We have seen, too, that meanings shift accordingly. Soon we will look more closely at some issues of interpretation and consensus. But first we need to discuss tone.

Reading or interpreting tone is something we do constantly in the course of conversation. Talking with others, we interpret irony, exaggeration, understatement, mock seriousness, and a dozen other styles of expression. When our coworker says, "I'll kill you if you're late tomorrow," we understand it as a figure of speech—or *hope* we do. When a friend steps in from a downpour and announces, "It's really nice out," we don't hurry to find our tanning lotion. Indeed, if we think of how most casual conversation is carried on, we will realize that a great deal of it involves communication by way of *tone*. Tone tells us how to interpret the obvious sense of a remark, whether to reverse its meaning, scale down its exaggeration, or take it at face value. In daily life, we are all experts at making these translations.

With reading, however, we face a greater difficulty. We do not have the author's speaking voice to go by. We have to do some guessing. The context—other words—provides our only clues. Sometimes, of course, the context makes our job easy. We turn to the humor column in our newspaper with the expectation that we will find irony there. The writer may begin by stating, "I was depressed yesterday. I decided that I would either shoot myself or go shopping." If we didn't know that the columnist was looking to be funny, we could guess as much.

But what about the piece that begins "America is a great country"? Our first impulse is probably to give assent: yes, of course, a great country. But what if the next sentence reads: "It allows more than 10 percent of its citizens to live in abject poverty"? Suddenly we must turn our expectations inside out: we hear irony, as the writer suggests that our greatness needs serious questioning. We could find dozens of examples in any newspaper of passages that need to be read with care, passages where the intended meaning depends not just on the words but also on the larger verbal context they inhabit.

Reading is not just negotiating the fine point of *what* gets said; it also requires close attention to the *how*. Sometimes—when reading an encyclopedia entry, say—we can relax our vigilance: a reference book insists on a matter-of-fact assemblage of information. We don't have to screen the words to try to decide the author's intent. Editorials, opinion pieces of all descriptions, speeches—indeed, *any* writing that seeks to persuade—these force us to read with all our faculties on the alert.

CHAOS OR CONSENSUS?

Considering the variables that make up even the simplest act of reading, it is hard to see how any two people could ever be said to read the same piece of writing. Strictly speaking, it is true: not only do different individuals respond differently to the same words, but any one person will probably feel or interpret the words differently at different times. This is even more true of electronic writing, where the reader may choose to follow hypertext links to other texts. Different readers may choose to follow different links, or the same reader may follow different links at different times. The text of *Walden* that you read in your high school English class is not the same *Walden* that you might pick up for pleasure after college or when you retire. Our experience changes us; our understandings and associations are never exactly the same from day to day. As the Greek philosopher Heraclitus once said, We never step twice into the same river.

This issue of the subjective response of readers is one that literary critics and theoreticians are fond of debating. Indeed, one group of thinkers takes an extreme position, arguing that since every reading of a work of literature is different there can be no correct interpretation. Who will judge between reader A, who believes Shakespeare's *King Lear* to be a satire, and reader B, who understands it as a tragedy? We cannot call the playwright on the phone to ask him what he meant. And even if we could, would his word be final? We cannot be sure that Shakespeare planned out what his play would mean, that he was not just writing down speeches and scenes as his inspiration dictated them.

In part, of course, this kind of questioning is an academic game. As readers we may not have identical inner reactions, and we may debate points of interpretation, but we tend to agree on the main substance of what we read. Few careful readers of Shakespeare will insist that *King Lear* is a satire. But in considering the *logic* of the extremist view we are brought face to face with the paradox of reading. To put it simply: language reaches our most private and subjective selves, and reading is the most solitary of acts; at the same time, language is a social instrument—a means for communication. Words isolate, and words bring us together. The philosopher is right in one sense: we cannot step twice into the same river. But the fact is that we do; at least we pretend that we do. We call it the Mississippi or the Ohio or the Kennebec. We draw it on maps and sail our boats down its waters. We read privately, but when we speak or write about what we've read, we look for agreement, for consensus.

Reading and writing are social acts often accomplished in solitude. When we speak or when we pass our writing to another person, we break that solitude and enter the social realm. In electronic writing, the reader often interacts with the text, by choosing which links to follow. The reader may even change the text itself, adding comments that may, in turn, become links. Reading, then, becomes literally a conversation between author and reader, and between the reader and other readers. Our expression becomes communication in any form of writing, which means that our meanings must be shared, carried across to others. For this to happen, there must be agreement—about the meanings of words, the rules governing sentence formation, and so on. There must also be a shared understanding of context. We need to be sure that the other person understands that we are being completely serious or tongue-in-cheek. When these rules are clear, then the paths of communication are open; then we stand a chance of finding agreement, consensus. Consensus literally means *shared sense.*

Soon we will take up some of the practical applications of these ideas. We will see what they mean in a classroom, how they affect us as readers and writers working to master a craft. But first we need to make a few additional points about reading.

READING IN THE INFORMATION AGE

In many ways, technology is changing the way we read and the way we write. The Internet has made it possible for writers to share texts in progress, to get feedback from readers even before a work is finished. As a matter of fact, some people view all electronic writing as unfinished. The technology makes it possible to change a text from moment to moment; the reader chooses which links to follow, so that each reading is, in essence, a new text; and the reader can respond, adding notes and comments to the text itself.

Writing and reading become social acts. The writer may include a link to his or her E-mail, or a comment block where the reader can ask questions of the author or add comments. On-line chat rooms turn conversations into multiauthored texts, often without any consensus or single point of view. And E-mail discussion groups allow for feedback and response as an integral part of the text itself. Reading and writing thus are part of an ongoing process, where both readers and writers take an active part in creating the text.

READING AS REREADING

Whenever this book speaks of writing it speaks of revision, and not only when it concentrates on process; writing *is* revision. When we become conscious of the act of written revision, we may learn to hear ourselves revise even as we *speak,* even in casual conversation. Almost everyone speaking crosses out one word and substitutes another, saying, "It was a small, I mean *tiny* dog . . . ." Sometimes we may say the same sentence over again, repeating it almost exactly but making little changes in word choice, in grammar, or in emphasis by pitch and volume—trying for more exact shades of meaning as we reach out to the listener.

It is less obvious but equally true that reading requires revision.

As writing is revising so reading is rereading. Even the most experienced of readers will misread on occasion. If we read actively, demanding coherence from the page before us, we will from time to time realize that we have lost this coherence, and we will need to go back to the text and start again. We lose track because our minds wander when we are tired, because a car backfires, or because we tune in to a conversation at the far end of the hall. We lose track because of imprecise knowledge of a word, because we miss the force of a grammatical turn or the sense of a transition, or because we do not share an association with the author.

We may misread because we do not share experience with the author. If an Argentinian uses the word *July* with the implication of a frigid climate, we from the northern hemisphere may miss something at first reading. We also misread because of bias or because we do not want to hear something the author wants to tell us. For all these reasons and a thousand more, we need to revise as we read; we must return to the text and question it, stopping to look up the meaning of a word or the date of a battle; we must try to pick up again where we left off. At times it is almost as if we were reversing a film a certain number of frames in order to look at a sequence again.

PUT THE BLAME ON BLAME

People often lose sight of the issues—readings and misreadings—by assigning fault. When we have trouble reading, we often think *either* "This is a stupid/obscure/lousy writer" or "I am stupid/This is not the kind of thing I can read." Casting blame lets us off the hook of a text. Casting blame is a kind of laziness because it suggests that we are surrendering. As always, of course, there are exceptions. When the writing is thoughtless or imprecise, we may be able to take the author to task: part of reading well is insisting on clarity. But we should not expend our energy on assigning blame; we should try to identify the problem and then move on. Everything is grist for the writer's mill. When we sit down to express ourselves, we will remember the ways that other writers have tripped us up—and we will seek to avoid them.

ACTIVE AND PASSIVE READERS

We must be active, not passive, readers. Much in our culture encourages passivity. When we grew up watching cartoons on Saturday mornings, we bathed in the glow of animations created to entertain us in order to sell us something. If we felt bored, we would switch the channel: therefore no one allowed us to feel bored. If we read the way we watched television, we would never get past the Archie comics.

Maybe we should call not merely for active reading but also for aggressive reading. We should look the text in the eye; if it will not look back at us, we should take it by the scruff of the neck and shake it. Or we should sit on a chair with a thousand-watt bulb and ask our questions: "What are you saying? Why aren't you making more sense?" But we must not merely question a suspect text; if we grill our reading like a detective, we must also be sure to investigate the investigator.

In practice, the active or aggressive reader is a series of detectives, one of them interrogating the text and the rest interrogating the interrogator. Suspect, detective, judge, and jury are all the same—which makes for difficult justice. If we ask the text to confess how it got from *A* to *B,* or why it lacks detail in support of *Z,* we must also ask if the question itself is appropriate. Are we sure that the interrogator is not making the mistake (omitting to notice the connective; missing the support offered) that he accuses the text of making?

The point is to be active, not passive; to be aggressive, not merely accepting. When we read that E. M. Forster gives two cheers for democracy, we must not simply record the number as a given. After we register the number we must inquire, *Why?* Why does Forster use the figure *two* instead of *three* or *one* or *twenty-seven?* Out of our experience we should recollect that the traditional number of cheers is triple—three cheers for the old school—and understand that Forster's approval of democracy implies limitation. But if we merely registered *two cheers* without actively inquiring about the phrase, without questioning the significance of the number—if we had been passive to it—we would have no limitation to look for. We would be missing the point.

The more active or imaginative we are in our reading, the more we tend to make our own essay as we respond to the writer's. This invention is not only inevitable with active readers but even a good thing—as long as we recognize what we are doing. Our interpretation, our *subjective* response, should not be whimsically private; we should always keep one eye on the probable consensus. Reading E. M. Forster on "two cheers," the reader may wonder what happened to the third cheer. She may think, "That cheer must be for the English class system!" But that is finally *her* conscious notion, not Forster's. Try to gauge at all times which part of your reaction is private and which part seeks the more objective view of the consensus.

CLOSE READING

When we have discriminated, as well as we can, the subjective from the objective, we can then analyze the text, reading with utmost care and concentration to see just how the writer has caused our responses. This kind of scrutiny is often called *close reading.* When we close-read, we approach a text with full attention. We make ourselves sensitive not just to the meanings and associations of the words and sentences but also to the fine points of the author's style. Is the author using different kinds of sentences, different rhythms, to get a message across? Do the word sounds contribute to the effect of the prose? What about punctuation?

Here, as an example, is a paragraph from the beginning of an essay entitled "The Golden Age, Time Past" by Ralph Ellison. Ellison is writing to evoke the atmosphere of Harlem jazz clubs in the 1940s:

> It has been a long time now, and not many remember how it was in the old days; not really. Not even those who were there to see and hear as it happened, who were pressed in the crowds beneath the dim rosy lights of the bar in the smoke veiled room, and who shared, night after night, the mysterious spell created by the talk, the laughter, grease paint, powder, perfume, sweat, alcohol and food—all blended and simmering, like a stew on the restaurant range, and brought to a sustained moment of elusive meaning by the timbres and accents of musical instruments locked in passionate recitative. It has been too long now, some seventeen years.

There is nothing difficult about the sense, or meaning, of Ellison's paragraph. But if we read carefully, slowly, allowing the phrases to sound in our ears, we can appreciate just how much the style—the phrasing, the rhythms, sounds, and sentence lengths—highlights the meaning.

For one thing, the whole paragraph imitates the feeling of a memory. There are three sentences. The first is short; it does the job of leading us up to the moment of recollection. The second, by contrast, shifts and flows, packing together the images and details from all the remembered nights. Reading it, we get the misty, dissolving sensation that comes when we think about the past. The third sentence brings us back, almost as if the author shook his head abruptly, to shock himself into the present again.

Now look at other fine points. The semicolon in the first sentence, for example, sets off and emphasizes the "not really." Read it out loud and you can feel the punch. It would not be the same with a comma, nor would we get the right effect if the author had tried to make separate sentences. The memory sentence then makes for a complete change; it is almost impossible to read it out with a single breath. Ellison forces us to move through it as if we were walking through a crowded room—which is, of course, what the memory is about. By the time we reach the end, with the "timbres and accents of musical instruments locked in passionate recitative," we feel the same strain of breath that the horn players must have felt. The short sentence that follows brings a nice relief.

We could go on and on. We could ask whether the many *s* sounds in the middle sentence add to the mood; we could analyze the changes in rhythm that Ellison uses to keep the memory sentence from falling apart. But I think the point has been made: style and content go hand in hand. To write well we must constantly try to bring the *what* and the *how* of our expression together. The more we close-read, reflecting on the choices made by other writers, the more choices we will have when we sit down to write.

PRACTICE IN RESPONSE

A class at a university in Rhode Island practiced and compared its own responses by reading Edward Hoagland's editorial "Walking the Dog" reprinted from the *New York Times*. Beginning the exercise, the teacher identified the essay as an editorial. After all, any reader encountering it under normal circumstances would come to it with such information. She also reminded her class that editorials speak like kings and queens, using *we* where the writer would say *I*. Otherwise, she said to her class, you're on your own.

She asked the class to write a page or so of notes as they read it. She asked them not to read through the whole editorial before beginning their notes, but to write as they went along, pausing after every paragraph to write about what they had just read—and to predict what would come next if they had any notion. She told her students: Don't spend more than ten minutes on this; you don't have to be correct; but be prepared to read it out loud to one another. She reminded them that in such an exercise there are no right answers, though it is always possible to misread. No one would be graded on correctness of response; the point of the exercise was to explore *differences* of response. This exploration, she said, should help us not only as readers in trying to understand our response and discriminate between the more subjective and the more objective, but it should also help us as writers who try to predict the responses of our readers. Here's the editorial she used:

Walking the Dog

We are in favor of cleaning up after them, but we are also in favor of dogs. Manhattan was once the home of whistling swans and seals and mountain lions, and, walking the dog, we remember this in our bones. Walking the dog, we feel occasionally that we are with a living ancestor, as children seem to do also. Children are born with a liking for dogs; and when we are out with the family dog, we seem to remember aptitudes of nose and leg that we no longer have.

For the dog, one purpose of our walks is checking out the gutter—the chicken knuckles and Reuben sandwiches there. As a student of fermentation (wine and cheese buffs have nothing on him), he is immensely cheerful as we go around the block. Also, he marks his territory. You might say it's like the trappings of wolf territoriality without the territory, just as for us it is a walk in the woods without the woods. He looks particularly for irregularities to mark: a shovelful of dirt next to a Con Ed excavation, a clump of grass, houseplants or Christmas trees that have been thrown out but still smell of earth. Males found females by the process, but the other social function—when dogs were wolves—was to reinforce the order of rank and rule within the pack, increasing the pack's efficiency on a hunt.

We are animals too. We confront a cold wind with our backs, and turn grumpy if somebody unexpectedly grabs hold of us while we are bent over a steak. But the spirit of both man and dog is sociable, and most people will never be too old to get a kick out of whistling to a dog and seeing him wag his tail. The point of having a descendant of the Lost Wolf for company is not to crush his spirit but rather to direct it so that he can live in, even delight in, the city. The eagles and wild swans are gone, and we have an idea that dogs and the saving irregularities they look for add life to New York City.

At the next meeting of the class the instructor asked two students to read their responses aloud. Bill Julio read:

> This "we" business sounds phony even if it is an editorial. I keep wondering "How does this guy know what *I* think?" City dogs to me mean those small furry balls that you could almost step on if you weren't careful, but I suppose there are police dogs and Great Danes, too. Though I don't agree that all kids are born loving dogs. My sister cried whenever she got near one. Maybe he's generalizing too much about things. Interesting, though, to think about feeling old human memories in our bones. Do swans whistle?
> This confuses me about mountain lions in Manhattan—I thought they lived out West.
> He is probably going to come out and say that dogs don't really belong with all this concrete.
> Litter, street garbage—it's mostly just disgusting. This writer is showing off when he talks about dogs as "students of fermentation," as if they were wine experts. Con Ed—who is Con Ed? He shouldn't assume we know these things.
> We are animals, he says. This is the oldest cliché in the book. The whole point is that we're *not* animals, that we have to keep animals. I start to lose interest. If we are all animals how come we write and read editorials like this? The argument for keeping dogs in the city is stupid—if it's just so that we can remember what we used to be like. What about the poor dogs, locked up in stuffy apartments all day?

When Bill finished reading a number of people raised their hands. Someone said: "Obviously not every kid in the world likes dogs—but there is a definite truth to what Hoagland is saying. Sometimes a writer has to exaggerate to make a point." Bill answered that he agreed, but that he had been trying to put down exactly what went through his mind as he read along. His teacher nodded. Other hands went up. One student said that she agreed completely with Bill's thought about dogs locked up in apartments all day. "That's not what nature intended," she said. "I can't respect a writer who thinks dogs are just there for people." Some others voiced agreement.

The teacher then asked Rachel Goldberg to read from her notes:

> Cleaning up after being sick? Shedding hair? What does cleaning up have to do with seals? Is a living ancestor like a grandfather or like a caveman? I can't believe that this is an editorial because it doesn't . . . argue. Is it about our own "aptitude" that this is about? Dogs in Manhattan—pooper scoopers!

I bet this article is from the time when they were passing the law about dog poop on sidewalks.

In the suburbs it's more like telephone poles and mailboxes, not sandwiches and chicken knuckles. Yuk! Chickens have knuckles? Is that what they mean by knuckle sandwich?

He marks off territory. This is by lifting his leg, right? Why can't he say so? Can the N.Y. Times use language like *piss?* For that matter, what's all this about *he?* Why do we always assume everyone and every animal is male? Do lady dogs do their marking in different ways? That might be a funny article. . . .

Grabs steak. Like a kid protecting a popsicle. Natural, I guess. Is it really animal? Or just self-defense? Countries do it, too. They grab other countries, go to war. Maybe we *are* all animals after all. I don't know. He gets to these "big" generalizations awfully quickly.

Rachel's remarks brought another show of hands. "You're right, all these guys are male chauvinists." "Girl dogs and boy dogs pee the same way—don't they?" "This piece only pretends to be about dogs. It's really about people and how they need to be reminded of where they came from." "I still think it's cruel. He says the dog is happy to be sniffing garbage and he sounds so superior. He'd be sniffing garbage too if he'd been locked up all day!" "I think he's really saying how all the wild things have been tamed, and how everything has become civilized."

The teacher let the discussion flow for a while, then signaled for silence. She asked everyone around the room to note quickly exactly what they had pictured when they first encountered the word *dog* in the editorial. Then, pointing to one student after another, she listened to the responses:

A poodle/"Clarabel," our setter/big dogs, two on a leash/one of those hot-dog type dogs with the little short legs/a German Shepherd/Lassie from TV/a part golden named Gussie/Frank/a whole line of mutts following each other down the street/a spotted dog—dalmation/"Buster"—our collie/Lassie/a friendly mutt/nothing, no picture/vague kind of city dog/one of those dogs on a dogfood commercial/Grandma's old shaggy dog . . . .

So—said the teacher after a sigh—when you look up *dog* in the dictionary, does what you find have anything to do with what the word meant when you read it on the page? Nobody even tried to answer. Several people shook their heads.

SIGHT READING

For the next class meeting, the teacher asked for a volunteer to bring in another editorial, so that she herself could read something aloud to the class—trying to say her responses as she encountered the sentences for the first time. They would continue their investigation of reader response with the teacher as Exhibit Number Two. She said that she would leave the room for a few minutes so that the class could decide what to do.

When the door had closed, Cathy Bates took the lead. She told everyone how her mother regularly sent her clippings from a California newspaper. It was a sure bet, she said, that their teacher would not have seen any of them before. Everyone agreed. One classmate cautioned that she should clip away all identifying marks, including the author's name.

On Monday, Cathy presented the teacher with the clipping. She had cut and pasted so that the piece had a title but no author identification. "I'm not sure that this is an editorial," said Cathy. "Does it matter?" The teacher assured her that it was not important *what* kind of writing was used—the results would be the same. She then explained that she would leave the room again, this time to allow Cathy to read the piece aloud twice. When the class was familiar with the text, the teacher would then re-turn and encounter it for the first time.

When the students let her back in, she read the following text. Here the newspaper material is in regular print, and the teacher's itali-cized impromptu associations follow each sentence in parentheses and quotation marks.

First she read the title:

Bad Luck Bob and His Dog

(*"Hey, this might be fun. I expected something dreary about parking laws or merchants' associations. 'Bad Luck Bob' suggests a story, a tall tale. Simple guy . . . not Maurice or Frederick, but Bob, good ol' Bob. Why 'bad luck'? Because he has bad luck, or is bad luck? I guess we'll find out. As for the dog—well, that's a friendly touch. A guy and his dog. There's something fa-miliar. I sense that I want to like Bob."*)

Bob Greene is the kind of guy who, if there were one hole in the ground within a 10,000-mile radius, would fall into it and break his leg. Then, when he got out of the hole and sued the hole owner, he would lose the case and be successfully countersued for falling into an unauthorized hole.

(*"I was right, this will be fun. The writer has a great sense of humor. He's absurd and exaggerated. But I'm tuning right in, not only because I want to know where the piece will go, but also because I identify. Don't we all some-times feel that we're Bob. I sure did yesterday—I got two parking tickets. But back to Bob. I'm drawn in, too, because I sense it's going to be about the little guy, the underdog. Lawsuits, countersuits—isn't that just the modern world. I get anxious just seeing the word* lawsuit. *But I have the feeling, I don't know why just yet, that the piece is going to make me feel better."*)

Later he would suffer a deadly deep-hole virus that would cause his hair, his teeth and his fingernails to fall out. He would lose his home and his life savings to medical bills and legal costs, his wife would run off with the hole owner and his carnivorous plant would try to eat him.

("I feel a slight sense of disappointment. He's going too far with the exaggerations. I don't feel that it's my life any more. Now it's a shaggy-dog story or something. I still want to know what will happen, but. . . . And, speaking of dogs, I've forgotten about the dog in the title. What else? Losing hair and teeth and fingernails. Well, hair is something men have to worry about. My husband—well, never mind, he wouldn't want me telling about his problems. Teeth, though. That's a nightmare I sometimes have. I'm able to reach into my mouth and pluck out my teeth. Horrifying! I guess we all fear old age, the body's collapse. The wife running off, and the plant—those details turn the whole business into a joke. Well, let's see where the joke will go.")

Believe me when I tell you that misfortune sticks to the man like drool to a baby.

("That's nice: I like the casual touch of "Believe me." It's a funny image, drool sticking to a baby. Funny, too, to find it referring to a guy who is older, who has a wife and loses his hair and teeth. Is there a message: are we all babies? No, I guess it's just a figure of speech. The author is trying hard to be memorable. Drool sticking to a baby is pretty good, though. It's kind of . . . universal. The baby can't help it, and neither can Bob, apparently.")

For those who may not recall Robert Alan Greene, he was arrested last March in Laurel Canyon Park for walking his dog.

("Aha! I'm surprised. The writer set me up, and he got me. The piece is suddenly turning around. Robert Alan Greene instead of Bob. The language of official papers, arrests, legal action. Very ominous. Now I don't know at all where this piece is going. Are we supposed to get all serious? Or are we going to jump back to Bad Luck Bob and carnivorous plants? I'm not sure I like being tricked. But it does wake me up. I mean, I am going to read on to find out what is happening. The author is holding me. Now I know that it's from California. Maybe it was a big story there, I don't know. Mostly I'm wondering how I should be responding, if I should relax and enjoy, or if I should be ready for something more disturbing. I do see, though, that the dog has finally appeared. It makes me think back to the title: Bad Luck Bob and His Dog.")

Forget that the park was probably the worst place on earth to be at the time. Dog owners were battling with children owners over the question of who ought to be leashed, the dogs or the kids, and Animal Regulation Cops were swarming over the hills like Jewish commandos at an Arab outpost.

("More switches. There's enough humor to make me think I should be reading for amusement—the business about dog owners and children owners is clever—but there's a certain amount of uneasiness, too. You can't just joke about the warfare in the Middle East—at least I don't think you can. My reaction now is one of confusion. It's a picture, half humorous, of a kind of battle scene. Dogs are being equated with kids. In some ways that's funny. In other ways, it's too true. I mean: I see mothers at the supermarket yelling orders to kids as if they were just animals that needed to be controlled. And then the part about Jewish commandos—it makes me edgy. I see too many

*images on the evening news—I can't find the humor there, no matter how
hard I try.")*

The teacher stopped reading. "It's a fairly long piece," she said. "It's
obvious that I won't be able to get all the way through. But maybe you get
the idea. I may be getting paid to teach you writing, and you may be
tempted to think that I have the answers, but I'm just another reader. There
is no reason to think that my responses are in any way better, more correct,
more *anything* than your own. They are different. I am older, I've had different experiences; I've probably read more, and I've had more practice at
finding my responses. Now, tell me who I was reading."

Cathy identified the writer as a columnist for the *Los Angeles Times*
named Al Martinez. The teacher praised the selection. "It's a lively piece of
writing," she said. "I hope you'll let me take it home and finish it." (See Exercise 2 for the complete column.)

A week later, mostly studying other matters, they reviewed the subject
of reader response by working together, instructor and students, on another
editorial brought to class by one student but unread by anybody else. For the
rest of the term, when the class talked about student essays or essays read in a
reader, they analyzed their own responses as readers. Writing, they tried to remember the potential responses of others and to respond to their own writing, and they reread and revised their own work. The teacher was satisfied that
the message was sinking in that there is no writing well without reading well.

EXERCISES

1. (a) Here are two passages of writing that are exceptionally attentive to word sounds and rhythms. Choose one passage and practice close
reading. Recalling the discussion of the Ralph Ellison passage (page 36), see
how many deliberate effects of rhythm and word sound you can locate. Heed
the shifts of tempo from sentence to sentence as well as the movement of the
whole. Make notes about what you find and be prepared to discuss in class.

> I grew up in N.Y.C., where I learned to drift with crowds, to
> be one shining particle in those streaming currents of phospho-
> rescence that merge and intersect around Fifth and Fifty-sev-
> enth, especially on late winter afternoons. As one sparkling cor-
> puscle, I delighted in the speed, the thrust, even the bumps and
> jolts of those other glittering corpuscles. Black, white, Hispanic,
> Asian, Native American, we made up one Amazonian blood-
> stream. In those crowds, I savored my anonymity, that deli-
> ciously sensuous private space where I could dream in public,
> sensing the outermost edges of other people's dreams: that
> woman striding past me in a green suede coat, lighting up a
> Mary J—the burned eggplant smell drifted back to me, spread-
> ing, smudging the purely olfactory calligraphy of her dream.

Long after she disappeared into the crowded distance, her dream flowed from her nostrils, enigmatic, persistent.

Susan Mitchell, "Dreaming in Public:
A Provincetown Memoir"

I came to reading and writing more or less naturally. As, for example, you might come to swimming early and easily. Which, matter of fact, I did; learning to swim at about the same time I learned to walk. I can very well remember the name of the man (he was the swimming coach at Rollins College near Orlando, where I grew up during the Depression years) who took me as a toddler and threw me off the end of a dock into a deep lake where I had the existential choice of sinking or swimming. And I chose to swim, thank you very much. His name was, I swear, Fleetwood Peoples. Could I forget a name like that? More to the point, could I invent that name? For reading we had all the riches of my father's one great extravagance—an overflowing library of some thousands of books. Books of all kinds in bookcases and piles and on tables everywhere in the house. Everybody read and read. And so did I. I remember reading Kipling and Stevenson and Dickens and Scott sooner than I was able to. And you could earn a quarter anytime for reading any one of any number of hard books that my father thought anybody and everybody ought to read.

George Garrett, "My Two One-Eyed Coaches"

(b) Write a description of your own that attempts to incorporate something you've learned from one of these passages. Read it to the class and see if others can identify what you have used.

2. Look back at the section "Philosophies and Politics" (pages 30–31), and then try to come up with three "loaded" words of your own. For each word write two sentences, one representing a neutral usage, the other a usage that may strike a reader as value laden.

3. (a) Look through some magazines and the op-ed pages of some larger newspapers. Find three passages from different writers where the reader is being trusted to interpret the tone (see pages 31–32).

(b) Write a paragraph of your own in which you require the reader to interpret tone.

(c) Write separate sentences that convey their meaning through irony, exaggeration, understatement, and mock seriousness. Be prepared to read your sentences aloud and to test reactions from classmates.

4. Find a passage in a newspaper or magazine that you believe will elicit diverse interpretations from your classmates. Write down some of the responses you anticipate, then read the passage out loud. Discuss your predictions and the various reactions with class members.

5. Here is the complete column by Al Martinez from the *Los Angeles Times*. Pick up where the instructor left off. Find three or four paragraphs to respond to (they should be in sequence). Try to capture your real reactions by noting not only associations and expectations but also the ways in which those are played on by Martinez.

Bad Luck Bob and His Dog

Bob Greene is the kind of guy who, if there were one hole in the ground within a 10,000-mile radius, would fall into it and break his leg. Then, when he got out of the hole and sued the hole owner, he would lose the case and be successfully countersued for falling into an unauthorized hole.

Later he would suffer a deadly deep-hole virus that would cause his hair, his teeth and his fingernails to fall out. He would lose his home and his life savings to medical bills and legal costs, his wife would run off with the hole owner and his carnivorous plant would try to eat him.

Believe me when I tell you that misfortune sticks to the man like drool to a baby.

For those who may not recall Robert Alan Greene, he was arrested last March in Laurel Canyon Park for walking his dog.

Forget that the park was probably the worst place on earth to be at the time. Dog owners were battling with children owners over the question of who ought to be leashed, the dogs or the kids, and Animal Regulation Cops were swarming over the hills like Jewish commandos at an Arab outpost.

Dogcatchers, as a police friend pointed out, are usually people who cannot qualify to be *real* policemen and take out their career frustrations on whoever happens to be in the vicinity during periods of high tension.

Bob Greene, of course, was the one strolling by.

The way Bob tells it, his dog Princess was on a leash. The way the animal cops tell it, Princess was walking next to him *unleashed* and was snarling and looking around for babies to kill.

An officer shouted for Greene to stop, but Bob said he had witnessed the "Gestapo tactics" of the animal cops before and was not about to submit to their torture and humiliation and gruesome death. So he told them that and kept going.

Bad news. Bob fell into the hole again.

"I probably shouldn't have said that," he reflected during a more reasonable moment the other day. "I have a big mouth."

The animal cops thought so, too. Greene says they waited in the bushes, jumped him, beat him and booked both him and the dog. The dog was later o.r.'d, but Greene was charged with resisting arrest and failing to keep his pet on a leash.

He requested a jury trial, acted as his own attorney and, of course, lost.

"I was a fool," Bob lamented.

Somewhere along the way, incidentally, he had mortgaged his house in Laurel Canyon to buy a sign-making business. The business naturally failed and he lost the house.

But wait. We're not finished.

Bob was arrested that first time on March 31. He remembers it because it was Palm Sunday, but that didn't do him any good at all. And it didn't improve his luck or his judgment. Four months later, he went back to the park and this time, he admits, was walking Princess *without* a leash.

"Bob," I asked him as gently as I could, "why in the dog-walking hell did you go *back* to Laurel Canyon after that first incident and not even put the dog on a leash this time?"

He thought about that for a moment, then shook his head sadly.

"I don't know," he said. "I guess it was just bad timing on my part."

Greene is 55 and, as one might expect, divorced. We met in the West Hollywood sign-making shop he once owned and now works for. He sleeps in a tiny room adjacent to the office. Princess and a stray called Barney sleep in the room with him when they are not out hunting babies.

"I'd do some things all over again now if I could," he said. I hope to God he would.

Sparing you the strange details of that second encounter at Laurel Canyon Park, Bob was subsequently charged with abandoning a pet, interfering with a dog officer and threatening a dog officer.

He is to appear in Municipal Court on those charges unless he is already in jail after sentencing on the first set of convictions.

"When I was found guilty," Greene remembered, "the judge gave me a choice of being sentenced right away or of waiting until October. I asked him what he would suggest and he said, 'Well, if I sentence you now, you'll go straight to jail.' So I said I'd wait until October."

Greene and others involved in the Laurel Canyon Park mess insist that he is being punished not for crimes he committed but for twice testifying before the Animal Regulation Commission on the excesses of the dog cops.

Maybe so, but if bad judgment were a felony, Bob Greene might be sitting on Death Row today.

As a final example of his synaptic lapses, I asked if he were going to appeal the first conviction.

"I sure am," he said. "A friend of mine is going to show me how to fill out the papers. I'm doing it myself."

Oh my goodness, oh my soul, there goes Robert down the hole.
Again.

3

Writing an Essay

This book began with the most general and incontestable assertions about writing—that its purpose is communication and that it can be learned. Then, in the second chapter, we talked about *how* we read and about the deep connection that is found between reading, writing, and thinking. Now we must attend to the most basic part of the writing process: getting the words onto the page. In most composition courses the student is asked to write a complete paper at the very beginning and to write additional complete papers every week or two throughout the term. It is time for some practical advice.

*An essay—or paper—has a purpose—*to give information, to define or to contrast, to explore, perhaps to persuade. A paper *shows* its purpose, both in its shape and in its statement, or the paper fails. In beginning a paper, we *find* that purpose, often in the act of writing; revising and finishing the paper, we make that purpose *clear* to the outside world.

In an essay we must support our purpose by detail; we must provide sufficient detail, and we must arrange the details into an order that expresses purpose. If we are writing five hundred words we must find a purpose limited enough to be supported adequately in two pages of typing. If we try brief surveys of grand topics—"Nuclear War," "The Problem of Welfare"—our five hundred words will remain abstract and superficial, lacking detail. If we choose a more limited topic—"Recruiting High School Seniors for the Army," "Applying for Food Stamps"—we can organize adequate detail into a shape that reaches an audience. We must limit not only topic but purpose.

Writing an essay we need to use both the critical and the creative sides of our brains. To accumulate detail, we can use the spontaneity we cultivate in daily writing. But to cut and to shape, to narrow and to focus, we need to cultivate other qualities of mind. We must develop a sense for order and shape, a sense by which we understand the whole paper as several units organized to become one larger unit controlled by one purpose. Finally the shape of an essay reflects the shape of our purposeful thought.

We must also understand that *our whole essay*—from our choice of words for the opening paragraph to our choice of detail for the concluding paragraph—*directs itself to the eyes and ears of other people.* We do not write for ourselves only. We need to persuade, to inform, to please, to convince, to charm, to arouse, to make an impression on *other people.* By definition a composition class presumes—as much as a newspaper presumes by publishing—that its writing directs itself from inside out, from writer to reader, from individual to world. Acts of language are social acts; it takes two to talk.

Once we understand that writing is directed to an audience—and not inward, where we can be sure that a generous interpretation will accept our intentions—then we can understand the function of good style and even of mere correctness. *Good style smooths the passage from writer to reader; good style is a convincing clarity.* Mechanical correctness removes impediments to understanding; even a mistaken *it's* for *its* can throw a momentary monkey wrench into the machine of comprehension. We must write well in order to make contact with our readers. We avoid clichés or extraneous information or misleading abstractions or dangling modifiers or incomplete arguments *for one reason:* all these flaws, errors, imperfections block the passage between the writer and the reader.

In later chapters, we will look into the choice of words, the making of sentences, the construction of paragraphs, and the different types of writing a student may undertake. First we must investigate how the whole essay is made. We must look into the process that will be the student's classroom task throughout the term: writing essays single in purpose, integrated in shape, and clear to others.

GETTING IDEAS FOR PAPERS

Writing begins with invention. Many writers find that getting started is the hardest part and they feel discouraged about learning to invent. Beginning writers commonly suspect that organization and clarity are qualities that can be learned by study but that originality depends on luck or genius—the inventor's spark of inspiration. Fortunately, however, this common idea is untrue; anyone can learn procedures that generate ideas. We need not be Thomas Alva Edison to invent a good paper: even for a literary genius, inspiration is 99 percent perspiration.

When an instructor assigns a free paper, both topic and organization are up to the writer. When an instructor assigns a general topic like "Public Transportation," the student needs to formulate and organize ideas on the topic. When an instructor assigns a form of organization—comparison and contrast, for instance—we need to generate a topic appropriate to the form and an idea by which to organize the topic. Then we must discover and organize the best details. Whatever the assignment, we need to discover details and set them in order.

Maybe the mind feels blank, at first, with an open assignment. Total freedom suggests no starting place. If we do daily writing, we can read over the pages and sometimes find a suitable subject to rewrite into a shape that will convey a purpose to the reader, or we can look over messages sent to an on-line newsgroup if we have access to one, for ideas that spark our imaginations. Otherwise, it is a good idea to consult our recent interests, or subjects of discussion or argument in other classrooms, with family or with other students. It is also true that we should simply keep our eyes open: essay topics float around us like motes in the air.

When the instructor assigns a topic or a pattern, the direction simplifies the process of invention. We generate ideas on a topic by narrowing it; reducing "Student Politics" to "Running for Class President" begins the choice of detail. We can call to mind incidents we have witnessed and slogans we have heard. When form is assigned, we must filter possible topics through this special entry gate: although we could contrast a small college with a large university, do we know enough about life in a large university (or a small college) to provide fair comparison? If we do not, we cannot write a decent comparison and contrast paper on this topic, which therefore fails to pass through the gate. If we are to analyze a process and think of writing a recipe for spaghetti sauce, can we really generate enough detail for a paper? Hot pepper and chopped carrots are not enough. And even if we add oregano, we may fail to keep our readers interested.

The true beginning of the essay waits for concentration on the task. Writers find many ways to begin, and in a moment we will look at several of them. First, we must emphasize how *not* to begin: *do not sit down with a few notes and a vague notion of topic and form to write the essay.* Many essays fail because beginners try to improvise the final essay at first sitting, attempting to find ideas at the same time as they organize and shape them. Too often, vaguely aware of shortcomings but despairing of making large changes, the writer merely makes mechanical corrections to this rough draft, such as correcting spelling and capitalization errors, and hands in a disorganized and incoherent essay.

Time spent in preparation is time well spent. It is wise to figure how much time we have and allot half to preparation and half to execution. When we begin by writing a whole draft, we start without a full supply of details. If we go back later with the idea of adding detail, we all too often try to squeeze in material that does not really belong. Detail should grow into place naturally; it should not feel taped on. Of course if we have the time and energy, we can look at a premature first draft as raw material, take it apart, and rewrite and reorganize it thoroughly. But it takes less time and effort if we prepare patiently and thoroughly before attempting a draft. A delayed draft is more likely to generate the material and a complete and coherent final revision. The longer we brood over an idea, the more details we are apt to accumulate.

Any advice on writing an essay, however, must recognize that different writers follow different processes. Indeed, the same writer, at different times, may find different procedures useful. Some writers, or maybe all writers on some occasions, will find it best to begin by writing several pages before the plan of the essay becomes clear in order to generate material. Some people think best in the act of writing. Later, they must return to what they have written in haste, to mine this material for the real essay. Attitude is important. *If we do not wait, think, and plan before attempting to write, we must use much of our writing time to generate raw material.* We must not write expecting merely to polish this material into a final draft. Revision more radical than polishing will be necessary.

Here are some ways to prepare for writing an essay, ways to get ideas, develop them, examine them, analyze them, and expand them. Later we will mention ways to select and organize these ideas.

Brainstorming

To brainstorm is to list ideas and details rapidly, without self-criticism, without attending to formalities or parallelisms or mechanical considerations—and without worrying about being silly: no one else need see the product. When we brainstorm, we fill a blank sheet of paper or a computer screen with fragmentary notes that we hope may lead to ideas on a topic. We write rapidly and uncritically, receiving the brain's topical snow flurries without trying to make sense or to give shape. The uncritical mind generates good ideas and bad ones together with a broad generosity.

Suppose the topic is comparing and contrasting bicycles and cars at a residential campus. Sitting down with a blank sheet, a student might begin with a list:

> bikes quicker no parking trouble
> but bike theft—chains and combinations
> healthy, keep in shape
> but carrying groceries?
> more car accidents; more serious?
> bikes ecology, energy saving
> winter ugh salt jeans
> bike cheap car expensive
> insurance gas parking fines
> car status symbol
> kind of car?
> old car repairs
> vans, hearses, old buses

When the mind compares and contrasts, it brainstorms ideas by flipping back and forth like a Ping-Pong ball—bikes are healthier, *but* you don't carry a lot of groceries on bikes; bikes save energy, *but* riding them in winter can be unpleasant. These alternatives are good raw material, but if we wrote an essay that swung from side to side so rapidly, the to and fro would only confuse the reader. After we list alternatives, we can organize coherently, often putting like with like—the advantages of cars in one paragraph perhaps, and the advantages of bicycles in another.

It is useful after brainstorming to look back at the list and highlight ideas that need thinking out. The creator lists; the critic reads the list and responds to it. We may put question marks by some notes to acknowledge that we are only guessing; are we really more likely to have an accident driving a car than riding a bicycle? To make such an assertion, we need the authority that comes from research. Sometimes we find an item, like "car status symbol," which can head a list for further brainstorming:

> car status symbol
> rich students—rich-seeming?
> money and parents
> some earn own money
> but—doing errands for others
> weekends? not on campus—
> getting away!
> sports cars, antiques, clunkers

When we brainstorm, we list a few words, sensing that if we needed to, we could expand any item. After we have accumulated much material, we could try organizing our notes and writing a draft—but chances are we will do better if we continue to delay the first draft, preparing further. Many professional writers make a practice of such stalling. They know that *once they have come up with an idea,* that idea will work like a magnet, drawing forth details from memory. The more we learn to trust ourselves as writers, the more faith we put in the capacities of the unconscious mind.

Sprinting

Sprinting—or free associating—is another technique for loosening the mind into discovery or invention; we can use it instead of brainstorming or in addition to it. Sprinting, we write a quick paragraph on our topic, writing as fast as we can for five minutes or so, beginning with the first thought that occurs to us and hurtling forward by association of ideas without pausing for logic or correctness. The results at times resemble (or *are*) nonsense, but every so often—often enough to make it worthwhile—some unexpected connection opens up a whole new set of possibilities. Even when it does not bring fresh insight, the process is a useful way to loosen up for writing. Before beginning an essay, we may try sprinting on our essay topic for our daily writing.

Sprinting resembles the method author Peter Elbow calls "looping," writing a series of ten-minute passages, each loop circling out of the passage before it. This technique is especially appropriate for endeavors longer than a weekly paper. We may follow Elbow and loop a second sprint onto our first one. Pausing to look back at our spontaneous prose, we should extract the essence of what we have written. Do these sentences lead toward something in particular? Is there a leading idea? Trying to answer such questions, we should write one more sentence that captures the best or most interesting idea of our paragraph. And next, using this sentence as our beginning, we should sprint again. Often a brainstorming list provides an initial range of topics, and a sprint or two will generate detail within the narrowing topic. Sprinting on the topic of cars versus bicycles during an in-class exercise, one student came up with "Funny how when I drive I hate bikers, when I ride I hate drivers . . . ." Her spontaneous expression made her realize that she had two different attitudes about the subject. She later made the idea of a double perspective the core of a short weekly theme.

Cross-examining

There are questions we need to ask ourselves when we gather materials for writing. If we cross-examine our notes and ideas before we begin a draft, we will save ourselves revising time. Not all questions will apply to all topics. But usually an array of questions directed at the topic undertaken will generate new ideas, details, and directions.

The Journalist's Six.   Anyone who writes for a newspaper or takes a journalism course learns to answer six questions at the beginning of a news story: Who? What? When? Where? Why? How? Here is how a news story in a Detroit daily begins: "A Grosse Pointe systems analyst missed out on a $1,000 first prize at a Pontiac radio station yesterday because he could not remember the lyrics of 'America the Beautiful.'" *Who?* "A Grosse Pointe systems analyst"; *What?* "Missed out on a $1,000 first prize"; *Where?* "At a Pontiac radio station"; *When?* "Yesterday"; *Why?* "Because he could not remember the lyrics of 'America the Beautiful.'" (*How?* does not fit without some stretching.) The journalistic formula anticipates the questions any reader might ask; newspapers cannot afford baffled audiences.

Although essays for freshman English are seldom news stories, if we ask the six questions before we begin to write, they will help us make contact with our audience. If we write about the old television series *L.A. Law,* we may find ourselves easily telling what it was, why it was the way it was, and how it formulated itself—but we may forget to tell when it was on the air, which will leave a question hanging for our readers. If we remember to answer the six questions, we will satisfy our audience's curiosity.

Questions of Form

Rhetoricians, who study effective speech and argumentation, long ago found that most presentations of material were organized according to certain basic patterns. These rhetorical forms can be as useful as the journalist's six questions. They, too, can be turned into basic interrogations—an idea-generating exercise that finds six new ways of asking "Is it bigger than a bread box?"

1. *Comparison and contrast:* What is it like or unlike?
2. *Definition:* What is it?
3. *Division:* What is it composed of? What are its parts?
4. *Classification:* What kind of thing is it?
5. *Process:* How does it work?
6. *Cause and effect:* What causes it? What effect does it have?

The same questions can help us to develop paragraphs when we revise (see Chapter 6).

Thus, if we were preparing to write about leaves changing color in autumn, consideration of rhetorical forms might lead us to write about the chemical *process* by which chlorophyll drains from the maple tree or about the temperature-related *cause* of the change or about the *classification* of different maples or about the *comparison and contrast* between two parts of the country or two kinds of maple tree. Considering these forms, not unlike the journalist's six questions, allows us to consider alternatives for the structure of our paper. We may choose a rhetorical form for our whole paper—*comparing and contrasting* Hogan's Heroes and M★A★S★H *or defining* the national debt—or we may simply use *analysis* or *classification* in a paper; calling something a "situation comedy," we classify a form of popular entertainment.

Selecting Detail

Invention generates detail; next we must select and organize what we have generated. To write a good essay, we have to organize details in the best order, and we must leave out any details, however attractive, that do not contribute to the whole. The whole essay embodies our purpose in writing it. The essay's shape is the shape of our thought, and focus or concentration is the architecture of purpose. The idea of focus, in Chapter 1, is perhaps the most important *structural* idea in writing an essay, unless it is the related idea of a thesis. With many essays it is possible to boil our purpose down to a single sentence that states a thesis: a summary or kernel of purpose, which our detail and argument support. A single governing thesis allows us unity and focus.

Sometimes—before we write or during revision—we find ourselves oppressed with too much detail. Writing is acquiring material (through brainstorming, sprinting, and rapid daily writing), and it is ordering and cutting that material. The writer must be a paradoxical combination of opposites: the big spender and the miser, the exhibitionist and the recluse. Cutting can take place when we organize our notes before writing, or it can come later. When we start to write, it is often hard to know which details are going to prove relevant. Many writers consciously write too much in their first drafts, knowing that they do not yet know what will be useful and knowing that they will later cut for focus and form, often with the help of a discovered thesis directed to a specific audience.

Suppose you describe a particular day. At the end of a vacation, you had a perfect (or perfectly horrible) day. On that Thursday, when you woke up, it was 8:35. You ate scrambled eggs with catsup. These details could be relevant, or they could be mere padding. Cut what does not contribute to the whole. But first, you must have a whole. The point of your paper could be the triviality of your day: a dog barked, the mail was junk, nobody was home when you telephoned your friends. The point is to have a point. Find one—or even make one up. The truth we want is truth-to-feeling; we are not under oath in a court. If we are remembering a sequence of events—A, B, C, and D—we can rearrange the sequence to make a piece of writing true to the feeling we want the whole to give. If event B happened second, but we see in retrospect that it was the emotional climax, we can change the sequence in order to tell the emotional truth. We can use C, A, and D in that order and save B for last. We are still writing out of our own life. We are telling the truth in a serious sense. Within the limits set by credibility, we can even combine different events into one or different people into the same character. Suppose in a family anecdote two uncles move in and out of a story, doing approximately the same things. In telling the anecdote, it might be more shapely and pointed—and just as true—to turn them into one person. This advice does not apply, of course, when the writer's relationship to audience—a report to a committee investigating a problem, a journalist's account of an event—implies a contract to tell the literal truth.

To make a point and to give our writing a shape, we must limit our material. Here we are back to unity. If we try to write about a whole summer, we are most likely to write disjointed paragraphs and be boring and superficial. We should find one event or one unifying device (a place, a person, an automobile, a time of day, a kind of food) to tie together different details. Contrast can make a glue as adhesive as similarity. We must find the detail and form that combined will embody the summer's spirit.

WRITING THE DRAFT

To write the draft, we first try setting our notes in order, notes derived from brainstorming, sprinting, or cross-examining. Orderly notes resemble an informal outline, reminders of what we need to say in the best order of saying. Writing a first draft, we waste time if we worry about finding the perfect beginning. Word processors make it easy to insert whole sentences or paragraphs or to move blocks of text around later, when we have decided on our focus and method of organization. If we do not immediately know how to begin our essay, we should plunge ahead anyway and worry about the introduction later.

What matters is the essay's shape of thought: *the shape we give the essay,* like the motion in the paragraph, *is the structure formed by our thought.* Our matter and our purpose determine our way of proceeding—or they ought to. An anecdote or a historical summary or an explanation of a process must use chronological order. In an argument that advances a thesis, the essay's order embodies persuasion—accumulating detail, proceeding by logic, and using various forms of persuasion or argument.

Our purpose is reflected in our essay's order of development. A different order of ideas can make a different statement, even when the ideas or details remain the same. In a reminiscence, if we begin with pleasant associations and move to horrid ones, we leave the reader with a negative impression; if we move from horrid to pleasant, we leave the reader feeling positive. We could accumulate identical details for each essay but make a different impression by our organization. We have to decide on the point we want to make. There are important associations that result from the order we give details. In a history essay, one student wrote:

> The rainfall in the Southern provinces is approximately two inches a year. On the average. What this means is that most years the country people starve in a drought; one year in five, they drown in a flood. However, the combination of surviving Indian ritual, and a local brand of Roman Catholicism, keeps the people remarkably cheerful and content.

For the same assignment, writing from the same source, another wrote:

> Indian rituals which still survive, combined with a peculiar indigenous Catholicism, keep the natives of the South apparently contented. However, the climatic conditions are deplorable. The rainfall averages two inches a year. This means that the peasants parch for several years in drought, and are drowned in floods the next one.

Both students' original notes for this passage were, approximately,

> Catholicism and Indian stuff
> happy
> rainfall
> floods
> starvation, drought

The two students were heading in different directions—the first toward an expository essay on daily life in the tribe, the second toward an argument for public works such as irrigation and flood control—but they started from the same information, which they organized or pointed in different ways. Their paragraphs embody the different shapes of their different thinking.

We need to make an order that is lucid and expressive. Too often, essays lack lucidity because they lack orderly development. One sentence should lead into another and lead the reader to follow the track of thought. Lucidity and expression carry out thought, writer to reader; we are not expressive if our message is garbled by repetition, by lack of transition, or by afterthought. We need orderly progress in all our writing in order to engage the reader. We must always assume that the reader cannot second-guess our intentions; a lucid structure makes intentions clear.

Beginnings

When considering structure we have to think hard about beginnings and endings for essays. Beginnings are like first meetings: they leave all-important impressions. And as with people, so with writing—there is nothing harder than overcoming a bad first impression. We are bored by vagueness, exhausted by pointless detail, and angered when we feel that our time is being wasted. Many home pages on the World Wide Web include large graphics files or video and audio files with no rhetorical purpose. These files increase the time it takes for the reader to access the page, and many readers are frustrated or angered by the waste of time and resources. Try, while writing, to imagine how your reader would respond. Ask yourself: would I really like to read an essay that begins like this? Sometimes we overexplain at the beginning of an essay and begin too far back. Trying to talk about something that we did last weekend we realize that it resembled something we did last summer; then we realize that last summer's feelings were like the feelings we had at age five when we started kindergarten or at age three when we moved to a new town. All these details may be valid, but to include them all would destroy the essay's shape. The bridge into the country of last weekend would be longer than the country itself. With enough self-questioning, we could begin every autobiographical paper with "I was born" or "My grandparents emigrated from Lithuania in 1905" or "Life for my peasant ancestors in medieval Turkey must have been difficult." Too much detail prevents the reader from perceiving the shape of thought.

Long bridges are not only the curse of autobiographies; the same malady can afflict all writing. In discussing how World War II began, we can begin with the fall of the Roman Empire. Or else we can fall victim to what might be called the closing funnel approach. Setting out to write about the disappearing whale, we begin the essay with the general topic of human destruction of the environment, narrow it to destruction of species, narrow it to destruction of whales, and then narrow it to the decline in population of one type of whale. The last category is the essay's focus; if we are not careful, we can spend three-quarters of our essay walking the bridge to our topic.

The good, sharp beginning narrows the topic. When we understand our writing's purpose, we can begin with reference to that purpose, or with a thesis we propose to explain. We can begin with something that arrests the reader and points to the main topic.

> Humpbacks are mammals, as all whales are; they breathe into huge lungs, bear live young, which they nurse for the better part of a year, and have vestiges of hair . . . .

In this research paper, the author catches our attention immediately with facts that will interest almost anyone, probably because they interested her and she shows it: *huge lungs, for the better part of a year.*

Editors of magazines sometimes refer to hooks, beginnings (or *leads*) to articles constructed to grab the reader by the hair. *Time* is good at hooks. Here are two opening sentences from one issue.

> The United States was founded on a complaint.

> When the young Chinese woman heard a mysterious voice asking, "What's under your pillow?" she felt sure that the answer was a "biological radio apparatus" put there by a special agent who suspected her of crimes against the state.

In the *Saturday Review,* Gordon Lish began an article:

> Like every interesting American, I live in New York City—

All immediately involve our interest, and none has a preamble. Two begin by startling us. A short sentence makes an unconventional assertion that arouses our interest. We will read the next sentence because we want to see what the writer will do. We are *hooked.* At other times a definition of the subject may be essential before we can begin.

> In its widest possible extension the title of this book—*Adventures of Ideas*—might be taken as a synonym for The History of the Human Race. . . .
>
> Alfred North Whitehead, *Adventures of Ideas*

Whitehead builds a swift bridge into his topic. He is free to get right to his point.

Purpose and context determine the kind of beginning. But in any piece of writing, the beginning focuses our writing; it requires special attention, and it requires brevity and incisiveness. Some information we need quickly; information that may be pertinent but not wholly necessary should be held back; information that is both pertinent and necessary but might make a tedious beginning can often be put off until later in the essay, when its relevance becomes obvious and it ceases to seem tedious.

One kind of opener, the overt announcement of what is to be done, is often boring: "I am going to show that the government of the United States is split into three branches, the executive, the legislative, and the judicial." Essays may be constructed analytically by delineating parts, but they should show and not tell. The essay that begins with the sentence above will probably take a paragraph each for the three branches and end, as boringly as it began, "I have shown that the government of the United States is comprised of the executive, the legislative, and the judicial branches." It is structure for people who have difficulty following the story line of a Disney movie.

Endings

Endings, like beginnings, must serve their purpose. In a long, complicated argument, we may be pleased to find at the end a succinct summary of the author's argument. It is like seeing an aerial photograph of country we have just walked through. But the short essay—the kind in which we are most interested in this book—rarely profits from summary and often withers by it. We should point the whole essay toward the last sentence, and when we have written it, stop writing. Often we conclude an essay and then continue writing. The essay writer must develop the confidence to let facts and arguments stand by themselves without epilogue. We should trust the intelligence of the reader. If the point has been clearly made, there is no gain from repeating it. People who moralize at the end of a story or summarize at the end of an argument are the same people who kill jokes by explaining them. In a report about Tracy Kidder's *The Soul of a New Machine,* which recounts the invention of a computer called Eagle, a student concluded:

> Kidder makes an adventure story out of unlikely materials, the marriage of business and technology, the interrelationships of a corporation and its research engineers. Both in the book and in the marketplace, the Eagle flies.

Unfortunately, this student felt the need to continue after her conclusion:

> *The Soul of a New Machine,* by Tracy Kidder, is a book that tells a story both unusual and exciting.

Her paper improved when, at her instructor's suggestion, she revised by crossing out her final paragraph.

Usually we should conclude a topic without seeming to draw attention to the conclusion. Part of a paper's unity is the resolution it comes to, all details organized toward an end. But this resolution can be violated by obviousness; anything that feels tacked on destroys a sense of unity.

Joan Didion, in an essay called "On Going Home," writes about the fragmentation of American family life. Visiting her parents in the house where she grew up, she encounters familiar details of her old life. She feels that she was "born into the last generation to carry the burden of 'home'" and clearly finds a value in the burden. Her feelings are complex, and she ends her essay not by summarizing her feelings or reducing them to abstraction but by turning to her own child and allowing her mixed feelings to show directly.

> It is time for the baby's birthday party: a white cake, strawberry-marshmallow ice cream, a bottle of champagne saved from another party. In the evening, after she has gone to sleep, I kneel beside the

crib and touch her face, where it is pressed against the slats, with mine. She is an open and trusting child, unprepared for and unaccustomed to the ambushes of family life, and perhaps it is just as well that I can offer her little of that life. I would like to give her more. I would like to promise her that she will grow up with a sense of her cousins and of rivers and of her great-grandmother's teacups, would like to pledge her a picnic on a river with fried chicken and her hair uncombed, would like to give her *home* for her birthday, but we live differently now and I can promise her nothing like that. I give her a xylophone and a sundress from Madeira, and promise to tell her a funny story.

Joan Didion, Slouching Towards Bethlehem

When Nina Chan first drafted her personal essay, she had no title and no ending. Her last paragraph attempted to summarize everything she had learned from her experience.

I now understand why my father acted as he did. He wanted me to discover for myself what was important. Making such discoveries is what growing up is all about. When I grow up I will not be the violinist my family wanted me to be. But I will be something else—I will be me.

When Nina reconsidered her draft in terms of focus and impact, she crossed out this passage. If she had done her work in presenting the situation, the reader would be able to draw these necessary conclusions. Just to make sure, however, Nina devised her title: "To Be (Myself) or Not to Be." And then, recalling what her teacher had said about using detail to convey emotion, she found a powerful and direct way to bring her essay to a close.

I think that thought often now—every time I look inside my closet and see my brown violin case packed away in the corner.

Knowing what we do about Nina's struggle, the simple image of the "brown violin case" conveys a great deal. Reading Nina's last words we feel a satisfying sense of completion, or closure. The brevity works. To say any more would be to undercut the power of direct statement.

Revising and Invention

Usually it takes several drafts to arrive at an essay that is worth finishing. Later in this chapter we will follow a student through typical changes. We have already looked at Nina Chan proceeding from an impromptu to a finished essay. Often we will need to revise our first draft in major ways for focus and clarity, removing some paragraphs and adding others, altering the order of details or paragraphs, developing and expanding. Finally, if we are persistent, we will accomplish a draft that is almost there—a roughly finished object that we may now polish and perfect.

In the next chapters we will concentrate on words, sentences, and paragraphs, providing tools for final revisions. But in this chapter on writing an essay, we must anticipate some advice. In revising, as in composing, we must invent. But in order to revise we must find fault with what we have written, and it is difficult to find faults that we have just committed. As the cliché would have it, we can't see the forest for the trees. If we have started writing our paper early enough, we can put time between the latest draft and the final revision; nothing is so helpful as a night's sleep.

First, we should check the drafted essay against the teacher's assignment; it is easy to drift away from original intentions. Second, it helps if we make a checklist of our own typical errors—we can collect them from our teachers' corrections on old themes—so that we can be on guard against them. Spelling? Look up every word that seems doubtful. If you are using a word processor, the computer spell checker program can help you to catch most spelling errors. Computer grammar checkers can help to find some kinds of common grammatical errors. Incomplete sentences? Comma splices or run-on sentences? Parts of sentences not going together? Check chapter 9. Examine the length of your paragraphs. Have you denied your reader the pause of paragraph breaks? Or have you made your paragraphs too short, only three or four lines long? Look at your essay for its sentence structure—many computer grammar checkers will help you examine the readability level, measuring factors such as sentence length and complexity. Many beginners make their essays boring by using too many simple or compound sentences in a row; their prose can start to sound childish. Vary sentence length and complexity. Try reading your words out loud to see what kind of rhythm they make. Would a longer sentence with subordinate clauses (see pages 138–140) offset the staccato sound of simple assertions? The ear, like the mind, must be kept alert. Experiment with different possibilities.

At the suggestion of your instructor, it may be useful at this time to get together with one or two other members of the class, to read and criticize one another's drafts. You can provide examples of audience for one another—models, anticipations.

Finally, look closely at your prose for clichés and empty expressions. Summon the Critic Inside for internal dialogue. The Critic Inside is our ideal listener, our writer's conscience, a voice embodying all that we have learned about clear and honest expression. A cliché discovered is an opportunity for new invention. If you have written that something is the *basic foundation* of something else, and you detect the cliché *basic foundation,* consider what kind of building base you are talking about. Is the *basic foundation* made of granite? Concrete block? Cinder block? Frozen baloney? Empty expressions give us the same opportunity. If you have written that a teacher was *awfully nice,* as critic you should cross it out; then as inventor you should fill the empty space. You should invent, out of memory, a detail or a story or a fresh expression or some quoted speech that *shows* the quality that *awfully nice* tried to *tell*.

A Note on Impromptus

This survey of essay writing emphasizes preparation over several days and advises sleeping on ideas, brainstorming, sprinting, cross-examining, drafting, and revising. It is good to have the time to follow these steps. But sometimes in the real world we are required to write thirty-minute essays on final exams or to put a letter in the mail by five o'clock—or to write an impromptu paper in an English class with only forty minutes for invention, drafting, self-criticism, and revision. We are unlikely to be able to sleep on an impromptu, much as we might like to. Nor are we able to spend much time brainstorming, sprinting, or consulting the Critic Inside. This chapter's advice is still useful, however, even when time is short.

The components of invention, organization, drafting, and revision remain the same whether we have a week or a quarter hour. If our time is brief, all components are reduced in length, and we must remember to follow our habitual methods *in proportion.* If we have learned to spend half our time in preparation and half in execution, we should keep the same proportion when we find ourselves with forty minutes instead of four days. Many beginners make the mistake of changing their methods entirely, feeling so cramped for time that they try to write a final draft right away. The result is panic, and a messy product.

If you have forty minutes, you should spend twenty minutes thinking and organizing and twenty minutes writing and correcting. Try brainstorming a list; try sprinting one small paragraph; circle the most inventive idea, make another list, and organize it into an informal outline. Try remembering the responses of other students to your earlier writing; if there were ways you missed your audience earlier, these are ways to watch out for. Do everything you would do at your desk over an optimal period—only squeeze the time.

Writing an impromptu in the time remaining, write slowly and deliberately—crossing out and correcting—but be legible. If you write on a computer, of course, you can correct, move, delete, or insert words, phrases, sentences, or whole paragraphs with ease. If you write with paper and pen, you should use alternate lines of lined paper. Then during your last-minute revisions, you can add missing phrases or sentences in the blank lines.

BIOGRAPHY OF A THEME

Gian Lombardo took composition in the second term of his freshman year in 1996, doing daily writing, exercises in and out of class, and a weekly essay. His first grades frustrated him: He could not break out of the discouraging C Zone. His teacher, Mrs. Zimbalist, wrote in comments that his worked lacked focus, that he had trouble with organization; she recommended that Gian outline carefully before writing and that he write complete rough drafts. "If you don't," she said, "you are using the word processor to cheat yourself."

When Mrs. Zimbalist assigned a fourth essay, Gian decided to get an early start for once and to try as hard as he could to follow the writing advice he had been transcribing into his composition notebook.

Mrs. Zimbalist explained that in this essay students should write about something other than their own experiences. Personal narratives, she explained, are only one of a great many different kinds of essay possibilities. She asked for a four- to six-hundred word essay making use of comparison and contrast. "You are free to choose whatever subject you wish," she said, "but try to avoid large-scale comparisons—between men and women, Democrats and Republicans . . ."

Some students had questions. Mrs. Zimbalist referred everyone to the definition of comparison and contrast in their textbooks. She reminded them that an essay must be governed by its purpose and that therefore they should find a comparison that could legitimately make a point, fulfill a purpose. Gian raised his hand. If they were not to write about personal experience, he asked, how were they supposed to know what they were talking about? Mrs. Zimbalist replied that the assignment did not prohibit them from writing about something they had experienced; the challenge was to be objective about it, to avoid the autobiographical temptation. "Don't tell us your feelings about the recent election," she said, "or what you did on election day. Tell us what happened in the election itself."

Gian left class and headed for his dorm. Though he would have liked to flop back on his bed for a short nap, he forced himself to sit down at his desk with notebook and pen. If he could just get a topic before the end of the day, he thought, then he could start collecting mental notes. "Compare, contrast, compare, contrast," he muttered, tapping the pen against his knuckles. It struck him right away that almost anything could be compared or contrasted with some other thing. Gian tried to focus on things that interested him, noting a few possibilities quickly:

> downhill skiing vs. cross-country
> Chinese vs. American cooking
> The music industry past and present

Gian wondered if that last notion involved comparison and contrast, then decided that it did. Past and present encompassed two very different approaches to musical expression. But none of these were quite the things he wanted to be thinking about. Gian then looked back through his notebook, glancing at some passages of his daily writing. There were jottings about old girlfriends, his father's football jersey, a trip he had taken with his uncle to Arizona—all of it was, of course, autobiographical. Maybe he could do an objective comparison of the Southwest and the Northwest . . . He tried brainstorming, writing notes without stopping to organize his thoughts, just as Mrs. Zimbalist had suggested. After a few minutes he had this list:

rugged land
few trees, lack of water
N.W. has too much water—why?
different places = different styles of living
different employment
S.W. has industry, auto workers went there
N.W.?
fishing, mountains, Seattle very "hip"—electronics industry, Microsoft . . .

But even as he wrote these phrases down, Gian knew that the topic was too big and did not much interest him. He looked at his watch. Ten minutes until he could go down to lunch. He had just enough time to check his E-mail before lunch. Sitting down at his computer, he was surprised to see that he had three new pieces of mail. There was a message from his father, reminding him to pick up football tickets; a question about chemistry from Tony, his lab partner; and—Gian smiled—a letter from his brother Todd, who was spending the year as an exchange student in New Zealand. He scrolled quickly through Todd's letter, deciding he would read and reply later. Then, saving that and Tony's question, he switched off the computer and headed for lunch.

After lunch Gian dragged himself to the library and worked on his chemistry set. It was a warm afternoon and he was having trouble focusing on the fine print in the textbook. He kept thinking about his brother being in New Zealand, wondering what that was like, wishing he could just get on an airplane and be off. Thank God for E-mail, he thought. And then he stopped, shook his head, and grinned. That was it! The perfect subject. He would compare E-mail with regular postal mail. Even without thinking it through, Gian knew he had a winner. This was a subject that people debated and got excited about. Pushing his chemistry textbook aside, he fished out his composition notebook and opened to a fresh page. For a few minutes he stared into the distance, then he wrote:

letters are slow in arriving
handwritten or typed
a whole long tradition, part of a different world
people saving letters, mom's bundles from her friends
waiting for the mail to come
harder to write because you have to gear up, make a deal out of it
E-mail always working, always there
casual—you just jot it out
you can save it, but usually don't
less exciting, generally

but sense of access makes up for that
E-mail belongs to new way of doing things
people interact differently now
imagine waiting 2 wks. for Todd's letter
What letter? He wouldn't write—he'd call
E-mail more like a phone in some ways

Gian stopped. He glanced at what he had scrawled and felt confident. There was, he saw, a great deal to compare and contrast. It would just be a matter of organizing what he came up with, and he was not too worried about that. When he had enough material, the rest would follow. He felt that he had done his work for the day; he could, as Mrs. Zimbalist suggested, sleep on it.

Before going to bed that night, Gian printed out Todd's E-mail—it was almost two full pages—and after reading it, he decided to reply at length later. He E-mailed Todd a short message saying that he had picked up the letter and that a reply would be coming soon. He was tempted, even then, to start adding things, but he knew that if he got going he would never make it to bed.

The next morning, before going down to breakfast, Gian opened his notebook and wrote for a few minutes:

> The world has changed and so have our means of communication. Years ago people used pen and paper and wrote letters, and these took days—even longer—to reach their destination. My mother and her best friend from college wrote to each other regularly, once a week, for many years (though now they call each other) and mom often refers proudly to her "correspondence." Now, though, millions of people have E-mail and it is very different. There is no paper (you can print a letter out, though), no handwriting, no mailman, no waiting—it is the preferred communication for today's busy world.

Enough. Gian was hungry. He didn't like that phrase "today's busy world"—it sounded like an advertising slogan—but he would worry about that later. He had just wanted to get some words onto the page; he always worked better when he had something to refer to.

After breakfast and his art history lecture, Gian went back to his spot in the library. He had his notebook with him and was planning to work at a rough draft. Before starting a fresh page or making an outline, however, he sat and stared at the short paragraph he had written earlier. Then, uncapping his pen, he circled two phrases: "The world has changed" and "today's busy world." Gian had an inkling that his essay had to be something more than just a compare/contrast menu, that the specific terms of difference had to be tied to some larger explanatory idea.

But what idea might that be? To say that the world was changing was hopelessly general. To say that it had become busy was a half-step closer, but it was still not enough. Then, as Gian sat with his notebook, other ideas started to occur to him. Letters, he thought, belonged to a world still dominated by distance and separation, and by a very different understanding of time. The whole point of sending E-mail to his brother in New Zealand was that he could get his message to the other side of the world instantly. That had to change how he—how everyone—thought about the world.

Gian felt he was starting to get somewhere. He wrote at the top of a notebook page: "Two Worlds." Then, setting his thoughts down quickly, he began:

> Living in today's world, surrounded by gadgets—VCRs, computers, beepers, answering machines—it's easy to forget that things have not always been simple. I pick up an E-mail from my brother in New Zealand and zap back a reply. The world seems small. But then I remember a visit my family took some years ago to Sicily, where my father's family still lives.

Gian stopped. He saw where his thoughts were leading and realized that he did not want to go in that direction—there was too much family material. He wanted to write about ideas, not about his grandparents and their way of living. He ripped out the page, crumpled it up, and started again:

> I've heard people say that E-mail is just mail delivered quicker and better. Wrong. That's like saying that driving a car is just walking with wheels instead of shoes, or something like that. Not only are E-mail and letter writing completely different processes, but their difference tells alot about where the world is headed in the upcoming millennium.

This opening felt right. Gian thought he saw how he might be able to generate a draft from this beginning. But now, instead of beginning another paragraph, he sketched an outline of sorts on the page. He did not want to forget the sequence he had in mind.

    I.   Opening—differences
         Connect to change in world
    II. Letters—handwritten or typed—are physical objects
         Distance determines time lapse between sending and receiving
         Writer figures on time lapse, writes for longer term
         Letters read, re-read, maybe saved
         Style more important
         General sense of importance about written letter
    III. E-mail—nothing exists unless its printed out
         Instant—powerful immediacy
         Geography irrelevant
         E-mail generally disposable
         Encourages chatter, excess
         I rarely keep E-mail

IV.   The difference shows how world is changing
       Seems smaller
       Time has speeded up, people doing many things at once
       More contacts and diversity than before
       More interesting? Or just busier?
       Less sense of importance about events
 V.   A trade-off?
       It has to be—there's no going back
       Keep in mind the advantages—past not golden
       Best of both worlds would be to keep the new but not lose
         touch with the old (the values)
       Possible? We must try

Setting down his pen, Gian felt elated. He had a sense, now, of how his ideas were going to unfold. He knew that he would be able to do a draft now in one sitting. He also knew that he had a dorm party to attend that night. Maybe Mrs. Zimbalist was right—that sometimes it was good just to let ideas sit. After mentally checking his calendar, making sure that he had the next afternoon free and clear, Gian closed his notebook.

When he sat down at his computer to write the following day, Gian felt more confident than usual. Not only did he have his main ideas more or less outlined, but he felt as if the time away from his first jottings had been productive, almost as if he had been working on things in his sleep. Now facing his task, he told himself that the important thing was to get the whole essay out, never mind how roughly, so that he could start to work on the fine points of organization and expression. He decided, therefore, that his first paragraph from yesterday would do just fine. Consulting his outline, he jumped right in at the second paragraph.

> Handwritten or typed, letters are things. They actually travel through space, and take time to do so. The distance determines the time, so that a letter to the next town is not the same as a letter across the ocean. Time and distance are important. The writer understands the delay and writes accordingly. The writer writes less about what's boiling in the kitchen (maybe) and more about his deeper thoughts and feelings. Letters are often better written, the writer takes her time, and style is key. The process encourages a certain amount of thought and planning. Because of this there is often a sense of importance about a letter. I study the envelope, read the letter more than once, and maybe put it away where I keep important things.
>   E-mail is very different

Here Gian stopped. He scrolled back to the beginning and read slowly over what he had written. The gist was there, but he could also feel what Mrs. Zimbalist called his Critic Inside going to work, commenting over his shoulder as he read. It was, he realized, the voice of Mrs. Zimbalist, combined with the voices of a few of his high school teachers. Gian decided to ignore it for now; he would let the roughness remain. Then, when he had everything written, he would print the essay out and let that critic do his job. Here is Gian's first draft, complete with the Critic Inside's comments and corrections. On pages 68–72 is the rewritten version, which Gian handed in, and for which he received his first B+.

```
Two Worlds
```

```
    I've heard people say that E-mail
is just mail delivered quicker and
better. That's like saying that dri-          grammar
ving a car is walking with wheels in-
stead of shoes, but that there is no
other difference. Not only are letter
writing and E-mail completely differ-
ent processes, but their difference
tells us alot about where the world          a/lot
will be heading in the new millennium.
    Handwritten or typed, letters are
things, they actually travel through         comma splice
space and time to get from here to
there. The distance determines the
time. A letter across town is not a          weak verb
letter across the ocean. Time and dis-
tance important. The writer figures on       fragment
the delay and writes differently. He
writes less about what's for dinner
and more about his thoughts and feel-
ings—though on the other hand that           vague
```

could depend on the person. People are

different the world over. Letters tend

to be better written. Style is key.

Because of this there is often a sense

of importance. I study the envelope,

the stamp, read it more than once, and

maybe I save it.

E-mail is obviously very differ-

ent. It is instant, travelling around

the world in an instant, and unless

you print it out doesn't physically

exist. Geography doesn't matter. The

ease of writing and sending make for a

different kind of thinking and style.

Often you just say whatever and zap it

along. E-mail, thus, matters less, or

it can. People don't usually save it.

They glance at it and if it's not im-

portant they don't save it.

The difference between E-mail and

letters points to a larger change hap-

pening in the world. Science and tech-

nology—communications—have not only

made things faster and more efficient,

they've shrunk the world as if by

magic. Time and distance used to be a

big deal. People travelled for days to

get places, letters did the same.

Things were harder. But maybe they

were also clearer, more important.

obvious

too casual

transition to "I"
feels sudden

repeated word

"you"?
"zap" too casual

too many short
sentences

paragraph idea
needs expansion

too casual

watch out for gener-
alization
vary sentence
lengths

Sometimes now everything feels too
easy. Maybe a letter to New Zealand
should take time. Maybe I *should* race
to the mailbox every day to see if it
has come. Where is the mystery?   *clarify*

    Still, it's a trade-off. Would we
go back if we could? Would we make
things harder just to have them more
real? I don't think so. I think we
need to be aware of the advantages,
but we can't let go of the things that   *maybe too general*
had value. We have to remind ourselves
about what really matters and what
doesn't. E-mail is faster, but when my
mother looks at her bundle of letters
from her best friend, she sees a lifetime of friendship there. We must be
careful.   *ending feels sudden*

    Two Worlds by Gian Lombardo

    Many people have said that E-mail
is just a faster way to deliver letters. Then again, there were probably
people who thought that driving was
just a modified way of walking. The
fact is that letter writing and E-mail
are completely different processes.
Their difference tells us a great deal

about where we may be headed in the
new millennium.

Handwritten or typed, the letters
that we put into envelopes and mail
are *things*. They travel through actual
space and take time getting from one
place to another. The distance of the
mailing determines the time, so that a
letter to the next town is very different from an air-mail letter across
the ocean.

The time and distance influence
the letter-writer. If I am writing on
paper to my brother in New Zealand, I
will be less likely to complain about
yesterday's dorm lunch. I will probably write about my relationships and
some things that I've been thinking
about. I will also take more care with
my style, trying to write in a way
that is interesting and worth rereading. People tend to regard letters as
important. My brother might save my
letter; he might read it back to me
years from now.

E-mail is very different. It is
instant, like a telephone call, travelling from point to point as an electronic impulse. If you don't print it
out, the message doesn't physically

exist—it exists, as they say, "virtually." With E-mail geography is no obstacle and time is not important. I
can zap a message to New Zealand whenever I want to, and it gets there as
fast as I can click the keys.

The ease of this kind of writing
and sending probably makes for a different kind of communication. I *can*
complain about the mystery meat—or am
more likely to. I can rattle on about
friends and movies and tell much more
than I might in a letter. This is, in
part, because I am not so focused on
style and profundity. The down side? I
might be less likely to say something
deeper. My brother might glance at my
letter, have a laugh, and then delete.
People seem to agree that E-mail is
faster and easier, but also that it
seems to matter less.

This difference sheds some light
on a larger change taking place in
our world. Science and technologies—
communications in particular—have accomplished wonders. They have sur-
rounded us with messages, images, and
data of all kinds. We are never more
than a few keystrokes away from the
information we want. But along the

way the world has gotten smaller,
less mysterious.

Time and distance used to matter a
great deal. People travelled for days
to get to places. For the generation
of our grandparents, things were much
more difficult—and they will tell us
this whether or not we ask. But they
also say that life did not feel so
crazy and scattered, that the world
made more sense. Maybe a message to
New Zealand *should* take weeks—maybe
that's what makes New Zealand New
Zealand. And maybe I *should* race to
the mail-box to see if my brother has
written, because when I'm waiting I'm
also missing him more.

But what if the choice were given?
Would we go back? Would we make things
harder just so that they would matter
more? I don't think so. The point,
just as with growing up, is to learn
what is important and what is not. We
should not sacrifice the possibility
of sending messages around the world
in an instant, but we should remember
what things used to be like and that
there were advantages to slower modes
of life. When I finish writing these
words I will check to see if my

brother has sent me any new messages
since yesterday. But I will also reflect on the shelf in my mother's
study, where she keeps the bundles of
letters from her college friend. She
tells me that every time she sees
those bundles there she thinks of a
lifetime of friendship. We should
never risk losing such a feeling—no
amount of speed is worth it.

EXERCISES

1. In class, imitate collectively how we choose a subject and narrow a topic. Narrow these general subjects into topics.

drug testing	environmental pollution
the plight of the aged	alternate energy sources
coming to college	college admission policies

Some subjects are broader than others, but all can be narrowed further.

2. In class, brainstorm details for a paper on a recent local controversy. (Look at the editorial page of the local paper for some ideas.) Then try to organize the details, using the blackboard. Or take the details home and elaborate and organize them for the next class.

3. Write a paragraph rapidly (sprint) in class, taking as a starting point one of the topics listed in question 1. Read the paragraph aloud for class discussion. Which sentence or phrase would profit from expansion and development?

4. (a) On your own, work up an idea that might be developed into a theme. (b) Accumulate details, brainstorming or sprinting if you wish. (c) Organize details, eliminating those that seem irrelevant, tailoring your material to your purpose. (d) Bring all material to class. Students can read their material one at a time for general discussion. Or the instructor may want to collect the material and copy some of it to use in the next class meeting.

The instructor may also ask one student to outline his or her topic for the rest of the class. Students will then have twenty minutes to sprint impromptu paragraphs. These may be compared and discussed.

5. Read the student essay below. (a) Does this essay answer the journalist's six questions? (b) How well does this student accomplish comparison and contrast? Might questions of form have helped this student revise? Does the theme show a purpose? Is it addressed to an audience? (c) Pretending that you are a teacher, correct this paper in the margins. Give it a grade. (d) Revise and improve one of the paragraphs of this essay.

Night and Day
Betty Hampers

There is a small ski area about five miles away from my home town of Easthampton, Massachusetts, called the Mt. Tom Ski Area. Besides its excellent slopes and trails, Mt. Tom is the only ski resort in my neighborhood that offers both night and day skiing. Although night skiing is convenient and fun, there are many advantages to skiing during the day.

One annoying problem that can be avoided by skiing during the day is the large crowds. In the daytime, most people are in school or working and therefore, aren't able to go skiing. That means the parking facilities are less crowded and the lift lines are shorter, giving you more time on the ski slopes. Usually the conditions of the mountain are best during the daytime. The surface powder is still deep and fluffy. At night, the slopes often become icy because the deep powder has been worn away.

Also, feeling the sun's warmth as you glide down the slopes makes daytime skiing quite enjoyable. When the sun is warm, you can shed some of those layers of clothing. Who knows, maybe you'll even get a suntan!

With all that daytime skiing has to offer, there are still some disadvantages. For example, because your friends are either in school or working, you have to ski alone. Skiing just isn't as much fun unless you have a friend to fall down and look like a fool with! The view when riding the chairlift is much more glamorous at night than in the day. The bluegreen and white lights you see from above look like the flashing eyes of some Hollywood monster.

However, I still haven't mentioned safety, the most important advantage to skiing during the day. In the daytime, the trails are much more visible. At night, they are dimly lit and can be dangerous if you're not careful. In case of injury, it is much easier to locate an emergency telephone than it is at night. For these reasons alone, I feel that daytime skiing is best.

6. Which of these beginnings are interesting and which seem potentially boring? Why? How might different purposes be served by different beginnings?

    a. When the United Nations met in September, its members were already agitated, anxious, and almost apoplectic.

    b. The origins of the missile crisis are already well known to the informed reading public.

    c. Bang!

    d. When I was born I lived in Cleveland. Then my family moved to Akron when I was two years old. After that we moved to Muncie, Indiana.

    e. The goat had three eyes.

7. Revise this beginning:

Every Easter we drove to my great Aunt's house in Troy to eat a ham for Easter dinner. Even when my father was a little boy, they had gone to Troy for Easter. Sometimes it would snow and we would be late. Once we blew a tire about half way, and the spare was soft, and we took at least an hour and a half to get it fixed.

Last year was my Senior year in high school, and my great aunt thought graduating from high school was a big deal, so I knew I would get a lot of attention when I got there. We have to pack because we actually stay over Friday and Saturday nights. Fortunately, for some reason, I packed my tennis shoes and my jeans. If I hadn't, I wouldn't have been able to play touch football decently, I wouldn't have wound up in the emergency ward, and I wouldn't have met Linda.

8. Consulting the margins of essays your teacher has returned with corrections, make a checklist of repeated errors. Bring it to class or conference to see if your instructor agrees with your self-assessment. Use your revised list when you write your next essay.

4

Words

THE SMALLEST UNIT

When we study writing we learn to swim by jumping into the lake; some of us swallow much lake water before we paddle to shore. How do we learn to write a paper of five paragraphs when we don't know what a paragraph is? How do we write a paragraph out of seven sentences when the concept of "sentence" remains fuzzy? With writing as with many endeavors, we start at the end because it is the only place where we can make a beginning. We must try everything at once. After we have made a start, only then is it possible to return to beginnings. Now we attend to words, sentences, and paragraphs. Presumably the student comes to this section after writing several essays. In this section we look at the smaller units of writing with the notion that having sketched out some larger shapes, we can concentrate on language for a while.

THE INSIDES OF WORDS

Words Themselves

It may seem difficult, at first, to think of words apart from contexts; *salt* does not stand alone; it is part of "salt and pepper" or "Please pass the salt." Words seem like drops of water in a stream that has its own wholeness and its own motion. But when you write well, each word is accurate and honest and exact in itself, and it contributes its special history to the wholeness of the stream of meaning.

The writer must be able to feel words intimately, one at a time. He must also be able to step back, inside his head, and see the flowing sentence. But he starts with the single word. He starts with tens of thousands of these units, and he picks among them. He may end by writing a passage like this account of man's first sleep on the moon:

> It was almost three-thirty in the morning when the astronauts finally prepared for sleep. They pulled down the shades and Aldrin stretched out on the floor, his nose near the moon dust. Armstrong sat on the cover of the ascent engine, his back leaning against one of the walls, his legs supported in a strap he had tied around a vertical bar. In front of his face was the eyepiece of the telescope. The earth was in its field of view, and the earth, "like a big blue eyeball" stared back at him. They could not sleep. Like the eye of a victim just murdered, the earth stared back at him.

> Norman Mailer, *Of a Fire on the Moon*

Until the end, this exposition seems simple and straightforward. Simple and straightforward it is, with the power of visual exactness, "his nose near the moon dust," and the unexpected detail, "a strap he had tied around a vertical bar." Mailer cements each word in place exactly and inevitably, with the help of rhythm and sentence structure. For now, just look at how he prepares for the last, emotional image with related words.

This passage, and much of Mailer's book, is about man and machine. The machinery is sophisticated, complex, overwhelming. Men are frail in comparison. The language begins to embody this idea by repeating the names of parts of the body: *nose, back, legs, face.* We have become accustomed to the jerking motions of the puffed-up spacesuits, as if we were watching robots. Now suddenly we see *nose* and *face.* We might be a mother looking at a sleeping child. From *face* we move to the most vulnerable and necessary of sense organs, the *eye,* first by way of a telescope's *eyepiece,* then by a visual comparison, easy to follow, of the earth to a *big blue eyeball,* which stares. We have departed from the astronauts' bodies and moved on to the emotional crux: the earth is dead, murdered by the astronauts who leave it behind for another destination, beginning the exploration outward, into the stars. Mailer makes his point not by telling us about it overtly, but by his control of language, his understanding of the insides of words, so that the movement from *nose* to *face* to *eyepiece* and *view* to *victim just murdered*—in each case a distancing movement—has an inner and emotional necessity.

Here is another example:

> All the warm night the secret snow fell so adhesively that every twig in the woods about their little rented house supported a tall slice of white, an upward projection which in the shadowless gloom of early morning lifted depth from the scene, made it seem Chinese, calligraphic, a stiff tapestry hung from the gray sky, a shield of lace interwoven with black thread.

> John Updike

This sentence begins a short story called "The Crow in the Wood." Updike exercises the possibilities of our language in rhythm, in variety of sentence structure, and in observation that is dreamy and precise at the same time. He does it with words. Instead of looking at everything he does, let us look at two words that stand out. *Adhesively* is a word we all know, from the noun or adjective *adhesive,* as a longer way of saying *glue* or *sticky.* Here the snow "fell . . . adhesively." Snow really cannot fall like glue, and so we have something apparently inaccurate; yet it is right, because the context prepares us. It is a *warm night;* the snow will be damp. And using *adhesively* rather than *stickily* shows that the snow is not gooey to the fingers but will readily adhere to something. What's more, the word's four measured syllables give us a sensation of slowness—we can feel the steady downward motion of the snow. *Adhesively* by its unusualness draws the right attention to itself.

Then look at the word *slice:* "every twig . . . supported a tall slice of white." Most of us would have said something about snow *piling* or *accumulating* on branches. But a "tall slice of white," besides being pleasing to the ear, is a brilliant image; the sharpness of *slice,* together with the image of whiteness, nearly dazzles the eye. With the word *slice* is an unspoken knife, just out of sight. And I think we have a moment's vision of an upright piece of white-frosted cake.

We could pick many more words for praise in the passages from Mailer and Updike, and maybe for blame as well (we will do that later). But the excellence here is perhaps like all excellence. These writers are *original, as if seeing a thing no one else has seen;* yet they report their vision in a *language that reaches the rest of us.* Here, again, we find the opposites we must combine. For the first quality, writers need imagination and freshness of perception; for the second, skill. Without both qualities, they could not write such a passage. Imagination without skill makes a lively chaos; skill without imagination, a deadly order.

No Synonyms

To appreciate the word—the *eyepiece,* the *eyeball,* the *slice,* the *adhesively*—writers and readers must first realize that no words can be exact synonyms. Some words are close to one another in meaning, close enough to reveal that they are not the same. Writers must know not just the surface definitions of words; they must go deeper and realize the families of contexts into which words have extended their associations—like *slice* with *knife* and even *cake.* These families are the connotations of the word and the associations we make with its denotation. We use *denotation* to mean the explicit or literal meaning of a word, *connotation* to mean a word's implications. The verb *to stagger* denotes an unsteady or irregular motion; one of its connotations is drunkenness. Associations are different from connotations. *Pepper* is not a connotation of *salt* but an association of it. Because we use the whole family, it does not matter that we discriminate connotation from association. But we must know the insides of words; we must be a friend of the family.

The verbs *to emulate, to imitate, to copy,* and *to ape* are synonyms by definition, but when we use them in a sentence, they carry slight differences in meaning. *To emulate* sounds fancy; also, it usually implies that the imitation involves self-improvement. *To imitate* is neutral, except that everyone knows that an imitation is not the real thing; inferiority shadows the word. *To copy* is to reproduce exactly; like *to imitate,* it states a lack of originality. *To ape* is to mimic, and to be comical or mocking about it. If you wanted to say that a young pianist imitated a famous virtuoso, but you carelessly used *ape* instead of *imitate,* you would grant her style the grace of a gorilla. Context is all; the inside of a word must reinforce or continue the force built by the context. When a sportswriter wrote that one middle linebacker aped another middle linebacker, he was being witty.

Dictionaries of synonyms and other books, especially *Roget's Thesaurus,* list words that resemble one another. Experienced writers can sometimes use a thesaurus to joggle their brain to find not a *synonym* but the *right* word. They will be aware of the insides of the words they discover. The thesaurus can be useful not for supplying words never heard before (we know words only when we have met them in sentences; some dictionaries supply examples of words in use) but to remind writers of words known in the past but not remembered when needed.

Sometimes an unsophisticated writer finds disaster in such a book. A thesaurus supplies us with words that *resemble* one another, but we must recognize the *differences* among them. When I look up *imitation* in my pocket *Roget,* I find under Verbs:

> imitate, copy, mirror, reflect, reproduce, repeat; do like, echo, re-echo, catch, match, parallel; forge, counterfeit.
> mimic, ape, simulate, impersonate, act, etc. (drama), represent, etc., parody, travesty, caricature, burlesque, take off, mock, borrow.
> follow in the steps (or wake) of, take pattern by, follow suit [colloq.], follow the example of, walk in the shoes of, take after, model after, emulate.

The editors separate the verbs into three categories of association, which ought to help the cautious writer, but it is difficult sometimes to defend their sorting out. Why does *forge* or *counterfeit* belong among the closer synonyms in the first group and *emulate* among the phrases in the third group? Why is *represent* among the comic or belittling words? Putting *ape* with *travesty* and *parody,* however, reminds us of the comic insides of *ape.* Beginning writers should certainly be wary of a thesaurus because if they believe too wholeheartedly in synonyms, they can produce a prose that means something completely different from what they intend. The sentence

> I walked in the flowers that bordered the garden, sniffing the sweet airs of spring.

could become

> I peregrinated in the flowerets that flounced the orangery, sniffing the saccharine ventilation of the vernal equinox.

Spoken by W. C. Fields, the second version could be perfect for its context, but otherwise it makes sense only as an example of how people misuse a thesaurus.

Using dictionary synonyms, you can test your sensitivity to the insides of words. Put the adjectives *false, fake, phony,* and *insincere* with the noun *laugh.* Everyone has heard laughs that are unreal, laughs that flatter, laughs that express the laugher's nervousness, or laughs at jokes that are not funny. If we wrote a description of such a laugh, we might want to write, "His laugh was false" or "His laugh was fake" or "His laugh was phony" or "His laugh was insincere." Each time the exact meaning differs. "His laugh was false" sounds direct and serious, a stern and objective judgment. "His laugh was fake" sounds harsher, a strong indictment of the laugher; it implies that the falseness was deliberate. "His laugh was phony" tells us more about whoever wrote the phrase. The choice of *phony* over *false* or *fake* or *insincere* makes the speaker imply something like "I am relaxed enough to be slangy." In contrast, "His laugh was insincere" sounds slightly pompous in its moral judgment—partly pompous, partly naive.

These attempts to name the associations that words gather, without setting the context that story or essay bestows, are speculation; but whatever the context, the words would all be different. Slightly, but genuinely, different. Katherine Anne Porter announced in 1961 that she had discovered "a law" that she put into "a little axiom":

> There is no such thing as an exact synonym and no such thing as an unmixed motive.

Literalness and Metaphor

Another way to become sensitive to the insides of words is to take them as literally as you can. When you read "Fog enveloped the city," try seeing a gigantic gray-brown envelope enclosing Los Angeles. You can see some silliness in literal images—but it is a silliness that can increase your sensitivity to words. Puns are another form of useful silliness. Punning is a relaxed playing with the sounds that sense is made of: words have meaning, but words also *halve* meaning.

Literal-mindedness, like all exercises that can improve your writing, can improve your reading as well. Literal-mindedness exposes mixed metaphors, careless phrases comparing things that are comic or gross or inappropriate when brought together. Metaphors usually become mixed when a writer uses the kind of clichés called "dead metaphors" without noticing their original meanings. Sometimes people write, "The door yawned open"; the would-be comparison of door to mouth is dead from overuse. Sometimes people write, "The door beckoned," and the dead metaphor has the door turn into a hand that gestures an invitation. Once a student wrote in a paper, "The door yawned and beckoned." Two clichés make a mixed metaphor, if we are carefully reading the insides of words: first the door is a huge, gaping mouth; suddenly an arm materializes between rows of teeth and motions us to enter.

When we take words literally, we respond to metaphor. We see the fog *compared* to an envelope. A metaphor is a comparison made without being stated. We *state a comparison* as a simile—"like a big blue eyeball"—and we *make* a comparison when we leave out *like* or *as.* Hamlet in his soliloquy wonders if he should "take arms against a sea of troubles," rather than against troubles as vast and overwhelming as the sea. It is futile to fight with the ocean. The futility is what Shakespeare had in mind. If you take the words literally, you might see an armored knight wading into the surf and slashing at the waves with his sword. The image shows an emotion that the abstract word *futility* would only name. The picture—which we receive by literal reading—gives us the emotion without losing the idea.

Sense Words

Words that carry feeling most strongly convey pictures and smells and touches and tastes and noises. Images are details of sense. The more sensuous words are, the more they reach us and move us. Updike embodies feelings of cozy shelter and of precise observation of the outside world. He does not tell us how to feel, but he arranges the sense details so that we will supply the inner response ourselves. Mailer does something similar with ideas. He does not abstract them from the actions. When he gives us an exact visual image of the astronauts trying to sleep on the moon, he gets us to feel their cramp and discomfort without ever using those words.

In his essay "Once More to the Lake," E. B. White needs to let his audience know that his son lacked experience of lakes; he therefore speaks of "my son, who had never had fresh water up his nose and who had seen lily pads only from train windows." Sense words *always* reach the reader with more strength than words of generality, like "lacked experience of lakes." The phrase "had fresh water up his nose" probably wakens a sharp sensation-memory in every reader.

Sense words carry feeling, and they fulfill purposes appropriate to different kinds of writing: for Mailer, the sense words embody a speculation; for Updike, they convey sensation to enhance the illusion of fiction. For Jane Addams, in this passage from *Twenty Years at Hull House,* images explain a scene at the same time as they express outrage over poverty in Victorian London:

> . . . On Mile End Road, from the top of an omnibus which paused at
> the end of a dingy street lighted by only occasional flares of gas, we

saw two huge masses of ill-clad people clamoring around two huck-sters' carts. They were bidding their farthings and ha'pennies for a vegetable held up by the auctioneer, which he at last scornfully flung, with a gibe for its cheapness, to the successful bidder. In the momentary pause only one man detached himself from the groups. He had bidden on a cabbage, and when it struck his hand, he instantly sat down on the curb, tore it with his teeth, and hastily devoured it, un-washed and uncooked as it was. He and his fellows . . . were huddled into ill-fitting, cast-off clothing, the ragged finery which one sees only in East London. Their pale faces were dominated by that most unlovely of human expressions, the cunning and shrewdness of the bargain-hunter who starves if he cannot make a successful trade, and yet the final impression was not of ragged, tawdry clothing nor of pinched and sallow faces, but of myriads of hands, empty, pathetic, nerveless, and workworn, showing white in the uncertain light of the street, and clutching forward for food which was already unfit to eat.

Notice that our sense of outrage, almost without exception, comes from the images chosen; we are not *told,* except when she writes, "that most unlovely of human expressions"; we are *shown.* If Addams used only ab-stractions like *degradation* and *extreme poverty,* we could forget them easily; we do not forget the man who devours the cabbage *unwashed and uncooked* or the hands clutching at inedible food.

Misusing the Insides of Words

Just as we can learn to embody feelings and sensations by being aware of a word's associations and connotations and by using language that ap-peals to the senses, so we can misuse words to fool ourselves and other peo-ple. By misusing the insides of words, we are insincere. The poet W. B. Yeats wrote, "The rhetorician would deceive his neighbors, / The sentimentalist himself." A rhetorician, in his usage, is something like a propagandist—one who manipulates words to achieve some end. Sentimentality means cheap or exaggerated feeling, emotion that is not genuine. Usually, the rhetorician who wishes to deceive others must first become a sentimentalist who de-ceives himself. In the advertising business, it is common wisdom that you have to *believe* in your product, so that grown people believe that Dento is superior to all other toothpastes. To con others, you begin by conning yourself, or you end that way.

Some propagandists deceive by will. The conscious manipulator sets out to change minds by slanting words to *seem* objective and yet to carry a disguised subjective content. Newsmagazines *(Time, Newsweek, U.S. News & World Report)* generally serve specific corporate or political interests. They are not neutral—what besides the naked fact *is* neutral?—and often convey subtle editorial comment within their reporting. Newspapers do the same, though the best editors try to keep the editorials editorial and the news objective. But even when you appear objective, you can select with bias.

One photograph of candidate Y looks flattering; another makes him look like an ass.

We will never destroy bias, but we can learn to see bias and not be deceived by reporting that is really editorializing. A few years back, one newsmagazine blatantly supported one presidential candidate. It openly supported him editorially. And in its news stories it supported him subtly, using the associations of words. Candidate A, it said, "in his rumpled suit slouched into the gleaming limousine." Candidate B, however, "strode smiling into his black sedan."

Now, a sedan may sound expensive, but it may also seem to suit the dignity required of a candidate for high office. *Gleaming limousine* is more lavish, more gloatingly rich. *Rumpled suit* and *smiling* are obvious contrasts. The most telling use of the loaded word is the contrast between *strode* and *slouched*. Who would vote for a man who slouched when he could pick one that strode instead? Yet in all fairness, can we say that the *news* in each sentence is different? In the flattest language, the sentence would read, "The man got in the car." The rhetoricians of the newsmagazine, playing on the separation between meaning and expression, flash us the sign: "Vote for B!" Because they pretend to objectivity, their use of sense words to influence opinion is underhanded.

Rhetoricians and propagandists—"spin doctors" as they are sometimes called—manipulate language and images for a living. We know their motives. But what about the thousand and one deceptions we all practice in daily life and the loaded words we kid ourselves with? We use euphemism to persuade ourselves that one thing is really another; a *janitor* cleans floors, but it sounds more lofty to call him a *custodian*. When we say that someone is *wealthy,* we avoid the plainer word *rich,* which has acquired overtones of vulgarity. If a real estate agent shows you a two-room shack converted from a chicken coop, he does not call it a *house;* he calls it a *cottage.* A Cadillac is never a *used car;* it is *previously owned.*

Often, a euphemism is more abstract or general than the plain word. The euphemism not only sounds fancier (mortician/undertaker; route salesman/milkman) but also has less color or imagery. H. L. Mencken, in *The American Language,* gave some historical background to American euphemisms.

> The tendency to engaud lowly vocations with names presumably dignified goes back to the Revolution, and has been frequently noted by English travelers, beginning with Thomas Anburey in 1779. In 1784 John Ferdinand Dalziel Smyth observed that the smallest American shopkeepers were calling their establishments *stores,* which indicated a large place to an Englishman. "The different distinct branches of manufacturers," he said, "such as *hosiers, haberdashers, clothiers, linen drapers, grocers, stationers,* etc., are not known here; they are all comprehended in the single name and occupation of *merchant* or *store-keeper.*" By 1846 the American barbershop had begun to be a *shaving*

salon and by 1850 a photographer was a *daguerrian artist.* By 1875 barbers were *tonsorial artists* or *tonsorialists,* and in the early 80s presentable saloon keepers became *restauranters* or *restauranteurs.* By 1901 the *Police Gazette* was carrying on a campaign for the abandonment of the lowly *bartender* and the adoption of either *bar clerk* or *mixologist.*

But euphemism is not only comical. We employ euphemism, frequently, when we want to conceal something painful. When we have a tomcat castrated, we hesitate to admit that we have cut off his testicles or even that we have castrated him; we have had him *altered.* We have a tooth *extracted;* it would be more painful to have it *pulled.*

Politics and political acts of destruction always bring forth the worst in our prose, as we struggle to justify ourselves. Hitler euphemistically labeled his genocide of Jews "the final solution." The most massive outrage ever perpetrated is cloaked in the tidy neutrality of an abstract phrase. One of the finest essays on the deeper implications of style is George Orwell's "Politics and the English Language," written in the 1940s. He says:

> Millions of peasants are robbed of their farms and sent trudging along the roads with no more than they can carry: this is called *transfer of population* or *rectification of frontiers.* People are imprisoned for years without trial, or shot in the back of the neck or sent to die of scurvy in Arctic lumber camps; this is called *elimination of undesirable elements.* Such phraseology is needed if we want to name things without calling up mental pictures of them. Consider for instance some comfortable English professor defending Russian totalitarianism. [George Orwell was English and was writing after Stalin's execution of the Kulaks and the mass murders of the Soviet purges of the late 1930s.] He cannot say outright, "I believe in killing off your opponents when you can get good results by doing so." Probably, therefore, he will say something like this:
>
> "While freely conceding that the Soviet regime exhibits certain features which the humanitarian may be inclined to deplore, we must, I think, agree that a certain curtailment of the right to political opposition is an unavoidable concomitant of transitional periods, and that the rigors which the Russian people have been called upon to undergo have been amply justified in the sphere of concrete achievement."

Meanwhile, the bullet enters the back of the head. Always be suspicious—as Orwell advises—when the words do not call up a picture.

Collecting Words

We must watch our words to see if we are using them with respect for honest expression. It helps to love words, and a love of words is something that we can develop. The growing writer finds pleasure in becoming a word collector, picking up, examining, and keeping new words (or familiar words seen suddenly, as if for the first time) like seashells or driftwood.

Think of the richness in *hogwash* or the exact strength in *rasp*. English abounds in short, strong words. You can collect words from books, of course, but you can also find them in speech; a sense of lively speech adds energy to the best writing. A writer listens to speech—others' and even his own—with a greedy ear. Primitive people and children love words as things in themselves and collect them as ornaments. To become a better writer, rediscover some of the pleasure from words-as-things that you had in your childhood but have probably lost along the way. Patrol the miles of speech looking for words like *flotsam*.

Sometime, when you are in the library, take down from the shelves one of the thirteen volumes of the *Oxford English Dictionary* and browse a little. The English poet and novelist Robert Graves says only one book is indispensable to the writer's library: the *OED*. In the thirteen volumes of the original, the editors tried to make the most precise possible map of the English language. They left out only recent coinages and words considered unprintable at the time of publication.

It is not only the *OED*'s completeness that makes it so valuable; it is the context given for each word. The editors try to supply a context for the earliest example of each shade of meaning for every word; for each word in the language the dictionary provides a small biography, or *etymology*. Words, like individuals and nations, have complex and fascinating histories. Suppose we look up the word *vegetable*. More than three columns of small print chronicle the life of the word, which began as an adjective meaning "having the vegetating properties of plants; living and growing as a plant or organism endowed with the lowest form of life." The earliest example is from 1400. The poet John Lydgate, a couple of decades later, wrote of the wind (spelling modernized): ". . . that is so comfortable / For to nourish things vegetable." When Andrew Marvell wrote "To His Coy Mistress" two and a half centuries later (1687), he used the adjective in the same way: "My vegetable love should grow / Vaster than empires and more slow." Six examples (complete with small context) come between Lydgate and Marvell.

Meanwhile, the noun *vegetable* got started in 1582, when an author named J. Hester spoke of "the Hidden Vertues of sondrie Vegitables, Animalles, and Mineralles." The reader can discover thirty-six contexts for the word *vegetable* as a noun from 1582 to modern times—and many shades of meaning. If you take pleasure in words, you will find your sensitivity to the insides of words increasing as you know more about the history of words. Meanings keep changing, of course, but old meanings live on as part of a word's connotative or associative life. So much of our history, external and internal, global and psychic, is coded into our words. The more you know, the more you respect the integrity of the word. (*Integrity,* as we find out when we check the O.E.D. originally meant "wholeness.") A word's wholeness includes all its possibilities: its family, its insides.

Words as Blanks

A frequent failure in our language, spoken or written, is our use of words that can mean anything the context requires. These words are like blanks for the reader or listener to fill in. Words of vague praise or blame— *lovely, nice,* and *terrible*—are frequent blanks. *Great. Terrific.* What does "nice hair" look like? Is it red or blond or white or black or brown? Long or short? Liveliness is specificity. Obscenities are common words as blanks, used without attention to their literal meaning. Vogue words are usually blanks also. *Awesome, wicked, psyched. Fink* was popular some years ago as a vogue word of contempt, no more precise than the *jerk* or *creep* of earlier generations. Yet once *fink* meant something exact: a man employed to join a labor union and spy for bosses. Words of complex history suddenly come into fashion and lose all color. *Funky* moved from black American speech into television—and no longer has anything to say.

Words and Associations

Words used as blanks get in the way of writing and thinking and feeling. Words mean things only by our agreement. If we start using *April* to mean *sunset* or *anything pleasant,* it will not be of use to us anymore. Our agreements about words are coded into dictionaries, which of course change as the words shift gradually in meaning because of historical change and the way that literary genius adapts old words to new conditions. Our agreements about words are also coded into the dictionary from which we really make our sentences—the dictionary (the computer) of the brain. This mental collection is even more complicated and useful for our writing than the dictionary on the shelf. The innumerable associations of the word *April* are stored in it, waiting to be used in the right way at the right time. The inside of a word is a huge room of possibilities, limited—because *April* does not include *August* or *catsup* for most of us—but multiple: flowers and showers, Easter, spring, seeds, vacation from school, Chaucer and Browning and Eliot for readers of poetry, ploughing or manure spreading for farmers.

Someone might associate *April* with catsup or cats or soup or a girl in the first grade who had that name. These associations are private. The few phrases I listed at the end of the preceding paragraph, however, are public or general. Other people can share them. A moment's thought will usually reveal to the writer, at least in revision, whether he is using a word privately or generally. "Tulips like catsup" would be a grotesque and inappropriate simile for most of us—despite the real color—though it might be a spontaneous expression of the writer who privately associated April with catsup. A writer must learn to suppress the highly private because writing must get through to an audience; you are talking to someone besides yourself; you have climbed out of the pure self-involvement of the crib and are trying to make human contact.

Words and Audience

But we must also remember, in choosing words, that an audience is not *everyone*. The larger the audience we try to reach, the fewer associations we can take for granted and the more limited our possibilities. If we are writing for a big newspaper, we probably do not assume that most of our readers associate *April* with Chaucer, Browning, and Eliot. An idea of the audience is crucial to our choice of words. Everyone makes this sort of choice in conversation: we use words with our best friend that we do not use with our grandmother; if we hitch a ride with a white-haired man wearing a blue suit, our words differ from those we would use if the driver wore reflecting sunglasses and an earring. If our vocabulary stays the same, chances are that we are being nasty in the sacred name of honesty.

To adjust our vocabulary to our audience is honest and not hypocritical; we do not speak of adjusting our opinions or beliefs. Our minds contain multiple possibilities of expression among which we choose. If we do not try to make contact with another, the notion of honest speech is meaningless: for speech is speech only when it reaches another person.

In writing we make the same choices. If we write a letter to the college newspaper, we choose the words from a collection different from the one we choose from when we write a thank-you letter to an aunt. A term paper in business administration requires a vocabulary different from the one for a term paper in literature.

The difficult, necessary task is to adjust our vocabulary to our audience with tact, humility, and appropriateness—but without hypocrisy. Sometimes it is merely a matter of common sense. If we are writing for an audience from the southern hemisphere, we must remember that *April* connotes autumn and falling leaves, not green and sprouting seeds. But common sense is easy, compared to the difficulties in learning the difference between appropriate tact and gross hypocrisy. When Nina Chan wrote her first essay, the one about the "land of opportunity for education" and so on, she was writing for a faceless audience—an audience that enjoyed clichés and formulas. In other words, she was not writing for anybody at all. Probably at that moment she did not believe that she could write with honesty for an audience that was a teacher or a fellow student. Probably Nina had no vocabulary of her own to fall back on at that moment but that of college pep talks and glossy brochures. But little by little, by becoming aware of the insides of words, she learned a lot about the insides of Nina Chan; and she learned to make the inside outside—to make connection with other people, to use words for social purposes, to *write*.

Revising Words

From the first notes for an essay to its final typing, words are the material we work with. When we brainstorm or sprint, we use the associations of words. When we develop ideas, when we expand generalities by detail,

our focus on individual words generates more words. But our local concentration on language increases as drafts come closer to the final draft. It
may be far along before we discover that *wage* may be more appropriate for
our context and audience than *salary*. It may take a final draft before we ex-
cise the blank word *aspect* and find a useful substitute. At the end we check
our sentences both to remove error and to find better language: more exact, more particular, and more original—in a word.

EXERCISES

1. Consider these three groupings of words that are similar in
meaning. Write a short sentence using each word accurately. Then write out
some of the same sentences inserting the other words. Be prepared to discuss
how the connotations of the sentence are changed by the substitution.

> **a.** relaxed, leisurely, slack, easy, undisciplined
> **b.** wise, learned, intelligent, educated, witty
> **c.** infirmity, debility, illness, disease, indisposition
> **d.** beautiful, pretty, pert, fetching, lovely

2. Try to read past the thesaurus words to uncover the proverb or
slogan.

> **a.** The event has not concluded until the corpulent woman
> descants.
> **b.** If initially you fail to attain your objective, venture, venture
> another time.
> **c.** An ornithological specimen enclosed in the manual digits
> equates to double that in the undergrowth.
> **d.** Precipitousness occasions depletion.

Write three other such transformed sayings and read them aloud in class
for class members to figure out.

3. Here are some fabricated sentences that mix metaphors and
misuse comparisons. Try the tests of literalness and metaphor (p. 79–80).
Rewrite each one for consistency.

> **a.** Theirs was a marriage made in heaven, a respite from the
> dog-eats-dog grind.
> **b.** The rush of emotion shielded him from spotting the truth.
> **c.** The fact that Bib was the mayor's son did not put obstacles
> in his path; he climbed the ladder to power on the wings of
> family connections.
> **d.** Trading on his considerable charm, Gary expects to win
> Ginny's heart and avoid the sour repercussions that dogged
> his earlier relationships.

> **e.** A flowering of poetic language cushions these pivotal expressions until they are all but camouflaged.

4. Look back at the section on sense words (pp. 80–81). Drawing upon your own experience, write three short passages that convey sensory information vividly. The first should summon up a moment from childhood, the second should invoke the natural world, and the third should enact some incident from the past twenty-four hours.

5. When prose gets out of control, there is often more than one thing wrong with it. In these passages of bad prose, find words used as blanks and as euphemisms. If you notice other faults, name them.

> **a.** Thank you for the information you recently provided in connection with your request for Gulf Travel Cards. The information contained in your communication, along with other data developed, has enabled us to reverse our previous decision regarding your Travel Card application.
> **b.** We will be experiencing a development of shower activity.
> **c.** The purpose of this program is to provide opportunities for teachers at undergraduate colleges and universities and at junior and community colleges to work in their areas of interest with distinguished scholars in their fields and to have access to libraries suitable for advanced study.
> **d.** The evidence developed was not corroborative of the allegation on which it was predicated.

6. Read several articles in a national newsmagazine (*Time, Newsweek,* etc.) and see if you can discover any instances of subtle (or not-so-subtle) bias. Your instructor might want to copy a single such article for everybody to read. Come to class prepared to discuss your findings.

7. In this paragraph, underline three words that the author uses with special skill—the way John Updike uses *adhesively* and *slice*—and be prepared to defend your choices in class.

> The top of the hill, pasture for one straggly cow, was clear of brush except for patches of dark juniper, in spreading flat circles ten feet across. Around the tumbled stone walls tall pines and maples held off an advancing army of small gray birch. At one side, by the bouldery path that had once been a town road, a little family graveyard lay on slightly tilted ground. A deer trail ran right through it, bright and twisted between the slate stones, and a birch had fallen and rotted out of its bark, leaving a print like a white hand.
>
> Thomas Williams, *Town Burning*

8. (a) Pick one of the following words—*chemical, comb, shield, car, slave, table*—or a word from a list your instructor gives you. Read the complete entry for that word in the *Oxford English Dictionary* and write a short report on its origin and later history. Compare the earliest usage with the present sense of the word. (b) Look through the *OED* and find your own word to trace. Prepare a history to present in class.

VERBS

Action and the Choice of Style

Verbs act. Verbs move. Verbs do. Verbs strike, soothe, grin, cry, exasperate, decline, fly, hurt, and heal. Verbs make writing go, and they matter more to our language than any other part of speech.

Verbs give energy, if we use them with energy. We could have said, "Verbs are action. Verbs are motion. Verbs are doing." But if we had written the sentences in this second way, we would have written dull prose. We could have gone even further into dullness and written, "Verbs are words that are characterized by action."

Try to use verbs that act. Yet sometimes we will need to write verbs that are less than active. Just as there are no synonyms, there are no two sentences that mean the same thing but are different only in style. A change in style, however slight, is always a change in meaning, however slight. Is it, therefore, possible to make a stylistic generalization at all?

Generalization does remain possible, with explanation and with room for exception. Both explanations and exceptions will follow in the sections on verbs and nouns, but let us start with a general explanation. Most of the time, the passive voice and weak verbs evade precision and commitment. Examples follow, in which weak verbs add static to statements and in which the passive voice avoids being wrong by evading a definite statement. These habits fuzz our prose with bad brain fuzz. To recommend that we use active forms of active verbs is to recommend energy and clarity, definite statement, and commitment. Style is morals.

Verbs with Nouns and Adjectives

Usually, a lone verb is stronger and better than a strung-out verb-and-adjective or verb-and-noun combination. People say, "I am aware of this fact," or "I am cognizant of this situation," when they could have said, "I know it." In these examples, we have a weak verb and adjective followed by a noun that means little but appears to end the sentence, to give the verb an object. The phrases mean something different from "I know it," but the difference is mere pomposity. "I am aware of the fact" differs from "I know it" because it shows us that the speaker thinks well of himself. "I am cognizant of the situation" is so pompous it may sound ironic; it would usually drip from the lips, or leak from the pen, of someone nervous about his intellectual status, like a television executive.

Look out for the verbs *be, is, are,* and *has, have* combined with nouns and adjectives. See if you do not gain by using the verb itself, clear and clean. Edit your writing to simplify your verbs. "He looked outside and became aware of the fact that it was raining" revises easily into "He looked outside and saw that it was raining" or, more simply, "He looked outside. It was raining." Instead of "We had a meeting," try "We met." The meaning is different, slightly, but if the second phrase is accurate, it is better—we save three syllables and add energy to our prose; when we cut to the essential motion, we add vitality. Instead of "They were decisive about the question of . . ." try "They decided to . . . ."

Now "to be decisive"—if we look at the insides of words—means something quite different from "to decide." The person who "is decisive" has vigor and intellectual intensity; she cuts through the uncertainties that surround a question and makes a choice firmly and quickly. If you are describing a committee meeting in which, after long discussion, the members reached a consensus or took a vote and decided to do something, "they decided" is the clearest phrase to use. Most of the time, when we use a wordy noun-adjective-verb phrase, we are merely trying to *sound* more complicated. We use the longer phrase just to *seem* to be considering fine points. The sensible rule: use the shorter, more direct verb ("they decided") except when the longer variation has a precision that your meaning requires. "They talked for two days about lowering the voting age, without coming to a conclusion. Then Senator Jensen returned from a junket. He spoke briefly. He was decisive. The measure carried by a two-thirds majority."

Verbs with Participles

The same advice applies to phrases that use verb forms ending in *-ing* (present participles). "They were meeting to discuss" can often become "They met to discuss," and "He is clearing his throat" becomes "He clears his throat." But the participle is different in meaning—it marks a different sort of time—and therefore can be useful when that difference is important. "She'll be comin' 'round the mountain" has more continuous motion in it than "She'll come 'round the mountain." Participles imply continuing action. But be sure that you *intend* the difference and are not just lazy. To say that the group "was deciding a topic" implies that it took some time; if you use this verb phrase, be sure that you mean to use it instead of *decided*. Apparently the mind finds it easier to be pale than to be colorful. Or maybe the mind finds it easier to avoid the extra vocabulary of verbs, sticking to *be* and *has* with nouns and adjectives. Whatever the reason, when we add little words like *is* and *has* to participles, adjectives, and nouns, usually we thin our prose into invisibility.

Verbs in the Passive Voice

A verb is in the passive voice when it acts on the subject; for instance, "The passive voice *is used* when the subject *is acted on* by the verb."

When writers use the passive, they usually subtract meaning from their prose. We say, "A message was received" instead of "They [or *I* or *you* or *he* or *she*] received a message." We suppress identity, which is a particular, and we put hazy distance between implied subject and definite action. The passive voice avoids responsibility. We might claim that "A dish was dropped in the kitchen" rather than name ourselves as the dropper. Omitting a doer diminishes a sentence. It can be politically useful: "PLO enclaves were bombed yesterday." Or as the president said when profits from secret arms sales were covertly diverted to a guerrilla army, "Mistakes were made." Many inquired: who made them?

Sometimes we use the passive voice from shyness, modesty, false modesty, or all three. It waters the soup. We sound as if we wrote labels for medicine bottles: "Doses may be administered three times daily. Dosage recommended for adults is . . . ." A depressed writer might say, making an argument: "It can be assumed that someone in college is fairly mature. It might be objected that . . . ." Here, the passive makes invisible dialogue, a pale argument between people who are not there. Scientific prose uses the passive by convention, establishing an impersonal tone. Sometimes writers on nonscientific subjects achieve a pseudoscientific tone by using the passive. "Crest has been shown to be a decay preventive dentifrice . . . ."

Occasionally the passive voice is right or unavoidable. Passives are used in a textbook whose author generally advises against passives.

> The author uses passives in the textbook.
> The textbook uses passives.
> Passives are used in the textbook.

In some contexts, the third sentence is best. The second is most terse, but it involves a hidden metaphor—the text must be compared to a person, if it "uses" something—which may weaken the sentence. The first correctly says that the author does the using, but it would be intrusive and wordy in some contexts to state the subject when the subject is perfectly obvious. The passive might be the least of three evils.

Good writers use the passive for variety in sentence structure, too. Rarely, but they do. In a paragraph about two groups taking opposite sides on an issue, in which all sentences have the active voice, the author looking for stylistic variety might insert the sentence "Arguments were put forward, on both sides, that would make a goat blush." When you use a passive for variety, be certain that you are not using it for any of the reasons that make passives bad: shyness or self-consciousness, false modesty, evading responsibility, or imitating scientific respectability.

Particular Verbs

We have been writing all along as if there were two classes of verbs: strong ones and weak ones. Of course language is more complicated than that, and not only because weak is sometimes better than strong, as we have suggested. Some strong verbs are stronger than others. "He moved" is stronger than "he was in motion." But in the right context, we might say with greater strength, "he crept" or "he slid" or "he hurtled." We would almost always want to say, "he crept" rather than "he moved, creeping." (A difference of meaning might, in some instances, make the second phrase useful).

Invisible Verbs

In the prospectus for a dissertation, a Ph.D. candidate wrote this sentence in which he misused verbs; in fact, he managed to write almost *without* verbs.

> Illustrative of what Kornhauser means by constraint imposed on professionals in organizations are the findings of Leo Meltzer in a survey of 3,084 physiologists in the United States.

The sentence has no strong and active verbs. *Means* is the closest. *Illustrative* is an adjective substituted for a verb. *Imposed* is a past participle that suppresses responsibility. *Are* is boring.

To rewrite the sentence in a language not far from the original but with more vigor and clarity, we can simply cut and rearrange. Edited in revision, the passage could read:

> Leo Meltzer questioned 3,084 physiologists in the United States; his findings demonstrate Kornhauser's contention that organizations constrain professionals.

Maybe *surveyed* is more accurate than *questioned,* but *surveyed* smells of jargon.

The last phrase of this revision may not mean what the original author had in mind. Did he mean that the institution imposed the constraint or that something else, unnamed, chose professionals in organizations, rather than others, to impose restraint on? The ambiguity in the original passage is real and serves no function; it is merely unclear. The second version is clearer, though without context it still raises questions. What is this constraint? What desires are held back? Does the author mean "constraint" as restraint or as compulsion? Does he mean all organizations—like YMCAs, universities, corporations, fraternities, bridge clubs, and nations— or specifically professional ones, like the Modern Language Association or the American Medical Association? We must make sure that our sentences leave no unanswered questions. The more straightforward our presentation, the easier it is—for us and the reader—to be sure of the sense. Clarity comes from vigor combined with detail. Verbs are the most vigorous parts of speech; by particularity, they add detail.

False Color in Verbs

The search for particularity and color can become obvious, and the prose can look silly. In the examples that follow, the faults do not lie in the verbs alone but in the whole style. Verbs are at the center of the action in our prose, however, for good or for ill. In the play *The Owl and the Pussycat,* a would-be novelist reads the first page of his manuscript to the girl who has invaded his apartment. When he starts by saying the sun *spat* on his protagonist, she flies into a rage. And so should we whenever we see language being abused. Men's action magazines are full of methedrine prose, violence done to language in the name of violence. In a thriller called *A Clash of Hawks,* the author's second sentence reads:

> The 200-foot-high derrick was a black, latticed steel phallus raping the hot, virginal blue sky.

If an author needs these overblown images to describe an oil rig, we have to wonder what language tortures he will resort to when he gets to a sex scene. But tough or sadistic writing is not the only kind of bad overwriting. Pretty writing may be worse.

> Songbirds trilled out my window, vines curled at the eaves, and Spring drenched the day with gladness.

Often a beginning writer tries to make the verbs describing dialogue too exaggeratedly active: *he whimpered, she snapped.* Almost always it looks too strenuous. We should use *said,* or nothing at all, most of the time. The emotion should be in the dialogue itself, in the speaker's words; if the reader has to be told, the emotion is not there. The trick is to convey energy with appropriateness. We may need to learn to do too much before we can learn to do the right amount. Newly wakened to verbs, one student wrote this passage:

> The train slammed to a stop in the station. Steam vomited from all apertures. Passengers rushed through the barriers and hurtled into the night.

It was a useful exercise because the student was searching through his mental dictionary for energetic verbs. But the color was more vivid than necessary, to the point of distortion. Steam gushing out at the base of an engine is not like vomiting; *vomiting* is too sick and unpleasant and bad-smelling a word; the writer used it only for its power, not for what it contributed to the picture. Though the general advice—choose color over pallor, energy over lethargy—holds true, one matter overrides all others, in any discussion of style, and that is appropriateness: context is all.

Fancy Verbs

Some verbs are too fancy for normal use. Writers use them when they think their prose ought to wear fancy clothes or when they do not fully trust what they are saying. *Depict* is usually inferior to *paint* or *draw* or *describe.* "He depicted a scene of unparalleled magnitude." Maybe that means "he painted a big picture" or "he told a good story" or half a dozen other things, but its real meaning is its would-be fanciness. Of course, *depict* is not the only culprit here—"A scene of unparalleled magnitude" sounds like something W. C. Fields might conjure up in an inspired moment. Indeed, the whole sentence is busy admiring itself in the mirror. *Emulate* would usually be fancy for *copy, ascertain* for *make sure,* and *endeavor* for *try.*

Made-up Verbs

Then there are the made-up words, neologisms, which sound fancy to the people who use them. When we are tempted to say *finalize,* we would do better to say *end* or *finish; make personal* is more accurate than *personalize.* In general, we should avoid verbs made of an adjective and an *-ize.* Advertising and politics have created many crude verbs, often using nouns as bases instead of adjectives. Some good old English verbs end in *-ize. Scrutinize,* deriving from the noun *scrutiny,* is a useful verb. *Finalize,* however, is used to sound fancier than *finish* or *end,* to give false complexity to a simple act. Therefore it is bad style, pretending to be something that it is not; it is a form of euphemism, a way of overdressing plain usage. The writer should search the language for the simplest and most direct way of saying and expressing, not make up a new word when an old one will do.

Revising Verbs

The section headings of these pages (Verbs with Nouns and Adjectives, Verbs with Participles, Verbs in the Passive Voice, Particular Verbs, Invisible Verbs, False Color in Verbs, Fancy Verbs, Made-up Verbs) can form a checklist for revising the draft of an essay. Scan your prose to see how you have been using verbs. Find substitutions that make your style stronger, more honest, and more precise.

EXERCISES

1. Read the following sentences and underline the weak verbs (verb-noun or verb-adjective or verb-participle combinations, verbs lacking particularity), and then substitute strong verbs. How do your substitutions modify the meaning of the sentence?

    a. The students are currently in the process of trying to make changes in the curfew rules.

    b. We were going from city to city in Europe, having a hard time with different languages and ways of doing things.

    c. Jeremy came across to those who didn't know him well as loud and pushy.

    d. I was getting around to improving my situation, which was slowly moving from bad to worse.

    e. In the hands of a good guitarist, the instrument can make pleasant or deliberately unpleasant sounds.

    f. Standing by the boathouse we were happy to watch the gymnasts go through their practice drills.

    g. Howard did not tell the truth often and was no better at being honest when he wrote his memoirs.

    h. When we went snorkeling, we looked at the most unusual kinds of fish and were surprised and excited.

2. Underline the passive verbs in these five sentences and then consider whether any of them are necessary or useful. Where they are not, revise the sentences using active verbs.

    a. This was how things stood when the time for decision drew near.
    b. Intelligence and perseverence are two qualities much sought after by employers in most fields.
    c. When an insult is given, or when you feel that you are not being treated in a respectful way, you should ask yourself if some response is not called for.
    d. As Jane Austen wrote at the beginning of *Pride and Prejudice:* "It is a truth universally acknowledged that a single man in possession of a good fortune must be in want of a wife."
    e. How it was between members of my family and how it is between us are two very different things.

3. Select one political news story and one feature story from your newspaper and underline all passive constructions in both. What do you notice about frequency of usage of the passive voice, and what reasons would you give for the difference?

4. Find three synonyms or close alternatives for each of the verbs listed below. For the first five verbs and their synonyms write sentences illustrating correct usage. For the second five verbs and synonyms write sentences that reflect misuse, however slight. Be prepared to read the latter examples in class, allowing others to pinpoint the errors.

    a. struggle
    b. assist
    c. recommend
    d. annoy
    e. communicate
    f. endeavor
    g. entice
    h. destroy
    i. create
    j. pretend

5. Look through the various example passages in this book and copy out three sentences that you think use verbs in a vivid and interesting manner. Bring them to class to read aloud.

    6. Here are four passages. Underline the verbs and decide in class how well each author uses them.

a. When it comes to the actual methods of consumption, asparagus eaters seem to be roughly divided into two groups. There are those who assume a crouching position and attack the vegetable with knives and forks. Lined up against this faction are those who believe the only way to eat asparagus is to throw back the head, grasp the stalk between thumb and forefinger and lower it slowly into the mouth, chewing steadily.

Diane White, "The Noble Asparagus" *(Boston Globe)*

b. A machine gun lashed at him from across the river, and he ducked in his hole. In the darkness, it spat a vindictive white light like an acetylene torch, and its sound was terrifying. Croft was holding himself together by the force of his will. He pressed the trigger of his gun and it leaped and bucked under his hand. The tracers spewed wildly into the jungle on the other side of the river.

Norman Mailer, *The Naked and the Dead*

c. The service shall be delivered in the following manner: Immediately before commencing to serve, the Server shall stand with both feet at rest behind the base line, and within the imaginary continuation of the center mark and side line of the singles court. The Receiver may stand wherever he pleases behind the service line on his own side of the net. The Server shall then throw the ball into the air and strike it with his racket before it hits the ground. Delivery shall be deemed complete at the moment the racket strikes the ball.

"How Service Is Delivered," *Official Tennis Rules*

d. Weighing the half-pounds of flour, excluding the scoop, and depositing them dust-free into the thin paper sacks held a simple kind of adventure for me. I developed an eye for measuring how full a silver-looking ladle of flour, mash, meal, sugar or corn had to be to push the scale indicator over to eight ounces or one pound. When I was absolutely accurate our appreciative customers used to admire: "Sister Henderson sure got some smart grandchildrens." If I was off in the Store's favor, the eagle-eyed women would say, "Put some more in that sack, child. Don't you try to make your profit offa me."

Maya Angelou, *I Know Why the Caged Bird Sings*

NOUNS

Particularity and Choosing a Style

Nouns are the simplest parts of speech, the words least tricky to use. Nouns are the names of things, *things* in the broadest sense: *table, elm, Nancy, rain, noun, Centerville, nation, hunger, nine o'clock.* If verbs supply the energy that makes prose go, nouns are the body of prose. Without nouns, nothing would be doing the going.

Many of the generalizations that apply to verbs also apply to nouns. We prefer as a rule the specific, the sensuous, the strong, the simple, and the colorful over the abstract, the general, the polysyllabic, and the fancy. We prefer *elm* to *tree, Nancy* to *girl,* and *nine o'clock* to *evening.* The more particular the noun, the clearer the pictures we make, and the more accurately we can represent feelings. Pictures carry feelings from writer to reader, as abstract idea words do not. Particulars make contact. A student wrote:

> I remembered the flowers that grew on some land near a relative's house . . . .

and revised it to

> I remembered a path of daisies that grew on a meadow near my Cousin Annie's farm . . . .

and the particularity is all gain. The first example was not bad style, but it was pale prose. The second by comparison is vivid.

But we also need to generalize, and we must express reservations. Sometimes the more general noun is more accurate and honest than the specific one. From a distance, you see *a man* or *a woman,* not *a sophomore* or *a mechanic. Town* may be more appropriate, in the right context, than *Centerville,* though it is less specific. We must keep in mind the advice to be specific; but, as ever, we must be wary that our rules do not lead us into absurdity. A student revised some daily writing into

> On Tuesday afternoon, October 13th, I read a sentence halfway down the first page of *War and Peace* which . . . .

Maybe in a particular context, such extreme specificity would be useful, but usually it would sound overly precise.

Also, we must remember again that the advice to cultivate one kind of style, at the expense of another, means thinking or seeing things in special ways. *A change in style, however slight, is always a change in meaning, however slight.*

Although most writing improves as particularity increases, there are exceptions to this rule. If we are philosophers seeking generality, *tree* might be preferable to *elm* and *humanity* to *Nancy and David.* For scientific summary, injunctions to *Be particular!* and *Avoid abstraction!* are useless.

> At first cats would not seem to offer a likely clue to human history. Yet when one considers that the writing of adequate histories of human populations began scarcely 200 years ago, that writing itself dates back only about 6,000 years and that for many populations historical, linguistic and cultural records are inadequate or nonexistent, cats appear in a different light. They have been associated with human beings for a long time, but they have never had any economic significance and only rarely have they had much social significance. Genetically they, unlike other domesticated animals, have been left

largely to themselves. The study of the population genetics of cats is therefore rewarding not only for what it reveals about the evolution of cats but also for what it suggests about the movements of human populations.

> Neil B. Todd, "Cats and Commerce" *(Scientific American)*

Todd writes vigorous expository prose, which must be abstract and concrete by turns to impart the necessary facts and perspectives to his readers.

The wise advice is simply to be as particular as the context allows us; when we are as concrete as possible, we have a better chance of connecting with our audience. Too often, we are vague and general, when we would say much more by discovering the concrete. Instead of saying

> When it got cold, the animals looked for shelter.

we could convey much more by a particularity:

> In October there was frost, and the sheep huddled in one corner of the barn for warmth, the cattle in another.

Abstract and Particular Nouns

Degrees of difference separate the noun at an extreme of abstraction from the noun at an extreme of particularity. S. I. Hayakawa, in his book *Language in Thought and Action,* speaks of moving up a ladder of abstraction, climbing from the most particular level, gradually discarding particularities, and arriving into the thin air around the highest abstraction. The number of rungs on this ladder is limited only by our ingenuity, but we can usefully distinguish three main degrees—the abstract, the general, and the particular.

Beginning with the abstract, we can move by degrees toward greater particularity. Take *animal, dog, spaniel.* One might become still more particular by adding an age and a color and by naming a breed of spaniel: "a five-year-old, rust-colored cocker spaniel." In contrast, one might become more abstract than the general *animal* by climbing the ladder into the thin air of *organism.* Or one might remain general by defining *dog* in scientific classification as *canine* and *quadruped.*

The more abstract a noun, the more difficult it is to use well: words like *emotion* (or *love,* for that matter) or *courage* or *hatred* or *responsibility.* To make these nouns work, you must provide a context with anecdote or analogy; you must put flesh on the bones. Usually an adjective in front of an abstraction does not do the work. The abstraction is lazy, retrieved by the writer from the attic of Big Ideas, and the adjective strives to do all the work; but adjectives themselves are often weak, and so we have two weaklings failing to budge the door that one strong noun could burst open.

Take the word *love* again. *Love* is thin and airy; it is pretty, but what is it about? Our affection for a pet salamander? The feeling of a grandfather for his granddaughter? Bert's obsession with the character of Charles Dickens? Mark and Nancy in the Oldsmobile? Married affection? *Love* is a grab bag of possibilities, only a bit less abstract than *emotion* or *feeling.* If we modify it with the adjective *intense,* we narrow its possibilities a little, but we do not really localize it. If we speak of *young love,* we are more particular—and yet we move toward cliché. Many clichés are adjective-noun combinations in which the adjective is a desperate, though habitual, attempt to rescue a bland abstraction—*blind faith,* for example.

Abstractions are usually lazy. The writer finds it easier to label the general category of a feeling than to search out the particulars that embody the feeling. Sight, taste, smell, touch, and hearing carry feeling from writer to reader—concepts do not. (And most writers using abstractions, we notice instantly, are not using concepts with the precision of a philosopher but vaguely and inaccurately.) Usually, we talk best about *love* when we do not use the word at all. If we use *Nancy* and *Centerville* and a *1989 Pontiac* and *rain* and *nine o'clock* and connect them with strong verbs, the reader may know what we mean by the big hazy word *love*—in this time and in this place.

Time and *place* are abstractions. Are they used appropriately here? Sometimes the abstract affords a setting for the concrete, as a black velvet background shows up diamonds. In other contexts, instead of *time* and *place* we would want to use more specific words—*end of high school, summer night, elm, Long Lake Road.*

Abstract Nouns: Beginnings and Endings

An abstraction can be explained by context, by analogy, or by anecdote. Some abstraction or generalization is necessary to any conceptual or argumentative writing. Only fiction, poetry, and autobiography can be free of it, and they do not always stay free. When we revise an essay, we should look most carefully to eliminate abstractions at two points—beginning and ending. Frequently, we introduce a subject with an abstraction—"I am going to tell a story that illustrates inequality"—and then we tell a story that illustrates inequality. If the illustration is clear, the introductory abstraction was unnecessary; what is more, it was probably distracting. When we announce that we are going to tell a funny joke before we tell it, we take the humor away. If the idea of inequality arises in the reader's mind—by name or not—from the anecdote, it will be much more powerful. Telling the reader the meaning of what she is going to hear bullies her; she is likely to resist.

Similarly, we often write anecdotes that trail off with an abstraction. Having told a perfectly clear story, we end, "which is an illustration of the inequality so prevalent today." Don't nudge your reader in the ribs, saying, "In case you didn't get it, this is what I mean." We summarize abstractly because we lack confidence in our own writing and in the reader's intelligence. Of course some stories need interpreting; that usually makes them less valuable. But if the road is clear, do not put up road markers; they are good only for stumbling over.

Invisible Nouns

So far, we have been talking about degrees of particularity and color, and we have admitted that some prose needs abstractions. The preacher could not have said, "All is vanity," if there had been an enforced commandment against abstractions. But some nouns are almost always useless. These nouns are invisible. When someone says, "The snow is gray in color," what is the phrase *in color* doing? It does not do anything for meaning or particularity. Maybe it contains a message informing us that the speaker is pompous.

Words like *nature* and *character*, which have perfectly good uses, also turn up invisibly in pale prose. Probably the snow was gray in color because of the urban nature of the environment and the frigid character of the weather. Probably it would have seemed too ordinary to speak of gray snow in the cold, dirty city.

We use invisible nouns with adjectives—much as we use invisible verbs like *be* and *do* and *has* with adjectives or nouns—to make a sentence *sound* grander than it really is or because we lack the vocabulary. Whatever the reason, we abuse the language. Some other nouns we render invisible are *sense, kind, action, situation, respect, regard, case,* and *element.* Look at this excerpt from the annual report of a large corporation:

> The President is pleased to report that, despite the unusual nature of the fiscal situation in the past twelve months, earnings have risen substantially above the margin foreseen by the Treasurer's Report of March 1981. In a marketing sense, the profitable character of the corporation proved itself under trying circumstances.

Circumstances is another invisible noun—at least as it is used here. Sensible writers avoid these words unless their contexts provide visible meanings. For instance, a *case* holds papers, *characters* speak parts in plays, and there are five *senses.* Edit invisible nouns out of your prose when you revise.

Making Bad Nouns from Verbs

Sensible writers also choose the plain noun, if it is adequate, over the fancy one, and they choose the old noun rather than making up a new one. Earlier we mentioned the verb *finalize,* which had been wrenched out of an adjective. It has been wrenched further into a noun: now and then we run across *finalization* when *end* or *finish* or maybe *finality* would do. Bad stylists will go to any lengths to complicate things. *Scrutiny* is a fine noun; *scrutinize* is a necessary and traditional verb. But recently a young man wrote on an application form that he submitted documents "for your scrutinization." The word means nothing more than *scrutiny;* it must have sounded more respectable to this writer.

Or maybe his vocabulary failed him. He remembered the verb *scrutinize* but forgot the noun *scrutiny.* And so he made up a new noun out of the verb. When you are tempted to make a new noun from a verb, go to the dictionary first. You know *unify;* when tempted to create *unifization,* go to the dictionary and you will find *unity* and *unification*—and clearer, more eloquent prose.

Fancy Nouns

Reading bad prose, we find thousands of examples of pomposity or fanciness, either neologism (new words generally invented, when old ones would do, out of a failure of vocabulary) like *scrutinization* or polysyllabic alternatives to simple words like *domicile* for *house* or *cessation* for *end.* These words parallel verbs like *masticate,* substituted for *chew.* The fanciness may arise from lack of confidence or ignorance or pretension or whatever. Probably we are more often lazy than insincere and simply settle for what we first think of. Whatever our motive or our failing, the result is the same; fanciness separates the thing described and the mental act of perceiving it. Feelings are kept at a distance. Fancy abstractions and clichés enable Orwell's Communist professor to discuss without feelings the murder of innocent people.

Revising Nouns

In revising, we should look to remove the lazy abstraction, as well as the invisible noun, the neologism, and the merely fancy noun. Cutting such a word leaves a hole, which we can fill with another noun or a phrase, to specify and bring down to earth the airy word we started with. Lazy abstractions are like clichés and jargon—and the three are usually discovered together—because they are instantly available to the tongue; they lie heaped together with clichés and jargon in the fore-room of the brain; we do not have to search for them with our intelligence or dream for them with our imaginations. Here is a passage from an essay.

> Financial problems were coming to a head in my family last spring and we didn't know if my sister and I could have the benefit of higher education. Then my grandfather got the surprise of his life when a large amount of money came his way when he least expected it. He got a sum from the VA, which he didn't know was coming to him. Through his generosity, we were enabled to arrange payment for tuition.

As usual with faulty prose, the faults do not lie in one part of speech alone. Some hunks of cliché are ready-made—*financial problems, coming to a head, benefit of higher education, surprise of his life, when he least expected it, arrange payment*—and combine with a dozen other signs of lazy thinking and evasion of feeling. Think of the emotional reality—the anxiety, the sudden jubilation—these phrases obscure with their familiar haze. Instead of *financial problems,* let us forget euphemism and talk about being in debt or having no money or losing a job or payments coming due—*anything* more particular. The ultimate particularity would probably sound as cold as a balance sheet (outstanding indebtedness $27,429.31; assets . . .), but we know a median lies between the bland, evasive euphemism of *financial problems* and the sterile figures. The median is actual circumstances and anecdotes; the median comes closer to the truth than the extremes.

Certainly *go to college* or *go on in school* is preferable to *have the benefit of higher education*. Then instead of speaking generally of *surprise*—an abstraction that takes the surprise out of surprise—why not show it happening? Describe the grandfather opening the envelope or picking up the telephone. Use dialogue. Or use some new analogy to express his feelings, instead of a useless cliché. How much is *a large amount of money* or *a sum?* Both seem genteel evasions for saying a specific figure, like *a check for $5,000.* But perhaps it seems crass to the writer to name the figure. Then at least some phrase could give a better idea of the numbers, so the reader can place the figure between $500 and $5 million or judge the amount of money by what it can do: "enough money to send us both through school."

The phrase *through his generosity* includes an unnecessary, labeling abstraction. We do not need to be told that he is generous. When we are bullied with the notion, we resist it. Maybe the old man just wants to boast that his grandchildren go to college. Finally, the last part of the paragraph has a pair of general nouns and a fancy verb in place of simpler and more natural language. It is pretentious to write, "we were enabled to arrange payment for tuition," when we could write, "we were able to pay for college."

The student, in fact revised the passage.

> My family was so far in debt last spring that we didn't think my sister and I could go to college. My father had borrowed money to get a fish and chips franchise, and lost it all in six months. My sister and I both took jobs in the summer. I was working twelve hours a day in the mill, and when I came home at night I was so mad and tired I just drank beer and watched the box. Then my grandfather telephoned my father and I saw my father suddenly start crying. The VA had just sent my grandfather a check he didn't know was coming, and it was enough to pay for us both. That night, we bought a bottle of Four Roses.

He changed verbs and other parts of speech, but the revision of his nouns is most useful of all.

EXERCISES

1. Take a careful look at your surroundings and see how large a list of nouns you can generate. Try in every case to be particular, writing "rocker" instead of "chair," and so on.

2. a. Write three pairs of sentences, in each case using general nouns in the first and concrete, or particular, nouns in the second. What are the effects of the substitution? Are there any instances where the general noun serves better?

b. Pick a passage from a magazine or a literary work and replace every specific noun with a general noun. Read both passages aloud and comment on the difference.

3. Consider the following nouns. For each noun find one that is more specific and another that is more general. If you can't find a word, use a short phrase.

  a. apple
  b. computer
  c. knife
  d. cat
  e. alcohol
  f. pasta
  g. pen
  h. relative
  i. salmon
  j. dance

4. Collect four or five clichés that combine an abstract noun with an adjective, like *blind faith, basic needs,* and *conflicting desires.* Look in the newspaper for accounts of political speeches, or read magazine advertisements. See how many alternatives you can find for each, always realizing that a different context will require a different substitute for these filler phrases. Thus, *basic needs* in different contexts might be revised into distinctly different phrases—like *minimum nutrition* or *attention and support.* Provide brief contexts, if you need them for clarity.

5. Study the following sentences. Underline the nouns that fail by invisibility, imprecision, fanciness, neologism, or excessive abstraction. Find substitute nouns that improve the sentences.

  a. I ran into the building and spent some time there.
  b. Who would you say caused this unfortunate thing to happen?
  c. Seth was not happy with our utilization of the funds he had allocated.
  d. My emotions for Tish have always been strong and I think the relationship we have is based on good feeling.
  e. The police agreed with the mayor: This was a situation and it needed to be monitored.
  f. Precipitation and generally inclement climate conditions have delayed our class trip.
  g. Relationships are a matter of togetherness.

6. Underline the nouns in these passages, and label each as abstract or general or particular, according to the context. In class, compare your judgments with those of other students. Be prepared to argue. These distinctions are often tenuous, but discussing the distinctions will sharpen your eye for the insides of words.

a. I myself, to come right down to it, have never been in love from afar, except perhaps for a handful of fleeting moments when a flickering shot of Wallace Reid driving over a cliff would make me feel queer. I know of women who have really mooned, and for years, over some such glamorous shadow, and it is highly possible that my own immunity is due to my sensual satisfaction, even vicarious, in such things as potato chips and Beluga caviar.

M. F. K. Fisher, "Once a Tramp, Always"

b. At 15,000 feet, its best operating height, the Kittyhawk IA could fly at a maximum speed of only 354 mph and climb to that height in 8.3 minutes, a longer time than the AGM2 Zero took to reach 20,000 feet. Empty weight was 6,350 pounds, normal loaded weight 8,280 pounds, which was the load carried in combat without drop tank or bombs, and maximum permissible weight was 9,200 pounds. Service ceiling was 29,000 feet. The IA climbed best at lower altitudes, but its best rate was only about 2,100 feet per minute at 5,000 feet.

John Vader, *Pacific Hawk*

c. It is a very small office, most of it taken up by a desk. The desk is placed smack in front of the window—not that it could have been placed anywhere else; this window looks out on the daylight landscape of Bergman's movies. It was gray and glaring the first day I was there, dry and fiery. Leaves kept falling from the trees, each silent descent bringing a little closer the long, dark, Swedish winter. The forest Bergman's characters are always traversing is outside this window and the ominous carriage from which they have yet to escape is still among the properties. I realized, with a small shock, that the landscape of Bergman's mind was simply the landscape in which he had grown up.

James Baldwin, *Nobody Knows My Name*

7. Look out your window and describe everything you see. Combine precision in your choice of nouns with accuracy and vigor in the use of verbs.

MODIFIERS

Qualities and Choosing a Style

Modifiers—adjectives, adverbs, participles, and sometimes other words—give quality to nouns and verbs. "The *huge, green* lion leapt *slowly.*"

Adjectives and adverbs *modify* nouns and verbs. Participles, and sometimes nouns, work in the same way: "the *grinning* lifeboat," "the hypothesis *constructed* on Thursday," "*rock candy* mountain," "*mouse* music." Used well, modifiers create distinctions in meaning and add particularity to the particular. They discriminate and promote precision.

But modifiers give us the greatest trouble of all parts of speech. A writer using clichés assembles prepackaged combinations of nouns and adjectives. A beginning writer, when she tries to write colorfully, may stuff her style into obesity with a fatty diet of adjectives.

Overuse or misuse of adjectives and adverbs makes prose weak and lethargic. Because they are qualities rather than actions or things, adjectives and adverbs are inherently weaker parts of speech. Yet once more, choosing a style *means* something. *A change in style, however slight, is a change in meaning, however slight.*

To choose vigor in writing is usually to work with fewer modifiers. A few great writers, like Faulkner, use as many adjectives as any beginner— but use them well and with great originality. Most of the best writers use them sparingly and then make them count. We are not saying that adjectives are unimportant to writing. They are important. But verbs and nouns carry the sentence; if they take charge properly, they liberate adjectives, adverbs, and other modifiers to do their proper work: to make the exact final discriminations necessary to honesty and fullness.

Using Modifiers Well

Ernest Hemingway is known for using adjectives and adverbs sparingly. Let us look once more at the passage that begins "In Another Country."

> In the fall the war was always there, but we did not go to it any more. It was cold in the fall in Milan and the dark came very early. Then the electric lights came on, and it was pleasant along the streets looking in the windows. There was much game hanging outside the shops, and the snow powdered on the fur of the foxes and the wind blew their tails. The deer hung stiff and heavy and empty, and small birds blew in the wind and the wind turned their feathers. It was a cold fall and the wind came down from the mountains.

Hemingway says *the war,* not *the long war* or *the distant war* or *the bloody, maiming, killing, useless, horrid, revolting war.* He uses *always* and *any more* as adverbs in his simple predicates. *Cold* is an adjective in the second sentence; *electric* is necessary to lights, at a time when electric lights were new; in a country at war they seemed especially unwarlike; *pleasant* is an adjective as restrained as the verbs *was* and *go.* Then the eye of the paragraph turns away from restrained thoughts of war and looks at the dead animals that substitute for dead soldiers; right away the verbs and nouns become stronger and more particular: *foxes, shops, powdered.* Then the adjectives, exact and strong, come marching in: *stiff and heavy and empty.* The last is especially vigorous. The adjectives used sparingly are used strongly and well.

Let us apply the same standards to the passage quoted before from a story by John Updike.

> All the warm night the secret snow fell so adhesively that every twig in the woods about their little rented house supported a tall slice of white, an upward projection which in the shadowless gloom of early morning lifted depth from the scene, made it seem Chinese, calligraphic, a stiff tapestry hung from the gray sky, a shield of lace interwoven with black thread.

Updike is sometimes condemned by critics for overwriting, for self-indulgence in description, for too much prettiness. Can you find anything here to back up such a charge? We can admire a writer, or a passage of his writing, and still find flaws.

What good does the word *secret* do us? It adds a little to the meaning—a kind of coziness—but the word seems there mostly to be pretty and because its *s* sound chimes nicely with that of *snow.* We might like the line better if it read, "All the warm night the snow fell so adhesively . . . ." *Warm* is connected to *adhesively,* but *warm* would be a stronger adjective if it were more isolated, if the next noun, *snow,* did not carry its adjective also. Then later, in one phrase after another, each noun takes one adjective, and although each adjective is defensible in itself, the effect is monotonously pretty: *tall slice, upward projection, shadowless gloom, early morning.* The mixture tastes too sweet. Rearranging clauses, putting an adjective after a noun instead of before it, putting two adjectives with one noun and none with the next—any number of minor reworkings could improve the passage.

The modifier in exposition or argument can help you or hurt you, just as in poetry and fiction. E. B. White, in a brief essay on schools, says that he always went to public ones; by contrast, he says, "my wife was unacquainted with public schools, never having been exposed (in early life) to anything more public than the washroom of Miss Winsor's." The sentence includes several modifiers—*unacquainted, public, exposed, early,* and *public* again—and yet it has vigor and clarity. The words express light disdain for the snobbism that White associates with private schools. The verb phrase *was unacquainted with* is preferable to alternatives like *knew nothing about* because *acquainted* is a word we use in more formal social contexts: "No, I am not acquainted with that person." In the small world of White's sentence, the past participle wears a monocle and looks down at the peasants. *Exposed (in early life)* suggests that public schools are a contagious disease, like measles. And the parenthesis *(in early life)* has a mock formality that agrees with the medical metaphor.

But the adjective with which White plays the best trick is *public,* which he uses twice: first with *schools* and then in the phrase "anything more public than the washroom of Miss Winsor's." *Public* then becomes associated with public lavatories; we wrinkle our nose in disdain. At *Miss Winsor's*—the name sounds upper class (maybe we think of the British royal family)—of course, the lavatory would be spotless and relatively private. What's more, it would not be a lavatory, john, W.C., or even bathroom; it would be a *wash-room*. By a turn on the adjective *public*—from describing schools to imply-ing lavatories—White makes his point most clearly.

In expository prose, adjectives usually narrow a noun's generality, to make the statement more specific. But if we do not watch ourselves care-fully, we'll let the adjective drift into one of its characteristic errors. Here is a passage of exposition from a student essay.

> If you approach the shore of a rocky island in your kayak you must paddle slowly and cautiously. Even a gentle breeze may crush the kayak against a sharp rock and sink the traveler, his vehicle, and all his very precious equipment.

Let us examine the modifiers. *Rocky* is necessary. *Slowly and cautiously* might become only *cautiously,* because *slowly* seems included in the idea of cau-tion. *Sharp* is useful to make the threat more particular. But *very precious* is not so useful; is the equipment any more precious by being called so? Does *very* do anything at all? The sentence would end more vigorously as three nouns in a series: ". . . the traveler, his vehicle, and his equipment."

One adjective in the piece makes a palpable cliché, *gentle breeze.* Yet the writer clearly wants, and needs, to tell us that the winds that can cause this accident need not be gale force. "Why not use 'gentle breeze,'" says the beginning writer, "because 'gentle breeze' is exactly what I mean?" But the problem is not *what I mean* but *what gets through:* the problem is communi-cation. All problems of writing are problems of audience, of the responses of readers. *Gentle* together with *breeze* simply repeats a commonplace, and the reader is unmoved. We would do better simply to alter the expectation slightly and speak of a *faint breeze, slight breeze,* or *tiny breeze.*

The Modifier and the Cliché

Beginning writers often misuse modifiers, especially as portions of clichés. In our minds we associate adjectives and nouns in pairs. Our minds are not only computer dictionaries but also junkyards of cliché. Thus the clichés listed in Exercise 4 on page 103 consist of adjective-noun combina-tions like *blind faith* and *basic needs. Gentle breeze* is another such combina-tion. Often nouns seem to imply adjectives, and if an adjective is implied by its noun, we should not use the adjective. If we think *grass,* we probably think *green.* We move in worn tracks. If we think *snow,* we think *white.* These weary associations are not really thinking; they are automatic re-sponses to stimuli. When the reader encounters a cliché, his mind shuts off, even if only briefly. The point of writing is to keep the reader engaged at every moment. To do this we have to be engaged ourselves, first as human beings, then as writers. The more we can be ourselves, the less we will re-semble a machine. If we remember more closely the grass and the snow we are describing, we will describe them precisely, out of our own memories, not out of the sad memory bank of other people's words. We might find an unexpected adjective for grass that is accurate for the grass at that place and that time. We might think of *harsh grass*. Or we might not describe the grass at all, or we might describe it in a clause or in a whole sentence. But we must avoid familiar associations; only the distinct particular takes our attention. Green snow is news.

The Modifier That Weakens the Noun

An adjective gives us the noun's quality or type: *white* snow. An adverb relates to a verb in the same way: he grinned *happily*. But each of these examples would be bad style in most contexts. In each, the modifier diminishes the word it should strengthen. *Snow* is whiter than *white snow*. *Snow* is white in the brain's computer-dictionary, so why color it, unless to suggest its opposite? To say *white snow* brings to mind snow that is gray with dirt. This suggestion might be just what the writer wanted. "White snow fell, that morning, on the trash of the old city." The contrast is part of the meaning; *white* takes its place, modifying *snow*, because of the later words *trash* and *city*. But most of the time, when a writer adds *white* to *snow*, he subtracts from his sentence. He adds *white* in an uneasy search for particularity; he lacks confidence in the insides of *snow*. The adjective overinsists on a quality already firm in the word.

If we know that the character grinned, must we be told that he *grinned happily?* It can only bring to mind that he *might* have grinned unhappily, which is a nasty thought; the author reassures us that this supposition is not so, but without the reassurance there would have been no supposition.

A beginning writer often goes through stages with adjectives, and different people have different problems with them. With some beginners, all adjectives are predictable.

> It was a long trip from the high mountains of the frozen north to the desert wastes of sunny Arizona, but it was highly educational and well worthwhile.

The problem is not primarily adjectives and adverbs, but thinking (or not thinking) in the old tracks.

Modifiers as Weak Intensives

We often misuse adjectives and adverbs as weak intensifiers. We say, "she moved gracefully," when we might say with more gusto that "she danced" or "she swept" or "she glided." We may use vague adjectives in place of specific ones or in place of clauses that could add color and precision. We say, "a tremendous amount," when *amount* is vague and *tremendous* is a weak and unspecific intensifier, or *really huge,* when we might say, *ten million* or *as long as a supertanker.* Here the specific number of the comparison carries color; the accuracy is one of feeling, not of dimensions.

Automatic Modifiers

Another misuse of adjectives and adverbs, a more advanced or sophisticated misuse, appears when writers suddenly appreciate bright colors in writing, especially when they try their hand at stories and poems. In this misuse, the symptom is not cliché but multiplicity. Nearly every noun carries its adjective, like a tote bag, and every verb wears an adverb for a cape. The style is flashy and overdressed. Here is part of a poem written by a student in a creative writing class.

> I woke suddenly from a ghost-ridden dream
> of old women, to find myself wandering vaguely
> on the far edges of the raw city where white skulls tipped crazily
> in the western sky, and dirty children ran by
> to the cave shelters of abandoned cars . . . .

The lines are improved by mechanically stripping them of modifiers. Should any be kept? Yes. *Abandoned* is necessary to the emotion in *abandoned cars.* If it is merely *cars* that are *shelters,* they could be the kind of comfortable, middle-class vehicles one drives to the supermarket. The *abandoned* makes the children take *shelter* in something more suggestive of a dump.

Certainly *old women* is different from *women.* The phrase is altered by leaving out the adjective; perhaps we should restore *old.* But the other modifiers are best exterminated. When revised, the poem read:

> I woke from a dream
> of old women, to find myself wandering
> on the edges of the city
> where skulls tipped
> in the sky, and children ran
> to the shelters of abandoned cars . . . .

Here only two modifiers remain from the thirteen in the original version. Certainly the spare version is better writing, and it was accomplished wholly by deleting modifiers.

Nouns as Modifiers

In the phrase *cave shelter, cave* was a noun used as a modifier. Writers use participles and nouns as modifiers—*sheltering cave,* as well as *cave shelter*—with the same dangers, and the same opportunities, that attend the use of plain adjectives. Keep the same cautions in mind.

It is an advantage of the English language that its grammar is not rigid. In some languages, a noun would have to undergo respelling before it could be used as an adjective. English accepts change. And because it accepts change, in speech and writing, the writer or the speaker can make shades of meaning more precise. Using nouns as modifiers, we can say, *house party, religion committee, death wish.*

We can also say, "this type grammar," or—as in Bergen Evans's example of tediously multiplied nouns as modifiers—"he absconded with the River Street fire house Christmas Eve party funds." Because English lacks grammatic rigidity, it is subject to abuses that can lead to chaos and disorganization. *Type* is frequently a filler noun, and when we use it as a modifier we make even less sense than we normally do. With Bergen Evans's example, as with too many sentences that are seriously intended, the proliferation of nouns as modifiers creates heaviness and awkwardness. Here a longer, complex sentence would be preferable: "He absconded with the funds that the River Street fire house had collected for its Christmas Eve party." The noun modifiers in "River Street fire house" and "Christmas Eve party" are reasonable, and they are not heaped on each other.

Be careful when you use nouns as modifiers. Sociologists are often prone to abusing this devise. One hears of the "city group research effort." By the third of these noun modifiers, the reader begins to feel afloat in a sea of possibilities. What will go with what? It is as if one were wandering inside a Chinese sentence, with no inflections, with no connectives, with no tense or number. Avoid afflicting your reader; confine yourself to no more than two noun modifiers in a row.

Revising Modifiers

When you revise your prose, question the need for every adjective and adverb. Can I do without these modifiers? Does the noun (like *postulate* in *basic postulate*) or the verb (like *run* in *run quickly*) do the job without the modifier? Or can I find an exact noun or verb to do the job in one word? Do I avoid a succession of adjective-noun combinations, the monotonous pairs? Do I, on the one hand, create a cliché by joining two words that are commonly used together? Do I, on the other hand, use the necessary modifier to make the discrimination or to add the expressive color?

Edit out all unnecessary modifiers; add necessary, useful, colorful ones.

EXERCISES

1. For each of the nouns listed below, find three adjectives, and for each of the verbs, three adverbs. Pick one pairing from each category and use them to construct an interesting sentence. You should have three sentences.

    a. armor
    b. parrot
    c. lips
    d. shrieked
    e. fastened
    f. spread

2. Study these sentences from student essays, underlining adjectives and adverbs that are redundant (like *pointed* pin) or else function as weak intensives (like *terribly* long).

    a. The small mouse ate the twitching insect very quickly.
    b. Joshua is a real nice counselor and does a good job with the harder tasks.
    c. We watched a scary horror movie, where an evil fiend went around with a very bright light and searched for his missing fingers.
    d. Bob doesn't have even the slightest idea about how very boring he has become on the subject of computers.
    e. You could describe Diane as a "very" kind of person—very tall, very smart, very nice, and very sexy.
    f. How did you get the great honor of leading the whole big group of graduating seniors across the stage?

3. Find a passage of descriptive writing that is rich in adjectives and adverbs. Rewrite the passage by eliminating all such modifiers—then describe the ways in which you have changed the meaning of the passage.

4. Go on a cliché hunt. Find ten adjective/noun combinations on the order of "gentle breeze" and bring your list to class to read aloud.

5. Underline adverbs and adjectives in these passages. Can you criticize or praise the author's use of modifiers? Isolate specific examples and write short comments.

> a. After the age when hunting was done by males and the gathering of vegetables and small animal food by females—always with close cooperation between men and women—the discovery of planting and herding and then of the animal-drawn plow assured a steadier food supply, which underwrote male enterprises: conquest, the building of cities, trade, and *the stratification of society*. But women's role continued to be circumscribed by childbearing; whatever a women did she had to do near home.
>
> Margaret Mead, "Needed: Full Partnership for Women"
> *(Saturday Review)*

> b. The needs of a society determine its ethics, and in the Black American ghettos the hero is the man who is offered only the crumbs from his country's table but by ingenuity and courage is able to take for himself a Lucullan feast. Hence the janitor who lives in one room but sports a robin's-egg-blue Cadillac is not laughed at but admired, and the domestic who buys forty-dollar shoes is not criticized but is appreciated. We

know that they have to put to use their full mental and physical powers. Each single gain feeds into the gains of the body collective.

Maya Angelou, "Mr. Red Leg"

c. Nick looked at the burned-over stretch of hillside, where he had expected to find the scattered houses of the town, and then walked down the railroad track to the bridge over the river. The river was there. It swirled against the log spiles of the bridge. Nick looked down into the clear, brown water, colored from the bubbly bottom, and watched the trout keeping themselves steady in the current with wavering fins. As he watched them they changed their position by quick angles, only to hold steady in the fast water again. Nick watched them for a long time.

Ernest Hemingway, "Big Two-Hearted River"

d. Personal consideration of various and sundry matters of considerable importance has led numerous observers to ultimately conclude that the final end of Western civilization is certainly closer to a realistic possibility than might earlier have been tentatively assumed.

e. All girls in this period of American Victorianism suffered in an environment that utterly discouraged the healthy development of their emotional lives. However, at least some enterprising girls with a full measure of curiosity were less ignorant—perhaps less virginal—than the popular mythology supposed.

Cynthia Griffin Wolff, *A Feast of Words*

6. You might make more exercises out of the five examples above. Here are some possibilities. (a) Discuss in class the modifiers in each passage. (b) In each passage, look at the verbs and nouns. Are they used well? (c) In example c, put an adjective with every noun that lacks one and an adverb with every verb. Make the additions as apt as you can, and see what you have done. (d) Try to rewrite passage a, omitting adverbs and adjectives. How much, and what, do you lose?

7. Pick one of the passages in Exercise 4 and write a paragraph to follow it. Stay as close to the author's style as possible; use similar kinds of adjectives and adverbs.

ORIGINAL WORDS: COMPARISONS

The Need for Originality

When we put words together—adjective with noun, noun with verb, verb with object—we start to communicate. We begin to show our own minds, or we show a dull copy of someone else's mind. Originality depends on clarity and vigor. One source of originality in language is comparison. To talk about metaphoric writing and originality, we must go over some old ground.

Formulas or clichés or trite expressions substitute for the originality that each of us can attain. A girl who was mourning the death of her grandfather wrote, starting her first term paper of the term, "A tragedy recently occurred in my ancestral home." In a conference with her instructor, the girl wept over the death, she was pale, her hands shook. Moved by her obvious unhappiness, her teacher was sympathetic. At the same time he recognized that her prose style was not adequate to the depth of her feeling. Her body showed her wretchedness, but her prose showed her reading of a weekly country newspaper. He saw no grief in her phrasing, only the set phrases of headlines or lead sentences in obituaries. Perhaps the formulas came to her pen so that she could avoid the pain that comes with the real feeling. Or perhaps they came because she did not know the difference, in words, between the formula that communicates nothing and the originality that communicates feeling. No feeling reaches her reader. Her audience, instead of feeling moved, is bored. Her teacher felt that writing about her grief might help her to understand it, might help her through her mourning. By asking sensitive questions he helped her to criticize her own expression of grief. He suggested that *A tragedy occurred* is a formula that denies the tragic and compared this formula to others, like *a catastrophe was averted* and *a blessed event took place.* The journalistic familiarity and the detached passivity of the construction block off any believable expression of emotion.

A phrase becomes a formula or a cliché not just because it is used commonly but also because it prevents feeling. The phrase *rain fell* is more common than *a tragedy occurred,* yet we do not think of it as a formula because we do not use it to keep feelings down. A psychiatrist described clichés as "the lies we tell ourselves that we *want* to hear." When the student wrote, "A tragedy recently occurred at my ancestral home," she was not lying overtly or intending to lie. It was not like saying that she did not chop down a cherry tree when she really did. The lie was internal, the lie of using language to avoid difficult reality, the lie of euphemism.

Overhearing Your Own Originality

Listen to yourself as you daydream or think idly. Are you reciting newspaper formulas or greeting-card verse? If you overhear yourself, in your own head, thinking trite sentimentality about your love, something is wrong. Find out what your real emotion is. Make it new. *Invent.* This does not mean that you should make up something that you haven't experienced—only that you should push yourself to discover the true specifics of your feeling. What is really there behind those bland formulas of affection?

In general, trying to *overhear* yourself is a good idea. On some days, you can listen to the dreaming voice easily; on other days, that voice seems mute; it is more likely that you are deaf. The dreaming language is clichés sometimes, sometimes puns or phrases with crazy originality. Sometimes the voice hums the tune from a song; when you remember the lyrics, a coded message is there. You may hear a country-western song about an abandoned lover, when you are feeling lonely or abandoned or when something inside you feels that you will be lonely soon. The puns and crazy phrases are codes, too. Look at them closely. They have information for you. They are spoken by your original self, which is looking for attention from your conventional self, the self trained by parents and school and television to think like a train on a track. The crazier the phrase, the more devious the pun, the deeper the source in the self. It is not for nothing that psychiatrists often ask their patients to free-associate: associations are like arrows pointing to the real. When the dreaming voice talks in clichés, the train track is getting in the way of the real voice because the real voice would tell us a truth that we might find painful.

Overhear yourself to know yourself. Then you can farm your daydreams for original verbal images that express feeling. The crazy image and the pun do not make good writing in themselves—though often they can be the leaping-off point in daily writing—but they do give clues to feelings that the conscious mind can follow. Here is an unrevised passage from a student's daily writing.

> I was taking out the garbage this morning and I heard (in my head) Fanny Davis's voice talking. She has a funny way of talking, Englishy but not really, and I knew it was her. She was saying, "I like to use the word 'to intimate' without any regard for its actual meaning." I kept stuffing the garbage bags into the cans, wondering why I made that up, and why I chose Fanny's voice. It's always sounded affected to me. But that wasn't the sort of thing she says. She talks about her family and the home on the lake up North and going skiing in Switzerland. I was feeling blue. Bob had gone to New York and I knew that Sally was there, his old girlfriend, and I worried about that. Then I started laughing, right at the garbage, because I saw that "to intimate" and "too intimate" are close, but "to intimate" is a long way from the meaning of "too intimate." I was blue because I was too close to Bob, and I could get hurt.

The girl had uncovered something—which she almost knew already—by overhearing a daydream pun and by figuring it out. We may start dreaming; we end up thinking. Now she might be ready to examine her feelings about Bob or her feelings about her past.

Looking for Originality

We can try to activate the daydreaming mind. We will not always succeed. The girl who wrote the paper beginning "A tragedy occurred" returned to the subject many times. The week after her initial paper, she wrote, "A month ago my grandfather died," and went on for a few rather dry sentences. Though the prose was colorless, it communicated more than her sentences about tragedies occurring at ancestral homes. Still, it had no images, no pieces of *sense,* no particulars.

Later, thinking about things she could associate with her grandfather, she wrote about "farm implements" that were "unused" and "hanging on the wall of the barn." Then she changed "farm implements" to "rake and hoe." Then she revised the sentence again and added an image that could come only from the imagination guessing into the unseen. "His hoes and rakes hang from pegs in the barn. Spiders will spin webs there while the iron turns red with rust." She had farmed the dreaming part of herself, with a selective intelligence, and wrote two sentences that in their details and associations began to embody her melancholy and loss.

Simile and Metaphor

Images are groups of words that give an impression to the senses. Most images are visual, but we can also make images of taste, touch, hearing, and smell. Images communicate feelings and locate them firmly, really making contact between writer and reader. Comparisons in simile and metaphor mostly use images; they become ways for us to show emotions and illustrate ideas.

Similes are comparisons that use *like* or *as,* little words that announce a comparison. Metaphors omit the announcement. We write, "Her face bloomed with affection," and the word *bloomed* compares the girl to a flower; the face-flower is pretty, it is coming into its maturity, and it is associated with spring or summer. The writer may wish to go on talking about the girl in similes that use garden images. Perhaps her dress *rustles like leaves* and her skin is *as soft as petals.* The difference between similes and metaphors is small—a signal is there or not there—but it is real; the simile, because it announces itself, is more reasonable, more conscious of what it is doing.

For clarity, we must distinguish this brief comparison from the word *comparison* as we used it in the last chapter, discussing comparison and contrast as a structure used in exposition. We must also distinguish it from the grammatical sense—the *comparison of adjectives.* A comparison between the gross national products of Greece and Turkey, or between *less* and *least,* is not like comparing an old cheese to an untidy hog.

Creating a new, verbal comparison—simile, metaphor, and analogy— is our most original act of speech; the originality comes from the dreaming part of the self. Although we cannot always manufacture metaphors at will, we can learn to be alert for comparisons, and we can stimulate their coming. The dead grandfather's funeral had happened during a thunderstorm. When the girl tried to write about it, she encountered the trite associations of thunderstorms and death. She began simply.

> The funeral was 2 P.M. He was laid out in the front parlor, which was always closed except for weddings and funerals. Fifty people were there, some crowded into the parlor, others backed into the living

room. The minister talked a little and read scripture. Then the sky
turned dark.

The prose is simple and direct but it lacks energy. "The minister talked a
little and read scripture" would probably be better if it included direct and
indirect quotation. "Then the sky turned dark." *How* dark? How did she
feel about the sky turning dark? We have the sense reading this prose that
the feelings (which she earlier misrepresented in journalistic clichés) are
still restricted, held back, reserved.

Suppose the sky turned "as dark as" something. If it turned "as black
as the ace of spades," we would be nowhere. What does the ace of spades
have to do with her grandfather or her feelings? Even if she had told us
that the old man was a poker-playing farmer, the simile is so hackneyed
that no one will see the black of the playing card when she says it. The useful comparison has to be new. But to say "the sky turned as dark as the soot
from a factory chimney" would seem inappropriate; what would a factory
have to do with a farm? The comparison must be more than new; it must
relate to the context: to her memories of the man, to the funeral, to the
idea of death. "The sky turned black as my grandmother's dress" would be
a better direction; but maybe that's too black, or the texture is wrong. Or
she might want to compare it to something she remembers and associates
with the dead farmer. "The sky turned black, like inside the barn after
milking."

Sometimes one phrase will not be adequate. You want your comparison to go on longer than that. "The sky turned dark. I could see a black
round storm cloud coming. I remembered leaning over the open well, staring down into the round black eye of the water." Here, we find a comparison within the comparison; the water is an *eye,* and the reader alert to the
insides of words might reconstruct the dead metaphor: *the eye of the storm*—
and revive it—although (or because) the author has not stated it.

Originality and Memory

To find the right comparison, we must draw on memory and daydream; imagination newly combines old things remembered; it is always
present and often hard to discover. Our memory does not consist only of
things memorized but also of everything that ever happened to us. We must
learn the path to this treasury. Memory is crucial to our writing, thinking,
and feeling. By scrutiny of the retained past, we begin to understand and to
express that understanding. In the floating world, we connect feelings in
the present to feelings about the past. We express these connections mostly
by making comparisons. In our own uniqueness we can each find something that the sky grew as dark as.

In speaking of originality and memory, we do not imply that originality applies only to autobiographical writing. Whether we write about
grandfathers or the gross national product, dinosaurs or television pro-

grams, we need original comparisons to make our prose lively enough to make contact with an audience. In an essay on economics called "The Technostructure," John Kenneth Galbraith contrasts *the man of intelligence* with his opposite; he could have used the abstract noun *stupidity,* parallel to *intelligence;* probably we would have remained content. But instead, he chose to brighten his prose with a figure: ". . . the same for the man of intelligence and for his neighbor who, under medical examination, shows daylight in either ear."

Galbraith remembers a familiar exaggeration of stupidity, as in *airhead,* and rewrites it in his own language by introducing a doctor's office. As we read his complex essay on economics, we are tickled momentarily by his comedy; it keeps us attentive.

Analogy

We use the word *analogy* for a comparison that makes or illustrates a point at greater length than a metaphor or a simile. An analogy can be extended into a whole essay; ministers' sermons are sometimes analogies—life is like the hundred-yard dash: birth is the starting gun, death is the tape, God is the judge. A whole book or system of thought can be based on analogy. Oswald Spengler, in *The Decline of the West,* at the beginning states an analogy that a civilization is an organism, that it is born, grows old, and dies; then he writes a long book to make a factual case for his analogy.

An analogy often runs through a paragraph like a thread in tweed, not separated into patches of assertion followed by comparison but interwoven. James Thurber wrote this paragraph about working with the editor of *The New Yorker,* Harold Ross:

> Having a manuscript under Ross's scrutiny was like putting your car in the hands of a skilled mechanic, not an automotive engineer with a bachelor of science degree, but a guy who knows what makes a motor go, and sputter, and wheeze, and sometimes come to a dead stop; a man with an ear for the faintest body squeak as well as the loudest engine rattle. When you first gazed, appalled, upon an uncorrected proof of one of your stories or articles, each margin had a thicket of queries and complaints—one writer got a hundred and forty-four on one profile. It was as though you beheld the words of your car spread all over the garage floor, and the job of getting the thing together again and making it work seemed impossible. Then you realize that Ross was trying to make your Model T or old Stutz Bearcat into a Cadillac or Rolls-Royce. He was at work with the tools of his unflagging perfectionism, and, after an exchange of growls or snarls, you set to work to join him in his enterprise.
>
> James Thurber, *The Years with Ross*

Thurber begins by announcing his subject, "Having a manuscript under Ross's scrutiny"; departs from it for the rest of a long sentence; returns to the manuscript for a sentence; then in the final three sentences develops his analogy, makes it funnier, and makes his point about Ross as an editor. He sharpens his points by contrasts: *mechanic* not *engineer; not automotive engineer* but *guy.* He then develops his analogy into impossibility (repairing a Model T into a Cadillac), exaggerating it out of all touch with reality; the customer joins with the mechanic to rebuild his torn-up machine. The analogy expresses feeling, it is witty, and it is a pleasure to read. Consider this alternative, omitting the garage and substituting abstraction and generality for analogy:

> Having a manuscript under Ross's scrutiny was an edifying if terrifying experience. He was a skilled editor, not an academic, but a practical man. When you first gazed, appalled, upon an uncorrected proof of one of your stories or articles, each margin had a number of queries and complaints—one writer got a hundred and forty-four on one profile. You beheld all your work torn apart, and it seemed impossible to put it together. Then you realized that Ross was trying to make ordinary prose into prose of the highest order. He was using his editorial skills with unflagging perfectionism, and, after an exchange of growls or snarls, you set to work to join him in his enterprise.

This gutted version is slightly shorter, but the cutting loses rather than gains: the paragraph diminishes in energy and expression.

The Unintended Comparison

With analogy as with other forms of comparison, you must be wary of the dead, the mixed, and the inadvertently comic. Often a writer will trap herself in an unconscious analogy expressing an attitude that she really feels but denies to herself. The disparity is as slapstick as a top-hatted man with his trousers missing. Here is an English critic, writing about American music in the London *Times Literary Supplement.* He writes in attempted praise of American energy and vitality, but other messages come through his bad prose.

> The American composer is neither enriched nor shackled. He had nothing to start from but old rags and bones of European culture that, imported to a new environment, soon lost their savor. Then gradually, in the pulping machine of a polyglot society, the rags and bones began to acquire a taste of their own.

Look at the main analogy, rags and bones. When they were imported here, they "soon lost their savor." Did the gentleman actually expect rags and bones to taste good? His idea of the American stew expresses his distaste; the analogy suggests eating the product of something like a paper factory: "in the pulping machine . . . the rags and bones began to acquire a taste of their own." The writer expressed his feelings, but he expressed feelings he didn't know he had. He appears to believe that he likes American music, but the unacknowledged Critic Inside is holding his nose.

To express a feeling without examining it is dangerous. Originality combines opposites: we dream—with our eyes open; we are inspired—then we scrutinize and revise. Scrutiny provides the motive for revision. We need to look at words—to see the connection among *rags and bones, savor,* and *taste*—and we will sometimes discover feelings we had not wished to acknowledge. Then we can revise ourselves or our prose or both. We must again float on daydream and memory for new words, and then put the new words under scrutiny again. Only by developing all these mental abilities—and this discipline—can we begin to be honest. The paradox is that to be sincere we must struggle; we must struggle to be spontaneous and then struggle to revise, refine, and order our spontaneity, in order to reach an audience other than ourselves. To speak our most intimate selves into the ears of others, we must revise.

One way to cultivate our sensitivity to the insides of words is to develop an ear for the unintended comparison. (The unintended comparison is often an overt, and sometimes extended, version of the dead metaphor.) On a Monday night football broadcast, Howard Cosell said of a new quarterback that he "walked in the wake" of a great predecessor. In this example, the unintended comparison approaches blasphemy.

The mixed metaphor is, of course, another consequence of thoughtless analogy making. *The New Yorker* regularly cites examples as humorous filler. Here is one of their findings:

> Saint Audrey and her board puppets have royally ripped their britches trying to ram more and higher taxes down our throats. Indeed, they have danced around the budget Maypole for too long. These same supervisors should now retreat, rethink, and reprogram. The time has come to fish or cut bait.

Looking for Analogies

We can think out an analogy more easily than we can create the lone metaphor, which to most writers seems a gift from the god within us, an inspiration. Suppose you are discussing what makes a love affair succeed. Suppose you decide that it takes a lot of work. The word *work,* itself a metaphor nearly dead, can lead you into analogy. What kind of work is it like? Is it like a nine-to-five job? You can make an analogy in the negative: "This work is no nine-to-five job." Is it like building a house? Rebuilding a destroyed city? Making the sets for a play? Sculpting a life-sized elephant out of used bubble gum?

Revising writing in order to reach an audience, we can use our clichés as clues to lead us toward inventing new analogies and metaphors. If we can learn to identify the worn out, we can create the original. Suppose that when we look over the draft of an essay, we discover the cliché of *clues* used above. By heeding our sense of the insides of words, we can discover a mystery story buried in the dead metaphor: clichés are the smoking guns that reveal the murderer—and oddly enough "the murderer" we discover in this analogy will become our original, invented comparison. If we convict the murderer of being a new metaphor, we have won our case. The defense rests.

The liveliest prose moves from analogy to analogy without strain. It takes practice to learn how to invent, and practice to learn when to stop inventing. When analogy shifts abruptly, the effect is usually ridiculous, and comic writers can use these sudden shifts to their advantage; if in one sentence you compare tennis with big-game hunting, do not compare it in the next sentence with knitting unless you want a laugh. Often a sentence or a paragraph of general summary or narrative separates passages of differing analogies, keeping them from clashing.

Here Edward Hoagland begins an essay called "The Courage of Turtles" with a bizarre comparison and goes on to make others.

> Turtles are a kind of bird with the governor turned low. With the same attitude of removal, they cock a glance at what is going on, as if they need only to fly away. Until recently they were also a case of virtue rewarded, at least in the town where I grew up, because, being humble creatures, there were plenty of them. Even when we still had a few bobcats in the woods the local snapping turtles, growing up to forty pounds, were the largest carnivores. You would see them through the amber water, as big as greeny wash basins at the bottom of the pond, until they faded into the inscrutable mud as if they hadn't existed at all.

(A *governor,* as Hoagland uses the word, is an automatic device attached to an engine to limit its speed.) Hoagland compares a turtle to a bird exactly because the comparison seems impossible. When he provides the bird-turtle with a mechanical device appropriate to tractor-trailers, he makes another impossibility. But by comparing the incomparable, Hoagland shocks us into seeing something freshly: both turtles and birds observe the world with an alert nervousness. When Hoagland goes on to speak of *virtue rewarded,* he makes an ironic comparison of turtles with downtrodden humans. He follows with a straight-forward but unexpected connection of turtles with bobcats and ends extravagantly by comparing turtles to kitchen utensils that have the power to disappear. The prose's energy derives from its quick assembly of details and outrageous, but accurate, comparisons.

Revising for Comparison

First, check your sentences to make sure that you are controlling the comparisons you make. Make sure that you do not inadvertently turn a quarterback into a deity or an art form into a bad smell. Second, see that you have not made cliché comparisons that no longer function, like "black as the ace of spades."

Then do the more difficult. *Add* simile, metaphor, and analogy. Most of us in our first drafts lack energy and feeling. Our prose resembles the pale version of Thurber after the analogy was deleted. The prose is too plain to reach the reader with excitement and precision. Float on memory and daydream to invent; scrutinize with critical intelligence to cut and to improve. Ask yourself if your invention is new, if it is appropriate, if it does not clash with anything else. In a paragraph of exposition, think if you can clarify by analogy. If you find a cliché or a dead metaphor, remake the old into something new. What was it like to have your prose edited by Ross? What was it like the day your grandfather died?

Revising Words

Cheryl Lewis, the student who had tried without success to write about her grandfather's death, eventually found another way to approach her subject. When her teacher assigned a short descriptive theme later in the term, Cheryl decided that she would try to describe her grandfather as she remembered him. Her first attempt began:

> My grandfather was a big man. He was over six feet tall and had white hair. But he did not look old. He was strong from working all his life and he stood very straight. His face was like leather. When he smiled or frowned, his wrinkles showed clearly. He usually wore overalls and a shirt, but sometimes he would walk around the house in his long underwear. Then you saw that even though his face and hands were brown, his feet were completely white. He liked to sit in the kitchen like that early in the morning, reading the paper and drinking coffee.

Several days later, Cheryl had a conference with her teacher. He praised her determination, her desire to master the subject and the emotions it aroused; he also agreed that this draft was better. She let her emotions show indirectly by allowing the description to speak for itself. *But,* he said, he still had some problems with this presentation. The picture in the reader's mind was not clear enough. "Let's look at the opening," he said. "If you can solve that you'll probably see what to do with the rest."

The teacher told Cheryl that she was not making use of some of the writer's best tools. "Precision tools," he said, "like images, adjectives, and adverbs." He reminded her of subjects they had covered in class discussions. Cheryl nodded. She said that she knew there was a lot she could do in the way of fine tuning. "I wanted to get my general impressions down first," she said. "If I spend too much time getting the first few sentences right, I freeze up." Her teacher acknowledged that perfectionism often led to writer's block, especially in the beginning stages of composition. But now that she had the essential shape, he added, she could turn her attention to more precise detailing. He reminded her that specific images and concrete words were the best way to make a connection with an audience.

Cheryl and her teacher talked about the opening passage. The teacher asked her a number of questions. "You say he was big," he said; "How big? Tell me so that I can see. Was he fat?" And: "He worked, but what kind of work did he do? What were his overalls like—rumpled, neatly pressed, dirty? Is there a better, less trite, image than leather for his face? What about those wrinkles? Is there some way you can describe those white feet? Can you compare them to anything?" Cheryl scribbled notes on her paper, but at that last question she looked up with a smile. "Albino fish," she said. "*What?*" Cheryl then explained how her grandfather had joked about his own feet—*he* had compared them to albino fish. "Perfect," said the teacher.

Cheryl finished making notes and looked up. "I think I'm starting to see what you're after," she said. "It's as if you want to *be* there." The teacher nodded. Then he made a suggestion. Cheryl was to sit down at home with her opening paragraph and try some of the brainstorming and sprinting exercises used by the class earlier in the term. She was to bring a page of ideas and images to class. "Check your memories," advised the teacher. "Try to reach back for some associations. Put down anything that comes to mind." Two days later Cheryl handed in her list:

> Grandma's kitchen, gramps leaning to get through the door
> reading the paper in longjohns (already mentioned)
> silvery hairs on his chest
> big belly—but hard
> Santa Claus?
> "A man needs to eat, needs energy."
> standing up and patting belly
> teasing grandma all the time
> loves jokes, loves to laugh
> boom, boom, boom—the whole kitchen rattles
> wrinkles tighten when he smiles
> I thought cheeks would break in half
> dressed he looked so brown, years in the sun
> but his feet—what a surprise!
> "albino fish" and how he wiggled his toes when he pointed to them

On the bottom of the page Cheryl had written, in exasperation, "Too much to tell!" When her teacher handed the sheet back the next day, her remark was circled. Beside it he had written: "Better too much than not enough!" In smaller letters: "Much better. Use some of these. Try to make every detail and action precise."

When rewrites were collected the following week, Cheryl passed in a much expanded essay. She was happier with the whole piece, but she especially liked her new beginning.

> My grandfather was a big man. He was tall enough to have to stoop coming through the kitchen door, and though he was not hugely fat, you could see that his weight made him do extra work. Sometimes at the end of a long day of driving the John Deere or mending fence he would come puffing from the barn. My grandmother was always after him to go on a diet. But he had an answer for that. "How can I work

if I don't have energy? Where does energy come from?" Or else he might stand up tall, stick out his chest, and slap his belly hard with his palms. "Pure muscle." Standing there in his longjohns, barefoot, he was a sight. He was like two different people put together to make one. His face and hands were dark, penny-brown, from working in the sun. The skin was hard, too. When he smiled I thought his cheeks might crack open. But what a shock it was to look down at his feet. "Like two albino fish," he would say, wiggling his toes furiously.

The teacher was pleased with the rewrite. He asked Cheryl if she could feel the difference herself. She could. "I also enjoyed the process of writing much more," she said. "It took a long time, but I felt *there,* really close to the farm and my grandparents."

"A few mere words," said her teacher. Then he took two minutes to point out the parts of Cheryl's description that he found especially successful. He praised the precision of the second sentence. Cheryl had managed to suggest the man's height, get him into motion, and introduce the kitchen setting; she had also given a sense of his girth. "I like your adverb *hugely* there," he said. "It tells us that he was big, *too* big, but that he stopped short of obesity." The next sentence helped the reader picture the kind of work he did—naming "John Deere" instead of writing "tractor" was good—but the focus, the real weight, was on the participle *puffing.* "Another nice choice," he told her. "Your words are starting to do the job they were meant to do."

"What else?" Cheryl's teacher said that he very much liked the sentence: "Or else he might stand up tall, stick out his chest, and slap his belly hard with his palms." The separated phrase defined the stages of the action very clearly, he explained. But it was the crisp emphasis, the clean word sounds of "slap his belly hard with his palms" that registered most vividly. *Slap* as a verb, *hard* as an adverb, and *palms* as a noun that was far more precise than *hands.* Palms, he said, forced the reader to visualize the action; the word established the position of the hands in space.

"I singled out a number of things here," said Cheryl's teacher. "I wanted you to know where you succeeded and why. You turned a vague, somewhat lazy piece of writing into something that begins to live on the page. You didn't do it by magic or voodoo, but by tuning in to every sentence. You made sure that you had something to say and that you said it as vividly and accurately as you could. You've got adjectives and adverbs working to sharpen your perceptions; you have in the cracking cheeks and those albino fish a pair of wonderful images. The playful sense of the toes wiggling *furiously* adds pleasure. And the *penny-brown* . . . ."

EXERCISES

1. a. Here are six common comparatives. Write two sentences using each, one in which you make an expected simile, one in which the terms of the comparison are more unusual.

> as long as   as green as
> as bright as   as sour as
> as wet as   as heavy as

b. Pretend that you are walking through a dark woods late at night. Find three similes that might express your feelings. Pretend now that you finally see the lights of your destination in the distance. Describe those lights by using three different metaphors or analogies.

2. Study the passage by Hoagland on page 120, then underline verbs, circle nouns, and enclose modifiers in oblong boxes. How does this writer make parts of speech work together—adjective with noun, subject with verb? Do Hoagland's metaphors and comparisons make use of all parts of speech? Which of these strikes you and why?

3. a. Write three pairs of sentences in which you make the same comparison as both simile and metaphor. Can you account for any difference in sense? Be specific.

b. Find a quoted passage in this book that makes use of simile and metaphor. Rewrite it, making similes from the metaphors and vice versa. Speculate on what changes in meaning or emphasis you have thus created.

4. In these passages, underline analogies, metaphors, and similes. Choose three examples that you particularly like, and explain your reasons for preferring them.

> a. But his position was weak. Like a cougar, the army was constantly perched above him, ready to pounce.
>
> John Gerassi, *The Great Fear in Latin America*
>
> b. After thousands of years we're still strangers to darkness, fearful aliens in an enemy's camp with our arms crossed over our chests.
>
> Annie Dillard, "Strangers to Darkness"
>
> c. Many of us grow to hate documentaries in school, because the use of movies to teach us something seems a cheat—a pill disguised as candy—and documentaries always seem to be about something we're not interested in.
>
> Pauline Kael, "High School and Other Forms of Madness"
> *(Deeper Into Movies)*
>
> d. I lay down on a solitary rock that was like an island in the bottom of the valley, and looked up. The grey sage-brush and the blue-grey rock around me were already in shadow, but high above me the canyon walls were dyed flame-colour with the sunset, and the Cliff City lay in a gold haze against its dark cavern. In a few minutes it, too, was grey, and only the rim rock at

the top held the red light. When that was gone, I could still see the copper glow in the piñons along the edge of the top ledges. The arc of sky over the canyon was silvery blue, with its pale yellow moon, and presently stars shivered into it, like crystals dropped into perfectly clear water.

Willa Cather, *The Professor's House*

e. Women have served all these centuries as looking glasses possessing the magic and delicious power of reflecting the figure of man at twice its natural size. Without that power probably the earth would still be swamp and jungle. The glories of all our wars would be unknown. We should still be scratching the outlines of deer on the remains of mutton bones and bartering flints for sheepskins or whatever simple ornament took our unsophisticated taste. Superman and Fingers of Destiny would never have existed. The Czar and the Kaiser would never have worn their crowns or lost them. Whatever may be their use in civilised societies, mirrors are essential to all violent and heroic action. That is why Napoleon and Mussolini both insist so emphatically upon the inferiority of women, for if they were not inferior, they would cease to enlarge.

Virginia Woolf, *A Room of One's Own*

5. Make up three paragraph-long analogies that express what it is like to go to school. Thurber's version of Ross as mad mechanic provides an example. Could you construct an analogy from work with a computer? From building a house? Work collectively on this exercise during the class hour. Be ready to read your best paragraph aloud to the class.

5

Sentences

STYLE AND THE SENTENCE

Outwardly, a sentence is a group of words with a period, an exclamation point, or a question mark at the end. This is like saying that a person is a mammal with two arms, two legs, a body and a head—it's true, but it's not enough. A sentence is also a verbal structure that reflects something about the world. It puts words in relation in order to map our understanding of the sensible structure of things. If we think any further along these lines, we will be in the realm of linguistic philosophy, so let's keep things simple. A sentence is a unit of expression; it arranges the parts of speech to mirror a perception or an understanding. We write *The dog crosses the road* and use a noun, a verb, and another noun to make a picture. Writing *I see the dog cross the road,* we make a different picture. If we then rewrite the sentence as *I remember that I saw the dog cross the road,* we have complicated things still further.

This chapter will focus on the unit of sense that is the sentence—on its underlying logical structure as well as the different kinds of modifications that alter the sense and enable a more precise communication of meanings. To learn about these modifications—how and when to make them—is to learn effective style. And effective style is the main goal of our instruction.

Of course, we have been listening and speaking all our lives, and we will learn far more about sentence structure by paying attention to what we do, and what others do, than by studying types of sentences. But the study will help us bring things into focus; we will be better able to *control* the style of our sentences to express feelings and ideas. Not least, we will grasp the variety of possibilities and learn to keep our expression fresh.

PARTS OF SENTENCES

Before we look into the types of sentences, we need to know something about the parts of sentences and the names of those parts. For conve-

126

nience we will use standard names for the parts—like *subject* and *predicate.* Once learned, the names will save time; *elbow* is both clearer and less wordy than *that joint in the middle of the arm.*

Sentences have two main parts, subjects and predicates. The *subject* is what we make a statement or ask a question about. Usually the subject is a noun or a pronoun like *she* or *who;* but on occasion the subject can be something else that substitutes for a noun, like a clause or a phrase. (Even a verb can be a subject: "*Is* is a verb. *Is* is the subject of these sentences.") In these sentences, the subjects are in italics:

> *The frogman* dived.
> *The theory* was valid.
> *Who* committed this brutal crime?
> *Whoever committed this crime* must be insane.
> *Watching pinball machines light up* gave him a headache.

In the following sentence the *simple subject* is *woman,* and the *complete subject* is *the woman in the blue house by the river:*

> The woman in the blue house by the river wrote bizarre sentences on the walls.

The *predicate* is the verb along with its modifiers and complements. The predicate is what the sentence says about the subject; most often, the predicate is the action that goes on in the sentence. In these sentences, the simple predicates are in italics:

> The frogman *dived.*
> The theory *was* valid.
> Who *committed* this brutal crime?
> Watching pinball machines light up *gave* him a headache.

The *simple predicate* in the next sentence is *wrote;* the *complete predicate* is *wrote on the walls with invisible liquids.*

> The woman in the blue house wrote on the walls with invisible liquids.

Objects come in four forms: direct objects, indirect objects, objects of prepositions, and complementary objects. The *direct object* is the part of a sentence that the predicate acts on. Here, the direct objects are in italics:

> She designed the *atomic reactor.*
> The president washed the *dishes.*
> *What* did the elephant say?
> Underline the *predicates.*

An *indirect object* usually comes before a direct object and tells us to whom or for whom (or to what or for what) the predicate acts.

> She gave the *team* a case of beer.
> Sam wrote *her* a new song.

Most of the time, the indirect object replaces a prepositional phrase using *to* or *for.*

> She gave a case of beer *to the team.*
> Sam wrote a new song *for her.*

In the last two sentences *team* and *her* are *objects of prepositions,* nouns or noun substitutes that a preposition relates to another word or word group. Here are more prepositions followed by objects:

> When you are defenestrated you are thrown *out a window.*
> Hulk Hogan was barred *from the premises.*

Another construction has two objects, in which the second modifies or describes the first. The second, or *complementary object,* may be a noun or an adjective. In these examples the complementary object is in italics:

> They made her *bartender.*
> He called her a *humbug.*
> Margaret painted the tree *purple.*

Complements follow linking verbs like *is* and *become* and *appear.* When they modify or describe the sentence's subject, we call these words *subjective complements.* These words can be adjectives or nouns:

> She's an *artist.*
> They appeared *pretty.*

A *phrase* is a group of words that work together as a unit but lack a subject and a predicate. There are several kinds of phrases, defined by the word introducing them:

Prepositional phrase	The bat *in the attic* is not a vampire.
Verbal phrase	More and more people *will be buying* subcompact cars as gasoline prices again rise.
Infinitive phrase	Hockey fans tend *to enjoy violence.*
Gerund phrase	*Establishing a Fascist state* requires ruthlessness and ambition.
Participial phrase	*Doubting the medical assumptions of his time,* Pasteur sought further knowledge about what causes disease.

A *clause* is a group of words that contains a subject and a predicate. A clause may be *main* (also called independent) or *subordinate* (also called dependent). A *main clause* can be a simple sentence in itself.

> *The thin dog barked.*

A *subordinate clause* is not a complete sentence and cannot stand by itself; rather, it works as a noun, as an adjective, or as an adverb within a sentence.

Noun clause	*Whether the new league will flourish* is a question that no one can answer with certainty.
Adjective clause	The cricket, *which appeared to be wearing a tiny tuxedo,* did not answer his naive questions.
Adverb clause	She ordered the troops to attack *when it became apparent that to delay any longer would be suicidal.*

Each of these last two clauses is a *modifier.* A *modifier* is any word, phrase, or clause that functions as an adjective or adverb. It quite literally *modifies,* or changes the meaning, of the noun or verb in question.

> The bat *in the attic* is not a vampire.

Here the prepositional phrase *in the attic* does something to, *modifies,* bat; it tells us *which* bat. If we say *the vampire bat is in the attic,* then the word *vampire* is an adjective that modifies *bat.*

> The vampire flew slowly around the room after he assumed the form of a bat.

Here we have three modifiers, all acting as adverbs. One modifier tells us about the way the vampire flew: the single word *slowly;* then a prepositional phrase tells us where: the vampire flew *around the room;* then a subordinate clause tells us when it happened: *after he assumed the form of a bat.* Manner, place, and time; how, where, and when.

Now that we have the names of parts, we can examine types of sentences.

TYPES OF SENTENCES

Simple Sentences

A sentence is simple as long as it remains one clause, containing one predicate. *John laughed* is a complete, two-word sentence, simple and common in its structure: subject/verb. We could add modifiers, *Big John laughed loudly,* or a prepositional phrase, *John laughed at her,* and the sentence would remain simple.

A sentence can be quite long and yet still be simple. This sentence is simple but elaborates the predicate with prepositional phrases:

> *Phil runs/with his wife/at Waterman Gymnasium/before classes.*

We can add as many modifiers as we wish; the sentence will remain simple unless we add a subordinate clause.

A subject can be long, too.

> *The ape-man in the gray loincloth, a wooden spear in his hand,* attacked.

Either subject or predicate can be compounded and the sentence remains simple.

John *and his zebra* cried.
John *laughed and cried.*

Or the verb can be elaborated.

The ape-man *attacked swiftly, with a sharp cry, from behind the rocks.*

Or we can have a direct object, and the object can be elaborated.

The ape-man attacked *the sluggish warriors, those intruders tired from their lengthy searching.*

Or the simple sentence can have all its parts elaborated and remain simple.

The ape-man in the gray loincloth, a wooden spear in his hand, attacked the sluggish warriors swiftly from behind the rocks, the boulders shining in the hot sun.

The basic sentence is still *The ape-man attacked,* though by this time we have more definition for each of the parts, more information, and too many adjectives.

Compound Sentences

A compound sentence has two or more main clauses, each containing a subject and a predicate, each describing an action complete in itself. Compound literally means "put together" or "added together." The clauses in the compound sentence are joined by a connective—*and, but, or, nor, yet, for,* or *so*—or by a semicolon or colon.

The economy stagnates and prices rise.
We can lower the price of admission or we can stage fewer plays.
He never went to the snake house again; he had been revolted by the alligator.

The clauses in each of these sentences are independent. Each sentence could become two sentences, with minimal change in meaning.

The economy stagnates. Prices rise.
We can lower the price of admission. We can stage fewer plays.
He never went to the snake house again. He had been revolted by the alligator.

In the compound sentence, notice that the two complete clauses are nearly equal in importance, or *coordinate.* A compound sentence, of course, can have more than two parts.

Clemens pitched a curve, the runner on first sprinted toward second, and Barrett ran to cover the base.

But a string of coordinate clauses is usually boring.

There was more crime in the street, the criminals were running around free, the judges were letting people go, nobody was safe in the streets, criminals were out on bail, murderers were on parole, and nobody did anything.

Complex Sentences

If, however, one part of the sentence depends on the other—if the one is the cause of the other, for instance—we have a complex rather than a compound sentence. We call the clause that depends on the other for explanation or completion the *subordinate clause.* A complex sentence would be

Because the economy stagnates, high-priced items find few buyers.

The first clause in this sentence is subordinate. It cannot stand alone.

We can vary sentences even when we use only simple clauses and compounds of equally complete clauses. But the complex sentence provides further variety and allows us to emphasize the relationship of ideas to others in the same sentence. If we combine the two simple sentences

We were good friends. We saw each other only in the summer.

alternately into two different complex sentences, the results have different meanings:

We were good friends, although we saw each other only in the summer.
Although we were good friends, we saw each other only in the summer.

Complex sentences allow us to establish a precise relationship among ideas.

Clauses introduced by relative pronouns, *that, which,* or *who*—sometimes called *relative clauses*—are subordinate to a main clause; they depend on it.

Do you remember the face of the man *who sold you this ticket?*
The king executed the horse *that had thrown him.*

In other sentences, we attribute cause or sequence, and we do it by a conjunction like *because* or *after.*

Because the Girl Scouts had proved to be unscrupulous, the neighbors destroyed the cookies they had purchased.
After the movie ended, everyone in the audience left.

Many other conjunctions—like *although, after, if, since,* and *when*—can introduce subordinate clauses, each with its own precise meaning to be used by the careful writer.

Compound-Complex Sentences

Sometimes we can combine compound and complex sentences, using at least two main clauses and one subordinate clause. In each sentence below, the clause in italics is subordinate; the main clauses are in roman type.

> The young heiress jumped under the covers *when her uncle walked in wearing his gorilla suit,* and she refused to come out.
> *If you had only proofread the article more carefully,* Mr. Crumbly would not have been so insulted, and we wouldn't have this lawsuit on our hands!

Incomplete Sentences

Another type of sentence commonly used is the incomplete sentence, or fragment. It is incomplete because it lacks a subject or a predicate. *John laughed* is a brief but complete sentence. Neither *John* nor *laughed* would be complete by itself, but we could use either word alone in the proper context.

> She thought about whom she might ask to the picnic. Harry? Harry was too grubby. John? John.
> When she saw him she covered her mouth and, though she tried to suppress it, laughed. Laughed. He could not believe it.

Often the incomplete sentence is a phrase or a clause of several words.

> The essay by Ellsberg shows control of sentence variation. Like the variety in his first paragraph.

Although this combination of sentence and sentence fragment makes sense, we should revise it if we intend to write formal prose. We have several ways of working the meaning of *Like the variety in the first paragraph* into a longer sentence:

> Ellsberg's essay shows control of sentence variation, an attribute obvious in his first paragraph.
> As we can observe reading his first paragraph, Ellsberg's essay shows control of sentence variation.

The incomplete sentence is informal and we should usually avoid it when we write essays. Often we use it in speech, where tone of voice or facial expression or gesture completes meaning. But when we write, only the marks on the page carry meaning for us. As writers we must make connections for the reader, fixing meaning with word choice, word order, and punctuation. Frequently the incomplete sentence leaves the reader baffled. But not always. We use the incomplete sentence with many common phrases like *No comment, Not at all, Of course,* and *But not always.*

Students writers usually make sentence fragments accidentally, without noticing that their sentence lacks a main verb. Such fragments creep up on us even when we think we are paying attention.

> Among my favorite foods, English muffins, hot from the oven, dripping butter and honey.

> When I climb onto my moped and drive out of town, away from the
> noisy dormitories and the silent library, onto the dusty back roads.
> Which she often does, although I don't approve.
> While I was growing up.

These sentence fragments hang in air. They give information that goes nowhere, that holds something back from the reader. They leave unanswered questions: *why, where, what?* Each can become a whole sentence when we supply what was missing.

> Among my favorite foods *are* English muffins, hot from the oven,
> dripping butter and honey.
> When I climb onto my moped, *I* drive out of town, away from the
> noisy dormitories and the silent library, onto the dusty back roads.
> *She drove home last night,* which she often does, although I don't approve.
> *I fell down and skinned my knees all the time* while I was growing up.

The first rule is clarity.

Students who have difficulty identifying fragments, and who write them unknowingly, should look carefully at the review of sentence fragments, pages 284–286, and do the exercises there.

Another common problem with incomplete sentences is that they tend to avoid committing themselves. If we take notes on a history lecture, using fragments rather than sentences, we may look at them a month later and read something like *Too many wars. Bad economy.* Unless we remember the context, these phrases may leave us puzzled. They could imply that the number of wars, at some time in history, destroyed a nation's economy. Or they could imply that bad economy created the wars. Or both. With neither a verb nor the expected order of subject and object to complete the action, the meaning is left vague. Of course it is ambiguity—uncertain meaning—that appeals to the part of our mind that likes to absolve itself from responsibility.

> The recession put everybody out of work in Flint. All those rich peo-
> ple in Cadillacs driving past the homes of the unemployed.

Here the sentence fragment avoids the responsibility of explicit connections and leaves the meaning unclear; an incomplete sentence leaves the thought illogical. Are the rich people responsible for the unemployment? Should the rich people take detours to avoid the workers' parts of town?

We must remember, at the same time, that writers *can* use the sentence fragment *when they know what they are doing.* If the prose is informal enough, the sentence fragment allows yet another possible variation in rhythm and structure. It isolates a fragment in time because the period creates a pause longer than the pause inserted by a comma or a semicolon.

> We were going to be consumed by fire once more, and once more
> the world would let it happen. As usual. What was true yesterday will
> be true tomorrow.

Elie Wiesel, *A Beggar in Jerusalem*

We must be careful to use incomplete sentences only in an informal con-text or deliberately, like Elie Wiesel, to establish pause and emphasis. A care-less writer may make clauses into sentences (with periods and capital let-ters) without purpose and with choppy results.

> He was a writer. Which is a difficult profession.
> She looked tall. Although she was really only 5 feet 3 inches.

Avoid incoherent sentences like these. These sentences need to become complex, with commas replacing periods.

> He was a writer, which is a difficult profession.
> She looked tall, although she was really only 5 feet 3 inches.

EXERCISES

1. In these sentences, identify subjects, predicates, objects, indirect objects, and objects of prepositions:

- **a.** The Empire State Building is no longer the tallest building in New York.
- **b.** When we sent three rock stars into space, we opened the way for new imagery in pop lyrics.
- **c.** Which of the fifty states spends least on education?

2. In these sentences, identify phrases as prepositional, verbal, in-finitive, gerundive, or participal:

- **a.** Remembering the tradition of the Old South, Rhett was unable to dishonor his name.
- **b.** The senator from Arkansas tried voting the way he felt.
- **c.** In the morning, the sun will be drying the dew off the grass.

3. Combine each of these groups of simple sentences into one compound or complex sentence. In the resulting long sentences, discern any differences in meaning from the originals. Try both compound and complex; is one more effective than the other? Why?

- **a.** The hurricane struck the island at four yesterday afternoon. Mr. Potts couldn't find his Lear jet.
- **b.** Henry ironed his shirts. He ironed pillowcases. He ironed his thumb and a small corner of the wall above the ironing board.
- **c.** The ram was named Chauncy. He butted Mrs. Grace. She carried a bag of groceries. The freezer is now full of mutton.
- **d.** A boa constrictor slowly emerged from the piano. It played a Bach concerto. It went to sleep on the keyboard.

e. Their mother bought Crunchy Bits every Saturday. She went shopping. Crunchy Bits is the only cereal with an inflatable bowl in every box.

4. Identify each sentence as simple, compound, complex, compound-complex, or incomplete. Rewrite each sentence into one of the other types. Decide whether each revision is more or less effective than the original.

> **a.** Because Margaret had brought the elephant into the house, Sandy had to take her sculptures down to the basement.
> **b.** This sentence, for example.
> **c.** Rocking back and forth on her heels, the professor lectured.
> **d.** The man in the Foster Grants strolled down the crowded street, a beret on his head, a cane in his hand.
> **e.** Always cheerful, Mr. Sputter the mailman smiled, although a German shepherd hung by its teeth from his sleeve.
> **f.** Without hesitation, thinking only of the box of jewelry, Branny dashed through the rising flames.
> **g.** He grabbed the chicken feathers and threw them off the cliff, screaming and dancing all the while, although the rites were not yet due to begin and he, a crazed poet, was forbidden to take part.

5. Here are five contexts, each including an incomplete sentence. Which fragments succeed and which fail? Revise the failures into successes. Try revising (a) and (b) as an in-class exercise; compare results.

> **a.** Henry Moore was born in 1898, in a country not known for sculpture since the Middle Ages. Son of a coal miner, raised in Yorkshire, trained to be a teacher, when Moore learned that he could attend an art school on an ex-serviceman's grant.
> **b.** Nevertheless, advocates of strip mining persist in their rhetoric. We hear of "vast untapped natural resources." It makes strip mining sound like pouring a glass of beer. Instead of destroying the earth.
> **c.** When I came back from Canada, my friends were all tanned. Everybody. I looked like a pale dime in a pile of rich, copper pennies. And I felt like ten cents.
> **d.** They looked up and saw it. The second stage of the launch vehicle.
> **e.** Whenever the Congress decides to tangle with the president, and the people need tax relief or something of that order of magnitude, although the country needs immediate help, and the newspapers are all complaining, except that nothing ever gets done.

CLARITY, COHERENCE, UNITY

To be understandable, our sentences must hang together. *Clarity* and *coherence* are needed in writing at all levels—from words to sentences to paragraphs to essays to whole books. We start pursuing clarity when we choose the right word; when we bring that word together with a second word, we begin to pursue coherence. Phrases and clauses must cohere; they must show connectedness in the logic of the sentence and in the larger unity of sentence and paragraph.

We first discover clarity and coherence most obviously in the next-to-smallest unit, the sentence. We must make clear sentences before we can make clear paragraphs or clear essays. Unity, clarity, and coherence—we must define these goals before we enumerate ways to reach them.

One way of trying to define a quality—something as abstract as *unity*, as *clarity*, as *coherence*—is to look at its opposite. Here is an incoherent sentence.

> The attention brought to Campus Management's mismanagement of its rental property at 410 Observatory makes a convincing case for the need of a strong and active tenants' organization in Ann Arbor.
>
> Editorial, *Michigan Daily*

Nothing holds this sentence together; it lacks unity and sprawls disconnected across the page. When we try to rewrite it, we run into difficulty because before we revise, we need to know what the writer wants to say. What does he mean when he asserts that "attention" itself "makes a convincing case"? Perhaps he confuses two ideas. (In another chapter, we will look into logic and speak about clarity as it relates to methods of thought; see pages 233–234.) Maybe the meaning is something like this: "When we see how this property is mismanaged, we realize that we need a strong and active tenants' organization in Ann Arbor."

Here is another incoherent sentence.

> It seems to be delivering a message right up to the end, but to decipher it, one has to dig deep within his subconscious and then he may not be sure of the nature of the manner in which it has affected him.
>
> Film review, *Ann Arbor News*

It is hard to rewrite empty phrases like "the nature of the manner." Vague, shifty, and incoherent pronouns—*it, one, he*—cause confusion here. Maybe this sentence could become two sentences. If we put a period after "within his subconscious," we could make a sentence like "Even then, one may not be sure how the filmmakers have done their digging."

Or take a sample from a student paper.

> All these shortages are eventually going to put people in a position which forces them either to take some type of action that will level off the population somewhere, or people are slowly going to make life difficult for the whole human race.

Reading this, or the earlier examples, we long for the fresh air of sense. All of these examples have faults in punctuation and grammar—but with one common result: the sentences are unclear. The writers were unable to use language to make their thoughts clear to another person.

When we speak of unity, clarity, and coherence, and later when we speak of variety, we use different words as approaches toward the same goal. It would be difficult to find a clear sentence that was not also coherent and unified. Coherence makes unity, which is necessary to clarity. Varied sentences can help win the reader's attention; but we pursue our three qualities all at once, in the act of writing and thinking. In this book, we discuss grammatical errors and proper grammar mainly toward this end. When you read advice on not misplacing modifiers or on avoiding the comma fault or the sentence fragment, remember that the goal is not mere correctness but unity, clarity, and coherence—qualities we cultivate in order to make contact with other people.

Unity: Coordination and Subordination

The poet W. B. Yeats said that a finished poem made a noise like the click of the lid on a perfectly made box. Good prose makes that noise too, no less loudly and clearly than poetry. A good passage of prose resolves rhythm, emotion, and idea into a pleasing whole—a unity.

Our tools for achieving this unity are the types of the English sentence. A good simple sentence is direct and clear; but the simple sentence will not always embody a complete thought. Writers can choose among simple sentences, compound sentences, and complex sentences—and variations within each type and a combination of the latter two types. Beginning writers usually run to simple sentences and collections of simple sentences bound together, which become compound sentences. But often we want to express certain exact relations that require the complex sentence. Think of it as using the right tool for the job at hand. Usually, the beginning writer needs to practice the art of the complex sentence, the art of subordination.

Subordination, often using conjunctions, saves words and makes connections between ideas. *Coordination* happens when phrases work together like equals, like *co*workers.

I climbed the mountain and worshipped the sun.

When we use *subordination,* one clause leads the other; the subordinate clause hangs from the main clause, depends on it, is underneath—*sub,* as in *sub*marine—the main clause.

When I climbed the mountain, I worshipped the sun.

Here, *I worshipped the sun* is the main clause and *When I climbed the mountain* is a subordinate clause. The main clause could stand by itself. *I worshipped the sun* could be a perfectly fine, coherent, simple sentence. *When I climbed the mountain,* all by itself, is only a sentence fragment; it does not stand by itself; it hangs from, it depends on, it is subordinate to a main clause.

We could write:

Hamilton was tired of the game. He took out his doughnut cutter.

These sentences are correct, and they are understandable, but too many of them in a row would be boring, and they might not give us a complete idea. We could write:

Hamilton was tired of the game, and he took out his doughnut cutter.

This version is a compound sentence, two whole and simple clauses joined by *and*. This sentence differs from the earlier version by enforcing, with its grammar, the notion that the two statements are intimately connected. But with a conjunction and a complex sentence, we could make the connection more explicit.

When he tired of the game, Hamilton took out his doughnut cutter.
Because he tired of the game, Hamilton took out his doughnut cutter.

Syntax, like words, has insides. Think of syntax as the invisible system of logic—the blueprint—that makes the sentence make sense. Each arrangement of words into a sentence makes a gesture of meaning. The last two examples, with subordinate clauses beginning with *when* and *because,* make alternatives to the simple sentences or to the compound sentence. The subtle logic of the meaning is different in each case. We could also make alternatives to the sentence by using a participle.

Tired of the game, Hamilton took out his doughnut cutter.

In all the examples but the complex sentences, the closeness of the two notions implies a connection between them but does not state it. The explicit conjunction makes a statement. If we want to emphasize cause, we can use the conjunction *because.* If we want to emphasize the time element, we can use the conjunction *when.* The writer has to decide, with each sentence, how much to tell the reader, and with what precision.

Subordination: The Correct Conjunction

When we make complex sentences by using words that imply sequence, cause, or other forms of subordination, our sentences will be whole and solid only if the context supports the idea we have expressed. We achieve unity only if we are sensitive to the insides of syntax and use conjunctions responsibly. Beginning writers frequently violate this duty, however. If a writer omits something important, the conjunction may appear illogical; with all the information, the conjunction would have made sense. If we read,

The work was hard; however, John was an extraordinary worker.

the word *however* is illogical. The hardness of the work should not be set in opposition to John's ability. If we read,

> The work was hard; however, the pay was good.

however functions logically: pay is compensation for difficulty. The first sentence omits something like this:

> The work was so hard it was difficult to imagine anyone doing it; however, John was an extraordinary worker and therefore he could do it.

Here the positive assertion of the second half of the sentence (however . . . extraordinary) balances the negative suggestion of the first half (so *hard it was difficult to imagine anyone doing it*). The two parts of the sentence go together, and the conjunction earns its place.

Probably the most important function of conjunctions is to establish relationships and notions of cause and of time. And they save words. Always be careful, however, not to use them falsely, as transitions, when you do not intend such a relationship. The commentary supplied on football games yields an example. The announcer blends two sorts of information into one sentence, with brevity but without logic: "And of last year's graduating class two-thirds went on to graduate school while down on the field O'Leary makes three yards on an end-around."

Other forms of subordination—without using conjunctions—save words and strengthen sentences. Subordinate phrases and clauses, used as modifiers, give our prose density and variety.

In the *absolute construction,* we omit the connective and the verb, or sometimes a preposition, and modify directly and clearly. The absolute construction is in italics in this sentence:

> *Day done,* he raised his pitchfork to his shoulder.

Here we have cut from "When day was done" or a longer construction.

> *The desk ordered, pencils sharpened, paper blank,* he was ready for a day of combat with the English language.
> The fullback twisted and plunged, *his legs pistons, his head an iron wedge.*

Using an adjective with a prepositional or comparative phrase gives us a construction very much like the absolute.

> Spring air, *thick with odor of lilac,* moved through the gardens of Montgomery.

Similar in effect is the *appositive,* a construction that identifies the word preceding it.

> Joe, *the mailman,* said hello.

The appositive is more direct than the adjective with prepositional phrase and briefer than clausal versions. "Fred the horse thief walked in" is more concise than "Fred, who is the horse thief, walked in." In relative phrases not in apposition we should also omit words when the relationship is clear without them. Any unnecessary word, in writing, makes it more likely that the reader will become bored and inattentive. Say "The flowers she picked were lying on the newspaper," not "The flowers that she picked . . . ." This device is often useful in expository prose. "He had taken a position that was both unworthy and untenable" becomes more forceful when we say, "He had taken a position both unworthy and untenable."

The participle is also helpful. Participles are verb forms used as adjectives, *usually* ending in *-ing, -ed,* or *-en.*

Breathing heavily, he plopped down on the bench.

Breathing modifies *he.*

The *broken* umbrella was afraid of the rain.

Broken modifies *umbrella.*

Impressed by her credentials, Mr. Jefferson stroked his *unshaven* chin, muttering, "Yes, yes, just what we have in mind."

Impressed modifies *Mr. Jefferson,* and *unshaven* modifies *chin.*

To save words, we can frequently use participles in modifying phrases in place of whole subordinate or independent clauses. Of course in saving words we must be careful not to sacrifice meaning; using a participle, we must make clear what it modifies, which is usually the noun nearest it in the independent clause. Participles can be past or present:

Tiring of the game, Hamilton took out his doughnut cutter.
Tired of the game . . . .

Coordination: Punctuating Compounds

We have concentrated on forms of subordination only because subordination is more complicated than coordination and needs more practice to become habitual. But compound or coordinate sentences form an important part of our prose style. And often when we use coordinate clauses, we find ourselves confused about punctuation.

We use a comma, generally, when the two independent clauses in a compound sentence are long.

The man wore a green bandanna around his neck, but his wife wore a Brooks Brothers suit and a black silk tie.

Short compound sentences, however, need no commas. "He was fat and she was thin." The contradiction inside *but* often suggests a comma's pause, but it is a matter of ear, of judgment, rather than of rule. "He was thin, but he was tall" draws more attention to the speaker's insistence on two opposed ideas than does the same sentence without a comma—"He was thin but he was tall"—which seems more matter-of-fact, more conversational. Context, as always, determines choice.

Compound sentences are loosely held together; a semicolon can substitute for the connective *and*. The semicolon implies the close relationship between two clauses, which *and* also implies, but the semicolon makes a different rhythm by substituting a pause for a connective word. It is a useful variation, especially in more formal writing. Avoid tacking together random compounds, many clauses all in a row. Prose that repeats the same loose structure comes to feel too lax. We are all familiar with the speaker who cannot pause.

> I saw her and she was carrying a kitten and it had a crooked tail and I think it was part Siamese and . . . .

Some of the same boredom afflicts us when the writer multiplies compounds; the redundant rhythm puts the ear to sleep.

> I saw her and she was carrying a kitten. It had a crooked tail and it was part Siamese. The cat was making tiny squeaks and struggling in her arms. She smiled and then she let out a shriek. The cat had clawed her and jumped out of her arms and run away.

It is easy enough, without radical change, to introduce variety; we vary the type of sentence, using some subordination, and we vary the punctuation in the compound sentences.

> When I saw her she was carrying a kitten with a crooked tail. It was part Siamese. The cat struggled in her arms, making tiny squeaks. She smiled. Then she shrieked. The cat had dug its claws into her, jumped out of her arms, and run away.

The variety we choose can be more or less expressive. In this small anecdote the action in the last sentence may be best expressed by three brief clauses, which were there in the original version. However, the long compound has more effect when it follows the two short sentences—two periods make the rhythm choppy with pause—than it had when it followed other compounds. It is like coming from a dark theater into daylight; the light is brighter because we are used to darkness. The pause between "She smiled" and "Then she shrieked" gives us the surprise we want. In a small way, the grammar and the rhythm add to the feeling, or the expression, which is the meaning.

We use conjunctive adverbs—like *however, still, certainly*—to join independent clauses, not to join subordinate clauses or phrases. Clauses that follow these adverbs must be complete. Subordinating conjunctions—*although, when, because*—lead to subordinate clauses, and conjunctive adverbs—*moreover, also, finally*—and coordinating conjunctions—*and, but, or*—indicate the equality of independent clauses. When these independent clauses are made up of few words, we usually employ a semicolon before the adverb and a comma after it: "Universal Airlines gained two points yesterday; however, it had lost three the day before."

When we join two or more clauses in a compound, we use a connective word or a semicolon, except on rare occasions when we join brief clauses by commas. The classic example is Julius Caesar's "I came, I saw, I conquered," in which the commas make the pauses appropriately brief. Periods—"I came. I saw. I conquered."—make too much space between these clauses. Remember that if the clauses are long, a comma will not hold them together by itself. We need a comma *and* a connective or a semicolon. In

> The hair fell to the floor of the barbershop, the man with the broom was dozing in the corner.

the comma is misleading. The sentence could be made into two sentences. Or a semicolon, which is always a safe choice, could take the place of the comma. Or we could insert the word *and* or *but* after the comma.

The distinction between *long* and *short* in this advice is vague and must remain so. It is clear that with clauses as brief as

> John blushed, Sara wept, Linda shrieked, the whole class erupted at once.

the commas work. In the bad barbershop example, the comma does not work. When you come to clauses of middling size, you must decide. It could be the comma splice between brief sentences, acceptable in the most informal prose:

> I climbed the hill, Susan climbed with me.

or preferably the semicolon:

> I climbed the hill; Susan climbed with me.

or a subordinate phrase:

> I climbed the hill, Susan with me.

No easy rule will decide among these arrangements. Context and tone as well as audience and purpose should dictate the choice. The writer must become aware of the alternatives, then work to refine her sensitivity to the differences.

Students who make inadvertent comma splices should look at the review section, pages 286–288, which gives advice on how to avoid them and provides exercises.

The insides of syntax and punctuation show themselves in slight differences in meaning. The first version of *I climbed the hill* is rapid and idiomatic and informal. The semicolon in the second example increases the pause slightly and adds formality. A period would make the longest pause and create a choppiness, perhaps even an overly simple tone—that boring monosyllabic simplicity we remember from learning to read in the early grades. (All comments on the implication of these forms are generalities, not rules; a context could make the choppiness rhythmically satisfying.) The final example is closest to everyday speech. The first example, by omitting the connection, is a tighter unit.

We have been talking as if *and, but,* or *or* either takes a comma or does not, depending on how long the clauses are or on whether the sense will benefit from a pause. Sometimes when the clauses on each (or either) side are long, we may want to use the semicolon, even when we use a connective. This punctuation allows us to take a longer breath yet still indicates a close relationship by keeping the two clauses in the same sentence.

> The block was dilapidated, gray, the houses raw and the sidewalks sprouting grass; but he knew he was home.

This semicolon before the connective is more common with *yet* and *so.* We can write:

> The lion was sleeping in the corner of the cage, yet his feeder approached him warily.

But we are more likely to use the greater pause:

> The lion was sleeping in the corner of the cage; yet his feeder approached him warily.

When we use adverbs as connectives—words like *however, therefore,* and *consequently*—we always use a semicolon.

> The lion stirred awake in the corner of the cage; consequently, his feeder threw down the pail of food and ran away.

Notice that the adverb connective takes a semicolon in front of it and a comma after it. Or we can make the two clauses into separate sentences.

REVISING SENTENCES I

To make a point about variety and sentence structure, an instructor asked his students to write a single descriptive or narrative paragraph in the last few minutes of class. He then photocopied several of these to use in small discussion groups for the next meeting. The point, he explained, was to discuss the passage and to look for ways to improve the sentences. "My hunch was right," he said. "When you write quickly, most of you tend to write in choppy little bursts." Here is one paragraph he used:

> Exercise is a pain. Being in school makes it especially hard. I should jog, but I have trouble getting motivated. I noticed that two other girls in the dorm were runners. I saw them going out separately. Then I had an idea. I saw them both in the lunch line one day and asked them to sit with me. Then I explained my situation. I asked if either

or both would like to go jogging regularly. Both of them—Tina and
Janey—said they would. They didn't know each other, but now they
had met. The plan worked. Three mornings a week we all go out
jogging together. Then we get bagels at Hunneman's. Funny thing,
we're getting to be friends away from jogging.

The group, which included Michelle, the writer of the passage, spent
part of the class hour working individually, each person looking for ways to
improve the prose. Then they pulled into a small circle for discussion. The
teacher asked them to work cooperatively, using what they knew about
different possibilities of sentence construction, to make the most interesting
version they could.

Since the students had been working on the passage by themselves,
they all had ideas about how to improve it. "The problem," said Judd, "is
that the sentences just go *dah-dah-dah,* you know what I mean? I could
imagine a robot voice reading them out—no offense." Michelle laughed.
She assured everyone in the group that she had written the passage quickly
and did not mind hearing that it had problems.

"Here," interjected Sam, "listen: *Getting exercise is hard enough as it is,
but being in school makes it harder still.*" He looked hungry for approval.
When people nodded, Sam looked pleased. The group fell silent, waiting
for him to continue, but he shook his head. "Sorry, that's all I've got."

Hilda raised a hand tentatively. "OK, let's leave the next sentence
alone, then do a combination, like this: *But when I noticed two girls from my
dorm going out in running clothes—separately—I got an idea.*"

"I like that 'separately,'" said Michelle, "the way it stands out—separately. So, what if we did some more combining in the next part? *When I saw
them both in the lunch line one day, I asked them to sit with me.* Then maybe we
could add a question: *Would either or both of them like to jog with me regularly?*

"Yeah, yeah—" Judd was nodding. "I like it. Now keep those other
dashes: *Both of them—Tina and Janey—said they would.* Then: *They hadn't
known each other before, but now they met. My plan had worked.*"

"That's OK—" Shyla looked thoughtful. "But if you listen to those
sentences you can hear that you need a longer sentence to round things
out." She read the three previous sentences and paused.

Molly looked at her paper, then read out: "*Having become friends, we
run three times a week, ending up at a table at Hunneman's with bagels.*"

"I'm sorry," Hilda said, "but that doesn't get it. The idea that they've
become friends is the payoff. You should save it, don't you think?"

The group tried out various suggestions, until Sam hit on something
that everyone liked. At that point Michelle, who had the neatest handwriting, copied the consensus version out to give to the instructor.

Getting exercise is hard enough, but being in school makes it harder
still. I should jog, but I have trouble getting motivated. But then I noticed two girls from my dorm going out in running clothes—separately—and I got an idea. When I saw them both in the lunch line

one day, I asked them to sit with me. Would either or both of them like to jog with me regularly? Both of them—Tina and Janey—said they would. They hadn't known each other before, but now they met. My plan had worked. Three mornings a week we head out together, getting our exercise, and then we gather over bagels at Hunneman's, getting to be friends.

EXERCISES

1. Look at these sentences from student papers for clarity, coherence, and unity. Rewrite each of them. If you have to, make assumptions about the writers' intended meanings.

    a. It is hard for a graduate to hold down both a teaching position and work for their degree.
    b. He takes one student, Mike, who says he can trust anyone and also that he only has acquaintances and no friends since when is unclear.
    c. When a friend of mine, Robert Olds, who I had known for years converted to Christianity in high school and I began to resent him.

2. Make the following sentences more concise.

    a. When he had finished eating the birthday cake, he stretched out on the sofa.
    b. The magnetic pole, which is not the same as the North Pole, governs the compass.
    c. United States Customs destroys tons of food every year. These fruits and meats are illegally imported.
    d. A vacuum-cleaner salesman, who was nearly 7 feet tall and who smiled continuously, fell down the cellar stairs.

3. Revise each of these passages into one complex sentence. You will have to make your own assumptions about relations of cause and time. Do more than one version if you can see different meanings.

    a. It was raining. It was about seven o'clock the next morning. The Jeeps sloshed through the street outside the window. We couldn't sleep. We had breakfast. We all felt hungry. All there was was some beans and brown bread left over. We felt better. The sun came out about nine o'clock.
    b. She packed her suitcase. It sat open on the bed. She folded a red sweater. She put the sweater in the suitcase. Her mother stood near the window. She looked out at the stark trees. Her arms were crossed in front of her. Her face drooped. She was sad.

    c. Mark sits at his desk. His electric typewriter is blue. It is a portable. He received the typewriter on his last birthday. His birthday is in March. He types five words. He pauses. He drinks coffee. Suddenly he gets an idea.

4. Analyze two or three of these passages. Decide how each sentence is put together, and identify the variety of sentences in each paragraph. Is the writer using the best tool for the job? Praise or criticize.

a. Down the hall in Apartment 2 the reporter found a very "strong case." There were holes in both the floor and the ceiling, big enough for the biggest rats. Cockroaches crawled up the kitchen wall. A curtain divided off a section of the room for a bedroom, and out from it peeked an old woman. She smiled at the visitors and watched them with interest. Isabel Sánchez, the head of the house, was pointing out some more ratholes. A teen-age girl sat staring at a television set whose screen was filled with a constantly wavering, almost undistinguishable cowboy movie, spoken in Spanish. The reporter walked to the kitchen to watch the cockroaches, and observed that some dishes were sitting on the table that contained the remains of rice and beans.

Dan Wakefield, Island in the City

b. The greatest sea power in Europe and the greatest land power faced each other in war. The stake was the leadership of Europe. Each was fighting to strengthen her own position at the expense of the other: in the case of the sea power to hold her widely separated empire; in the case of the land power to challenge that empire and win one for herself. Both, as the war began, were uneasily conscious that an important and even decisive factor might be an Asiatic nation, enormous in extent of territory, which had a foothold in Europe and was believed by many to be interested in watching the two chief Western powers weaken and perhaps destroy each other until in the end she herself could easily dominate Europe.

Edith Hamilton, The Greek Way

c. Many women have given their lives to political organizations, laboring anonymously in the background while men of far less ability managed and mismanaged the public trust. These women hung back because they knew the men would not give them a chance. They knew their place and stayed in it. The amount of talent that has been lost to our country that way is appalling.

Shirley Chisholm, Unbought and Unbossed

d. There under a spotlight, two Oriental gentlemen in natty blue suits were doing some amazing things with yo-yos. Tiny, neat men, no bigger than children, they stared abstractedly off into space while yo-yos flew from their hands, zooming in every direction as if under their own power, leaping out from small fists in arcs, circles, and straight lines. I stared open-mouthed as a yo-yo was thrown down and *stayed down,* spinning at the end of its string a fraction of an inch above the floor.

Frank Conroy, *Stop-Time*

e. The American does not enjoy his possessions because sensory enjoyment was not his object, and he lives sparely and thinly among them, in the monastic discipline of Scarsdale or the barracks of Stuyvesant Town. Only among certain groups where franchise, socially speaking, has not been achieved, do pleasure and material splendor constitute a life-object and an occupation. Among the outcasts—Jews, Negroes, Catholics, and homosexuals—excluded from the communion of ascetics, the love of fabrics, gaudy show, and rich possessions still anachronistically flaunts itself. Once a norm has been reached, differing in the different classes, financial ambition itself seems to fade away. The self-made man finds, to his anger, his son uninterested in money; you have shirtsleeves to shirtsleeves in three generations. The great financial empires are a thing of the past. Recent immigrants—movie magnates and gangsters particularly—retain their acquisitiveness, but how long is it since anyone in the general public has murmured, wonderingly, "as rich as Rockefeller"?

Mary McCarthy, "America the Beautiful" *(On the Contrary)*

5. Take one of the passages above and rewrite it completely by using different kinds of sentences. Stay as close to the author's intent as possible. How do the new sentences change the meaning?

Grammatical Coherence

The good prose already quoted exemplifies unity in the structure and arrangement of sentences through agreement, consistency, and coherent conjunctions. But we need to consider further various grammatical areas of agreement and consistency essential to good writing. Disagreement and inconsistency can sabotage even the most interesting ideas and alienate the most attentive reader.

Misplaced Modifiers. Placing modifiers properly is essential to unity in content and construction. We must always be careful that a clause *does* modify the word that its position makes it appear to modify. As we have seen, the dangling participle, with its often comic effect, destroys unity.

Being six years old and rusted through, I was able to buy the car for a song.

Arranged in this way, the participial phrase *being six years old and rusted through* modifies *I;* it implies that *I* was six years old and rusted through. Here the best solution would be a subordinate stating clause.

> Because it was six years old and rusted through, I was able to buy the car for a song.

A similar mistake is the dangling appositive.

> A good teacher, his superior saw to it that he was promoted.

This order would imply that *his superior* was *a good teacher.* Solutions:

> He was a good teacher; his superior saw to it that he was promoted.
> Because he was a good teacher, his superior saw to it that he was promoted.

Yet another kind of misplaced modifier is the dangling participle, often introduced by a preposition.

> Tall and strong, the job was easy for him.
> On achieving the age of twenty-seven, his parents threw him out of the house.

The syntactic logic in the preceding sentence forces us to picture twenty-seven-year-old parents expelling a small child—probably not what the author intended.

> Hopefully, this book will be done by late July.

Hopefully is a dangling adverb that is common to everyday speech, but that disfigures formal prose. Does the book really hope? The simplest rewriting would be

> I hope this book will be done by late July.

In all such misreferences, ambiguity is a possible problem; the reader may not be able to tell what we really *did* mean. We lose clarity, we lose coherence. Even if our *intended* meaning is apparent, however, misapplied language is a flaw that cannot be excused as informality. The reader is dismayed by the frayed edge left by incorrect order. We write with correct grammar in order to reach our audience—and grammar (like everything else having to do with language) is a social act.

For the unity of a sentence, nothing is more important than the precise placement of all modifiers. The dangling construction is a common error; we all fall into it from time to time. We also make mistakes—sometimes amusing ones—merely by misplacing modifiers. For instance, this sentence appeared in the classified ads of a newspaper.

> For sale: Piano by owner with large curved legs.

In an earlier edition of this book, I (D. H.) perpetrated this sentence:

Look at the examples elsewhere in this book of carelessly constructed sentences . . . .

Students who dangle modifiers, or have other problems with agreement (see what follows) should look at Chapter 9, especially pages 289–297. There is some help on punctuation on pages 299–312.

Errors in Agreement.   These errors are common when we use indefinite pronouns. *One* and *none* and distributives like *each, every, everybody, nobody,* and *everyone* all take singular verbs. Here are typical errors.

Everyone says they had a good weekend.
Everybody had their tennis racket with them.

Common speech accepts most of these errors in agreement; but formal writing rejects them. We should write:

Everyone says he had a good weekend.
Everybody had his tennis racket with him.

We should write *he* and *his* to be correct in grammar. Grammar in this standard use of *he* and *his* may, however, conceal sexism. No one has yet found a satisfying alternative that does not seem at times confusing or awkward. We can use *she* or *her* when context and audience allow; we can use the bulky *he and/or she* and *him and/or her,* but the reader quickly grows impatient. We can rephrase the sentence to omit pronouns; we can use the plural.

Everyone should remember to take her personal belongings from the bus.
Everyone should remember to take his or her personal belongings from the bus.
Take all personal belongings from the bus.
People should remember to take their personal belongings from the bus.

Frequently our writing becomes awkward, not because we use a singular pronoun together with a plural one, but because we use singular nouns with plural pronouns or other mixtures of singular and plural.

Although a person may not be hungry, a piece of pastry can stimulate their appetite.

Maybe *his appetite,* maybe *her appetite,* but not *their appetite.* We could say *their appetite,* correctly, if we used a plural in the first part of the sentence:

Although people may not be hungry, a piece of pastry can stimulate their appetites.

Vagueness of Pronoun Reference.   This error is more insidious than disagreement because it is harder to detect in a draft. We misuse *this* and *that* by using them without having a clear connection to an earlier reference. Thus, we destroy unity, clarity, and coherence. We say:

> When I went home at Christmas, the tree wasn't up yet and my dog was sick, my mother had to have an operation, and my father was worried about money. This bothered me.

What bothered you? *This* properly refers to one thing, and the reader is forced to choose at random among the items listed. The author might have talked about *These things,* for instance. Or we say:

> When the Panama Canal opened for shipping, the elapsed time for sending merchandise coast to coast in the United States diminished by 80 percent, and the cost accordingly. That pleased manufacturers especially.

Was *that* the time? The cost? Both? The last sentence, lacking clarity, fades into vagueness and disconnection.

Often we misuse reference by confusing parts of speech and ignoring antecedents.

> My father is a doctor and that is the profession I want to enter.
> Because we put wire fencing around the chicken yard, they cannot escape.

Each of these sentences is understandable, but each is sloppy and improperly connected. *That is the profession* fails to connect: a *doctor* is a person; *medicine* is a profession. In the second example, chickens are not mentioned; *they* can refer to chickens only by association with the phrase *chicken yard.* We reach an audience with these sentences in the sense that people can understand what we are getting at, but there is a price to pay. Part of any reader's response will be annoyance at our sloppiness. This annoyance is an impediment to connection; it gives us a social problem.

The sentences could be revised as follows.

> Because my father is a doctor, I want to enter the profession of medicine.
> Because my father is a doctor, I want to be a doctor.
> Because we put wire fencing around the chicken yard, the chickens cannot escape.
> Because we put wire fencing around their yard, the chickens cannot escape.

Consistency of Tenses.   The tense, or time, is the form by which a verb signals past, present, or future. We should stick to one verb tense in describing one action. An account of something that happened to us usually sounds best in the past tense but occasionally fits the present. Summarizing a book, we use either tense, often the present. But choosing past or present (a decision determined by context) matters less than sticking to the tense we start with. In careless writing, we drift back and forth without noticing it.

> The maple turned red in September, a bright range of reds from near-gold to near-Chinese. The sky is blue, and the maples show fiercely against it, making the colors more deep. In October the first frost came, and . . .

The second sentence should take the past tense to agree with its neighbors. On rare occasions, and usually at a paragraph break, we can change tenses. A leisurely description moves into sudden action, and a break from past to present is a good way to signal this change. Be careful if you try this device; and know that you are doing it.

Consistency of Point of View. Shifts in tense violate unity, and so too do other sudden shifts. Pronoun disagreement, already discussed, makes a shift in number. We must not shift the person of the sentence, unless there is compelling reason to. We might carelessly write:

> First you put on your skis, one at a time for most people, and then we take a quick look at the slopes.

The *you* and the *we* are inconsistent. Either pronoun will do.

Equally, we do not move from active to passive in the same sentence, unless there is a compelling reason. We need not say:

> We looked forward to the party and it was greatly enjoyed.

The reader is whirled through time and grows dizzy. Instead, say:

> We looked forward to the party and enjoyed it.

Do not shift from one mood of the verb to another—for instance, from an imperative command to an indicative statement of fact. Do not say:

> Keep your eye on the teacher and you should take full notes.

The sentence gains unity if it is one or the other.

> Keep your eye on the teacher and take full notes.
> You should keep your eye on the teacher and you should take full notes.

When it is half each, it is a minor monster, a mermaid with a human face and scaly fins.

All these instructions ask the writer, for the reader's sake, to keep his voice coming from the same place, in the same tone, with the same number and gender and mood. It is disconcerting—finally impossible to follow—when a voice comes from high and from low in the landscape, from past and from present in time, from singular and from plural in number. As ever, we write well to make connections. Inconsistency and incoherence curse the work of most beginning writers. Here is a paragraph from an essay in which the author lost clarity and coherence by neglecting grammatical unity. He (or she) had no single point of view. The inconsistencies in this passage occur from sentence to sentence in the paragraph, as well as within individual sentences.

The mountain from a distance is long and low, about 8 miles in fact, and when you climb it you find that it is covered with tiny bushes. The climbing itself went easily, and it was fun for everybody. I was there by 6 A.M., and all through our climb by three in the afternoon.

In revision, the writer found unity, clarity, and coherence:

From a distance the mountain shows itself long and low, 8 miles long and only 3,000 in elevation at its highest. As we drove close to it, and began our climb, we discovered that its sides were dense with small bushes. All of us enjoyed the easy climb, which took us from six in the morning until three in the afternoon, when we drove west again, into the setting sun, and back home.

EXERCISES

1. Rewrite the following sentences, removing errors and ambiguities.

    a. Stopping by the bookshop window, the display of thrillers looked exciting.
    b. Either Adam loved his first wife, or didn't know how to show it.
    c. Helen called to tell him that the book was wonderful, that the publishers were interested, and he should hurry up and write another.
    d. Having hit all the bars in town, my friends were still nowhere to be found.
    e. A genius while still in kindergarten, his father worried that he might have troubles with his relationships with his classmates.
    f. Intelligent, pretty, sympathetic, a good dancer, Jane was known to everyone in the dormitory.
    g. She danced to prove she didn't care, and implying she did.
    h. Without knowing which one was best, the chocolate-covered one looked mouth-watering.
    i. Thinking of him at every turn, she went from city to city.
    j. Either you come inside, or get a spanking.

2. Rewrite these sentences so that each is consistent and coherent.

    a. We all went to the concert and a huge brawl was seen there.
    b. Joshua reads all of the papers, studies the scores, and knew the players just from their numbers.
    c. Promising to give her what she wanted, they were married soon after.

d. When old, jogging won't seem so easy for me.

e. The woman with the pierced nose offers to buy dinner for everyone, and with us agreeing, left.

f. Nowadays every person does their own cooking.

g. Ralph's pair of running shoes were left on the radiator, stinking.

h. On entering when the gates are closed, the dogs must remain inside.

[The following examples have been cited in *Verbatim,* a magazine about language.]

i. The women included their husbands and children in their potluck suppers.

j. Even more astonishing was our saving the lives of little babies who formerly died from sheer ignorance.

k. I can't blame you for wanting to go outside and sit on your ten-minute break.

l. In some countries a person cannot slaughter any animal unless rendered unconscious first.

Structural Unity

Many attributes that give stylistic finish and polish come from the organization of the sentence, rather than from the words the writer uses. Ranging from the definable *parallelism* to the more intangible *rhythm,* these structural attributes are harder to define than grammatical unity. Though their absence does not *prevent* connection with the reader, their skillful use brings pleasure—and pleasure is the very stuff of connection.

Parallelism. Parallelism is essential in formal prose; sometimes we use it in informal prose as well. Parallel constructions are phrases or clauses within the sentence that repeat the same word forms (nouns, verbs, adjectives, and the like) in the same order to perform the same function.

He quit the job because the boss was cruel, the pay was meager, and the work was dangerous.

the boss was cruel/the pay was meager/the work was dangerous

After the conjunction *because,* each subordinate clause follows the pattern of article/noun/past tense verb/predicate adjective. Parallelism is not a grammatical necessity, like agreement. But it helps us to manage sentences and to *clarify* our intent.

We use parallelism most obviously when we introduce the parallels with pairs of words: *both/and, either/or, neither/nor, not/but, not only/but also, first/second.* The sentence beginning with one member of these pairs should pivot on the other; and the parallel clauses should use the same form. Do not write:

Not only did he run into the fire, but also carrying a can of gasoline.

This nonparallel construction is comprehensible but ugly. What's more, it feels stylistically uncontrolled. These clauses are not parallel because the second uses a participle instead of an active verb, like the first clause. We could rewrite it:

Not only did he run into the fire, but also he carried a can of gasoline.

If we are stringing many clauses together, any departure from the parallelism destroys unity.

His reasons amounted to these: first, the overwhelming size of the debt; second, that the company was ill managed; third, having so little leisure in such a job.

The sentence can be rewritten in numerous ways; for instance,

His reasons were first, that the debt had grown huge; second, that the firm was ill managed; third, that the job afforded little leisure.

The parallelism would remain the same—and we would still want parallelism—if we dropped the enumerations.

His reasons were that the debt had grown huge, that the firm was ill managed, and that the job afforded little leisure.

The briefest way to write the sentence would be to make parallels in the predicate subordinate to one *that,* by using the verb *to be* once and then implying it elsewhere.

His reasons were that the debt was big, the firm ill managed, and the job time consuming.

Context is also important. The writer would naturally wish to sound more relaxed and talkative writing a letter to a friend, more concise composing an official memorandum. The more concise the sentence becomes, the more formal the prose.

With *either/or, not only/but also,* and similar correlative expressions, be sure to place the words to correlate the same parts of speech in each clause. We frequently misplace our *eithers* and *onlys.* Too often we say:

Either she ironed all morning, or she watched television.

Because the verbs are being related, the sentence should read:

She either ironed all morning or watched television.

Here are other ambiguous uses followed by clear ones.

Either the professor was asleep or drunk. *The professor was either asleep or drunk.*

They not only ran to the grocer, but also to the florist. *They ran not only to the grocer but also to the florist.*

In making a list, either use an article or a preposition once, at the beginning of the list, or use it throughout. Either

> The soup, spaghetti, lamb, and salad . . .

or

> The soup, the spaghetti, the lamb, and the salad . . .

but not a mixture:

> The soup, spaghetti, the lamb, and salad . . . .

At any rate, do not attempt such mixtures in formal prose. For rhythm and emphasis, in informal prose or in a poem, you might depart from parallelism and profit by the departure. The rule of thumb remains—know what you are doing and why you are doing it.

When one or more prepositional phrases contain several words, parallelism always repeats the preposition. Say:

> Through wind, through sleet that stung his cheeks, and through snow . . . .

Do not say:

> Through wind, sleet that stung his cheeks, and snow . . . .

When you use long clauses, introduced by parallel conjunctions, repeat the conjunction. With long clauses, we need the repetition for clarity.

> Although the sun had gone down more than twenty minutes ago, and although shadows thickened in the field, he kept on ploughing.

When we use short clauses, we need only the first conjunction.

> Although day was done and night approaching, he kept on ploughing.

Also, use parallel parts of speech. Verbs go with verbs in a parallel, nouns with nouns, and adjectives with adjectives. We often violate this rule in making lists:

> From a distance, he looked tall, gray, well dressed, and a foreigner.

Instead of *a foreigner,* which is a noun, the sentence should fulfill its unity with the adjective *foreign.* A common departure from parallelism pairs an infinitive and a participle.

> He talked to prove he was intelligent and showing off his cultural background.

This writing is stylistically inconsistent, jarring the ear like an untuned piano. We should say:

> He talked to prove he was intelligent and to show off his cultural background.

Two participles would be stylistically acceptable, but the infinitives make a more vigorous sentence.

Another frequent lapse in parallelism is to omit a *to* when infinitives follow one another. In formal prose, we preserve the *to* for all infinitives in a series even when simple verbs follow one another. We do not say:

To see, want, and buy is the essence of the American consumer.

We say:

To see, to want, and to buy is the essence of the American consumer.

The longer the clause, the more upsetting it is when we omit a *to.*

His desires were few: to live on the ocean, to spend at least a portion of each day sketching the seabirds, to sleep alone, and cook for himself only.

Unity departs when the *to* is omitted before *cook.* Yet in informal prose and speech, we occasionally do something that resembles our practice with articles and prepositions; the *to* remains with the first infinitive and is understood with the rest.

He wanted to move back, get a job, buy a convertible, and drive through town in style.

As with the rule on prepositions and articles, the word *to,* once omitted after the first use, may not slip back in again.

Constructions on two sides of coordinates should agree. If we find ourselves writing,

Either he was rotten or a badly misunderstood young man.

we should improve it by keeping the parts of speech parallel:

He was either rotten or badly misunderstood.

The same rule applies even when pairs like *either/or* are not used. Sometimes we make sentences like this one:

He hoped that she would come and she would wear the blue dress.

The first clause uses *that* and the second violates unity by omitting it. The sentence should read:

He hoped that she would come and that she would wear the blue dress.

The word *that* can safely be omitted when no parallel clause is used. *He hoped she would come* by itself is fine, but when "he hoped" more than one clause, we need parallel *thats.* In the single clause, follow your ear.

Emphasis. Because emphasis works to construct a sentence firmly, emphasis promotes unity. When we use emphasis well, we make a unity between sentence structure and meaning and between sentence structure and appropriate emotional tone. Repetition, order, and contrast are three means of achieving emphasis.

Parallelism is emphatic, and parallelism is a form of *repetition*. Where the politician's speech as a whole gathers speed by repeating a phrase—like "and what is your answer to *this,* Mr. President?"—the sentence gathers firmness by repeating parts and structures. The repetition creates dramatic heightening, like quickening drumbeats on a movie sound track.

> We must agree that *the present administration is* bankrupt, *that it has* no cash reserves of the spirit, *that its morale* is a total liability.

Careful development in the sentence can contribute emphasis. This is emphasis by *order.* For emphasis, we put the most important words in the sentence at the beginning or at the end—and they are often best at the end. (See Concluding the Sentence, pages 160–161.) These sentences emphasize beginnings:

> Slowly, as though the engine were harnessed to elderly coolies, we crept out of Granada.
>> Truman Capote, "A Ride through Spain"

> Tears, blinding tears, were running down her face.
>> Thomas Hardy, *Tess of the D'Urbervilles*

These sentences save emphasis for the end:

> I keep wondering if there is an afterlife, and if there is will they be able to break a twenty?
>> Woody Allen, "Selections from the Allen Notebooks"

> One day, perhaps, the earth will have turned into one vast featherbed, with man's body dozing on top of it and his mind underneath, like Desdemona smothered.
>> Aldous Huxley, "Comfort"

> His form had filled out, his wrinkles were gone, the dull eyes had regained their fire, and there, sitting by the fire, and grinning at my surprise, was none other than Sherlock Holmes.
>> Sir Arthur Conan Doyle, "The Man with the Twisted Lip"

When a sentence like Conan Doyle's is long and delays its most crucial or dramatic part for last, we call it a *periodic* sentence. We postpone the most important part of a sentence—often the simple predicate—by using clauses or phrases or parenthetical remarks, in order to build suspense and gain attention. Periodic sentences promise that something is coming, but hold it back, teasing us, so that the tension holds our interest and the resolution achieves greater power.

> That the spring was late this year, that the dogwood never bloomed, and that the flowers struggled wanly out of the garden, all of these

failures must have contributed to the moment when Frederick, suddenly and without warning, shot his wife.

When we have several details or ideas to present in a sentence, the emphatic order is the *crescendo*. If one of the details is a surprise—something that may seem out of place but really belongs there—it should come last. Otherwise the order is simply that of intensity.

> I would appreciate consideration for any opening on your staff, and believe that I could bring to your firm unusual combinations of energy and caution, originality and reliability, youth and experience.

> The President has tricked the workers, ignored the military, soaked the rich, and plundered the poor.

It is always the last word or phrase that rings in the reader's mind. Even if it is not the most important, it naturally comes to seem so.

Departures from an emphatic order destroy unity by appearing accidental. A periodic sentence feels constructed and planned, sturdier than a loose sentence, which trails off into "many other instances of this kind." An emphatic order makes us feel control, not randomness. It is one more device contributing to the click of the box.

Varying sentence types can also become emphatic (and thus variety can lend its power to unity) when we shift suddenly from one sort of sentence to another. This is *contrast*. Most commonly, we see a short sentence provide emphasis after several long sentences.

> We were told to avoid the kids who played at the far end of the park, for they had a reputation for making trouble. We were also warned more than once to watch out for the older girls who gathered near the high school. There was no end to the instructions and warnings we were given. We ignored all of them.

By contrasting sentence types, we build emphasis into the developing of the paragraph. We need to be sure, however, that we are highlighting the right point.

Balance. Balance and parallelism are related; both have to do with repetition. Both create emphasis. But parallel construction is a matter of maintaining equal grammatical structure, and balance has to do with getting the sentence parts, each with its own weight, into proportion. Balance is style; it is not grammar, nor can it be described grammatically. (Parallelism is style, too, but it can be described grammatically.) A balanced sentence is one in which the main parts of the sentence have approximately the same rhythm and importance. A balanced sentence need not have two parts in balance; it may have three or four or more. Balance is similarity and *sense;* parallelism is similarity and *structure.* A balanced sentence is not precisely parallel in detail, in its two or more parts, but its parts must be similar in structure. Here are examples of balance and parallelism, with the parts printed on separate lines.

Balance

In his day, Frank built model airplanes of balsa wood and went to
the movies on Saturday;

now, at the same age, Jim cruises around in his own car and flies to
New York for the weekend.

Freda said it was dangerous,
but Jill insisted on going.

Balance and Parallelism

The Grogs wanted only to share and be reconciled;
the Kogs wanted only to kill or be killed.

Parallelism Without Balance

People possess four things
that are no good at sea:
anchor, rudder, oars,
and the fear of going down.

Antonio Machado

The foxes have their holes and the birds have their nests;
but the Son of Man has no place to lay his head and to rest.

New Testament

The old pine-tree speaks divine wisdom;
the secret bird manifests eternal truth.

Zen proverb

Rhythm.　Rhythm and resolution, which we name together because
they seem related, are more difficult to define or exemplify than any other
words used in this book. By rhythm we mean sounds and pauses pleasingly
arranged, an emphatic arrangement we might want to tap our feet to. The
Hemingway passage quoted on page 14 succeeds by its rhythm. Here is another example of superb rhythm, quite different from Hemingway's, more
lush and energetic.

> Witches, werewolves, imps, demons and hobgoblins plummetted
> from the sky, some on brooms, others on hoops, still others on spi-
> ders. Osnath, the daughter of Machlath, her fiery hair loosened in the
> wind, her breasts bare and thighs exposed, leaped from chimney to
> chimney, and skated along the eaves. Namah, Hurmizah the daughter
> of Aff, and many other she-devils did all sorts of somersaults. Satan
> himself gave away the bride, while four evil spirits held the poles of
> the canopy, which had turned into writhing pythons. Four dogs es-
> corted the groom.

Isaac Bashevis Singer, "The Gentleman from Cracow"

We find pleasure in the rhythmic combination of words, just as we find pleasure in the rhythms of music or in repetition of line or color in painting. In this example there is a lively pace, an alternation of short and long word clusters that gives us a body sense of wild confusion—which is just what the passage is about. In general, rhythms satisfy our elementary need for order, like the cycling of seasons and tides. But if rhythmic pleasure is essential to the satisfaction of good style, we must remember that the rhythms of words cannot be separated from the meanings of words. Sound and sense go together.

When we are writing, our ears are perhaps our most delicate, and valuable, piece of equipment. We acquire a good ear by reading and rereading the great masters until their cadences become part of our minds. The stored memory of a hundred thousand sentences becomes the standard of the our own ear, just as all the sentences we have ever heard pattern all the sentences we will speak. Craftsmanship comes from studying the accomplishment of the past and then practicing to equal it. To become potters, beginners will learn about clay, about glazes, about wheels and kilns. But they will also look at pots, even feel them—early Greek vases, Native American coiled clay cooking pots, Babylonian wine jugs, bowls, and basins made by their teachers. They will discover the uses, the shapes, the colors, and the techniques that determine good pots. Then they will make their own. Developing sensitivity to good writing tunes the ears of apprentice writers until they learn to produce their own good writing.

Resolution. Resolution (sometimes also called closure) is the art of ending a thing so that the reader feels satisfied. Resolution partakes of sound, sense, feeling, and emphasis. The periodic sentence, holding back its emphasis until the end, is an obvious method of achieving resolution. Here is another periodic sentence.

> Without schooling, without friends, without money, without the accent that is necessary for success in Britain, he arrived in London.

This device of delayed delivery is so pointed that we cannot do it often and must usually rely on more subtle resolutions. No rules can govern resolution or rhythm because each click of the box is original. But reading and paying attention to examples can help us achieve mastery. The more we know the materials that make style, the more extensive our ability to improvise. Look at the passage by F. Scott Fitzgerald on page 176 and see the slow, rising beginning; the calm plateau at the center; and the slow, peaceful descent at the end. Then contrast it with the more formal and complicated prose of Isaiah Berlin on page 176. Each sentence is its own little dance, in which variety arrives at unity by way of improvisation; and each sentence relates to every other sentence as part relates to part, so that the paragraph is a round of dances that become one dance.

Concluding the Sentence. We have been speaking—in the sections on emphasis and on resolution—about ending the sentences well. No sentence can have resolution if it trails off in flatness or emptiness. Let us look at some common failures. In conversation and in unedited writing, we frequently start a sentence with high energy and then collapse when we try to conclude it: we have a subject, but we haven't the faintest notion for a predicate. We say,

> The high level of heroin consumption in this country

because we are worried. But we do not know exactly what to say about it, so we reach around for a predicate filler, to end our sentence:

> is a matter of the utmost importance.
> requires our immediate attention.

Sometimes a writer will string such sentences together—all strong subjects with weak predicates.

> The high level of heroin consumption in this country is of paramount concern to us all. The solution will require the utmost in international cooperation. Firm international controls are of the utmost necessity. The identity of heroin-producing nations is a matter of public knowledge. The destruction of crops at their source is one way of dealing with the problem.

Each sentence achieves the art of falling. These dancers trip on their skirts. The writer has a partial idea—like a sentence fragment—but makes it into pseudocomplete sentences with trite predicates. The mind that writes such sentences seems to be disorganized or lazy about organizing. The unresolved, trailing-off sentences communicate a vacuum. Yet, with a little attention, the writer could have talked plainly, with decent whole ideas and an accompanying fullness.

> The high level of heroin consumption in this country requires international controls to destroy the crops at their source in the heroin-producing countries.

We used only a third of the words in this version, and the sentence is unified.

There are no ready formulas for ending sentences, but there is at least one big *don't*. The filler predicate is certain to destroy any possibility of an ending that satisfies us by its rhythm and resolution. Avoid it.

REVISING SENTENCES II

One instructor, for a weekly assignment, asked students to hand in a theme on the subject of television watching. Reading the papers over, the instructor saw an opportunity to follow up recent class discussion of sentences. He asked one student if he could use a paragraph from her paper as an example.

At the next class meeting, the teacher wrote the following on the blackboard:

The remote-control button has had an untold impact on the way we watch television and on our minds. We push the button and the image on the screen changes: there is a car chase, a dog food commercial, a news special. The person watching starts to lose track of what he's seeing and its meaning. Everything will come to seem equal in some way. How can you go from a sit-com with a laugh track to a special on starving people in Africa? You can't, inside. Or you shouldn't be able to. But the more you change the screen, the more you have started to forget that there's a difference. And after a while the pictures of the starving person mean less.

The teacher asked his class to take a few minutes to reflect on the passage, both on the statement it was making and on the way that the statement was being made. He suggested to the students that they consider some of the fine points of grammar—agreement, consistency of tense, and point of view—as well as structural matters like parallelism, balance, and resolution. Heads turned to the blackboard as class members started to read.

Twenty minutes later, the instructor saw so many hands waving that he set up a procedure. "First," he said, "let's look at grammar and construction; then we can worry about elegance." A number of students kept their hands up, and soon they were pointing out certain basic inconsistencies. "The pronouns are flipping as fast as the channels," said someone. "It's true," the writer said. "We, he, you. . . . Maybe I should avoid the tube myself." The teacher asked the group which pronoun would be most effective. There was a long pause. Then one girl suggested using *you.* "That would make it more direct," she said, "the author talking right to the reader." Another student immediately objected: *you* would make the piece sound condescending, like a lecture. "She should include herself; she should say *we.*"

The teacher turned around and studied the board. "It's a hard one to call," he admitted, finally. "But I think I lean toward the plural *we.* It's more inclusive, and it also combines—better than *you*—with a more neutral subject like 'the watcher' or 'the viewer'; it would be hard to use *we* or *you* in every sentence." He then asked for other observations.

"Tense agreement," said a girl in the front. She pointed out the switch to *will* in the fourth sentence and the use of the past tense *have started* in the eighth. "Both should stay in the present."

The teacher then brought up the matter of sentence structure. After a lull, several students raised their hands. One student thought that the first sentence needed work, that the prepositional phrase *on our minds* sounded weak. He looked down and read from a note on his paper: *a tremendous impact not only on the way we watch TV but also on our minds.* He said that he wanted to add another sentence to emphasize the connection, to make it clear that watching television can alter the way we think about things. "Something like: *We don't often realize the extent to which our contact with the medium can influence us.*" The teacher signaled a pause while he wrote the sentence on the board. "Good idea," he said. "What else?"

This time a student from the back spoke up. He said that he saw a place to use parallelism. The second sentence could make a stronger assertion. He read out his version: *When we push the button, the image on the screen changes: there is a car chase, there is a news special on starving people, there is a happy soft-drink commercial.* Asked why he made the changes he did, the student explained. First, he said, by repeating *there* the writer could isolate and emphasize the changes on the screen. He had made the new order and put in new examples to highlight the absurdity. "Going from images of starving people to images of Fizzy-pop makes more of a statement; it gets the idea across more powerfully." He indicated that he would change the order later, too, in the sentence about the sit-com.

The teacher glanced at the clock on the wall. "I want to point out a nice example of a parallel construction in 'The more you change the screen, the more you start to forget that there's a difference.' Let's make that *there is,* which is stronger. Now I'm going to take the last five minutes to write out a version that uses your suggestions."

> The remote-control button has had a tremendous impact not only on the way we watch television but also on our minds. We don't often realize the extent to which our contact with the medium can influence us. When we push the button, the image on the screen changes: there is a car chase, there is a news special on starving people, there is a happy soft-drink commercial. The viewer starts to lose track of what he's seeing; he mixes up the levels of significance. Everything comes to seem equal in some way. How can a person jump from a special on starvation in the Sudan to a sit-com with a laugh track? He can't, deep down. Or he *shouldn't* be able to. But the more we change the screen, the more we begin to forget that there is a difference. And after a while the image of the starving person just might come to mean less.

EXERCISES

1. Decide whether each of these sentences shows parallelism, balance, both, or neither.

> a. Inspiration is the beginning of a poem and it is also its final goal.
>
> Stephen Spender, *The Making of a Poem*
>
> b. I saw a new heaven and a new earth, for the old heaven and the old earth had passed away.
>
> Revelations
>
> c. The superior man understands what is right; the inferior man understands what will sell.
>
> Confucius

d. There are two ways of avoiding fear: one is by persuading
ourselves that we are immune from disaster, and the other is by
the practice of sheer courage.

Bertrand Russell, *Unpopular Essays*

e. The camera can be lenient; it is also expert at being cruel.

Susan Sontag, *On Photography*

f. Wherever new lines of communication have opened up,
wherever ideas new to a people have taken hold of their imagination, people have been able to change.

Margaret Mead, *Aspects of the Present*

g. A man may take to drink because he feels himself to be a failure, and then fail all the more completely because he drinks.

George Orwell, "Politics and the English Language"

2. Choose five of the sentences in Exercise 1 and, using them as
models, write five sentences of your own. For example, taking sentence (a)
as a model: "Understanding is the first step in education, and it is also its
desired result."

3. Rewrite these sentences from student essays, using parallelism
and balance to improve them.

a. Mary Pickford was America's sweetheart in her early films
and wore long blonde curls and little girl dresses and a
sweet, innocent smile and she was thirty-five years old.

b. The development of nuclear power promises an undreamed
of future, and we must be aware of the potential hazards of
nuclear waste.

c. Some estimates of adult illiteracy in the United States put it
at twenty million, but twenty-five million is the figure favored by others.

d. Television commercials urge children to consume sugar ce-
reals, candy, and sweet drinks and the principles of good nutrition are ignored.

e. My little sister stopped being cute at twelve; she borrows
my clothes; she whines at my mother; my father buys her
anything she wants.

4. Rewrite these sentences to improve emphasis. For instance, the
first sentence might read: "Worst for me among all childhood diseases was
measles." Compare your versions with those of your classmates. Discuss
how different constructions allow for different shades of meaning.

a. I had all the usual childhood diseases, but measles I remember as the worst.

    b. Because of the availability of handguns, violent crime in the United States is increasing.

    c. I needed glasses and couldn't even see what was written on the blackboard or read the posters behind the lectern.

    d. They served exotic fruits for dessert, pomegranates, persimmons, pineapples, and mangoes, and I didn't know how to eat them.

5. Revise the following passage so that it has a more satisfying rhythm; for example, the first sentences might become:

> The old man lived in the gloomiest part of the forest in a house made of crude bricks.
>
> The old man lived in a house made of crude bricks in the gloomiest part of the forest.
>
> In the gloomiest part of the forest, in a house made of crude bricks, lived the old man.

The old man lived in the gloomiest part of the forest. He had a house there. It was made of crude bricks. All kinds of trees grew around the house. There were oaks, fir trees, and kinds that had no name. They shut out the sun. Only scattered patches and changing shapes of sunlight showed on the ground. The old man didn't mind. He had lived in the city for many long years. He had grown to hate the neurotic scurrying about. And the hypocritic smiles and cement-block faces.

6. Revise these sentences so that they are resolved more concretely.

    a. The Boer War was a conflict which was a matter of the utmost importance.

    b. *Moby-Dick,* a masterpiece of the nineteenth century, is a great piece of writing.

    c. The dark-haired girl that he had only glimpsed before was very attractive.

    d. If David and Susan don't manage to compromise somewhat, they'll have trouble.

    e. The dog was strangely reserved, almost sinister; Dan didn't like it much.

7. Look through a local newspaper—especially the op-ed page—and find three examples of periodic sentences. What effect does the writer hope to make by holding back?

Unity of Tone

Earlier, we called some words *fancy,* and we alluded to formal and informal styles. Now, in a chapter on the sentence, we will consider the levels of diction, the tones of voice our prose can aim for. By choice of words and syntax, our writing can vary in tone as much as we vary our voices in speech by loudness and pitch. (Think of how "hello" can be said: neutral, questioning, sarcastic, loving, exclamatory—all by the tone with which we pronounce two syllables.) Among other tones, we can in our prose sound calm, precise, strident, humorous, angry, intimate, distant, or reasonable. We think of tone now, as we consider unity in sentences, because consistency of tone is another means of holding our writing together, another means to unity. Tone is the way we fix on our audience, or the way our audience understands and responds to the feelings with which we write.

In the chapter on words, we mentioned formality and informality, fanciness and colloquialism, which pertain to the tone of diction. In this chapter, we mean the tone of syntax and the tone of sentence structure.

Formality and Informality. Choosing a tone requires *tact*. You do not use the same vocabulary, sentence structure, or organization of thought on contrasting occasions. Audience determines tone; tone is the writer's choice of a connection with the reader. The doctor delivering a paper to his colleagues writes a formal and scientifically exact prose; the same person, contributing to an alumni newsletter, writes a relaxed and conversational prose. If one style wandered for a moment into the opposite, we would have disunity.

> The amino acids were observed to disappear from the patient's urine, which was a helluva note.
>
> "Pa" Barker writes that he and his child bride have settled into suburbia where they are expecting obstetric surgery.

The alumni note could be an attempt at humor, much of which depends on disunity.

Of course *formal* and *informal* are relative, and many points fall between the extremes. We must think about three things; first, what distinguishes formal from informal; second, the occasions requiring or suggesting different tones; third, how much unity of tone is appropriate to an essay or a story and how much variety it will tolerate, accept, or enjoy.

We can start with formal and informal prose writings as touchstones or concrete reference points for our abstractions. For formal prose, look at this passage from Ecclesiastes (9:11) in the King James translation of the Bible, which always combines vigor and formality.

> I returned and saw under the sun, that the race is not to the swift, nor the battle to the strong, neither yet bread to the wise, nor yet riches to men of understanding, nor yet favour to men of skill, but time and chance happeneth to them all.

Now look at this passage from a contemporary literary essay, in which the writer has used repetition, parallelism, and appropriate diction to convey controlled feeling and conviction:

The greatest American industry—why has no one ever said so?—is the industry of using words. We pay tens of millions of people to spend their lives lying to us, or telling us the truth, or supplying us with a nourishing medicinal compound of the two. All of us are living in the middle of a dark wood—a bright Technicolored forest—of words, words, words. It is a forest in which the wind is never still: there isn't a tree in the forest that is not, for every moment of its life and our lives, persuading or ordering or seducing or overawing us into buying this, believing that, voting for the other.

Randall Jarrell, Kipling, Auden & Co.

For informal prose, here is a passage from James Thurber's *The Years with Ross.*

Ross began as a dice shooter in the AEF, and ended up with a gambling compulsion. Nobody knows how many thousands of dollars he lost in his time at poker, backgammon, and gin rummy, but it ran way up into five figures. He finally gave up sky's-the-limit poker, but would often play all night in Reno or Colorado, on his trips West, in games where the stakes were only a dollar or so. He must have won at poker sometimes, but I don't think he ever really got the hang of the game; certainly he didn't bring to it the intuitive sense he brought to proofs and manuscripts. He once told me about what he called the two goddamdest poker hands he had ever seen laid down on a table. "One guy held a royal flush, and the other had four aces," he said. When I asked, "Who got shot?" he looked puzzled for a moment and then said, "All right, all right, then it was a straight flush, king high, but I've been telling it the other way for ten years." His greatest gambling loss occurred in New York, in 1926, when he plunged into a poker game with a tableful of wealthy men. He got off to a lucky start, and was two thousand dollars ahead and going to drop out when one of the players said, "Winners quitters, eh?" Ross, who was drinking in those days, stayed in the game, kept on drinking, and lost thirty thousand dollars.

In diction, formal prose avoids the slangy, the colloquial, or the eccentric. A writer attempting a formal style sometimes falls into temporary informality because he cannot think of the appropriate word, because his vocabulary is inadequate, or because he is too lazy to look for the word. Writing a research paper on exports from a small nation, we want to imply that the minister of the treasury lacked financial integrity; but "lacked financial integrity" is a pompous formula. What do we say of him? If we call him "a crook," we will intrude an alien vocabulary into this paper. The slang is like tactlessness. The best solution is to say something particular and avoid the generality. Perhaps we can say that he was convicted of taking bribes.

In a more informal context, *crook* might be just the right word, bringing in a slangy touch of roughness. Tact is all. And it is like social tact, which is often called hypocrisy. When you see an old friend for the first time in six months, you may call him all sorts of names that you would not use in front of your priest. When you are introduced to the Romanian ambassador between the acts of the ballet, you do not use the same gruff slang you would use with your old friend; you are more apt to say something original, like "How do you do, Mr. Ceascu?" If you called him "you old son of a bitch" (which is no more original, of course), you would have a social problem. Writing a résumé or a letter applying for a job, if we turn slangy or idiosyncratic—writing *thru* for *through;* saying *guy* or *gal*—we make a noise like someone who does not know how to act, perhaps someone difficult to put up with in the office. Awareness of audience indicates the writer's sensitivity to the world outside the self: to other people.

Formality Gone Bad.   We can help to define our terms by looking at what they are not. The virtue of informality can slide into the vice of slackness, excess, or vagueness. The virtue of formality can wiggle in a hundred directions into the vices of pomposity, fanciness, pretense, jargon, and meaningless abstraction. George Orwell turned a good formality into a horrid one by rewriting the passage from Ecclesiastes that we quoted earlier. His modern version is the High Abstraction of academic sociology. Orwell takes

> I returned and saw under the sun, that the race is not to the swift, nor the battle to the strong, neither yet bread to the wise, nor yet riches to men of understanding, nor yet favour to men of skill; but time and chance happeneth to them all.

and turns it into

> Objective consideration of contemporary phenomena compels the conclusion that success or failure in competitive activities exhibits no tendency to be commensurate with innate capacity, but that a considerable element of the unpredictable must invariably be taken into account.

Orwell's parody, which would pass for good prose with many people, sounds untouched by human hands, like a monstrous frozen dinner fabricated from sawdust and boiled crayons. The Orwell parody cannot be called formal. Because of its imprecision, it could be called sloppy, but not informal; imprecision is a quality in most bad prose, whether it is formal or informal in its intent. This parody ridicules a stiff prose style that *passes for* formality among many writers.

Pompous Language.   We use pompous language to paint over a reality we wish to avoid seeing. In Chapter 4, we mentioned euphemisms; sometimes, whole sentences are euphemistic. The airline has the flight attendant say, "Would you care to purchase a cocktail?" instead of "Do you want to buy a drink?" because the second sentence sounds crass, plain, and blunt. For the same reasons, *beverage* is often substituted for *drink*. These words are fancy substitutes for plain talk, and we use them (or they are used on us by commerce) for deceit. They are a vice that formality sometimes supports.

But they are not genuinely *more formal. Wealthy* is not more formal than *rich;* it is just fancier. *Rich* is not slang; it belongs in the most formal discourse. It is plain, and formality can include plainness without disunity. It cannot, however, include slang without upsetting its wholeness of tone. Think of the difference between *crook* and *rich.* And think of the difference between *tool* and *implement.* Like *rich, tool* is plain and perfectly suited to formal discourse; *implement* is polysyllabic and general, and often a pompous alternative to *tool.*

    Formal and Informal Sentence Structure. The question "Do you want to buy a drink?" is neither formal nor informal in itself. "Would you care to purchase a cocktail?" is pompous. "Want to get sloshed?" is slangy, which is not the same as informal. We could use "Do you want to buy a drink?" in a context that was either formal nor informal because its words are plain. Informally:

> The woman came down the aisle looking tidy and cheerful. In back of the makeup and the hair, which looked as if it would break off in chunks if you touched it, perhaps there was a living woman, somebody with a name like Eileen or Carol. She wanted to say, "Do you want to buy a drink?" But the airline had enameled her talk along with her hair. "Would you care to purchase a cocktail?"

More formally:

> When you arrive at the age of fifty, your ability to choose has narrowed, and you find yourself on a narrow road, lacking the old opportunity to expand or wander, facing instead the one bleak point at journey's end. When you were young, you questioned: Do you want to be an actor, or a poet? Will you live in London, New York, or Paris? Now you are no longer young: Will you eat lobster for dinner? Do you want to buy a drink?

The difference here is less a matter of vocabulary than it is of sentence (and paragraph) structure. The difference includes words also, but the difference in vocabulary is relative. *Tidy* and *cheerful* could go in either passage. The idiomatic gesture of *along with* in the first passage is relatively informal; perhaps *as well as* would be the formal equivalent. *Chunks* has an informal sound. But the sentence structure in the second passage—complex, pointed, controlled—mainly accounts for its greater formality.

    Informality Gone Bad. The fault typical of informal prose, when it goes bad, is incoherence. It does not hang together. (Pompous formal prose, or jargon, at least *seems* to hang together.) Here is a journalist's parody of what the Gettysburg Address would have sounded like if President Eisenhower, who was famous for his meandering style, had delivered it.

> I haven't checked these figures but 87 years ago, I think it was, a number of individuals organized a governmental set-up here in this

country, I believe it covered certain Eastern areas, with this idea they were following up based on a sort of national independence arrangement and the program that every individual is just as good as every other individual. Well, now, of course, we are dealing with this big difference of opinion, civil disturbance you might say, although I don't like to appear to take sides or name any individuals, and the point is naturally to check up, by actual experience in the field, to see whether any governmental set-up with a basis like the one I was mentioning has any validity and find out whether that dedication by those early individuals will pay off in lasting values and things of that kind.

Well, here we are, at the scene where one of these disturbances between different sides got going. We want to pay our tribute to those loved ones, those departed individuals who made the supreme sacrifice here on the basis of their opinions about how this thing ought to be handled. And I would say this. It is absolutely in order to do this.

But if you look at the over-all picture of this, we can't pay any tribute—we can't sanctify this area, you might say—we can't hallow according to whatever individual creeds or faiths or sort of religious outlooks are involved like I said about this particular area. It was those individuals themselves, including the enlisted men, very brave individuals, who have given this religious character to the area. The way I see it, the rest of the world will not remember any statements issued here but it will never forget how these men put their shoulders to the wheel and carried this idea down the fairway.

Now frankly, our job, the living individual's job here, is to pick up the burden and sink the putt they made these big efforts here for. It is our job to get on with the assignment—and from these deceased fine individuals to take extra inspiration, you could call it, for the same theories about the set-up for which they made such a big contribution. We have to make up our minds right here and now, as I see it, that they didn't put out all that blood, perspiration and—well—that they didn't just make a dry run here, and that all of us here, under God, that is, the God of our choice, shall beef up this idea about freedom and liberty and those kind of arrangements, and that the government of all individuals, by all individuals and for all individuals, shall not pass out of the world-picture.

Oliver Jensen, "The Gettysburg Address in Eisenhowese"

And here, in case you do not remember it, is Lincoln's formal original.

Fourscore and seven years ago our fathers brought forth on this continent a new nation, conceived in liberty, and dedicated to the proposition that all men are created equal.

Now we are engaged in a great civil war, testing whether that nation, or any nation so conceived and so dedicated, can long endure. We are met on a great battlefield of that war. We have come to dedicate a portion of that field as a final resting-place for those who here gave their lives that that nation might live. It is altogether fitting and proper that we should do this.

> But in a larger sense, we cannot dedicate—we cannot consecrate—we cannot hallow—this ground. The brave men, living and dead, who struggled here, have consecrated it far above our poor power to add or detract. The world will little note nor long remember what we say here, but it can never forget what they did here. It is for us, the living, rather, to be dedicated here to the unfinished work which they who fought here have thus far so nobly advanced. It is rather for us to be here dedicated to the great task remaining before us—that from these honored dead we take increased devotion to that cause for which they gave the last full measure of devotion; that we here highly resolve that these dead shall not have died in vain; that this nation, under God, shall have a new birth of freedom; and that government of the people, by the people, for the people, shall not perish from the earth.

The parody is twice the length of the original, yet it does not convey any more information. In fact, it is much less specific—substituting nebulous phrases like "this big difference of opinion, civil disturbance you might say" for clear and simple ones like "a great civil war." The sentences wander and repeat themselves ("It was those individuals themselves, including the enlisted men, very brave individuals . . . ."). The writing is so diluted and directionless that we don't feel the speaker cares for the subject; we don't believe that he is genuinely moved. One fault that helps to create this impression—a fault common to many writers—is repeating pointless qualifications like *I think, I believe,* and *I would say.* Many people mistakenly think that such qualifications make writing more informal and natural. But these personalisms are understood without being said, and they make one feel that if the speaker (or writer) is so tentative about speaking his mind, then he is probably not certain of it.

Mixing Formal and Informal Diction. We would write more easily if prose were either informal or formal, if nothing lived between the poles. But most good prose lives in the temperate regions on either side of the equator. The informal essay enjoys an occasional periodic sentence or unusual word. The formally deft argument uses a sudden colloquialism with charm and wit.

A sentence by E. B. White exemplifies the mixture a witty writer can make. White has been talking with appropriate disdain about a pamphlet on writing that, among other things, admonishes us, "Whenever possible, personalize your writing by directing it to the reader." *Personalize* is a slimy word. As White says, "A man who likes the word 'personalize' is entitled to his choice, but we wonder whether he should be in the business of giving advice to writers." The word is used commercially to mean an imprinted name—*personalized stationery,* for instance—and does not mean *to make personal* or *to direct toward* another person. White's comment, after he quotes the advice, is this sentence:

> As for us, we would as lief Simonize our grandmother as personalize our writing.

The mini-analogy expresses White's feeling: it would be monstrous to *personalize our writing*. He compares the offensive diction to an unnatural act. At the same time, he uses a cunning and *personal* oddity of diction. The plain way to say the sentence is "we would as soon Simonize our grandmother," but White uses the old-fashioned *as lief*. And *lief* butts against *Simonize,* the old-fashioned word against the trademark. The bizarre mixture of dictions—the *dis*unity—makes its point.

And so the mixture of dictions can be expressive as well as comic. Often it is chiefly comic. W. C. Field's polysyllables are comic because he uses high words in low matters—or for low purposes, like conning people.

Revising for Unity. Achieving unity in our writing usually requires revision. Go over your prose, thinking of it as something that ought to be as whole and as shapely as a clay pot or a well-designed sports car.

Read your sentences aloud to yourself or to a friend. Look for rhythm and resolution, paying special attention to the ends of your sentences. Look for parallelism, emphasis, and balance. Repair any grammatical disunity that may have crept in. Look for places in which your tone shifts for no good reason, and make appropriate repairs.

EXERCISES

1. Simplify the following sentences, eliminating excess verbiage and pretentiousness.

    a. Given the preponderence of avian life in the orchard, we thought to locate our temporary canvas domicile across the road.

    b. We subscribe to the belief that the damage incurred to our furnishings was largely owing to your negligence.

    c. Sobriety would be indicated if you expect to be transporting my daughter home after the gridiron event.

    d. My lower appendage does not have a great deal of mobility, confined as it is by the plaster cast.

    e. Despite my warnings against excessive speed, Jared utilized the full capabilities of the automobile in that regard.

    f. Indicate the vicinity of my abode.

    g. By no means a true bibliophile, he kept his choicest volumes arranged in order of their pecuniary value.

    h. I was happy to see that Cheryl had through a program of vigorous calisthenics removed much of her excess poundage.

    i. His investment in the emotional complex of their relationships, which had been ongoing for somewhat over five years, was minuscule.

2. Looking into textbooks, magazines, newspapers, or college catalogues, find five sentences in which the writer uses a pompous or fancy
construction in place of a plainer one. Rewrite for plainness, and speculate
on the reasons behind the pomposity. Bring both the original sentences and
your rewrites to class; be prepared to discuss your findings in small groups.

3. Take this passage from Ecclesiastes (2:18–19) and create a parody like George Orwell's (see page 168).

> And I hated all my labour wherein I laboured under the sun,
> seeing that I must leave it unto the man that shall be after me.
> And who knoweth whether he will be a wise man or a fool?
> Yet will he have rule over all my labour wherein I have
> laboured, and wherein I have shown myself wise under the sun.
> This is also vanity.

4. Write a short account of a real or imagined accident in three
tones of voice: for (a) a letter to a relative, (b) an accident report for an insurance company, and (c) a story in the school newspaper.

5. In these passages, analyze diction and structure for formality
and informality. Be prepared to find some mixture.

> a. It was during the Lebanon crisis, an earlier one, the Lebanon
> crisis of 1958. Every American aircraft in Europe stood at the
> ready. With no war on we milked any crisis or incident or ex-
> ercise that came along. Troops were being flown from Ger-
> many down to the Aegean. Tactical squadrons were ferrying
> over from the states. I remember one story, and this is just an
> aside, about a flight of four ferry planes, F-100s, crossing the
> Atlantic, when the lead pilot started hallucinating. His heating
> system had jammed at full. He was dehydrating. He thought he
> saw an airfield below him. He saw the runway and the control
> tower, and there was nothing any of his flying mates could do.
> He simply peeled off for a landing and went in.
>   Pilots liked to tell such stories. They circulated quickly
> around an airbase, throughtout a command. Each man told it as
> if he'd been flying in the next plane. Pilots grew animated
> when they told crash stories, their flat hands swerving, plung-
> ing. These stories always ended with the same line. "He bought
> the farm. He bought the goddam farm."

> James D. Houston, "The Window of War"

> b. "Omit needless words!" cries the author on page 17, and into
> that imperative Will Strunk really put his heart and soul. In the
> days when I was sitting in his class, he omitted so many needless
> words, and omitted them so forcibly and with such eagerness
> and obvious relish, that he often seemed in the position of hav-
> ing short-changed himself, a man left with nothing more to say

yet with time to fill, a radio prophet who had outdistanced the clock. Will Strunk got out of this predicament by a simple trick: he uttered every sentence three times. When he delivered his oration on brevity to the class, he leaned forward over his desk, grasped his coat lapels in his hands, and in a husky, conspiratorial voice said, "Rule Thirteen. Omit needless words! Omit needless words! Omit needless words!"

E. B. White, The Elements of Style

c. This is a society which has little use for anything except gain. All is hacked down in its service, whether people, ideas, or ideals. The writer, say, who achieves some entrance into the mainstream of American letters is almost immediately in jeopardy of being stripped of his insight by the ruffians of "success." A man who writes plays and poems, for instance, is asked to be a civil rights reporter, or write a dopey musical—if he is talked about widely enough—if not, there is no mention of him, and perhaps he is left to rot in some pitiful mistake of a college out in Idaho. A man who writes or makes beautiful music will be asked to immortalize a soap, or make sounds behind the hero while that blond worthy seduces the virgins of our nation's guilt. Even a man who is a great center fielder will still be asked to kick up his heels at Las Vegas.

Leroi Jones, Home

VARIETY AND UNITY

We write varied sentences according to the demands of thought and expression. Subordinate clauses often make needed qualifications in longer sentences that in their progress imitate the process of thinking. The simple, succinct sentence embodies the rhythm of a single idea. If our prose has unity, clarity, and coherence, it is usually varied in its sentence structure as well.

But not always. We get in a rut. We lack experience of the long, periodic sentence, or even of the complex sentence, and we tend to fall into a monotony of construction. It helps us, in revision, to look for variety of sentence structure, and if we lack this variety to see if we can appropriately impose it.

Unity and variety need each other. They are the two poles, and the world spins between them. Without variety, there is nothing to be unified. Identically constructed sentences strung together in a row have the unity of glass beads on a string. When we learn how to read, "See Spot run" sentences have this unity, which is perhaps why we want to leave first grade for the second. Paragraphs of successive compound sentences are similarly boring. In this passage from a student essay, the writer, lacking confidence in his ability to use complex sentences, writes beads-and-string prose.

> Student government at the high school level is pointless. Principals never allow students any power. School boards are the same. Every year people get elected and nothing happens.

We could revise this passage, for variety, into these sentences—which also supply greater unity and clarity:

> Student government in high school is pointless because no high school principal is prepared to grant real power to students, and no school board would support a principal who experimented with student power. Although elections take place every year, office without responsibility makes nothing happen.

By using different sentence types, we can vary the speed and style in our prose, and at the same time make it more precise. If for no other reason, we must vary our sentences to keep the reader interested and involved. Monotony destroys attentiveness; if the reader sleeps, our clarity is wasted. But variation also allows us to be subtle; it increases the range and conciseness of our expression. The means are not separate from the ends. *A change in style, however slight, is a change in meaning, however slight.* You will find meanings that you cannot express, cannot convey, unless you can find in your box of varied sentence structures the shape you require.

Long Sentences

Short sentences are easy. They are also useful when they are mixed with longer sentences of different types. Longer sentences give us more trouble; the more parts a machine has, the more things can go wrong. But to become skillful writers, we must be able to handle varieties of the long sentence.

In the most controlled prose, in the long sentences made by writers being formal, clause follows clause, the sentence is compound as well as complex, and absolutes, participles, and appositives combine with prepositional phrases—a combination of combinations that includes, balances, and ultimately unifies.

If we took the preceding sentence and separated it into one independent clause for each idea, we might end with something like this:

> Some prose is highly controlled and each sentence is long. This happens when the writer is being formal. There are many clauses. The sentence can be compound and it can also be complex. The sentence can also include absolutes, participles, appositives, and prepositional phrases. This combination makes the sentence inclusive. It gives it balance, and it gives it unity.

This version uses seven sentences and fifty-nine words. The earlier version was one sentence and forty-four words. The gain in brevity is trivial, but the shorter version is more accurate. Subordination adds accuracy, not only by bringing form and content into agreement, but also by making direct syntactic connections instead of continually stopping the flow of sense and picking it up again with a pronoun.

But we don't need to make such sentences up; we can find them in the work of many writers.

> In the early morning the distant image of Cannes, the pink and cream of old fortifications, the purple Alps that bounded Italy, were cast across the water and lay quavering in the ripples and rings sent up by sea-plants through the clear shadows.

> F. Scott Fitzgerald, *Tender Is the Night*

The passage begins and ends with prepositional phrases (*In the early morning . . . through the clear shadows*) and in between are more of them, and adjectives, and a varied use of verbs: *bounded, cast, lay quavering.* The sentence follows the logic of looking; it is a sequence of carefully organized perceptions. The verbs, which follow one another in time, have as subject the three phrases and clauses before—an elaborated subject, which includes the verb *bounded* as well as nouns and adjectives. Then we move into more prepositions and nouns, another verb, preposition and noun, preposition, adjective, and noun. The verbs at the center carry the sentence: they direct the movement of the inner eye.

Fitzgerald's prose is ornate and well ordered, but not so formal as the prose of certain essayists and historians. Here is part of a paragraph by one of the masters of the essay form.

> The concept of the perfect society is one of the oldest and most deeply pervasive elements in western thought, wherever, indeed, the classical or Judaeo-Christian traditions are dominant. It has taken many forms—a Golden Age, a Garden of Eden in which men were innocent, happy, virtuous, peaceful, free, where everything was harmonious, and neither vice nor error nor violence nor misery was so much as thought of; where nature was bounteous and nothing was lacking, there was no conflict, and not even the passage of time affected the full, permanent and complete satisfaction of all the needs, physical, mental and spiritual, of the blessed dwellers in these regions. Then a catastrophe occurred that put an end to this condition; there are many variants of this—the flood, man's first disobedience, original sin, the crime of Prometheus, the discovery of agriculture and metallurgy, primitive accumulation, and the like.

> Isaiah Berlin, "Vico and the Ideal of the Enlightenment"

Most of us are unlikely to compose sentences as long and complicated as the second in the paragraph, but we might study Berlin's technique for a moment just to see what a skilled stylist can do with this fundamental unit of prose. Let us look at the whole in terms of its clusters of sense. "It," writes Berlin, referring to the idea of the perfect society, "has taken many forms," at which point he begins to itemize. But he only reaches the second in his list, "A Garden of Eden," before he begins listing *its* virtues. The dwellers, he claims, were "innocent, happy, virtuous," and so on; he then switches to the negative in order to underscore a set of conditions that did *not* prevail. Positive and negative lists are roughly in balance: the positive list has more terms; the negative list uses more words. Then, as if we have not had enough heaped on our plate, Berlin inserts a semicolon and pushes on. Another list, this one again comprised of negatives, begins the second half of the sentence. Then, cleverly ("Not even the passage of time affected the full, permanent and complete satisfaction . . ."), the writer turns the negatives back into a list of positive virtues. By the time we finish the whole sentence, we have been carried through a logical system that makes either side of the semicolon a reverse image of the other. Thus: Positive Negative; Negative Positive.

The long, complex sentence lends itself especially well to organizing things that are related to one another, like events in history, plots of stories, or arguments with several parts. The art is to distribute the parts of the sentence so that the underlying logic shines forth clearly.

Mixing the Types

We can manipulate the types of sentence we use for variety and to create an expressive effect, to establish a mood, or to emphasize a point. Here are some examples. Keep in mind that the passages get their effect not by the sentence structure alone but also by the word associations and ideas. Sometimes, for the sake of sense or mood, we manipulate phrases to achieve more regularity than variety.

> In a little house on the mountain slopes above Delphi lived an old woman with her witless son. The house consisted of a single room; one wall was the mountainside itself, and always dripped with moisture. It was really not a house at all, but a ramshackle hut which herdsmen had built for themselves. It stood quite alone away up in the wild mountain, high above the buildings of the city and above the sacred precincts of the temple.
>
> Pär Lagerkvist, *The Sybil*

The sentence structure here is simple and stable. The construction is uncomplicated and regular. All the sentences except the first are regular in word order, beginning subject-verb and continuing evenly, without parenthetical expression or phrases set off by commas or any other complications in the syntax. The syntax is as undisturbed as the scene. The sentences are medium in length and similar in length, establishing a rhythm that reinforces the stability and simplicity in the scene described. We participate in the rhythm of untroubled isolation. That rhythm is established, even more, by the uniform length of the main phrases within the sentences. If we listen to ourselves reading the passage, we will find that natural pauses divide the phrases in this way:

> In a little house on the mountain slopes above Delphi/
> lived an old woman with her witless son./
> The house consisted of a single room;/

one wall was the mountainside itself,/
and always dripped with moisture./
It was really not a house at all,/
but a ramshackle hut which herdsmen had built for themselves./
It stood quite alone away up in the wild mountain,/
high above the buildings of the city/
and above the sacred precincts of the temple./

It has just enough variation to avoid monotony. The even length contributes not only stillness to the scene but also our sense of the narrator's
calm, unemotional objectivity.

The following passage from Annie Dillard's *Pilgrim at Tinker Creek* ex-
hibits different sentence constructions, with different effects:

> When I slide under a barbed-wire fence, cross a field, and run over a
> sycamore trunk felled across the water, I'm on a little island shaped
> like a tear in the middle of Tinker Creek. On one side of the creek
> is a steep forested bank; the water is swift and deep on that side of
> the island. On the other side is the level field I walked through next
> to the steers' pasture; the water between the field and the island is
> shallow and sluggish. In summer's low water, flags and bulrushes
> grow along a series of shallow pools cooled by the lazy current. Wa-
> ter striders patrol the surface film, crayfish hump along the silt bot-
> tom eating filth, frogs shout and glare, and shiners and small bream
> hide among roots from the sulky green heron's eye. I come to this
> island every month of the year. I walk around it, stopping and star-
> ing, or I straddle the sycamore log over the creek, curling my legs
> out of the water in winter, trying to read. Today I sit on dry grass at
> the end of the island by the slower side of the creek. I'm drawn to
> this spot. I come to it as to an oracle; I return to it as a man years
> later will seek out the battlefield where he lost a leg or an arm.

As with the Lagerkvist passage, we can put the Dillard paragraph into long
lines to see its structure more clearly and to understand how her complicated sentences work.

> When I slide under a barbed-wire fence,
>   cross a field,
>   and run over a sycamore trunk felled across the water,
> I'm on a little island shaped like a tear in the middle of
>   Tinker Creek.
>
> On one side of the creek is a steep forested bank;
> the water is swift and deep on that side of the island.
> On the other side is the level field
> I walked through next to the steers' pasture;
> the water between the field and the island is shallow and
>   sluggish.

In summer's low water,
flags and bulrushes grow along a series of shallow pools cooled
by the lazy current.

Water striders patrol the surface film,
crayfish hump along the silt bottom eating filth,
frogs shout and glare,
and shiners and small bream hide among roots from the sulky
green heron's eye.

I come to this island every month of the year.

I walk around it, stopping and staring,
or I straddle the sycamore log over the creek, curling my legs out of
the water in winter, trying to read.

Today I sit on dry grass at the end of the island by the slower
side of the creek.

I'm drawn to this spot.

I come to it as to an oracle;
I return to it as a man years later will seek out the battlefield
where he lost a leg or an arm.

Dillard starts with a long, complex sentence of description, with three lively verbs in a subordinate clause, and then an elaborated predicate in the main clause. She follows this sophisticated sentence with two simple clauses, a compound joined by a semicolon. The next sentence elaborates the pattern of the second one. The fifth is long and rich, its mass of description tending to obscure the fact that its construction is simple, direct—and compound. Following it is the shortest sentence, and the simplest one so far, in the paragraph. Two sentences later, we find a sentence even shorter and simpler, followed by a compound-complex sentence of great sophistication, and a final image that is startling, almost shattering. Dillard plays the octaves of syntax like a skilled musician improvising at the piano.

Though our focus in this chapter has been on sentences, their use and construction, we should not forget those fundamental components—words. Though Dillard achieves much of her effectiveness here through her grasp of sentence variety, she is also an expert at finding the right word to evoke the sensation she wants. The fourth sentence is a good example. Dillard's water striders *patrol,* her crayfish *hump,* and her frogs *shout* and *glare.* Try substituting *walk, crawl,* and *croak* and *stare.* The sentence feels diminished. Writing that touches a reader depends, finally, on everything working together: words and sentences, rhythms and meanings.

Revising for Variety and Conciseness

Look over your own writing for the construction of sentences. Ask yourself if you vary enough to avoid monotony, if your variations are as expressive as they might be, and if your informal sentences are appropriate and sufficiently precise.

Also, see if you can be more concise. To revise for conciseness often requires compound and complex sentences or conjunction and subordination. Concision and precision go together. We ramble on, in our first drafts or in our daily writing, assuming connections and causes but not stating them. If we try to make our prose more concise, by writing complex sentences with precise conjunctions, we often discover that what we wanted to imply does not really derive from what we said. And so this device of revision—by adding the conjunction—becomes another way of testing the identity of expression and meaning. Precision of time and cause is a responsibility that the loose or compound sentence may evade. In an earlier example, a tiny revision illustrated a small gain in brevity and responsibility:

> I saw her and she was carrying a kitten. It had a crooked tail . . . .

became

> When I saw her she was carrying a kitten with a crooked tail.

Maybe the greatest change here is in the tone; the writer seems to be controlling something, not merely rattling on.

Here is a passage from a student essay in which the writer dumps things together without showing relationships. He wastes words by repetition, and he wastes the power in those words by poor organization.

> The building was still burning and firemen couldn't put it out. An hour or so went by. The National Guard looked nervous and young. They drove around in their Jeeps with their guns. They tried to look tough. We didn't know if their guns were loaded or not. They were scary just because they had guns but they looked scared themselves. They were about the same age as the students. Yet they were guarding them.

Because the relationship between remarks is often vague in this passage, we could not rewrite it with certainty unless we knew more facts or knew the feelings the author tried to express. Reading the passage, we may doubt that the student had arranged the facts in his mind with clarity or had understood his feelings. Later, he revised the passage, and his sentence structure accounted for much of the improvement—though as always with writing, the *whole* shapes everything that it contains; the whole is better, partly because of sentence structure.

> As we watched the building burn for hours, the firemen standing by helpless, we became aware of the patrolling Jeeps of the National Guard, young men the same age as the students they were guarding,

young men who tried to act tough but looked as frightened of their guns as we were.

He gained economy and vividness, and also clarity of thought and feeling.

EXERCISES

1. Revise this passage to introduce varied sentence structure. Use variation not just for its own sake but also to make the writing more precise. Remember that commas, semicolons, colons, and periods are aids to rhythm and therefore to meaning, to expressiveness, and to clarity.

> Every man who worked on the docks had to wear a hard hat. He also had to wear heavy canvas gloves. The hats protected the men from falling objects. Sometimes crates fell into the hole. Sometimes steel beams were swung down to the dock on cables. There was danger of metal splinters and serious abrasions. These dangers were increased because the longshoremen might work for twelve hours straight. They might work from 6 P.M. to 6 A.M. Some of the men also had jobs during the day. And many of the men drank heavily. This was because they got depressed. Sometimes there would be a shipment of whiskey. The men might pretend to have an accident. They would let a crate fall. It would break open. They would stash the unbroken bottles. And they would hide them. They would drink some when the officials were not around. The officials were paid by the shipping companies. They didn't want to be blamed for missing goods.

2. Find and identify, in the passage you made from Exercise 1, a subordinate clause, a main clause, an appositive, a participle, and an adjective with a preposition. If you cannot find one of each, revise the passage to include them.

3. Examine the following passages to discover how sentence structure and variation express content and tone. Try modifying the sentences and see whether the meaning of the passage changes. If so, how?

> a. For purposes of pedagogy, I have sometimes illustrated these tendencies by reference to a technically uncomplicated product, which, unaccountably, neither General Electric nor Westinghouse has yet placed on the market. It is a toaster of standard performance, the pop-up kind, except that it etches on the surface of the toast, in darker carbon, one of a selection of standard messages or designs. For the elegant, an attractive monogram would be available or a coat of arms; for the devout, at breakfast there would be an appropriate devotional message from the Reverend Billy Graham; for the patriotic or worried, there would be an

aphorism urging vigilance from Mr. J. Edgar Hoover; for modern painters and economists, there would be a purely abstract design. A restaurant version would sell advertising.

John Kenneth Galbraith, "The Technostructure"

b. There they were, those who had wangled their way into war, at the wrong place, doing, in excesses of patriotism or curiosity or self-proof, work that was the wrong work, at the wrong time. They were valuable in some terms I had not run into as an aircraft woman. There were fine editors, good writers, movie actors, poets, in the halls of the OWI at Carlos Place, and I realize now that I was as glamorous to them as they were to me. Somehow I had touched the war they had come to. I knew things I couldn't tell. Gaunt and nervous, aesthetically pleasing in the fashion that pleases at a given time, an object of interest, I had had the experience they had come to share. What I had learned to take for granted, service in the forces was, to them, a fascination. It made them seem somehow younger than I was. I had a sense of knowing things—oh, not events—civilians seem always to expect those—but gray expanses and hours, days, months, of damp indifference.

Mary Lee Settle, "London–1944"

c. Familiarity has perhaps bred contempt in us Americans: until you have had a washing machine, you cannot imagine how little difference it will make to you. Europeans still believe that money brings happiness, witness the bought journalist, the bought politician, the bought general, the whole venality of European literary life, inconceivable in this country of the dollar. It is true that America produces and consumes more cars, soap, and bathtubs than any other nation, but we live among these objects rather than by them. Americans build skyscrapers; Le Corbusier worships them. Ehrenburg, our Soviet critic, fell in love with the Check-O-Mat in American railway stations, writing home paragraphs of song to this gadget—while deploring American materialism. When an American heiress wants to buy a man, she at once crosses the Atlantic. The only really materialistic people I have ever met have been Europeans.

Mary McCarthy, "America the Beautiful" *(On the Contrary)*

6

Paragraphs

USES OF PARAGRAPHS

The paragraph is a small box of sentences, making a whole shape that is at the same time part of another whole. It is a miniature essay itself, with its own variable structure. The paragraph within the essay makes a sign for the reader; it alerts the reader to the part structure of an essay. Paragraphs give signals and directions and help to connect writers with audiences. Paragraphs are partly arbitrary, and they will vary in length and purpose according to the essay's occasion. Frequently a writer arrives at the best paragraphing only in late revision.

In that bible for stylists, *Modern English Usage,* H. W. Fowler writes, "The purpose of paragraphing is to give the reader a rest." We called the paragraph, in effect, a mini-essay; it is also a maxi-sentence: the blank space at the end of the paragraph, before we indent and begin a new one, is like the period ending the sentence, only longer. Paragraphs punctuate by visual arrangement on the page. Like a sentence, a paragraph tells us that something completes itself and that we have come to the end of a group of statements composing a larger statement. Like a sentence, too, a paragraph should close with the sensation of a click. Now the reader must pause a moment and see what the paragraph was doing.

Look at the preceding paragraph. Its organization is only one of many possible, but it is a common one. It begins with a quotation from Fowler, which announces its purpose. Then it compares paragraph and sentence. Fowler does not make such a comparison; our strategy takes its cue from Fowler's word *rest.* The last sentence suggests the function—pausing—that rest fills. The paragraph elaborates and supports the first sentence, and the pause at the end should grant us a sense of wholeness.

Paragraphs rest the eye as well as the brain. Unbroken print leaves no landmarks for the eye that wanders and returns; we sometimes find ourselves using a finger to keep to the correct line. Though context gives us other reasons for longer or shorter paragraphs, we should not forget that paragraphs are useful as visual aids to comfort in reading. Those little indentations are hand- and footholds in the cliff face of the essay.

PARAGRAPHS AS SIGNS FOR READERS

As readers we identify the paragraph by the visual sign of its indented white space. Our eyes register PARAGRAPH before our minds have a chance to consider the writer's reasons for pause or the content of the new paragraph. But the visual sign is itself information; it begins the new content by alerting us that something changes.

The paragraph holds and shapes; it manipulates the reader's attention. When as writers revising we consider our paragraphing, we must as always imagine ourselves readers. Because the paragraph gives the reader a break, writers can gather their materials into units small enough for separate comprehension, and by separating them can allow each collection its own space as part of the whole essay.

The paragraph, by embodying a sequence or development of thought, is more thoroughly directed to audience than the sentence is. Maybe our attention to paragraphing improves our thought, if we consider fullness of development a problem not of the essay but of the paragraph. For you beginning writers it may be helpful, learning development to concentrate on the smaller unit; or you may think of the essay's structure as an assemblage of paragraphs in an appropriate order. But paragraphing always includes an element of the arbitrary. Finally it is not so much an aid to the writer's thought as a means by which the writer shapes her material, however generated, toward an imagined audience.

Paragraphing therefore tends to find its form in late revision when we realize that one sentence—say, "These views, so diametrically opposed, may be reconciled if we look at diplomatic history"—might perfectly well come at the end of a paragraph that details the opposition or at the beginning of the next paragraph that does the reconciling. No rule of paragraphing will decide whether this sentence ends one paragraph or begins another; writers must decide, on the basis of a chosen approach to the reader.

The paragraph is a writerly device for leading the reader by the nose.

The reader, we must remember, has certain expectations: the reader does *not* expect, in the formality of a textbook, paragraphs as short as the last one. When we do such a thing we surprise the reader and therefore we had better have a purpose. Did we?

Nor, however, does the reader expect to find page after page without any paragraph breaks at all. In some old scholarly treatises, and occasionally in essays by modern writers like John McPhee, readers will find such unexpected solid pages of print—and they may find themselves turning blue from lack of breath. But John McPhee is so skillful at leading readers by the nose with firm but gentle transitions, beguiling them by a variety of sentence structure and fresh detail, that he manages the stunt. He performs like the child on the bicycle: "Look, Ma! No paragraphs!"

The tone of discourse makes for different expectations. When we read philosophy or the history of the Peloponnesian War in the fifth century B.C., where detailed elaboration is essential, we expect longer paragraphs; when we read a news story in an afternoon daily we expect shorter ones.

Always, we expect a paragraph to be a unit; if a brief newspaper story gives one paragraph to each sentence, this very repetitiousness is a unity. (And if it continues for too long, this unity becomes totally boring.) More likely the paragraph assembles itself as a unit in a familiar way—like an assertion with details following to support the assertion. (We will list and explore familiar paragraph patterns later in this chapter.) Sometimes a paragraph forms part of something ongoing, like a narrative; the break should happen where, if we had to pause for a glass of water, we would pause. (We would *not* pause, say, in the middle of a sentence.) We expect the beginnings and endings of paragraphs, most of the time, to make small signals of starting and stopping. We expect paragraphs to hold together, without loose, flapping parts. All of these expectations belong to us as readers; when we become writers, these expectations become devices for our use.

PURPOSE AND THE PARAGRAPH

Paragraphs advance the writer's purpose, and their shape must reflect that purpose in the development of the essay. As always, purpose adjusts itself to audience, as the writer improvises a structure. Development that follows rhetorical patterns, which we return to later in this chapter, often gives paragraphs an appropriate shape—but they are not the only common structures. A frequent paragraph pattern begins with a generalization, makes a necessary qualification, and then reaffirms the generalization by example. "The personal computer, used in conjunction with telephone lines, will revolutionize the habits of American consumers." This topic sentence makes an assertion that could be questioned; it acquires more authority if it is accompanied by a modest restriction: "We do not mean that Americans will no longer pick up a quart of milk at a convenience store, or that shopping plazas will become ghost towns." After this qualification, the paragraph might illustrate computer shopping at home with two or three examples.

Another common form of paragraph is the question and answer: "Will consumers find enough choice, if they shop by electronic catalogue? That will, of course, depend . . . ." Questions need not be literally posed; the same paragraph could begin, in a more formal prose style, "Some commentators believe that electronic shopping will overly restrict consumer choice." In either paragraph, the sentences offering question or objection may be answered or rebutted by sentences that develop the paragraph.

Some essays profit by several paragraphs in a row constructed on similar principles: query or objection followed by reply or rebuttal. Two or three such paragraphs should suffice; when a whole essay is so constructed, the effect is too mechanical, or perhaps too defensive. It is wise to vary the construction of the paragraphs, and to vary the position of the generalization that the paragraph validates or illustrates. Often a topic sentence can conclude a paragraph. The writer could begin an essay by describing a consumer sitting in a den at the keyboard, shopping for a lawn mower; this opening paragraph could end, after its narrative example: "The personal computer, connected to telephone lines, will revolutionize the habits of the American consumer."

UNITY IN THE PARAGRAPH

An effective paragraph marshalls its sentences toward a single main purpose. Every part is relevant and serves the whole. The writer must omit the odd fact that happens to be true but that is irrelevant to the topic. Odd facts or misplaced assertions break the thread of concentration.

> Learning to cook well requires more than just knowing how to follow a recipe. Cooking depends on a knowledge of ingredients, a sense of how different tastes combine, and an ability to imagine the effect of a range of combinations. Setting the table is more a matter of knowing what goes where, and which dishes and forks go with which dishes. You would never use a fish fork for pasta or a soup spoon for custard. The first two are skills that can be learned. Imagination is, like most artistic gifts, inborn.

The sentence that begins "Setting the table" does not fit here; it redirects the reader's attention away from the enumeration of attributes that is the point of the paragraph. Even though the writer soon returns to the topic, the coherence has been compromised. Unable to trust the paragraph, we are distanced from the assertions. The clear signal has been marred by static.

We must remain alert to maintain unity of subject matter in our paragraphs because the associations in our thought, which can lead us to new ideas and perceptions, can also lead us into irrelevance. When we begin to write about a subject, our mind drifts from one thought to another, by personal association. As we have seen in Chapter 3, this random, uncensored thinking can be useful for gathering material. But we must take care that it not lead to rambling disorganization.

Two kinds of writing need especially careful paragraphing. Exposition (which sets forth or explains) and argument (which attempts to convince or persuade) should lead the reader's mind by careful steps to understanding or agreement. Paragraphs in argument or exposition are mini-essays. They deal with one topic, with closely related data, or with an integral segment of a topic. The paragraph is homogeneous. It is orderly—

and we must remember that there are many varieties of order. (See Some Ways of Developing Paragraphs, pages 200–211.)

Unity and Topic Sentences

Probably the most common paragraph construction begins with a topic sentence, which brings to the paragraph not only order but also unity. The topic sentence announces the topic and an attitude toward it. The other sentences of the paragraph use a consistent order—often moving from the general to the specific—to explain, elaborate, or enumerate examples or analogies supporting the topic sentence. Then a final sentence draws the elaboration to a conclusion in a way that leads to the next paragraph. Here is a paragraph that begins with a topic sentence and moves from a general statement to particular examples.

> Boston is not a small New York, as they say a child is not a small adult but is, rather, a specially organized small creature with its small-creature's temperature, balance, and distribution of fat. In Boston there is an utter absence of that wild electric beauty of New York, of the marvelous, excited rush of people in taxicabs at twilight, of the great Avenues and Streets, the restaurants, theatres, bars, hotels, delicatessens, shops. In Boston the night comes down with an incredibly heavy, small-town finality. The cows come home; the chickens go to roost; the meadow is dark. Nearly every Bostonian is in his own house or in someone else's house, dining at the home board, enjoying domestic and social privacy. The "nice little dinner party"—for this the Bostonian would sell his soul. In the evenings, the old "accomodators" dart about the city, carrying their black uniforms and white aprons in a paper bag. They are on call to go, anywhere, to cook and serve dinners. Many of these women are former cooks and maids, now living on Social Security retirement pensions, supplemented by the fees for these evening "accomodations" to the community. Their style and the bland respectability of their cuisine keep up the social tone of the town. They are like those old slaves who stuck to their places and, even in the greatest deprivation, graciously went on toting things to the Massa.
>
> Elizabeth Hardwick, "Boston: The Lost Ideal"

Many variations on this order are possible and are desirable because a long essay composed of paragraphs equal in length and identical in construction would be boring.

Sometimes we find a topic sentence in the middle of a paragraph, where it provides summary or generalization tying together the particulars that come before and after.

> We hesitated before we stepped into the garden, so heavy was the odor of flowering quince. The garden was orderly, comfortable, and gorgeous, with little benches artfully placed for the weary guest. *Our host, as generous as he was clever, introduced us to his hobby.* We toured

among hardy perennials, and walked past annual borders. We strolled among fig trees, past palms, to a density of shrubs. We floated in joy on the tropical air.

Hermann von Kreicke, *The Migrant Swan*

At other times we find a topic sentence ending the paragraph, as a summary. We can create drama or tension by starting with description and detail and building to a conclusion.

Now and then there is a house of brick. But what brick! When it is new it is the color of a fried egg. When it has taken on the patina of the mills it is the color of an egg long past all hope or caring. Was it necessary to adopt that shocking color? No more than it was necessary to set all of the houses on end. Red brick, even in a steel town, ages with some dignity. Let it become downright black, and it is still sightly, especially if its trimmings are of white stone, with soot in the depths and the high spots washed by the rain. *But in Westmoreland they prefer that uremic yellow, and so they have the most loathsome towns and villages ever seen by mortal eye.*

H. L. Mencken, "A Libido for the Ugly"

Notice how this structure involves us. We are pulled into the movement by the piling up of details, not knowing exactly where the argument will lead us. The author carries us with him, and the conclusion arises from the material presented. The principle is the same as that of the periodic sentence; the most important information is used as the clincher.

For the opposite effect, look back at the paragraph by Elizabeth Hardwick. Paragraphs that begin with topic sentences differ greatly in rhythm and in tone from paragraphs that end with them. The Hardwick and Mencken paragraphs have different purposes, which make their different structures appropriate. Hardwick wants to inform and explain. She tells us our destination as we start; she begins with her primary idea and then fleshes it out. Mencken wants to persuade us to share not only his ideas but also his point of view. He wants us to share with him the stages of the perceptual process. He keeps us off balance at first and involves us in the accumulating fabric of thought and feeling.

Sometimes we even find a paragraph's topic sentence at the end of the previous paragraph. The paragraph break serves almost as a colon.

In general, chronology is the most satisfactory organization. *However, we must not rely on it alone.*

We would reduce our psychological world to the order of the clock. We would become slaves of "then" and "afterward." . . .

The first two sentences in the second paragraph elaborate the negative topic sentence, which ends the first paragraph but which could have introduced the second paragraph just as well.

Sometimes we have no topic sentence, or it is understood or implied as a transition can be understood. A writer may mention that he spent a day in Omaha, then follow with a paragraph:

> The visitor can enjoy the aroma of the stockyards. He can watch the rich sit at their clubs, drinking gin next to pools of chlorine, beside flat golf courses. The visitor can walk up the sides of ugly buildings on dry Sundays. He can watch grass grow, at least in early spring and early fall. He can listen to the medley of rock-station radios in several parks. He can try sleeping for a week or so, until he is able to leave.

He needs no topic sentence; we already know what the topic is. The topic is the place, and the paragraph has unity because we can see that every sentence describes an activity possible in this place.

In argument or exposition, topic sentences often have the flavor of philosophical propositions. For instance:

> When a man needs help, he must know where to turn.
> In the 1960s, the rock guitarist was seen as a kind of god.
> The paragraph is a unit of sense, a discrete idea or topic.

In narrative and descriptive writing, topic sentences often change the scene or introduce signposts in complicated country. Here are some sentences that could be lead-ins to new paragraphs.

> Finally, he thought it was time to return.
> The weather turned fine.
> When they turned the corner, the street changed abruptly.
> Election night began with a bad omen.
> When he heard footsteps outside in the darkness, he turned off the
>   oil lamps and reached for his gun.
> The final chapters seem pointless.

When we revise our prose, it is useful to look into our paragraphs for topic sentences. We do not demand that every paragraph have one—but the *idea* of a topic sentence is a means of focusing and unifying and is therefore essential to clear and forceful prose. We look for the topic sentence of a paragraph—overt or implicit, at beginning, middle, or end—to see if the paragraph is sufficiently unified and whether it has a reason for being.

COHERENCE IN THE PARAGRAPH

Frequently, in unfinished writing, a sentence seems extraneous or irrelevant; the writer has a use for the information, but he has been unable to build the sentence smoothly into his thought. If a fact does not belong in a paragraph, it causes disunity. If it only *seems* not to belong, it causes incoherence.

The writer must learn how to blend his information so that it co-heres in a meaningful whole: the relationship between the sentences must be clear. Here is an incoherent paragraph from some daily writing.

> I had been having severe headaches and frequent dizzy spells. I was terrified of doctors. I went to the health clinic. I waited three days. It was the time of finals and I was very busy. I saw a doctor. He pre-scribed some pills. The problems continued.

It is impossible to tell what the relationships are between the bits of infor-mation related here. Did the speaker wait three days before or after going to the health clinic? Did she wait because of her fear of doctors or because she was busy? Was she busy studying for finals or doing something else? Not only is the sense confused, but the rhythm is irritatingly choppy. Here is a revised and more coherent version of the passage.

> I had been having severe headaches and frequent dizzy spells, but I hesitated to go to the health clinic because I was terrified of doctors. It was the time of finals and I was busy studying for them, so I made the excuse to myself that I didn't have time and that there was nothing the matter with me, just fatigue. Finally, I went, although I waited three days before making an appointment. I saw a doctor, and after he ex-amined me he prescribed some pills. But despite the medication, the problems continued, even after I'd been taking the pills for two weeks.

Notice that much of the coherence comes from the use of conjunctions and subordinate clauses. Although most facts remain the same, the writer has given the reader a good deal more information because she has con-nected the facts in a coherent paragraph, using complex sentences and log-ical transitions. The revision illustrates how a writer can take a mere list of facts and, by keeping her audience in mind, build them into a statement that leaves no question unanswered. In revising, the writer found it neces-sary to add a few new facts—that she was busy studying for exams, that she took the pills for two weeks. In striving for clarity she realized that her au-dience would need to know them.

We achieve coherence in our writing when our paragraphs answer the questions that they raise in the reader's mind. If we merely write,

> I was terrified of doctors. I went to the health clinic.

the reader is going to ask, "If you're so afraid of doctors, what compelled you to go?" If we don't answer the invisible question, the paragraph will lack coherence, and the reader will be frustrated or confused.

Similarly, when we make a general assertion, we create the expecta-tion that we will defend it. The reader expects us to justify or explain a statement like "The public was responsible for the war's continuation" or "Statistics show us that the VHS tapes have driven out Betas." The reader does not, presumably, know as much as we know about our chosen subject; we must give the detail, background, statistics, reasons, or explanations that our audience requires and expects of us. We write exposition to deliver information or ideas to other people.

Coherence and Consistency

We should know a few more mechanical ways to maintain coherence in the paragraph. Just as we need agreement within a sentence, we need agreement within a paragraph. We should avoid changes in verb tense. It is easy, if we let our minds wander, to begin writing a passage or paragraph in one tense and then switch to another. The shift can work, if done consciously and for the right reasons. We may begin in the present tense to be dramatic and then slip into the past tense because the events described actually occurred in the past.

> He sits on the dock, his feet bare on the warm wood, his eyes half-closed in the hot sun, daydreaming about women in black silk dresses. Suddenly he felt a violent tugging on the pole, and a long shape thrashed in the water ten feet away.

Or we may begin in the past tense and abruptly shift to the present tense, without realizing it, because we want greater immediacy.

> He sat on the dock, his feet bare on the warm wood, his eyes half-closed in the hot sun, and daydreamed about women in black silk dresses. Suddenly he feels a violent tugging on the pole, and sees a long shape thrash in the water only ten feet away.

But usually such shifts are careless mistakes that proofreading should correct.

Another common violation of coherence is to shift pronouns within a paragraph. If we start with *we,* we should not switch to *you.* We must be careful, if we have chosen to use the formal *one,* that we do not fall back into *I* or *you.*

> But if *one* has experienced the mystical conversion described by adepts in almost every culture in the world, *one* may still fall back into the old dualities and pettinesses. But once *we* have felt that stronger intensity of being, *you* can never again remain satisfied with less. The ghost of that experience haunts *us* like a dead loved one.

Coherence and consistency of paragraphs are goals essential to the final shape and value of the essay. We may not achieve these goals until we have written several drafts. After we have sketched our rough ideas, after we have begun to find phrases and sentences to express the ideas, we must edit and revise, refine and shape, to make a point and to reach an audience by means of coherence and consistency.

Coherence and the Paragraph: Transitions

Transitions in our writing are devices for moving from one place to another. They range from single words like *but* to phrases like *on the other hand,* and to subtler devices like repetition or parallelism. Transitions are essential to the coherence of paragraph and paper. You might expect to find this topic with the previous chapter, on sentences, or further on, in connection with whole essays, but we put it here because transitions happen *within* the paragraph as a way to move from one sentence to another or *between* paragraphs as a way of moving from topic to topic while keeping the essay whole. *Transitions are thus essential to coherence in paragraph and paper.* A prose insufficient in transitions is like a road map with certain key routes erased. It leaps from subject to subject—place to place—without stated or implied connection. The connection remains in the writer's mind. The reader, like the traveler, gets hopelessly lost.

Overt Transitions.   Often a transition needs to be obvious to carry the reader along our passage of thought, to make sure we don't lose him. Perhaps we are making an overt contrast. To draw attention to the contrast, we say, "on the one hand . . . on the other"—which is trite but hard to avoid. Or we use the context of our discussion: "Although most transitions are best left implicit, some are properly overt."

Often we need overt transitions when ideas or actions conflict, when the essay's meaning depends on keeping the terms of opposition clear. Or if we are piling detail upon detail, we might want to use a transition that calls attention to our multiplicity: "not only . . . but also." Prose that explains, reasons, or argues frequently uses overt transitions.

> Viewed from a suitable height, the aggregating clusters of medical scientists in the bright sunlight of the boardwalk at Atlantic City, swarmed there from everywhere for the annual meetings, have the look of assemblages of social insects. There is the same vibrating, ionic movement, interrupted by the darting back and forth of jerky individuals to touch antennae and exchange small bits of information; periodically, the mass casts out, like a trout-line, a long single file unerringly toward Childs's. If the boards were not fastened down, it would not be a surprise to see them put together a nest of sorts.
>
> It is permissible to say this sort of thing about humans. . . .
>
> Lewis Thomas, "On Societies as Organisms"

Here Lewis Thomas uses "this sort of thing," at the beginning of a new paragraph, as an overt transitional phrase referring to the comparison made in the preceding paragraph.

Repeated Words or Phrases.   One way to achieve continuity within a paragraph (or between paragraphs), to make transitions between sentences and between statements, is to repeat words or phrases. One of the simplest of these devices, so simple that we might not think of it as one, is repeating pronouns. We use it for both economy and continuity.

> Not too long ago *a male friend of mine* appeared on the scene fresh from a recent divorce. *He* had one child, who is, of course, with *his* ex-wife. *He* is looking for another wife. As I thought about *him* while

> I was ironing one evening, it suddenly occurred to me that I, too,
> would like to have a wife. *Why do I want a wife?* [Italics added]
>
> Judy Syfers, "I Want a Wife"

But you should be careful when using a repeated pronoun because if it is repeated too often, the prose can become monotonous and confusing. You can get variety and clarity by occasionally using the name the pronoun refers to. A writer also has to make sure that the reader knows what each pronoun refers to. If we say, "Mr. Cortazar saw that the man was following him closely; he stared at him," it is not clear who is doing the staring. Here we may need to be more explicit: "Mr. Cortazar saw that the man was following him closely; Mr. Cortazar stared at him."

If we want to avoid monotonous repetition, we can use variations (near synonyms) for the key words in some places.

> His *sculptures* seem like men and women stripped naked. They are
> *works of art* that seem to lack all artifice, *plastic creations,* which, in their
> emotional if not in their physical presence, have the feeling of natural,
> organic creations.

These methods are commonly used for transition *between* paragraphs as well.

> . . . and the importance of spatial form in *modern* literature.
> *Modern* thought, as well, has used the metaphor of dimensionality . . . .

Parallel Constructions.   We can repeat structures as well as words. Parallel constructions (see Parallelism, pages 153–155) can fulfill a need for transition that is not only structural and logical but also emotional; passages with parallel sentences can work like sentences with parallel phrases, to produce a dramatic effect or to maintain emotional tension.

> Today, now that he is no longer among us, *who can replace* my old
> friend at the gates of this kingdom? *Who will look after* the garden until
> we can get back to it? . . . [Italics added]
>
> Albert Camus, "Encounters with André Gide"

> *We describe* how the poor are plundered *by the rich.* We live *among the
> rich.* Live on the plunder and pander ideas *to the rich. We have described*
> the *torture* and we have put our names under appeals against *torture,* but
> we did not stop it. (And we ourselves became *torturers* when the higher
> interests demanded *torture* and we became the ideologists of *torture.*)
> Now *we once more can analyze* the world situation and *describe* the wars
> and explain why the many are poor and hungry. But we do no more.
> *We are not the bearers of consciousness. We are the whores of reason.* [Italics added]
>
> Jan Myrdal, *Confessions of a Disloyal European*

Parallel constructions that repeat part of a phrase are common and useful transitions, especially in exposition and in argument.

> . . . and they never decided whether they were *Bulgarians or Americans, rich or poor, artists or dilettantes.*
>
> And we, on our part, could not decide whether they were *heroes or frauds* . . . .

On our part, in the last sentence, is an overt transition, referring us to the *they* of the previous sentence.

Transitional Words and Phrases. We use many transitional phrases to establish the relationship between sentences and between paragraphs and to prepare the reader for shifts in subject or meaning. The most common are words like *and, but, or,* and *for.* Some are words of sequence and time— *meanwhile, afterward, before;* of qualification—*again, also, nonetheless;* and of reasoning—*for example, because, therefore.* Although we often try to avoid phrases like these in fiction or narrative, they are often essential to clarify a sequence of thought in exposition or argument. These paragraph openings use common phrases to accomplish transitions; they are taken from *The Naked Ape* by Desmond Morris:

> *Up to this point* I have been concentrating on the social aspects of comfort behaviour in our species . . . .
>
> *In addition* to problems of keeping clean, the general category of comfort behavior also includes . . .
>
> *Because* of his exploratory and opportunist nature, the naked ape's list of prey species is immense . . . .
>
> *For the next major category,* that of parasites . . .
>
> *In order* to find the answer to this question we must first assemble some facts . . . .

We commonly use comparison and contrast for transitions, especially in criticism and analysis. The means of transition are relatively simple. We describe one of the objects for examination in one paragraph and then, in a following paragraph, compare and contrast traits of the other. When we turn to the second object, we often begin with one of the transitional phrases that make for comparison or contrast, like *similarly, in the same vein,* or *however, on the other hand, in contrast, contrary to.*

> Freud, *on the one hand,* gave a picture of the unconscious mind as containing primarily memories and the remnants of suppressed desires. He saw the sexual drives as being the foundation of the unconscious.
>
> Jung, *on the other hand,* claimed that Freud's depth psychology wasn't deep enough, that there was another aspect of the unconscious which contained spiritual drives as important as the sexual drives. . . .

Remember that even in expository prose it is better to leave out well-worn phrases *if the sense is just as clear without them.* Many times, we can cut out the obvious direction signals and rely on implicit transition. Such cutting is often the work of later drafts.

Some of the most obvious clues to transition—within the paragraph or between paragraphs—are words of sequence, like *therefore, later, so, then,* and *next.* They are so obvious that it is pleasant to do without them, if we can.

Implicit Transitions. The order within the paragraph can itself be a means of transition. It gives the paragraph motion; it gives a reason for one sentence following another: left to right, down to up, smaller to larger; or other sorts of order: color to shape, spring to summer to fall to winter; or orders of ideas: from more obvious to less obvious, from less complex to more complex. These motions are clear enough in themselves to allow the movement from subject to subject without explicit directions. We need not say, "after spring came summer," within a paragraph; we can presume that people are aware of the order the seasons follow. We would be more likely to move from rain and early flowers to the longest day of the year, to hot sun and to swimming and to no school.

Sometimes the rest between paragraphs acts as a transition. We take a breath, and we pivot on the pause. It shows that we are moving from one grouping to another. We don't always have to be reminded that we are moving. Sometimes we do, and sometimes we do not. We must learn to develop *tact* for transitions, also a sense for the multiple means of transition. Good writers uses implicit, overt, parallel, repetitive, and many other forms of transition, and he uses them in rapid sequence as he moves through his paragraphs and from paragraph to paragraph. Transitions in complex expository writing are constant and multiple, overt and implicit. Much that is implied depends on orderly thinking and a clear sense of what the reader needs to know.

EXERCISES

1. These sentences have been taken from two orderly paragraphs and rearranged. Try to restore them to sequences that make sense.

a. When I found that Cervantes, in his fondness for reading, read "even the bits of torn paper in the street," I knew exactly what urge drove him to this scavenging.

b. Islam takes the notion even further: the Koran is not only one of the creations of God but one of His attributes, like His omnipresence, or His compassion.

c. Once I had learned to read my letters, I read everything: books, but also notices, advertisements, the small type on the back of tramway tickets, letters tossed into the garbage, the back covers of magazines held by other readers in the bus.

d. This worship of the book (or scroll, paper or screen) is one of the tenets of a literate society.

e. Books declare themselves through their titles, their authors, their places in a catalogue or on a bookshelf, the illustrations on their jackets; books also declare themselves through their size.

f. My hands, choosing a book to take to the bed or to the reading desk, for the train or for a gift, consider the form as much as the content.

g. I judge a book by its cover; I judge a book by its shape.

h. Depending on the occasion, depending on the place where I've chosen to read, I prefer something small and cozy or ample and substantial.

i. At different times and in different places I have come to expect certain books to look a certain way, and, as in all fashions, these changing features fix a precise quality onto a book's definition.

Alberto Manguel, *A History of Reading*

2. Following the example of exercise 1, find two paragraphs in sources of your own and alter the sequences. Gather into small groups in class and exchange sequences. Rearrange and discuss.

3. Decide which sentence functions as a topic sentence in each paragraph. Could it be moved to another place in the paragraph? What would be the effect?

a. Skill is the connection between life and tools, or life and machines. Once, skill was defined ultimately in qualitative terms: How *well* did a person work; how good, durable, and pleasing were his products? But as machines have grown larger and more complex, and as our awe of them and our desire for labor-saving have grown, we have tended more and more to define skill quantitatively: How speedily and cheaply can a person work? We have increasingly wanted a measurable skill. And the more quantifiable skills became, the easier they were to replace with machines. As machines replace skill, they disconnect themselves from life; they come between us and life. They begin to enact our ignorance of value—of essential sources, dependences, and relationships.

Wendell Berry, *The Unsettling of America*

b. Writing has always been a means of expression for me and for other black Americans who are just like me, who feel, too, the need for freedom in this "home of the brave, and land of the free." From the first, writing meant learning the craft and developing the art. Going to school had one major goal, to learn to be a writer. As early as my eighth year I had the desire, at ten I was trying, at eleven and twelve I was learning, and at fourteen and fifteen I was seeing my first things printed in local school and community papers. I have a copy of a poem pub-

lished in 1930 and an article with the caption, "What Is to Become of Us?" which appeared in 1931 or 1932. All of this happened before I went to Northwestern.

Margaret Walker, "On Being Female, Black, and Free"

4. Analyze these paragraphs for their unity. (a) Do any of these
paragraphs have extraneous material? (b) Does each paragraph contain a
topic sentence? Underline topic sentences, and discuss in class. (c) What
does the position of each topic sentence accomplish, if anything?

> a. The sea, autumn mildness, islands bathed in light, fine rain
> spreading a diaphanous veil over the immortal nakedness of
> Greece. Happy is the man, I thought, who, before dying, has
> the good fortune to sail the Aegean Sea.
>
> Many are the joys of this world—women, fruit, ideas. But to
> cleave that sea in the gentle, autumnal season, murmuring the
> name of each islet, is to my mind the joy most apt to transport
> the heart of man into paradise. Nowhere else can one pass so
> easily and serenely from reality to dream. The frontiers dwindle,
> and from the masts of the most ancient ships spring branches
> and fruits. It is as if here in Greece necessity is the mother of
> miracles.
>
> Towards noon the rain stopped. The sun parted the clouds
> and appeared gentle, tender, washed and fresh, and it caressed
> with its rays the beloved waters and lands. I stood at the prow
> and let myself be intoxicated with the miracle which was re-
> vealed as far as the eye could see.

Nikos Kazantzakis, *Zorba the Greek*

> b. A philosopher—is a human being who constantly experi-
> ences, sees, hears, suspects, hopes, and dreams extraordinary
> things; who is struck by his own thoughts as from outside, as
> from above and below, and by *his* type of experiences and light-
> ning bolts; who is perhaps himself a storm pregnant with new
> lightnings; a fatal human being around whom there are constant
> rumblings and growlings, crevices, and uncanny doings. A
> philosopher—alas, a being that often runs away from itself, of-
> ten is afraid of itself—but too inquisitive not to "come to"
> again—always back to himself.

Friedrich Nietzsche, *Beyond Good and Evil*

5. Consider the different sorts of incoherence in each of the following paragraphs. (a) Which paragraphs can profit by reorganization? In
class, reorganize them. (b) Which paragraphs need further development in
order to achieve coherence? In class, speculate on the directions development might take. (c) What reasonable readers' expectations do these paragraphs violate?

a. The heavy wooden door was painted red, but the wood showed through in many places where the paint was flaking off. Dandelions covered the lawn, but there were few weeds in the dark grass. A white and black cat lay curled by the door. Three huge oaks threw their shadows across the wide lawn. Far off, a deer was watching from the edge of the woods. There was no knob on the door.

b. The days were unusually hot and humid, even for that part of the state. Joe didn't want to go to the beach. His girlfriend, Linda, did. She wasn't a good swimmer. She loved to swim. Joe was working on his car. He was a fanatical sports enthusiast.

c. He had found that the wolves subsisted mainly on a diet of mice. Farley had been dropped in the middle of the Canadian tundra. He discovered that the hunters were lying, and that they themselves were the insane murderers. Hunters had been complaining that the wolves were slaughtering thousands of caribou for the sheer pleasure of killing. He had made an astonishing discovery. He had been assigned to investigate the killing of caribou by timber wolves.

d. Robert and Daniel crouched in the cave, listening for the sound of approaching footsteps. He thought the troops must have left the area by now. For the moment he was reassured by the silence, but he worried about the sharp pain in his knee, and he wondered if he would be able to walk on it if he had to. He was glad to have his old friend with him. He looked at him. Their gazes meeting, he felt tears come to his eyes from straining to see in the half-darkness, and from thinking where he and his friend had been just yesterday.

e. When the gate opens at last, four thousand music lovers push, crush, and shove each other forward in an immense mass. The sun glares down, the musicians struggle to tune their sweaty instruments, and the ice-cream salesman exhausts his stores in twenty minutes. Finally the music started at 1:30.

6. In the following passage, study the transitions—from sentence to sentence and from paragraph to paragraph. Write brief comments remarking on links as you find them. Try removing a few sentences or a paragraph and describe how coherence is violated.

Merely as an observer of natural phenomena, I am fascinated by my own personal appearance. This does not mean that I am *pleased* with it, mind you, or that I can even tolerate it. I simply have a morbid interest in it.

Each day I look like someone, or some*thing*, different. I never know what it is going to be until I steal a look in the glass. (Oh, I don't suppose you really could call it stealing. It belongs to me, after all.)

One day I look like Wimpy, the hamburger fancier in the Popeye the Sailor saga. Another day it may be Wallace Beery. And a third day, if I have let my mustache get out of hand, it is Bairnsfather's Old Bill. And not until I peek do I know what the show is going to be.

Some mornings, if I look in the mirror soon enough after getting out of bed, there is no resemblance to any character at all, either in or out of fiction, and I turn quickly to look behind me, convinced that a stranger has spent the night with me and is peering over my shoulder in a sinister fashion, merely to frighten me. On such occasions, the shock of finding that I am actually possessor of the face in the mirror is sufficient to send me scurrying back to bed, completely unnerved.

All this is, of course, very depressing, and I often give off a low moan at the sight of the new day's metamorphosis, but I can't seem to resist the temptation to learn the worst. I even go out of my way to look at myself in store-window mirrors, just to see how long it will take me to recognize myself. If I happen to have on a new hat, or am walking with a limp, I sometimes pass right by my reflection without even nodding. Then I begin to think: "You must have given off *some* visual impression into that mirror. You're not a disembodied spirit yet—I hope."

And I go back and look again, and, sure enough, the strange-looking man I thought was walking just ahead of me in the reflection turns out to have been my own image all the time. It makes a fellow stop and think, I can tell you.

Robert Benchley, "My Face"

7. In this passage, underline the topic sentence of the first paragraph. (a) How does the paragraph grow from this sentence? (b) Is every other sentence in this paragraph related to the topic sentence? (c) How do the sentences proceed? Underline transitions. (d) Do you find implicit transitions in this paragraph, and later between paragraphs? Find the basis for each implicit transition.

We may have a lot to learn from watching movies, but we're very good at seeing through them. People know how to jeer at the old-fashioned propaganda turned out by Hollywood for nearly half a century, from D. W. Griffith's (racist) *Birth of a Nation* in 1915 to Doris Day's (sexist) comedies of the early 1960s. "It is, generally, a bad time for illusions," writes Mickey Rooney, brooding over the disappearance of "nice clean movies" and "the illusion of the great star." Most would agree, but not mournfully. Having had our consciousness raised over the past fifteen years, we are proud enough of our awakening to shrug off all our naive dreams.

For example, it is now doubted that a lot of wishing and a little struggling invariably pay off. (The success of *Rocky* is only a fluke.) According to the old movies, success always comes to the peppy and the resolute. Those kids in the chorus get that bilious entrepreneur to lighten up and tap his feet, and so it's on to Broadway! That earnest lawyer-fella touches the hearts of decent folks all over, and so it's on to the White House! While artists usually succumb to the agonies of Genius, inventors, athletes, scientists, and businessmen, people with a Great Gift or a Great Idea, end up quickly vindicated and beloved, looking benevolent in powdered hair.

At the same time, many movies dramatized the sorrows of the wealthy, as if to assure us that we were better off as we were—with the sun in the morning and the moon at night and a diet of Spam. Throughout the Depression, the movies implied that money was poison, that only regular folks knew how to have fun, that the rich and their lackeys seemed faintly European, or worse. And in later films like *Caught, Humoresque, Young Man with a Horn,* and *A Place in the Sun,* among others, a humble person's romance with someone wealthier leads straight to disaster. Although the travails of the rich continue to provide Americans with a vindictive thrill, class conflict is no longer part of the story. When we see a bunch of stuffed shirts vexed by some happy-go-lucky man of the people, we sense that the moment is old-fashioned, as in *Heaven Can Wait* (based on *Here Comes Mr. Jordan,* 1941) or *Hair* (which alludes heavily to *Hallelujah I'm a Bum,* 1933). . . .

From the 1940s through the early 1960s, the movies taught that women who worked in office buildings were always sad. Whether boss or secretary, the working woman continually fought the melancholy of life without a man. The secretary was a little better off, since she at least could serve the guy of her dreams, concealing her adoration under brisk efficiency. The female executive was far more wretched. She had to strain to seem commanding, like an adolescent knowing that his voice might crack at any moment. Her employees were always handsome men, strolling into her office, leaning on her desk, every suave phrase really meaning: "How about it?" After fighting these assaults for a while with clipped retorts and starchy looks, she would finally give in, loosen her collar, let down her hair, and murmur, "Darling!" in the arms of her rightful master.

Mark Crispin Miller, *Boxed In: The Culture of TV*

DEVELOPMENT IN THE PARAGRAPH

Once we pass beyond the single sentence, we become involved in development and its problems. As we must develop paragraphs to substantiate generalizations, so too we must develop paragraphs to make our associations clear to the reader. Frequently, we lack fullness of development because we do not take the reader into account. We put forward a generalization, perhaps, and a conclusion that we have arrived at, but we do not lead the reader through the thinking that proceeds from introduction to conclusion. Perhaps in our own thinking we have leapt from generalization to conclusion by intuition—but the reader will not necessarily leap along with us.

Eventually, as we go over development, we will need to investigate length and order. But first, we must look at methods for developing paragraphs.

Some Ways of Developing Paragraphs

We can develop a paragraph in countless ways. No list can be comprehensive. But looking at some methods of paragraph development can help us to see the range of possibilities. The type of development we choose—the *how* in the paragraph—depends on the material we are using—the *what* in the paragraph—and the purpose we have in mind—the *why* of the paragraph. If we are listing Paraguay's annual imports, we develop by listing and not by comparison and contrast. *The container takes its shape from what it contains.* One of our tasks in organizing a paper is to find the means of development that is *most appropriate to our material.*

Earlier in the chapter we spoke of improvised shape, like generalization followed by qualification followed by example, or question and answer (objection and rebuttal). We have also mentioned chronology and spatial sequence as useful ways of organizing paragraphs (see also pages 208–210). We need to consider a few more. On occasion the reader must learn *what* something is; the writer must develop a paragraph by means of *definition.* Sometimes a reader needs to know what something is *like* or *not like;* the writer must develop a paragraph of *comparison* or *comparison and contrast.* Sometimes the reader needs to know the *parts* of a thing, what makes it up; the writer must supply *analysis.* Or the writer must use *classification;* he must name the species of something, perhaps; is it animal or vegetable? Sometimes writers develop our notion of a thing by discussing its *cause* and its *effect.*

These different ways of approaching and organizing a subject are called rhetorical patterns. They can serve as models for whole essays, but more commonly they provide the shapes for whole paragraphs; they are like blueprints for the basic ways in which thought moves. They suggest various means of development. When we find an unsupported generalization, we discover an opportunity for development, making use of the rhetorical pattern of example. But all processes of writing can help paragraph development. When we revise we should be alert for the journalist's six questions—who, what, when, where, why, and how—and for opportunities to reach our audience by explaining, which is after all the function of exposition.

We may organize a paragraph to *define* or *elucidate:*

> An addict does not merely pursue a pleasurable experience and need
> to experience it in order to function normally. He needs to *repeat* it

again and again. Something about that particular experience makes life without it less than complete. Other potentially pleasurable experiences are no longer possible, for under the spell of the addictive experiences, his life is peculiarly distorted. The addict craves an experience and yet he is never really satisfied. The organism may be temporarily sated, but soon it begins to crave again.

Marie Winn, "Television Addiction"

The paragraph begins in the negative, dispelling a common assumption, and defines by isolating distinctive features.

Or we can develop paragraphs to *compare* and *contrast:*

In other respects, the film follows Hearst's career with mixed fidelity. The plot adjustments are significant. Both Hearst and Kane were only children, born in 1863, and both were expelled from Harvard. Hearst's father and mother were not, like Kane's, poverty-stricken boardinghouse keepers. George Hearst was a well-to-do farmer's son, whose silver strike at the Comstock lode made him a millionaire, and whose later interest in the Homestake Mine still further increased his massive fortune; he became a senator and earned a respected place in the *American Dictionary of Biography*. In the film these parents are left a deed to the Colorado Lode by a defaulting boarder, Fred Grange, and the Kane fortune is thus founded not by the acumen and push of a paternal figure but by blind chance.

Charles Higham, *The Films of Orson Welles*

Comparison and contrast works when we talk about a relationship or conflict and are not merely separating facts about two or more subjects. Here, the first sentence states the mixture that is the paragraph's topic, and the rest of the paragraph gives examples of each ingredient in the mixture. Notice that the paragraph, when it compares and contrasts Hearst's life with Kane's, carefully maintains the order in which it first mentions them: Hearst-Kane. This order helps to avoid confusion, and makes for coherence.

We can also build paragraphs that *analyze:*

The "me decade" did not result from a sudden effusion of selfishness or decadence; it is the logical consequence of a public surface tolerance combined with a loss of individual historical depth. In a sense, people become more like one another (wear the same clothes, go to the same schools, read the same books, are informed by the same media, go to the same parties, are "liberated" into the same mores). In another sense, they lose the social inheritances that, while differentiating them from one another, also instilled in them profound common values. Inwardly, each is animated by nothing more profound than personal preference and idiosyncrasy. Homogenized yet fragmented, the society of the supreme "me" (find yourself, be true to yourself) is the logical expression of a materialistic humanism.

Michael Novak, "On God and Man"

We analyze when we need to explain or to demonstrate the mechanism of a process or an act. We tell how it works rather than what it is. Novak points out possible reasons for the modern cult of the self, and then argues step by step to show the larger causes that underlie the reasons.

We can also develop paragraphs to *classify:*

> We can thus say that while the average human being is a mixture, some people are mainly "digestion-minded," some "muscle-minded," and some "brain-minded," and correspondingly digestion-bodied, muscle-bodied, or brain-bodied. The digestion-bodied people look thick; the muscle-bodied people look wide; and the brain-bodied people look long. This does not mean the taller a man is the brainier he will be. It means that if a man, even a short man, looks long rather than wide or thick, he will often be more concerned about what goes on in his mind that about what he does or what he eats; but the key factor is slenderness and not height. On the other hand, a man who gives the impression of being thick rather than long or wide will usually be more interested in a good steak than in a good idea or a good long walk.
>
> Eric Berne, "Can People Be Judged by Their Appearance?"
> *(A Layman's Guide to Psychiatry and Psychoanalysis)*

Berne separates people into groups according to their bodily appearance, relating psychological classifications to physical ones.

This paragraph, from an essay about television advertising, is developed to show *cause and effect:*

> There is good reason to suspect that this manic obsession with cleanliness, fostered, quite naturally, by the giant soap and detergent interests, may bear some responsibility for the cultivated sloppiness of so many of the young in their clothing as well as in their chosen hideouts. The compulsive housewife who spends more time washing and vacuuming and polishing her possessions than communicating to, or stimulating her children creates a kind of sterility that the young would instinctively reject. The impeccably tidy home, the impeccably tidy lawn are—in a very real sense—unnatural and confining. Yet the commercials confront us with broods of happy children, some of whom—believe it or not—notice the new fresh smell their clean, white sweatshirts exhale thanks to Mom's new "softener."
>
> Marya Mannes, "Television Advertising: The Splitting Image"

In her argument, the writer observes negative results of advertising, where an image of cleanliness leads to a slovenly reality. The process resembles that of *analysis,* which also seeks after causes.

We may organize a paragraph to *make an assertion and give reasons:*

> The country is vastly indebted to him [Louis Brandeis] for his creative work in the field of labor relations, in dispelling misunderstanding between management and labor, and in making collective bargaining an

effective instrument for industrial peace. He successfully arbitrated or conciliated many labor disputes. In 1910 he was arbiter of a serious strike in the New York City garment trade. Not content with settling the immediate dispute, he devised the famous "protocol" for the permanent government of labor relations in the industry, with provision for the preferential union shop, for a Joint Board of Sanitary Control, and for a continuing Board of Arbitration composed of representatives of the public as well as of the employers and the union. The procedures thus developed and successfully tested served as a model in other industries. For several years he served as impartial chairman of this board of arbitration.

Irwin H. Pollock, *The Brandeis Reader*

The writer begins with a contention and then substantiates it by reciting information on which he bases it.

We can *make a statement and then give relevant facts:*

Gandhi recognized that the whites in South Africa thought they needed protection against a majority consisting of Negroes and Indians. The province of Natal, in 1896, had 400,000 Negro inhabitants, 51,000 Indians, and 50,000 whites. The Cape of Good Hope Colony had 900,000 Negroes, 10,000 Indians, and 400,000 Europeans; the Transvaal Republic 650,000 Negroes, 5,000 Indians, and 120,000 whites. In 1944, the five million Negroes hopelessly outnumbered the million and a quarter whites.

Louis Fischer, *Gandhi: His Life and Message for the World*

This last category resembles the one before it, except that *facts* (or statistics) take the place of *reasons,* which are arguments based on a value put on events.

Or we can *list:*

Now the leadership elements of the Democratic Party began to filter through the suite of the nominee in a parade that was to last the rest of the day, to assist him in making up their mind. First of the big-city leaders to arrive was David Lawrence of Pennsylvania. Following him came the New York crowd—Wagner, Harriman, DeSapio and Prendergast; then William Green of Philadelphia; then DiSalle of Ohio; then Bailey and Ribicoff of Connecticut; then all the others.

Theodore H. White, *The Making of the President 1960*

First, White tells us what sort of men they are whose names will follow, then the occasion that brought the men together, and then the names.

Even in the examples chosen, these methods are not exclusive. One paragraph may use more than one method, or one method may involve another. "Relevant facts" usually come in "lists." In the next paragraph, the author develops the idea primarily by an assertion followed by reasons, and his final sentence is a list.

If conventions epitomize the mythology and legendry of American national politics, then Chicago epitomizes the convention city. For one hundred years, ever since the nomination of Abraham Lincoln at the Wigwam, it has been the favorite city of political convention-goers. Counting notches for fourteen Republican and nine Democratic national conventions in the last twenty-five quadrennials, Chicago can boast that here were first named all the following Presidents of the United States: Lincoln, Grant, Garfield, Cleveland, Harrison, Theodore Roosevelt, Harding, Coolidge, Franklin D. Roosevelt, Truman and Eisenhower.

> Theodore H. White, *The Making of the President 1960*

A writer can make clear by *elaboration or rephrasing:*

The "duende," then, is a power and not a construct, is a struggle and not a concept. I have heard an old guitarist, a true virtuoso, remark, "The 'duende' is not in the throat, the 'duende' comes from inside up, up from the very soles of the feet." That is to say, it is not a question of aptitude, but of a true and viable style—of blood, in other words; of what is oldest in culture; of creation made act.

> Federico García Lorca, "The Duende: Theory and Divertissement"

Here, because the word names something more spiritual than intellectual—something harder to define than a concept—the author does not try so much to define and to elucidate as to name and rename, to offer description and metaphor, until we begin to comprehend the intangible.

Notice that the progress within these quoted paragraphs is the motion of thought. The exact detail, the example that locates the general in the particular, the comparison, the logical steps—these motions develop the thought and unify the paragraph at the same time. Paragraph development makes coherence.

Development: Length and Completeness

Paragraphs will vary in length, following no set rule. The length must be *adequate;* we must take the time and space to flesh out arguments, to justify contentions, to explain theories, or to describe characters. We discussed this need for completeness in Coherence in the Paragraph, but we must repeat it here. The writer must never forget that the reader is another person, who must be given reasons if he is to be persuaded of our opinions and must be given details if he is going to see what we see. We must not simply assert, "President Smith is the worst, most dishonest president we've had," and then propose to limit his power. We must tell *why* he is so bad. We must supply reasons, facts, arguments, details *adequate* to the assertion. We must develop the paragraph to make our assertion coherent.

Undeveloped paragraphs bedevil beginning writers. Many times paragraphs remain undeveloped because the writer does not adequately imagine the reader. Here is a paragraph from a student paper.

> When you study dance, you learn either modern or classical ballet.
> Some people prefer one kind of dance and some another. I learned
> modern dance and I prefer it.

The writer continued the paper by describing the pleasures of modern
dance. But her opening paragraph is undeveloped and lacks a sense of audience because it begs either for definition or for comparison and contrast.
One or two sentences of development, giving the reader an insight into the
difference between forms of dance, would establish the necessary background for the discussion of modern dance.

Less frequently, writers are afflicted with too much disorganized detail, so that the writing loses force. Another student wrote this in a paper:

> I bought my first car with money I earned working for a summer in a
> tuna canning factory. I was anxious to keep it running in top condi-
> tion. It was a 1973 VW bug, with a good engine (from a 1975 VW
> van) and a pretty good body, with just a little rust below the doors.
> My friend repainted it for me, bright red, and we rebuilt the engine
> and almost set the garage on fire. The upholstery is in terrible shape. I
> change the oil and the oil filter every 1,500 miles and the car gets
> about 25 miles per gallon, but the windshield wipers don't always
> work, and the insurance costs a lot.

We must keep in mind what is important and what is not. We must give
reasons, but only so many as we need to make our point. With too many
reasons the reader will be confused, be bored, or feel bullied.

To decide whether our detail is adequate—neither too little nor too
much—we must develop judgment and tact; we must look at what we have
written not only as writers but also from the point of view of readers.

Because adequacy always depends on context, it is useless to lay down
rules for paragraph length. Different kinds of writing, however, usually
need paragraphs of different lengths. Generally the more formal the writing, the more lengthy the paragraphing. In narrative and fiction, we use
paragraphs with more varied lengths, and in informal writing our paragraphs shorten. Newspaper writing breaks up the solid column of print by
making a paragraph out of every sentence or two.

In exposition, or in research writing, we may move from topic to
topic by long paragraphs that introduce a subject, elaborate it, enumerate it,
explain it, or conclude it. We may frequently write paragraphs as long as a
typewritten page. But if the paragraphs get much longer, we should cut
them down. We can always find a place where we can make a break that is
not wholly arbitrary and give the reader a rest. One argument might make
a six-page paragraph, but it would be tiring to read. If we were to look
back at it, we could find the steps in the argument. We could break between one step and another, even though the pause in reasoning is small. In
a long description, we can break between one part of the subject and another. Talking of a barn, we can break between remarks about the colors

things have, about the shapes they take, and about the uses they are put to. Suppose we want to write equally about ten houses in a block we grew up on. Ten tiny paragraphs would be too choppy; one paragraph would occupy two pages of solid print. Here, we can subdivide our houses by talking about one side of the block and then the other or by making a division for three architectural styles or different shades of paint or lengths of time houses were occupied by the same tenants.

Some paragraphs must be short. When we write dialogue, we show a change of speaker by indenting a new paragraph.

> "Did you go downtown after lunch?" He was tapping the arm of his chair with his index finger. Behind his glasses his eyes wandered.
> "Yes," she said. "I suppose I did."
> "Why?"

But such paragraphing is mechanical. In descriptive or expository or narrative writing—usual ingredients in essay or autobiography and frequently in story—short paragraphs feel choppy, a rash of blurts, like someone who talks in the manner of a machine gun. When we move from dialogue to description or narration, we should provide a change of pace by keeping the paragraphs relatively long. The long paragraph is a rest, a relief after several short ones: here is a bed big enough to lie down on. We do not want

> The room was large, the chairs comfortable. He sat down on the overstuffed sofa.
> All around him the ticking of clocks wove a mesh of sound. There was dust on the windowpane, and the rugs were shabby.
> Dark pictures hung on the walls, and the woodwork was dark.

It is too much like standing up and sitting down all the time. We want to relax and read the description straight.

> The room was large, the chairs comfortable. He sat down on the overstuffed sofa. All around him the ticking of clocks wove a mesh of sound. There was dust on the windowpane, and the rugs were shabby. Dark pictures hung on the walls, and the woodwork was dark.

Such a paragraph might continue for another five or six lines.

It is tempting to be dogmatic: "Outside of dialogue, keep your paragraphs between 200 and 250 words." Life would be more comfortable, and writing easier, if simple prescriptions solved our problems. Although a highly formal essay might follow some such rule, most good modern writing has much more variety to it. As it is hard to type the best contemporary stylists as formal or informal, so it is hard to put limits on paragraph size. Although formal writing leads toward a more uniform length of paragraph, it can use something as short as a one-line paragraph. A skillful writer may make a long statement in periodic sentences, a 350-word paragraph that concludes with a flourish, and follow it by a paragraph that reads, in its entirety,

On the other hand, maybe this reasoning is haphazard.

The writer may then write another long paragraph. The one-liner has been a change of pace—at the same time restful, offhand, and refreshing: it keeps readers on their toes.

On the other hand, look at these paragraphs of description, more nearly equal in length:

> The river widens; islands appear; but there is no solitude in this heart of Africa. Always there are the little brown settlements in scraped brown yards, the little plantings of maize or banana or sugar cane about huts, the trading dugouts arriving beside the steamer to shouts. In the heat mist the sun, an hour before sunset, can appear round and orange, reflected in an orange band in the water muddy with laterite, the orange reflection broken only by the ripples from the bows of the steamer and the barges. Sometimes at sunset the water will turn violet below a violet sky.
>
> But it is a peopled wilderness. The land of this river basin is land used in the African way. It is burned, cultivated, abandoned. It looks desolate, but its riches and fruits are known; it is a wilderness, but one of monkeys. Bush and blasted trees disappear only toward Kinshasa. It is only after nine hundred miles that earth and laterite give way to igneous rocks, and the land, becoming hilly, with sharp indentations, grows smooth and bare, dark with vegetation only in its hollows.
>
> Plant today, reap tomorrow: this is what they say in Kisangani. But this vast green land, which can feed the continent, barely feeds itself. In Kinshasa the meat and even the vegetables have to be imported from other countries. Eggs and orange juice come from South Africa, in spite of hot official words; and powdered milk and bottled milk come from Europe. The bush is a way of life; and where the bush is so overwhelming, organized agriculture is an illogicality.

> V. S. Naipaul, *The Return of Eva Perón*

These even, full, adequate paragraphs march in rank and in good order, helping to convince us—even by their shape itself—that they are calm, logical steps in a progressive statement of thought or opinion. At the same time, the writer creates tension within the paragraphs by setting up contrasts—river and shore, vegetation and cultivation, native agriculture and imported culture.

The variety and unity of the paragraph resemble the variety and unity of the sentence. The effective contrast, when the one-line paragraph follows the complex one, resembles the pleasure we take in a short, simple sentence after a long, complex sentence. A writer can mix a pleasing variety of sentences and paragraphs without violating the unity that holds the essay together.

Development: Order and Clarity

If we do not want to irritate or confuse our readers, our information or argument must be orderly. Things must follow one another with a sense of purpose. Purpose makes clarity. We cannot say, "Oh, I forgot to say . . ." or leave out steps in our progress. We must move in an orderly way, from earlier to later, from less to more important, from periphery to center, from smaller to larger, or from larger to smaller. Sometimes we will want to move from center to periphery, from present to past. But we must not scatter our sequence—from larger to smaller to larger to larger to smaller to largest to larger to smallest to large. We may want A B C D E F. On occasion we may want Z Y X W V, but never A Q I X L D.

The order in the following paragraph is fine; we move from generality in the topic sentence to particulars that describe and substantiate it.

> Winter is a catastrophe. Life on skid row is lived out of doors, and the cold and the snow bring with them intense suffering. The men often get drunk enough to lie in the streets in the midst of a storm. The first time one sees a body covered with a light blanket of snow, stretched out on the sidewalk, the sight comes as a shock and a dilemma. Is the man dead or just drunk? Or worse, the habitués are so obsessed and driven that stealing goes on in the dead of winter, and a man who needs a drink will take the shoes of a fellow alcoholic in the middle of January.
>
> Michael Harrington, *The Other America: Poverty in the United States*

The following paragraph, organized in a different way, moving from pieces of information to a general conclusion, is also well constructed.

> Last January as he was about to leave office, Lyndon Johnson sent his last report on the economic prospect to the Congress. It was assumed that, in one way or another, the Vietnam War, by which he and his Administration had been destroyed, would come gradually to an end. The question considered by his economists was whether this would bring an increase or a decrease in military spending. The military budget for fiscal 1969 was 78.4 billions; for the year following, including pay increases, it was scheduled to be about three billions higher. Thereafter, assuming peace and a general withdrawal from Asia, there would be a reduction of some six or seven billions. But this was only on the assumption that the Pentagon did not get any major new weapons—that it was content with what had already been authorized. No one really thought this possible. The President's economists noted that plans already existed for "a package" consisting of new aircraft, modern naval vessels, defense installations, and "advanced strategic and general purpose weapons systems" which would cost many billions. This would wipe out any savings from getting out of Vietnam. Peace would now be far more expensive than war.
>
> John Kenneth Galbraith, *How to Control the Military*

The organization in this paragraph, however, is not satisfactory:

> The birds often flock in huge numbers on trees, sometimes breaking limbs off. They may bury a car parked below them in white dung.

> Starlings can be a terrible nuisance. The dark purplish-black pests may tear up a whole lawn in the process of searching for worms and insects, particularly as winter approaches and live food gets scarce. Their antics can drive a homeowner out of *his* tree. In large enough numbers, they can create a din of voices that blocks out all other sounds in the area. Their cries are strident and irritating.

Here the order is unclear. In this paragraph we move from specific to specific to general to specific to general to specific to specific, without meaningful progression. It would make much better organizational sense to begin, "Starlings can be a terrible nuisance," and to end, "Their antics can drive a homeowner out of *his* tree."

In writing a paragraph we usually have to settle on some controlling principle of order or sequence and then keep to it.

Development: Order and Forcefulness

Clarity is not our only consideration when we organize paragraphs; we must also organize for appropriateness and forceful effect. Look again at the paragraphs by Hardwick (page 187) and Mencken (page 188), keeping in mind the discussion of topic sentences. Look at the order in the paragraphs compared with the effects achieved. By their positions the topic sentences give *force* to these paragraphs.

Or take the method that lets us order according to spatial proximity. It can be more than a means to clarity; it can direct the reader's attention significantly and achieve dramatic effect. Here is a passage from *Gandhi* by Louis Fischer.

> At Rajghat, a few hundred feet from the river, a fresh pyre had been built of stone, brick, and earth. It was eight feet square and about two feet high. Long, thin, sandalwood logs sprinkled with incense were stacked on it. Mahatma Gandhi's body lay on the pyre with his head to the north. In that position Buddha met his end.

Notice how the paragraph moves gradually closer to its subject, like a camera that dollies in for a close-up in a film. We start from far back and gradually zoom in. If the author had described the body of Gandhi first, and then its surroundings, the passage would be less forceful. Again, it is the principle of the periodic sentence applied to the paragraph.

When we consider how we organize our paragraphs, we must always consider our *purpose* in writing. In expository writing, we want to be sure that the reader knows what we are doing at all times. We therefore want to avoid listing statistics before telling what they demonstrate. Imagine the other paragraph quoted about Gandhi with the first sentence placed at the end.

> The province of Natal, in 1896, had 400,000 Negro inhabitants, 51,000 Indians, and 50,000 whites. The Cape of Good Hope Colony had 900,000 Negroes, 10,000 Indians, and 400,000 Europeans; the

> Transvaal Republic 650,000 Negroes, 5,000 Indians, and 120,000 whites. In 1914, the five million Negroes hopelessly outnumbered the million and a quarter whites. Gandhi recognized that the whites in South Africa thought they needed protection against a majority consisting of Negroes and Indians.

The revised order makes the paragraph confusing and pointless. The reader does not know what is going on until he finishes reading the paragraph.

And yet if our purpose in writing is to create an ominous or tense atmosphere—in narrative, perhaps, either fictional or autobiographical—we might want to list unexplained details first, waiting for the end of the paragraph to offer an interpretation. This suspenseful order would give our paragraph *force*.

> The forest, all at once, had grown silent. The monkeys had stopped their chattering, and the birds darted their heads apprehensively. The wind in the trees became audible, and then, faintly, the sound of drumming rose from the village enclosure. It could only mean that Godzilla had awakened once more.

Imagine how anticlimactic it would be in a film to show the monster suddenly appearing and then to pan around the trees. It would not make emotional or dramatic sense.

THE ORDER OF PARAGRAPHS

Ideally, the developed paragraph represents a neatly balanced unity of thought or feeling and form. The content makes the paragraph, and paragraphs become ways of organizing the subject's complexity (for writer and reader) into comprehensible units. One significant breakthrough in the writing of an essay comes when we see how the various parts fit together, and which element best combines with which. From small bits and linkages we assemble larger structural shapes; these in turn are joined to make the focused whole. Between the detail and the overview comes the paragraph. The paragraph gathers detail into narrative shape; it directs the reader's attention; it narrows the focus. Consider these notes for an autobiographical essay:

> going to Cape Cod with my family
> packing, driving
> traffic jams at the bridge, dad getting tense
> first view of water
> arriving
> boogie boarding, collecting shells, biking
> went again recently—almost ten years later
> changes: more crowded, cluttered, expensive
> went back to old store, saw postcards from old times
> sudden memories: how we fished for stripers, cookouts on the beach

now places have laws, restrictions
still, people seem to be relaxing and having fun
the overall spirit is probably the same

Before we order the whole essay, we need to make links among some of these units in an informal outline. If we have the notes on file cards—some writers swear by this method—we have only to set them out in sequence. If we list things in a column, as above, we may wish to use letters and numbers, connecting like to like. But how we arrange the items will depend on the shape we imagine for the piece. One possibility might be to stick with a strict chronology, moving the memories of fishing and cookouts up, using them not as memories but straight narrative elements. The essay could then end with the writer looking at old postcards and reflecting that in spite of the changes, the spirit of summer remains a constant.

But maybe this feels too linear, too predictable. Another essay might use this same material to emphasize the workings of memory. A natural beginning would have the writer visiting the Cape in the present, seeing old postcards, and then flashing back to recollections from childhood days. No doubt there are other ways to organize the same basic elements. The point is that the writer needs to decide what feeling, or effect, she desires to create in her reader, and to work from there. Does she want to have the reader think more about change, or the continuity that overrides change, or the strange way that time burnishes what once may have seemed commonplace experiences? (See exercise 1 at the end of this section.)

Many a beginning writer, or a writer who has not learned to paragraph, might write the essay following the order in which her notes originally appeared. The result would be chaos, moving back and forth in time by random association. That is the way people talk, thinking of points afterward and crying, "Oh, I forgot to say . . . !" But writing is harder and requires organization. The paragraph is our middle unit of organization between sentences that incorporate raw data and the finished, shapely essay. In developing explanation or narration, the pause lets the reader know that a limited subject has been dealt with and that we now move to another topic—perhaps arising from the last one, perhaps in contrast to it, certainly different. The paragraph becomes a unit of meaning. The look of it on the page makes a statement; it tells us that a topic, or a detachable unit of an argument, or that an event, or a detachable unit of an event, is complete here. Like commas and sentence structure, paragraphs create meaning in our prose.

To make statements with paragraphs, we must be able to construct good ones. The paragraph must have *unity,* and unity often requires a *topic sentence.* The paragraph must have *coherence* within itself, and a series of paragraphs must cohere to form the essay; coherence requires *transitions.* Finally, we must learn to *develop* the paragraph until it is adequate in its fullness and in its *length* and until it presents its material in the best possible *order.*

Make sure that your paragraphing is useful, to the mind that understands and to the eye that reads. Consider your paragraphs for their unity and variety, their coherence and adequacy of development, and their clarity and effective ordering. Consider their internal organization and their transitions, both internal and between paragraphs, both overt and implicit.

In late drafts of a paper, think of what your paragraphing communicates to a reader. Do your paragraphs give the right signal? Read as if you were someone else, and decide if your paragraph can be improved for clarity's sake—in shape, in wholeness, in development, in transition, in order.

REVISING PARAGRAPHS

When his teacher assigned an informal topical essay, Mark Matson decided to write about his recent visit to the town where he had grown up. This is his first version.

> I got the shock of my life when I went back to visit my old home town. I had heard about the new factory and how it had made a big impact, but I didn't realize what that could mean. Riding in on the train gave me my first clues about what to expect. But it was when I strolled around looking at familiar places that I found some of my worst fears about life coming true.
>
> I read a lot of newspapers. I know about the destruction of the ozone layer and the effects of acid rain and problems with crowding in the cities, but mostly I think of these as affecting other people. When I get depressed by the news, I find myself thinking about Garwood, the perfect small town. At least I used to.
>
> I had so many memories of the place. I remembered big trees, nice houses and lawns, friendly people, and a quiet, relaxed feel in the air.
>
> But riding in on the train made me think about those newspaper stories about crowding, smog, and so on. I looked out the window and saw new subdivisions and malls where there used to be open fields. And there were cars everywhere. I remember when it was so quiet that you could play ball in the street.
>
> As I walked away from the station I started to get depressed. I realized that nothing stands still. Here was a place that I had kept frozen in my heart. I really expected that it would look the same. Now I had to face the truth.
>
> The streets were crowded. There were new stores everywhere; everything was glass and metal. The traffic downtown was terrible, with horns honking. The smell of car exhaust was overpowering. The worst thing was the river. I walked over the bridge, and when I looked down I saw that the water was brown and covered with a kind of foam. I remembered when it was blue and clean. We used to swim there.
>
> Whose fault was it? Well, there is never any easy way to point the finger. But in this case we ought to take a good hard look at the price of progress. Building the Aerodyne factory in Garwood is progress. It has brought new people and a great deal of money to the area. The price is the loss of a way of life and the arrival of all sorts of modern ills, like pollution and crowding. I am sorry I visited. It would have

been nicer to keep certain images the way they were. When I think of Garwood now I have the feeling that something has been stolen from me.

Mark's teacher was not happy with this first version. He noted in his comment that the subject was promising, as was Mark's way of weaving observations and reactions together with the narrative of his arrival. "But," he wrote, "you are not getting the best use from your arrangement." After cautioning Mark about a number of problems and rough spots—tired expressions like "shock of my life," and too many abrupt short sentences in paragraphs five and six—he addressed himself to the core weakness: structure and paragraphing.

"Take this apart," the teacher suggested, "and look at the different pieces. Try to decide which perceptions are the most important. Is there some way that you can strengthen both the continuity and the sense of contrast between memory and reality? Why not mention Aerodyne earlier—by name—and let the reader get some idea of the culprit? Think about our class discussions on paragraphing. *Comparison and contrast* will obviously be useful. How about *analysis* or *cause and effect?* Maybe you can clarify the link between the new plant and the changes you saw in the town. Some more use of *assertion* might organize your final paragraph better. Overall, stay with a logical sequence (for example: expectation, arrival, shock, and reaction) and try to keep your own movements consecutive (on the train, at the station, walking into town, crossing the river) so that we can follow."

Mark broke his essay into small chunks. He underlined the parts that he thought were more important and looked to see if they were connected in some logical way. He circled every sentence that was about a memory and thought about ways to bring the recollections together. Then Mark wrote out the different kinds of paragraph organization on a separate sheet. He looked from the sheet to his essay, back and forth, and considered how to tighten individual paragraphs. He also paid close attention to beginnings and endings of paragraphs; he penciled in ideas for stronger connections. After making many such notes, and after two frustrating false starts, Mark came up with what he felt was a much more unified essay.

> I read the newspaper every day, not because I want to, but because I think that we have to be informed about what is happening in the world. The news is never good. A typical front page will have reports on pollution, corrupt officials, drugs and murders, and ongoing wars in the Middle East.
>
> When I put the paper aside, I usually feel depressed. I try to think about these different problems and about what can be done to make the world better. But usually I start thinking about escape. And when I do, I picture Garwood, the perfect small town. I grew up there, and I dream about going back.

That is, I *used* to dream about going back. Recently I took the trip: I found out that certain dreams are better left untouched.

Riding in on the train, I sorted through my memories and fantasized about what I would find. I pictured the quiet, tree-lined streets, the neat houses and lawns, the small shops with friendly owners, kids with dogs, you name it. I must have been thinking of one of those old barbershop calendars.

Before the train even reached the station, I knew that I was going to have to readjust my ideas. We were rolling through the outskirts—there never used to *be* outskirts—and I felt my heart sink. Where were the farms and open fields? All I could see through the window were shopping malls and subdivisions. I almost looked at the train schedule to make sure that this was the right stop.

Then I remembered. Before my family moved away there was a lot of talk and argument about the new Aerodyne plant. Some people said that if the company built in Garwood it would be opening the door to big city problems. The newspaper called it a "Pandora's box." Other people argued about the benefits: new business, expansion, and revenue.

There's no question about those benefits, but they look suspiciously like the evils that came out of the box Pandora opened.

The plant was built on top of Sear's Hill. Hundreds of workers and their families were brought in. Smart developers bought up the farmland on the west side of town and put up tract housing. Shop owners thought about ways to expand. People started to see dollar signs.

Walking up toward town from the station, I felt like a visitor from another galaxy. Everything was changed. Somebody had waved a wand and covered the old town with glass and steel. The streets were wider; parking meters were growing where the trees used to be. I actually saw a traffic jam at the intersection of Main and Wilder.

These changes shocked me, naturally, but the real shock came when I crossed the far end of Wilder and started over the bridge. I looked down at the river below and nearly got sick to my stomach. The blue water I remembered, where we swam and fished, was dirty brown. Dead brown. Some awful kind of foam was gathered behind the rocks and logs. I didn't have to look up the hill to know where the mess was coming from.

For so many years I had kept Garwood frozen in my mind as an ideal place to live. It was my mental retreat. Whenever I got depressed by the ways of modern life, I dreamed of going back. No more. They say you can't go home again, and they're right. When I think of Garwood now I feel as if something has been stolen from me.

EXERCISES

1. Reread the section entitled "The Order of Paragraphs." Rearranging the Cape Cod notations, write two different passages. Be prepared to explain how your sequencing of paragraphs changes the effect of the whole.

2. Develop one of these topic sentences in a short paragraph, using one of the methods discussed in the chapter.

> **a.** We live in a highly competitive society.
> **b.** Green is a cool color.
> **c.** Sitting by the fire on a cold winter night is a pleasure I miss at school.
> **d.** It is not difficult to make bread.
> **e.** The man was dressed in a most peculiar fashion.

3. Read these paragraphs and comment on their methods of development (see pages 200–205).

> a. I can easily walk ten, fifteen, twenty, any number of miles, commencing at my own door, without going by any house, without crossing a road except where the fox and the mink do: first along by the river, and then by the brook, and then the meadow and the wood-side. There are square miles in my vicinity which have no inhabitant. From many a hill I can see civilization and the abodes of man afar. The farmers and their works are scarcely more obvious than woodchucks and their burrows. Man and his affairs, church and state and school, trade and commerce, and manufactures and agricultures, even politics, the most alarming of them all,—I am pleased to see how little space they occupy in the landscape. Politics is but a narrow field, and that still narrower highway yonder leads to it.

> Henry David Thoreau, "Walking"

> b. On the twenty-ninth of July, in 1943, my father died. On the same day, a few hours later, his last child was born. Over a month before this, while all our energies were concentrated in waiting for these events, there had been, in Detroit, one of the bloodiest race riots of the century. A few hours after my father's funeral, while he lay in state in the undertaker's chapel, a race riot broke out in Harlem. On the morning of the third of August, we drove my father to the graveyard through a wilderness of smashed plate glass.

> James Baldwin, "Notes of a Native Son"

> c. One holds the knife as one holds the bow of a cello or a tulip—by the stem. Not palmed nor gripped nor grasped, but lightly, with the tips of the fingers. The knife is not for pressing. It is for drawing across the field of skin. Like a slender fish, it waits, at the ready, then, go! It darts, followed by a fine wake of red. The flesh parts, falling away to yellow globules of fat. Even now, after so many times, I marvel at its power—cold, gleaming, silent. More, I am still struck with a kind of dread that it is I in whose hand the blade travels, that my hand is its vehicle, that yet again this steel-bellied thing and I have conspired for a

most unnatural purpose, the laying open of the body of a human being.

Richard Selzer, "The Knife"

d. I am forty-two as I write these words, and I know full well now that my father was an alcoholic, a man consumed by disease rather than by disappointment. What had seemed to me a private grief is in fact a public scourge. In the United States alone some ten or fifteen million people share his ailment, and behind the doors they slam in fury or disgrace, countless other children tremble. I comfort myself with such knowledge, holding it against the throb of memory like an ice pack against a bruise. There are keener sources of grief: poverty, racism, rape, war. I do not wish to compete for a trophy in suffering. I am only trying to understand the corrosive mixture of helplessness, responsibility, and shame that I learned to feel as the son of an alcoholic.

Scott Russell Sanders, "Under the Influence"

4. Look at the length of paragraphs in these examples. Do the authors provide variety in length and type of paragraph? Do any paragraphs seem choppy? Are transitions adequate? Make notes in the margin for class discussion.

a. What, in our human world, is this power to live? It is the ancient, lost reverence and passion for human personality, joined with the ancient, lost reverence and passion for the earth and its web of life.

This indivisible reverence and passion is what the American Indians almost universally had; and representative groups of them have it still.

They had and have this power for living which our modern world has lost—as world-view and self-view, as tradition and institution, as practical philosophy dominating their societies and as an art supreme among all the arts.

By virtue of this power, the densely populated Inca state, by universal agreement among its people, made the conversation and increase of the earth's resources its foundational national policy. Never before, never since has a nation done what the Inca state did.

By virtue of this same power, the little pueblo of Tesuque, in New Mexico, when threatened by the implacable destroying action of government some twenty-five years ago, starved and let no white friend know it was starving. It asked no help, determined only to defend its spiritual values and institutions and its remnant of land which was holy land.

If our modern world should be able to recapture this power, the earth's natural resources and web of life would not be irrevocably wasted within the twentieth century, which is the prospect now. True democracy, founded in neighborhoods and reaching over the world, would become the realized heaven on earth. And living peace—not just an interlude between wars—would be born and would last through ages.

John Collier, Indians of the Americas

b. Pop stands for mutability and glitter. Its mode is the 45 single and the pinup, and its value is measured by record sales and the charts. Pop is about dreams and escapism and ecstatic moments; it believes in clichés and its philosophy is "give the people what they want." It is egalitarian by nature—anyone can make it—and capitalist.

Rock is about the search for permanence within the free-floating values of the marketplace. It is about tradition (blues, country, and folk roots), and it is hierarchical in that it believes in geniuses and heroes. Its mode is the long-playing album and the in-depth interview. Rock wants deep emotion and catharsis and truth; it has a religious element that pop does not. Rock believes in originality and self-expression in defiance of crass commercialism.

If this seems to suggest that pop means shallow and rock means depth, consider which is the more profound experience—Smoky Robinson's "The Tracks of My Tears" or Led Zeppelin's "Stairway to Heaven"? And yet the one is a pop, the other a rock classic. And far from being rigid categories, pop and rock often intertwine—where would you put "River Deep Mountain High"? Where would you put Prince? How do you classify punk?

Mary Harron, "Pop as a Commodity"

5. The phrases listed below might be the informal notes for an essay. Arrange them into several groups, each capable of becoming a paragraph. Then write a brief paragraph starting with topic sentence (a) or (b).

    a. Pets should be allowed in the dormitory.
    b. Pets should not be allowed in the dormitory.

dogs vs. other animals
sanitation and health laws
noise, barking during the night
exercise and traffic
responsibility for feeding and care
roommates and allergies
community considerations
student life and its demands
safety
school vacations and care
abuse of pets and negligence
companionship and loneliness

6. Here is a short essay on baseball. We have mixed up the paragraph order and lettered the paragraphs in the mixed-up order. See if you can restore them to their original sequence.

a. At any one point, there's anticipation, deliberation, preparation: "Now" is a building-up. "Now" is never only for itself. It's cumulative "progressing," in strife, to form the game's unfolding. Nor are any two games alike, any more than two art works that push themselves into being through the resistance of time, incident by incident, in head-on conflict by two complicated machines designed to win through accidents and opportunity. "What's happening" is contingent. There's a whole game to be gotten through.

b. This is to see baseball as an artwork-in-the-making affair, totally unrehearsed, improvised by more than eighteen men, who thrust in their various skills while the moving parts pass through innings, highlighted by crucial plays, to the conclusion being thereby created.

c. The game in progress is a structure-in-the-becoming; if you see it, through time, as a whole, all the separate episodes can come flashing together, and interlock, to shower aesthetic illumination on a drama of its own devising.

d. Like literature, music, opera, theater, and the dance, baseball takes place in time. (Architecture, sculpture, and painting don't—they're purely spatial.) The performer and the observer, while a game is in progress, look back and look ahead: the present action is laid out in a shifting, dramatic time field. A rhythm, of sorts, weaves its way through the "accidents" on the playing field. A current play, involving positioning and decisions, is affected by what was previous in the game, and is having its effect on what's to come later; the game may be seen as an organic unit. Every pitch has its place in there, somewhere.

Marvin Cohen, *Baseball the Beautiful*

7

Argument and Persuasion

EXPOSITION

Before we turn to the subject of argument and persuasion, we must give some consideration to exposition. Exposition is explanation—exposing a subject for an audience, making it clear. The word itself comes from the Latin verb meaning "to set out," and it becomes an English noun meaning "something displayed for public inspection." Expository writing is far and away the most common mode of expression. We write exposition not only in college; most writing required in professional life is expository—in business, in teaching, in technology and science, in law and medicine. When social workers deliver papers, when geologists make reports, when hospital officials release information on new diagnostic equipment, when marketing managers report on the activities of their competition, they write expository prose. Newspapers, brochures, and guidebooks are all exposition.

We might, therefore, think of exposition as the foundation on which most essays, including those of the argumentative or persuasive sort, are built. Its strategies are many, but principally exposition makes use of the rhetorical patterns discussed in Chapters 3 and 6. Taken together, these basic patterns are an archive of the most natural ways to present information. Each can be seen to answer one of the reader's basic questions. *Example* answers "For instance?" *Classification* answers "What kind is it?" *Division* answers "What are its parts?" *Cause and effect* answers "Why did it happen?" *Process analysis* answers "How did it happen?" *Comparison and contrast* answers "What is it like? What is it unlike?" *Definition* answers "What is it?"

In itself, exposition is not argument, although it usually forms part of an argument. Argument lacking explanation moves toward bombast or harangue because it presents unsubstantiated opinion. The rhetorical patterns will surface again and again as we work to bring the reader over to our point of view.

ADVANCING OUR POSITION

Now we turn our attention to argument and persuasion, a large category of writing useful far beyond the classroom. Like the other modes we have studied, argument and persuasion make use of certain patterns and habits of thought. Many of these are second nature to us; we resort to them without thinking as soon as we want to convince someone to do something or to agree with us. We argue and attempt to persuade when we give our friends reasons for taking a particular weekend trip. We do the same when we try to sell ourselves on the merits of one course over another. The basic procedure is simple: we line up the best reasons we can think of, and we try to anticipate objections so that we can counter them with convincing assertions. Writing to argue and persuade, we use the same tactics, only in a more formal manner.

The terms *argument* and *persuasion* are similar, but they are not synonyms. Persuasion has a more general application: when we persuade someone, we move them; we bring them over to our way of doing or seeing things. Argument is a means of persuasion, the setting out of a logical structure by which we move the other person to accept our view. The steps of an argument are like the rungs of a ladder; by climbing them the person arrives at a new position. Our position.

In the first paragraph we used the phrase "to sell ourselves" to characterize the process of persuasion. The verb *sell* gives us another way to look at the matter. Argument and persuasion are, in effect, the selling of a point of view. We approach the undecided or doubtful party—sometimes it is ourselves we are trying to convince—like a car dealer moving in on a prospective customer. "Look," we say, "you won't find a better value than this." We go on to itemize: it has this and this and this and this . . . (we describe). You may think the Flamethrower gets better mileage or has a longer warranty, but in fact . . . (we compare and contrast). Our engineers and researchers have been testing this model over a specially designed course . . . (we use process analysis). Their tests have shown that the specially designed suspension system, because it uses a new alloy . . . (we use cause and effect).

The point should be clear: while persuasion and argumentation have goals different from exposition, they make use at every turn of expository tactics. Indeed, without an expository foundation, most argumentative writing would collapse into bombast. Exposition provides the underpinnings for the built-up structure of persuasion.

In writing expository prose, we assemble details—facts, anecdotes, descriptions—to understand or to explain, not to take a position and support it. On occasion, we might seem to argue that something is superior to something else—say, the Cubist painters to the Impressionists—when we are really only giving our personal preference. If we explain our own likes and dislikes, we write exposition; we do not argue that anyone else should feel as we do. Exposing a preference is valid exposition. When we read someone else's praise of duck hunting, we can enjoy and understand it, without feeling any pressure to bag a bird for ourselves.

The honest writer, then, argues on behalf of genuine beliefs; she does not claim to hold positions just to score a point. She avoids the favorite devices of the rhetorician and sentimentalist. The loaded word—when the dictator's police shoot "unarmed civilians" or "a traitorous rabble"—or loaded syntax—when the beer company's advertisement asks, "As a lawyer, what do you think of Fitz's?"—can combine to make a whole essay into a loaded argument, or propaganda. Words and phrases seem to say one thing and really say another. In good writing, we must avoid such subterfuge.

Persuasion, perceptible and imperceptible, is an element we live in; we breathe it in with our oxygen. We live in a country that promotes a marketplace of goods and ideas, and persuasion is one of our national industries. Although political speeches and newspaper editorials are obvious exercises in argument and persuasion, we are influenced to a far greater degree by the ubiquitous claims of advertising. We are subject to it daily on television and radio, in newspapers and magazines, over public address systems, and on billboards. Thousands—hundreds of thousands—of people spend their working lives trying to persuade us to buy this new car over that one, this scented cat litter, this diet plan. We are the audience addressed by this mammoth industry; we are the readers whose responses they predict—and bank on predicting. As we study argument and persuasion in English composition, we can start to identify and understand how those arts are practiced on us in daily life.

Argument is not only external but also internal. In our everyday lives, we argue with ourselves as we approach decisions: Look for a summer job or enroll in a computer course? Major in marketing or Chinese? Buy new running shoes or wear out our old ones and save the money? Every time we use the word *should* to ourselves we lurk in the vicinity of an argument. Argument does not have to be a matter of loud voices and thumping fists; argument can simply test alternatives. We ask ourselves: *this* or *that?* And as we do so we inevitably ask *why?* If we tune in closely to our normal thinking process, we will find that much of it includes this internal debate. We are arguing our way forward through the day, making choices, giving reasons; every move we make is an argument won.

USES FOR ARGUMENT

Knowing how to argue is a useful skill. We use it on ourselves in order to arrive at decisions; we use it with others as we discuss business strategies or policy changes on committees, as members of the local PTA, a law office, an environmental action group; we use it as fundraisers for a cause, like saving whales; we use it in applying for foundation grants and in drafting a letter to the editor of our hometown paper; we use it when we discuss child abuse, toxic waste, tax cuts, pothole repair, working mothers, and university investment policies. Our ability to express opinions persuasively—to present our views systematically as arguments—will allow us to make some difference in public life. If we lack the necessary skills, we are condemned to sit at the sidelines. Instead of doing the moving, we will be among the moved; more persuasive voices will convince us of what we must do.

Most of the time, in writing argument, we work with debatable material. We cannot prove our thesis as a mathematician or philosophical logician can, by manipulating his own terms. We cannot measure results in a cyclotron like a physicist. We end with probability and persuasion, not with certainty or proof. If we had verifiable certainty then argumentation would not be necessary: the verification would speak for itself. The *proof* we arrive at might be called "the agreement of reasonable people," which just happens to be one of the old-fashioned senses of the word.

Matters of fact are rarely arguable. When we disagree about the running time of the Boston Marathon, how many films Clark Gable made, or the population of Minneapolis, we can look it up. Disagreement about facts is pointless. And it is likewise pointless to argue about personal preference or taste. We either do or do not like gulf shrimp, punk rock, jogging, or polyester suits. There is little hope, and usually little purpose, in trying to persuade others to feel as we do.

But opinions—about value or worth, about meaning or interpretation, about solutions to problems—are arguable. We *differ* in our views about two-career marriages, bilingual education, book censorship, burning the flag, and a thousand other things. We have our own ideas about what is right, and we usually have reasons for thinking as we do. Through persuasion and argument we try to convince our parents, our friends, our employers, our neighbors, or our legislators.

AUDIENCE IN ARGUMENT AND PERSUASION

Argument is a process by which we persuade ourselves or others. Most argument in writing is, of course, directed outward, though we may have had to go through some inner debate in order to clarify our position to ourselves. Once we know what we believe, we face the next stage of the process: we must determine how to bring others around to our view. And while the steps of argumentation tend to follow a pattern of logic, the specific application of that pattern depends entirely on whom we are trying to reach. A presentation on the perils of toxic waste disposal will be slanted one way to a group of environmentalists, another way altogether to lawyers representing the chemical industry. Before we can shoot, we have to find the target.

The first requirement is that we establish a believable, trustworthy presence. Our tone must meet our audience as equals, as if we were face to face. We must not speak down, as if to young children, nor should we appear to be hiding anything. Our tone must show our argument as fair, as open to modification or to further discussion. Argument needs to imply the process of dialogue, in which the other side has a voice. When we present the opposition's view, as we often do in the course of making our points, we must treat it with respect, just as if we were hearing out the objections of an audience member. We gain nothing by being curt, shrill, or dismissive.

The tone of address to the audience is fundamental. To find it we have to feel respect for the opposition. Often it helps to imagine a single person whose views and opinions differ from our own but whom we value as an adversary. We might think of a skeptical teacher or a friend with good debater's instincts. We write to convince, not to alienate. We lose our chance for a hearing unless we establish rapport and maintain it. Rapport depends first on identifying audience and then on using common sense in addressing it. When we give examples of the occasions for persuasion, we categorize by audience. An argument for breast-feeding over formula feeding addressed to suburban American mothers would be very different from one addressed to Third World mothers. A plea for more police foot patrols would take a different form if we proposed it to residents of an urban neighborhood with high crime statistics than if we made the suggestion to a suburban neighborhood worried about taxes.

One important reason for locating the audience for the argument, aside from establishing an appropriate tone, is to help us to set out the context for the information. An argument moves forward from point to point, in sequence, giving facts and reasons. To know what to say and what to omit, or how precise to get, we have to know whom we are trying to convince. Recall the example of toxic waste disposal cited earlier. Not only is it essential that we know the disposition of the audience—whether its members are environmentalists or corporation lawyers—but we must also know its level of competence. If we put together a mass of technical statistics for newly joined members of the Sierra Club, we risk losing their attention. We would risk the very same—or worse—if we presented the corporation lawyers with a beginner's lecture on the inadvisability of putting poisons in the earth.

The best way to assess an audience is to become it. Imagine for a few moments that you *are* the person you would like to reach. What kind of background information would you need? What would be the tone and approach most likely to make you prick up your ears and listen? What are some objections you might raise as you listened or read? Can you, as the writer, defuse objections in some way—by putting them into your essay and addressing them? Maneuvers like this are not only practically useful but also help develop the elasticity of mind that is an asset in all argumentative writing.

REASONABLENESS IN ARGUMENT

Most of the time, we persuade by being reasonable—and also by *seeming* so. The *being* comes from clear thinking and argumentative structure; the seeming is a matter of tone. We will *be* reasonable if we write with clarity and avoid typical errors of thinking (these will be taken up later). We will *seem* reasonable by refusing to be dogmatic or overly assertive, by allowing time to opposing points of view, and by writing with the modesty that distinguishes between fact and opinion. This does not mean that we should continually qualify our remarks by tagging them with phrases like *in my opinion;* it is more a matter of attitude. If we are writing about the Indiana Pacers and we assert that they ended the season badly, with a 44–58 win/loss record, we are not being dogmatic. If we come out and say "The Indiana Pacers are a terrible team and their disastrous season shows it," then we are airing our own feelings; there is no necessity or logic in the utterance.

Of course it is natural to mix fact and opinion when we write. We are obligated for the sake of honest writing only to know which is which. A fact is information that can be documented from historical and scientific sources. ("Truth" is illusive; the scientific "facts" of one century may look like errors to another; a "fact" is what we can reasonably accept as true.) A fact is also a statement of personal experience that can be accepted as reasonable. "It rained all day, May 31, 1921" can be a fact; a check with the weather service of the place in question can bring confirmation. To say "Hester looked intelligent" is opinion, or surmise, and not fact. When we refer to someone else's documented opinion—"her minister thought that Hester looked intelligent"—we are on the border between fact and opinion.

When we quote the minister, we have quoted an outside source, and this makes us appear objective; the source itself, however, is subjective, offering only opinion. On the one hand, we can use such a reference to help persuade, provided we do not lean on it too heavily. On the other hand, if we try to make the minister's opinion the fulcrum for our essay ("But contrary to her doctor's statement, we know from her minister that Hester looked intelligent. Therefore . . ."), the opinion will not move the rock of legitimate doubt and the essay will collapse. We have let ourselves seem unreasonable.

For persuasive argument, we must discover a tone that uses fact when it is relevant, inserts opinion modestly and reasonably, allows time for doubts and objections, and builds a sequential argument by paragraph steps that the reader can follow. Conviction is one thing, belligerence or insistence another. It is the difference between "Let me show you how I think and maybe you will begin to think as I do" and "Agree with me or else you're a fool!"

In the debate about cutbacks in federal funding for social programs, together with increases in defense spending, it is common for partisans of one side or the other to pretend that their opponents are warmongers who despise the poor or else bleeding hearts who think we need no army to protect ourselves. Telling arguments acknowledge that the opposition has its points. Here are sentences from two essays with different emphases:

Although a strong defense is necessary for a country like the United States, which has worldwide interests and influence, we will jeopardize our future security if we neglect the real needs of the poor and education for the next generation of Americans.

Of course there is a degree of poverty and suffering that any government must guarantee to alleviate, but without a believable force for defense, the United States will find itself lacking the prosperity that can supply the alleviation.

In each passage the writer attempts to acknowledge the opponent and to indicate that the writer's mind is not closed to other kinds of reasoning. As readers we nod and think, "Yes, that sounds reasonable."

For a purer and more sustained example of argument, we might go to the op-ed page of a newspaper. This particular column ran side-by-side with another column, which was entitled "Missing: The Influence of Black Women . . . ." This column's title read ". . . and Men, Too." The author is identified as William Raspberry, "a syndicated columnist."

If I could offer a single prescription for the survival of America, and particularly black America, it would be: Restore the family.

And if you asked me how to do it, my answer—doubtlessly oversimplified—would be: Save the boys.

So much of what has gone wrong in America, including the frightening growth of the poverty-stricken, crime-ridden and despairing black underclass, can be traced to the disintegration of the family structure.

Everybody knows it, but too many of us have been reluctant to talk straight about it. We know that children need intact families that include fathers. But we fear to say it lest we appear to be blaming hard-pressed single mothers for the very problems they are struggling to overcome.

The point, however, is not to assign blame but to encourage analysis that can lead the way to solutions.

Nathan and Julia Hare put it this way in their book "The Endangered Black Family":

There is nothing wrong with being a black-female single parent—and one rightfully makes the most of any situation in which she finds herself. But there is something wrong with why a black woman is so much more likely to experience the single-parent situation, why one race can freely imprison, send off to military duty, unemploy and otherwise destroy the oppressed black woman's eligible male supply.

Also, there is something wrong with glorifying this problem instead of rising up to change it. People will speak here of 'options,' but forced or unintended options must be called by some other name.

That's from a pair of radical black social scientists. Now hear this from white ethologist Phon Hudkins: "The family is the only social institution that is present in every single village, tribe or nation we know through history. It has a genetic base and is the rearing device for our species.

And from conservative Richard John Neuhaus, editor of the *Religion & Society Report:* "Millions of children do not know and will never know, what it means to have a father. More poignantly, they do not know anyone who has a father or who is a father. . . . It takes little imagination to begin to understand the intergenerational consequences of this situation."

It strikes me as it strikes these writers—as it struck Daniel Patrick Moynihan a quarter century ago—that children unlucky to be born into a single-parent households are, if not doomed, at least at serious disadvantage.

Hudkins believes the disadvantages include not just poverty and crime and hopelessness, but also poor health produced by the stress of family-lessness.

The question is what to do about the children of deteriorating and never-formed families. The first thing to do is to provide as much help as we can for these feckless children in their present circumstances: education, mentoring, role-modeling, job training, help toward self-sufficiency. The second is to devise policies to restore families. Hudkins, who has been ridiculed for his contention that female dominance is eroding America's strength, has it right in the prescription he offered in a recent open letter to the president:

> If families are to be formed and survive, young males must be prepared for skilled jobs to support these families. In order to do this, we must target our government aid and our compensatory education and training programs for disadvantaged young males.
>
> We can't rescue America's families unless we make up our minds to save the boys.

Boston Globe, July 18, 1989

In this essay, Raspberry is not so much arguing systematically as attempting to persuade the reader that his point is sound. Still, we can note a few things about his procedure that will be useful when we set out to practice argumentation. The first consideration is tone. Raspberry is open and direct; he addresses the general reader of the newspaper. The diction is simple, neither pompous nor condescending. With his second sentence he uses the second-person pronoun "you," thus making a connection through direct address. And in his fourth paragraph he once again reaches out. "Everybody knows it," writes Raspberry, thereby including us in the upcoming debate.

But Raspberry is not just being friendly. It is the purpose of his column to capture the attention of a constituency. Raspberry wants to reach those reasonable, well-meaning people who without reflection hold a particular view about the plight of single mothers with families. His point is that to remedy that plight we must bring it into the open, into the public eye; too many of us, however, fear to discuss the situation as it needs to be discussed because we fear to look as if we blame "hard-pressed single mothers for the very problems they are struggling to overcome."

Once he has identified and addressed his audience, Raspberry sets out to change minds. He does this not through a logical sequence of arguments but rather through a powerful appeal to common sense. Raspberry quotes from three different sources; with each quotation comes an identification. First we hear from "a pair of radical black social scientists," then from a "white ethologist," and finally from a "conservative" editor. Raspberry is, in essence, giving us views from all parts of the spectrum: the left, the scientifically neutral, and the right. The sources are all presented as respectable public figures—and as thinkers who have all come to the same conclusion. Raspberry has thus saved himself the work of arguing. He says, in effect, "If reasonable, thoughtful people from all parts of the political spectrum come to the same conclusion in this matter, it must be the right conclusion." He finishes by spelling that conclusion out unambiguously.

Later in this chapter we will discuss the use of sources in building arguments. For the present, as we look back on Raspberry's presentation, let us focus most closely on his use of tone and address to build consensus.

TIME FOR THE OPPOSITION

When we hope to persuade, we need to pay court to the opposition—and the opposition is a portion of our audience. We need to imagine possible rebuttals of our position, so that in our argument we can anticipate them. This is the first principle of debating: the good debater is one who has planned counterarguments for every attack on his position.

Sometimes we can take on the objections directly. Suppose we are arguing that television news is an abomination, that television newscasters have become celebrities, that they are hired for looks and personality rather than for their competence as journalists. We might say, "Networks claim that because television is a visual medium, on-camera appearance is basic to a reporter's ability to communicate with the public. But . . . ." Then we could contradict by means of anecdote, example, or appeal to a hypothesis. To acknowledge possible objections in this way weakens their effectiveness even as it makes the position advanced sound reasonable and open-minded.

Thinking of opposing arguments is also a natural system for generating and gathering ideas. We must put ourselves on the other side and consider the evidence that argues against our thesis. To find out the probable objections to our argument about newscasters, we have to make an effort to think like an executive at a television network: what would such a person say to defend the network's hiring policies? If we argue that possession of handguns should be illegal, we must consider the argument that Americans have a constitutional right to bear arms. If we contend that impounded dogs and cats should not be used for laboratory experiments, we must answer the argument that by sacrificing unwanted animals we may save human lives. By considering the counternotions, we can develop our argumentative material and discover the form that our argument must follow to convince the audience. The internal antagonist—the voice that keeps saying "Yes, but what about . . . ?"—is essential to good argument.

As we consult this internal antagonist, we may find ourselves succumbing to the Ping-Pong effect: for every assertion we formulate a counterassertion. While such a to and fro is an excellent way to explore all sides of an issue and locate the argumentative possibilities, it should not provide the form for our essay. The reader would quickly get a crick in the neck from looking this way and that. Don't say:

> It has been argued that smokers have a right to smoke in public places because they are members of the public. But what about the non-smoking public whose rights to breathe clean air are infringed upon?

Such a volley may work once, to introduce a conflict of views, but if it were sustained for more than a paragraph, the reader would quickly grow restless. Often it is best, in avoiding the Ping-Pong tactic, to lump all opposing ideas together, perhaps in one paragraph, and then answer them in another. Or we might acknowledge and counter an argument in the flow of one sentence:

> Although smokers claim the right to smoke in public places, they forget that nonsmokers have a right to breathe uncontaminated air.

Our most persuasive argument, in the long run, derives from praise for our point of view, rather than blame for the opposition. If we record too many opposing arguments—more than we need to overturn the objections—our own position may start to blur out of focus; we lose unity, and we may lose the sound of conviction. Usually we deal with opposing views obliquely, raising them in dependent clauses while allowing the main clauses to carry our argument: "Although smokers claim the right to smoke in public places, they forget that nonsmokers have a right to breathe uncontaminated air." This device raises the issues that belong to the opposition but keeps our direction clear.

Giving time to the opposition allows us to sound open-minded. No one wins an argument by asserting that the other point of view is wholly invalid and that anybody who disagrees with us is ignorant or stupid. We must admit the facts and give credit to valid lines of reasoning; if we do not, we undercut our own validity and lose our audience, especially the one we most want to reach—the misguided fool who disagrees with us.

One thing we should remember as we generate ideas and strategies by giving time to the opposition is the usefulness of sources. We can usually make a good deal of headway on our own, by putting ourselves in the position of the adversary. But sometimes it helps to confront the position as it has been worked through, or argued, by another writer. Fortunately there is no shortage of material: almost any topic we can think of has its *pro* and *con* partisans. A library search will generally yield books and articles in newspapers and journals representing any point of view we desire. But we must be aware of certain dangers. If we consult the views of others before we have formulated our own clearly, we risk losing the tone of independent conviction that marks good argumentative writing. It is all too easy to start parroting the arguments and sequences of another thinker. We need to be aware of the hazards of plagiarism: not only is it wrong—and punishable—to use another writer's words without attribution, it is also wrong to take the structure of another's argument as one's own. We are far less likely to face this risk if we work out our pattern of arguments and counterarguments *before* we look elsewhere.

Once we do have our basic thoughts in order, however, a check of the documented positions of others can help us a great deal. We may discover lines of argument or objection that we had not considered and that may have a place alongside ours. Or we may, like William Raspberry, find that certain positions have been summed up by others with eloquence and conviction. Our essay may profit from direct incorporation. We might want to write, "The position against gun control has been summed up most persuasively by Max Bulet in his book *Our Right to Murder . . .*" and then go on to quote the passage. This tactic is most effective when we use it to highlight counterargument. We might follow the quotation giving Bulet's position with a sentence signaling our rebuttal: "Bulet's argument depends on several fallacies . . ." or "What Bulet neglects to tell his reader . . . ." When we argue against a clearly stated position, one that can be attributed to a spokesperson, our own points stand out in greater relief. At the same time we show the reader that we have made time for the opposition.

Using the clearly stated arguments of another writer on our own behalf, as part of *our* argument, is less advisable. Though the points may be good, we surrender authority. The reader is likely to think, "This other person says it better than the writer; why don't I just read *her* article?" We must at all costs avoid undermining the reader's faith: when we argue, not only must we take control, but also we must keep it.

THE ORDER OF ARGUMENT

Once we have gathered valid support for our argument—first by debating with ourselves, *then* perhaps by checking the stated views of others—we face the task of organization. A few pages back we cautioned against using the structure of the Ping-Pong game. There are other kinds of order to consider.

Audience and purpose interact to determine the shape of argument. In any list of argumentative details and evidence, some will make a stronger case than others; some will be more interesting or appealing to our audience. Generally, we want to save the best, the strongest, for last. One good way to order argument, therefore, is by increasing intensity. After we introduce the issue—"The administration claims that the need to raise teachers' salaries and improve facilities will require an increase in students' fees next semester"—we counter it with facts or statistics in order of increasing importance, as we see them or as we understand our audience to see them. Thus we might write: "But our faculty salaries are already higher than those at other colleges in the state, and the computer center houses equipment that pays its own way with time-sharing. Many students depend on government loans, which become less available, and they will leave school if tuition increases. The administration's well-paid faculty will teach to classrooms full of machines and empty of students." The persuasive effect derives from the crescendo.

Another shape of argument states its main thesis at the beginning, at center stage under spotlights: "Next year's planned increase in tuition and board will contribute to the downfall of this institution." After introducing our argument with a thesis statement, we continue by acknowledging points that argue against our view and by countering them. We then conclude with a summary that rises to our most persuasive point: "Tuition hikes will deny many students, who have already taken on extensive loans and extra jobs, the opportunity to finish their education. The tuition increase will discriminate against the people whom this university was intended to serve." The conclusion echoes the thesis statement in its force.

Most arguments are structured as variations of one of these two patterns. The important thing is to set out the terms of the debate early on: we can begin with a statement of the opposing view and then proceed to take apart its premises, or we can assert our own position and rebut possible objections. Either way, we must lead the reader from point to point in such a way that the conclusion will come with a sense of finality. Ancient rhetoricians used to close their arguments with the initials Q.E.D. (*quod erat demonstrandum*), meaning "as has been demonstrated." We want to leave our reader with the same confident click.

To write argument, we can first turn again to the rhetorical patterns discussed in Chapter 6, this time in the new context of argument and persuasion.

Example is the backbone of argument, the support it requires to become convincing. If we try to persuade people to contribute to the public library system, we may list examples to show what money can achieve.

We argue by *example:*

> . . . to acquire new library materials, from books to computers; to increase hours providing more services; to expand children's programs by adding new staff; to improve facilities allowing community groups to use the library for film festivals and lectures; to preserve old books and manuscripts; and with climate control to prevent further deterioration of the library collection.

We argue by *classification and division:*

> In seeking candidates for membership in the Sierra Club, we look for
> people who have demonstrated an interest in the outdoors or in pro-
> tecting the environment. We send you this invitation in the hope that
> you are such a person. . . . Whether you particularly enjoy hiking,
> backpacking, camping, canoeing, whitewater rafting, or simply appre-
> ciation of nature. . . .

From a letter of solicitation, the Sierra Club

To persuade people to become members of a special group (*classification*)
this letter goes on to identify the characteristics and interests of that group
(*division*).

We argue by *cause and effect:*

> Despite a thirtyfold increase in outlays on social programs for the
> poor, the condition of impoverished blacks in the United States has
> been steadily deteriorating since the launching of the War on Poverty
> and the Great Society in the 1960s. These redistributionist schemes,
> by destroying incentives for work, thrift, and family support, have
> created in our inner cities a tragic wreckage of demoralization, rage,
> unemployment, and crime, raised the illegitimacy rate to fifty-five
> percent of all black births, and driven fathers altogether out of the
> ghetto family and national economy.

George Gilder, "But What About Welfare's Grim Side?"
(The New York Times)

We argue by *comparison and contrast:*

> Unlike the Bulldog I, an expensive proposition for the home com-
> puter because it requires a large initial investment, the Mastiff III
> plugs into the family television set. It is compatible with many Mastiff
> programs and can grow with your family, whereas the Bulldog I lacks
> flexibility.

We argue by *process analysis:*

> Put into practice, computer-aided robotics could mean startling
> changes in farming before the end of the century. The dairy barn of
> the future, for example, might look like this:
>
> Cows wearing identification tags walk through the door and are
> "recognized" by an electronic sensor. They amble to their permanent
> feeding stations and eat a ration tailored to their individual needs,
> weather conditions, and milk production. Sensors implanted in their
> bodies weigh and check the animals for nutrient levels and early de-
> tection of disease.

G. V. Perkins, Jr., "What's New in Agriculture"
(The New York Times)

And we argue by *definition,* which includes other rhetorical patterns:

Either America is an open society or it isn't. If it is, the country has nothing to fear from such political and literary luminaries as Nobel Prizewinner Gabriel García Márquez, playwright Dario Fo, Salvadoran insurgent leader Guillermo Ungo and Chile's widowed First Lady Hortensia Allende. But the Reagan Administration has refused to grant all of the above—and dozens more—the entry privileges customarily accorded other figures of their stature. The country seems more of a closed company with ever-slamming door. The exclusion of famous people deters thousands of others from the arduous and humiliating application process, where detailed probes are made into political and affectional ties. No particular threat to national security need be divined: radical thinking, organizational affiliation or sexual preference is enough to keep the Administration's critics out.

Editorial, *The Nation*

The writer defines open and closed societies by listing controversial visitors to whom our country is a closed door. A society that excludes possible critical visitors is not an open one.

LOGIC AND EMOTIONALISM

If we wish to persuade, we must be reasonable: we must appear logical. Argument may be fueled by feeling, but in persuasion the appeal to emotions is dangerous. If our appeal appears to violate reason the reader loses confidence. The photograph of a weeping child does not provide a *reason* for doing whatever the caption asks. After all, a caption writer could use the same melancholy photograph to illustrate the hardships faced by refugees on either side in any war.

Whether we think to ourselves or on paper in a public forum, we must avoid illogic in order to think well. All of us know some logic, perhaps without giving it the name; often we use the name of common sense for thought we accept as reasonable. For example, common sense tells us not to generalize from particulars. Suppose I read in the paper about a drunk teenager who killed a pedestrian in a hit-and-run accident. Suppose I told you about it and added, "Therefore, we should raise the drinking age to protect society from drunk teenagers." You would be right to ridicule my logic: I would be guilty of violating common sense by arguing from insufficient evidence. One teenager cannot be made to stand for all.

The use of an anecdote or example is not necessarily generalizing from a particular; it depends on how we do it. If I had been modest in my declaration, I could have said, "I know that we cannot generalize from one case, but this sort of news item seems characteristic. There have been a great many fatalities involving drunk teenagers. A careful look at the statistics might cause us to reexamine the laws." Here the anecdote is used to introduce an issue that may be debated in less subjective terms.

When we caution against emotionalism, we are not blaming feelings but their misuse, as when emotionalism appeals to feeling in order to disguise a defect in thinking. If we say,

> The United States needs a strong defense. Anyone who is against the draft is a traitor to those who have sacrificed their lives to preserve freedom.

we give no reasons to support our claim. With words like *traitor* and *sacrifice* we name-call and breast-beat. Charged words persuade only the already persuaded; they alienate those we wish to reach. This writer's counterpart on the other side of the fence might write,

> Anyone who advocates the peacetime draft wants America to rule the world for the sake of the military-industrial complex.

A writer can defend either position without resorting to loaded language:

> With our commitment to free enterprise or capitalism, in a world that contains many opponents of free enterprise, we would be naive to reduce our armed forces unless we can be certain that our opponents will do the same. Although all sensible people dread the possibility of war, it can be argued that we can prevent war only by preparing for it.

In this fragment of argument, the writer carefully avoids the unfairness of loaded words and gives the antagonist at least the benefit of a dependent clause.

Loaded words, begging the question, and unsupportable claims for cause and effect all contribute to errors in thinking; we may lump them under one general label—*emotionalism pretending to argue.* Soon we will look at the related subject of logical fallacies, which we are more apt to fall into if we are arguing from feeling. We must watch ourselves carefully for bad thinking and bad writing whenever we take on a heavily charged issue: abortion, capital punishment, school prayer, disarmament, pornography, or freedom of speech.

STYLE IN ARGUMENT

Loaded words make bad prose. To avoid fooling ourselves and trying to fool others, to appear reasonable, we have to apply to argument the stylistic standards of clarity and forcefulness discussed in the chapters on words and sentences. When we use a passive verb instead of an active one, we may detach our subject from responsibility and distort our argument. At the very least we weaken the tone of conviction essential to making a strong case. If we write in the passive mood,

> Mistakes were made . . .

or

> Toxic wastes were dumped at the site over twelve years . . .

we avoid placing responsibility. *Who* made the mistakes, and *who* did the dumping? The active mood supplies a subject and attributes responsibility:

> The Boxtex Company dumped toxic wastes at the site over twelve years . . .

Abstract nouns and euphemisms can also combine with the passive to diminish the force of concrete and direct expression:

> A process of repatriation was employed . . . .

To argue with clarity, we must use conjunctions with care; we should never imply cause or sequence that evidence cannot support:

> While record companies are making ever larger profits from sales of rap music, reports of violent crime among juveniles are on the rise.

The reader of this sentence might mistakenly conclude that its two parts are casually linked: either that the record companies are somehow capitalizing on the incidence of violent crime or that the crimes themselves are encouraged by the contents of the music. Neither inference is necessarily supported by the facts.

It is difficult, in working on a paper in argument, to discover our own errors, especially when we feel strongly about the subject. Often we misuse verb forms and abstract nouns in early drafts of an argument without knowing it. It helps to find a clearheaded friend to read the draft for us. It likewise helps to set the paper aside for a time, then to return to it with the eye of the Inner Critic. Many argumentative errors are not merely mechanical; they are learned errors—fallacies—by which we fool ourselves. Here is a passage of would-be argument from an impromptu essay:

> The governor wants to raise the state drinking age to twenty-one. Adults drink as much as they want and get bombed on cocktails when they get home from the office, but they want to stop kids from having a casual beer. It is true that teenagers are picked up for driving under the influence and getting involved in car accidents. Everybody should be more careful and drunk driving is to be avoided. But there is no reason why teenagers should not relax on weekends with a few beers.

There is no argument in this passage; assertion and innuendo reek of special pleading. The writer avoids the connections implicit in his sentences; he ought to confront weekend relaxation with the argument about highway deaths, but he does not want to make the confrontation. If he wishes to work on his thinking, he can find much to say that is reasonable, even persuasive, on behalf of his point of view. If the author revises these sentences for their prose style, the argument will improve. Bad style allows the illogic of emotionalism to wander into common fallacies of thinking.

COMMON FALLACIES IN THINKING

When we discussed rhetorical patterns earlier, we described them as mapping the sequences that thought naturally follows. We can make use of the same analogy to explain logical fallacies. Briefly: they are misreadings of the map, wrong turns taken. The path of a fallacy often looks like the other, desired path, but it leads us away from clarity and common sense. If we recognize some of these fallacies, or false paths, we stand a better chance of avoiding them in our argumentation.

Many common fallacies in thinking are misuses of *induction* or *deduction*. We meet them every day in newspapers and advertisements and in the rhetoric of political campaigns. *Inductive reasoning,* or *induction,* draws general conclusions from particular examples or evidence—Sherlock Holmes's speciality.

> Because the plums were in the refrigerator when I left, and because George was the only person remaining in the house, and because the plums have disappeared, and because there are plum pits in the sink, I conclude that George ate the plums.

Deductive reasoning, or *deduction,* in contrast, applies a general truth to a specific instance. We deduce by three-step thinking called the syllogism. The most famous syllogism is probably "All men are mortal. Socrates is a man. Therefore, Socrates is mortal." No beginning philosophy course is complete without a nod to this sample of deductive reasoning.

We use both induction and deduction in our thinking and our writing. From time to time we misuse or misapply the logical form and fall into error. A common slip, as in the example of the drunk teen driver, is that we arrive at a general statement from a sole supporting fact or from too narrow a range of particulars. These are errors, or fallacies, of induction. When we generalize too rashly from a particular, we sound silly. We claim that New York City is a rotten apple because one taxi driver was rude to us. We claim that motel chains are dishonest because an aunt was short-changed in San Diego. We generalize poorly when we do not collect sufficient evidence; we assume that because X happens once or twice, X will always happen.

This caution should not be construed as advice to avoid the particular. Often an argument takes on persuasive power because we present a specific bit of evidence—carefully—as typical of the generalization. The argument's effectiveness, however, depends on the general validity of the assertion; a generalization is never demonstrated by one particular. If we began an essay on public television by describing one offensive commercial, and said, "Therefore we must have at least one national network without advertising," we would be illogical. But if, after mentioning the particular commercial, we listed other offensive advertisements, noting a trend, and gave statistics on the programming time devoted to commercials, perhaps we could make a generalization that would appear to follow.

Deduction, too, can lead to fallacy when we misuse it. The most common problem is the overinclusive premise or conclusion. "Everybody who goes to medical school is out for money." "Lawyers are all corrupt." "All people who drive BMWs are yuppies." The next link in the argument would likely be "*X* goes to medical school . . . ." But these assertions do not resemble "All men are mortal." This latter is true beyond dispute; none of the others stands on similarly solid ground. The writer must be wary of bold assertions; logical cross-checking is essential.

Another false step commonly taken begins with wrongful or arbitrary associations. Politicians thrive on guilt by association. Because socialists believe in free medical care, a wily campaigner may insinuate that *anyone* who believes in free medical care is a socialist. If we attach a negative emotional association to the word *socialist,* then our thinking may be affected. If the rival candidate is not a socialist, or inclined to socialist views, then we have been misled.

A linked fallacy, which also depends on association, attacks the person instead of the issue. The name given to such bad argument is *ad hominem,* which is Latin for "to the man." We often resort to this tactic in argument when we lose our tempers or when our logic deserts us. When someone defends cutting down trees to make a parking lot, we attack *him* instead of questioning the need for additional parking spaces. We say, "You're in favor of this plan because you like carbon monoxide more than maple trees." Name-calling may satisfy something in the name-caller, but it avoids thought. A friend says, "I believe in a socialist form of government because the profit motive, which is basic to a capitalistic system, robs us of our humanity and corrupts our intelligence to serve materialism." We rebut, "You always were nuts."

Argument ad hominem—as long as we are using Latin terms coined by ancient scholars of rhetoric—can be construed as a species of *non sequitur,* which means "it does not follow." It does not follow that *X* wants to cut down trees because he loves carbon monoxide. Common sense tells us that nobody loves, likes, or even tolerates this poison. When we commit a non sequitur, we give a statement or idea that *appears* to grow out of an earlier one (by causation, by chronology, by logic), but which upon examination fails to make the trip:

> He was a doctor and therefore an all-round man.
> She left an hour ago, although her car wouldn't move.

Comedians sometimes use the non sequitur to humorous effect. Woody Allen is a master:

> I believe my consumption has grown worse. Also my asthma. The wheezing comes and goes, and I get dizzy more and more frequently. I have taken to violent choking and fainting. My room is damp and I have perpetual chills and palpitations of the heart. I noticed, too, that I am out of napkins.

Non sequiturs sometimes result when we try to make complex sentences in pursuit of conciseness: "My uncle was born in 1902 in Miami, where he sells lawnmowers and garden tools."

When we use the rhetorical pattern of cause and effect, we sometimes unintentionally create the non sequitur or the related fallacy of *post hoc ergo propter hoc*. We needn't be scared away by the Latin. The literal meaning is "after this, therefore because of this." When we fall into this fallacy, we mistake sequence for cause. We assume that if *B* follows *A*, *A* must cause *B*, but our assumption is not logical and often leads to confusion. If we say, "Cousin Eveline visits and I get a headache," we are suggesting a cause-and-effect relationship. In fact, Cousin Eveline may be a delightful person, and the headache may be from a cold contracted the same day. We need to monitor sequential links to make sure that we are not suggesting cause where none exists.

Another instance of misapplied causation is *begging the question*. In this error the arguer assumes the truth of a premise that readers may question. The arguer could try to prove the assumption but does not. Instead, he merely repeats it—it is so because it is so. Someone might say, "The rising incidence of lymphatic cancer proves that early advocates of the test-ban treaty were correct." This writer neither demonstrates that lymphatic cancer *is* rising nor shows that nuclear testing causes the disease. Causation asserted but unsupported indicates sloppy thinking. Sometimes misused conjunctions beg the question: "Although middle-aged, he wore Levis." Again, an untenable connection is advanced through a careless expression.

We don't want to instigate a witch-hunt for fallacies, but several more need to be mentioned before we look at the process of argumentation. One of these might be called the either/or fallacy, and for a good example we can turn back to the quotation from *The Nation* we used (page 233) for an example of argument by definition. Although the passage defines what it means by a closed society, it begins with an example of the either/or fallacy: "Either America is an open society or it isn't." There is an attractive, no-nonsense tone in this introductory sentence; but in fact it *is* nonsense, for it implies that there are no degrees between one extreme and another. If the United States and the Soviet Union are both closed societies, as the 1984 editorial seemed to assert, does the writer really wish to imply that there is no difference in degrees of openness? We should be alert whenever we make a statement using strongly polarized terms; not every instance of this fallacy uses either/or. "Because Herbert Perkins is not a superb human being he is a rotten person."

Finally, we should beware of using analogies as if they were facts. Analogies themselves can be most useful in argument; they can illustrate the sense in which we mean a statement that might otherwise seem tenuous or elusive. But we must be sure to use them as clarifications or elucidations and not as statements of fact. Suppose we want to write about different civilizations that seem to have features in common—like beginning, development, fulfillment, and decay. To carry this idea to a reader, we invent an analogy: each civilization is like an organism—it is born, it grows up, it matures, it becomes old, and it dies. So far so good. We embody the abstract thought, associating it with concrete organisms. But many writers become so accustomed to a dominant analogy that they begin to take it literally. Arguing later that our own civilization must end, we say, "Like all organisms, our society must come to death." The argument is invalid because a civilization is not literally an organism, and therefore we have not proved that what is true of an organism will be true of civilization. Remember: the analogy is not the thing itself.

LOOKING FOR AN ARGUMENT: PROCESS

In Chapter 3 we watched Gian Lombardo as he worked up a theme looking at the pros and cons of E-mail. Now we will follow another student through some of the stages of writing a paper in argument.

When his teacher assigned an essay in argument, Jerome Williams did not go through his usual period of indecision. For once he knew exactly what he wanted to write about. A week earlier his father and his older brother had argued (his brother called it an argument; his father kept calling it a "friendly discussion") at the dinner table. The subject was drugs and gang violence. The whole family had watched a television special the night before. Afterward, Jerome's father and brother had expressed different views about what should be done to remedy the situation. Jerome's father said that criminals and offenders only understood one thing—force—and that the government had to take action. More police protection, stiffer penalties, more prisons—nothing else would work. If that meant raising taxes, he said, then so be it. Jerome's brother was against such a solution. He argued that the only answer was to legalize drugs and make them available as liquor is. The profit motive would disappear, the gangs would disband, and the streets would be safe. "You're a dreamer," his father said.

Jerome had listened as his father and brother went back and forth, arguing and trying to convince each other of the rightness of his position. He had a hard time making up his mind. He was surprised to find that some of his brother's arguments made sense, and his father was not able to rebut them. Jerome felt that this was an issue that concerned many people in his city; he wanted to think his way through to a clear position of his own. What better way than by writing an argument paper?

When Jerome first sat down with pencil and paper to work out his ideas, he did not know which side he wanted to argue. His first step was to make a list. On the left side of the page he wrote *arguments for legalization,* on the right side *arguments against.* He then tried to replay the discussion as he remembered it, listing his brother's points on one side, his father's on the other.

Arguments for legalization:	*Arguments against:*
1. Eliminate profit motive	1. Drugs addictive and dangerous
2. Reduce gang presence	to users
3. Free up funds and resources	2. Legalizing sends message that it's
used in war on drugs	OK to use drugs
4. Control sales and distribution	3. More people would use drugs
5. Ease strain on prison system	4. Strain on hospitals, families;
6. Safer neighborhoods	problems at the workplace

When he had written out his lists, Jerome sat and stared at his paper. He wasn't sure what to do next. The listing hadn't given him his answer; he found himself as divided as before. When he was writing down his brother's reasons, he had sided with that position. When he wrote the counterarguments, *those* seemed most convincing. He knew one thing, though. Sitting and staring all night was not going to get his paper written. Jerome therefore decided that he would argue his brother's case: he would take a stand *for* the legalization of drugs. The points he had listed seemed strong, and besides, there were more of them; he could appear to be overpowering the opposition.

The question was how to get started. He knew that it was not enough just to write out the arguments for one view, then the arguments for the other. He also knew that he should avoid the quick back and forth, where each argument immediately matches up with a counterargument, like a high school debate. His teacher had said that this argument should read like an essay. "The shape itself should be persuasive," he had said.

Jerome used some time walking around the house, ending up in the kitchen with a glass of milk and a piece of cold chicken. He was tempted to find his brother and ask him for advice, but then he stopped himself. This was *his* argument, *his* essay, and he had to work things out for himself. But the thought of his brother was enough to suggest something: as Jerome was rinsing out his glass, the word *Prohibition* popped into his head. He suddenly remembered one of the points his brother had been making. During Prohibition, he had said, it was against the law to make, sell, or consume alcohol. But what were the results? Those who wanted to drink drank. The illegality of alcohol made it attractive; bootleggers organized into criminal gangs in order to control sales; gang warfare was rampant. . . .

Jerome felt he had what he needed. A comparison would allow him to give his argument some shape. He could end by saying something along the lines of "It didn't work then, and it won't work now." He was ready to go back to his room and get to work. He knew from experience with writing papers that his best strategy now would be to sprint a short rough draft. If he got that right, then he could come back to fill in details and look for ways to polish. Jerome sat down and got to work:

There are many good arguments for keeping drugs illegal and for imprisoning users and dealers. Drugs are addictive and dangerous; some people feel they are immoral. Widespread use of drugs like cocaine and its derivative crack puts a strain on hospitals; it causes untold damage within families. Not least, it affects productivity at the workplace. Some people believe that to legalize the drugs or to lessen the penalties would send a message out that it's OK to use drugs. The drugs would be cheaper and more people would try them. More people would get addicted and the problems would worsen.

But then, people said similar things back in the 1920s when Prohibition outlawed the manufacture, sale and consumption of alcohol. If alcohol were available, people would become drunks. Families would be destroyed, and so on. What happened? The illegality just made the product more attractive. Those who wanted to drink were going to find a way, they were going to pay more. Selling bootleg alcohol became very profitable. So profitable, in fact, that the criminal types got interested. Gangs formed; gang-wars were fought over control of territory. Thugs like Al Capone became millionaires. Why? All because people were willing to pay money to take a drink.

Sound familiar? The situation is in many ways similar to the one we face today. Urban areas have become war zones as rival gangs shoot it out to decide who is going to control the crack and cocaine sales in a certain area. Innocent people are shot daily. The government responds by bringing in more and more police. But what is the effect? Our prison system can't begin to cope; offenders cop plea bargains and are back on the street immediately. Taxpayers foot larger and larger bills. Prohibition was a disaster, and so is the present situation.

There is only one logical solution: To treat these drugs as we treat alcohol, to control quality, price and distribution. With the profit motive removed, gangs will stop terrorizing our neighborhoods. The streets will belong to peace-loving citizens again. Sure, some people will get addicted and will pay the price. But isn't this true of alcohol as well? The money now spent on massive police enforcement and on the legal costs can be spent on the creation of treatment centers. After all, there is no stopping people from doing what they want to do. We are responsible for our own decisions. Everyone knows that these drugs are addicting and that they can lead to death. Everyone knows that cigarettes cause cancer. The only answer is to give people a choice. And to launch an ambitious program of education. When the facts are known, most sensible people will say no.

Jerome stopped writing. He had the feeling that something was wrong with his approach. When he read his words over, they seemed to make sense until the last paragraph. He didn't like what he was saying; he didn't know if he believed the conclusions he was reaching. The analogy with Prohibition was effective, a good organizing tool, but the more he looked over what he had written, the more he felt bothered. Then he realized what it was: in his heart of hearts he did not believe that alcohol and cigarettes could be equated with crack and cocaine. Alcohol and cigarettes were bad, sure, and when abused over a period of years could cause grave health problems. But were they really in the same class as drugs? From what he had heard and read, Jerome knew that the drugs, especially crack, brought on intense and disorienting reactions. Great pleasure, but then, very soon after, horrible pangs. Crack was extremely addictive. He read that the deprived user would do *anything* to get more. He had never heard of anyone killing for a cigarette or a drink.

As he thought about this, Jerome became convinced that the analogy was not workable. The risks of having a drug like crack available to anyone over a certain age (how else could they legislate it?) were too great. Obviously, too, minors would get hold of it, just as they now get hold of alcohol. How would he feel about living in a society where a great many people were walking around under the influence of a powerfully addictive and potentially deranging substance? *Scared.*

Jerome found himself in a dilemma. His argument essay was due in two days, and he had just realized that he did not believe in the position he planned to present. It was easy enough, he supposed, to come up with more arguments to strengthen the antilegalization case, but then he would have to find another way to give his paper shape. He hated to throw out the Prohibition comparison; did he *have* to? Maybe not. Jerome stopped and picked up what he had written. He had an idea. Maybe he could keep the analogy and simply turn it around, saying something like *those people who propose legalization like to point to the failure of Prohibition, but what they don't understand is that alcohol and narcotics are very different.* Jerome sat down and took out a fresh sheet of paper. He liked the twist; in some ways it was better than the original line of argument. It also reproduced the progress of his own thinking. He had started by believing the analogy; the fact that it didn't hold up had convinced him that the position was wrong. Maybe he could do the same kind of thing in his paper.

Jerome tried sprinting again. This time he began by presenting the prolegalization view as clearly as he could, first summing it up, then bringing in the comparison with Prohibition. Reading over what he had written, Jerome was satisfied that he had given fair time to the opposition. In fact, he thought, the case sounded quite convincing. Now it was time to change the reader's mind. He wrote:

> The comparison between the current drug crisis and the situation during Prohibition is a good one. In both cases we find people undeterred by laws, risking imprisonment to buy their alcohol or their drugs. In both cases we also find a substantial increase in crime as gangs form and attempt to control lucrative illegal sales. Our history books tell us that Prohibition was a great failure. What does that say about current drug laws?

This kind of reasoning is fine—up to a point. There is just one hitch: alcohol and crack are not the same thing. Liquor, though damaging when abused, is familiar. We know what it does and we have ways of dealing with that. Millions of people drink in social situations and never become alcoholics. Crack and cocaine are different. They are highly addictive and they cause violent changes in personality. We have not even begun to understand the kinds of damage they do to the body and mind. If we legalize these drugs, arguing that adults can make free and responsible choices, we are making a great mistake. Maybe normal adults can make such choices, but is a person with a desperate craving for a high a "normal" adult?

Jerome wrote quickly. He knew that some of his sentences were rough, and that certain links would have to be tightened. But he felt confident. In the several paragraphs that followed, he set out some problems with current drug policy: ineffective policing of neighborhoods, crowded prisons, plea-bargaining loopholes in the legal system. . . . Then he reiterated his major point: that a society had a moral and legal obligation to promote the safety and well-being of its citizens; that while there were serious problems with meeting the legal part of that obligation, this was no reason to give up on the moral consideration. The only answer was to work harder, to ask for the leadership that would find ways to confront and solve the drug crisis.

Jerome was tired but satisfied. He knew that he had not said everything there was to say and that there was probably a better order for his arguments. But he also knew that the argument was now his, not his brother's or his father's. He had learned from their exchange of views; but he had worked his points through for himself. More important, he now believed what he had written; it was not just argument for the sake of writing a paper.

The next day, Jerome went to the school library. Now that he was sure about his views and his process of argument, he wanted to read what others had written on the same issue. The library, as always, was intimidating, with three floors of stacks and an enormous room for periodicals. Jerome suspected that the material he wanted was in journals and newspapers: this was a recent controversy. He also knew from past experience that the best policy was to stop at the reference librarian's desk.

The librarian first showed Jerome how to do a computer search. Looking under the key words *drugs* and *narcotics,* they found a handful of listings. The librarian explained that periodical entries in the database only began with 1987. She printed out a column of references and then directed Jerome to the *Readers' Guide to Periodical Literature.* He paged through several of the volumes, beginning with 1986. Checking under the same key words, he found a great many entries; subheadings in bold type helped him to narrow his search. He jotted down the titles of several promising articles, noting their date and place of publication. Twenty minutes later Jerome seated himself in a window seat with a stack of journals.

Not all of the articles turned out to be relevant to his subject, but those that were had all sorts of usable material. Jerome began making notes; from time to time he copied a quotation, making sure to write the name of the author, the article, and the publication under each citation. He had worked too hard for his ideas and he was not going to risk any appearance of "borrowing." Still, Jerome often had to wonder. He came across ideas and arguments that were very similar to the ones he had come up with on his own. Who owned these ideas? Did anyone? He could only conclude that common sense was universal; a certain overlap was inevitable. He had to make extra sure that someone else's words did not stray into his paper without acknowledgment.

Jerome read through four articles. Two were general feature stories on the nation's drug crisis; one was a ranting call for universal legalization of everything (useful to attack? he wondered); the best of the group was a piece from *The New Republic* entitled "Crackdown." Indeed, the authors, James Q. Wilson and John J. DiIulio, Jr., argued at great length a position quite similar to his own. Jerome found himself writing a number of quotations in his notebook. At a certain point he started to worry: not that he was reproducing Wilson and DiIulio's argument—there were significant differences—but that he was finding more and more documentation that he would have to attribute. He did not want to spend half of his paper quoting others. But their arguments were good ones that he had not thought of; not to include them would weaken his case.

Jerome finally decided to use two of the points from the article in his own argument. He would give proper credit, but he would keep the discussion to a minimum. He knew that competing voices could undermine the force of an argument. His teacher had urged independent thought in this assignment.

When Jerome had copied out the quotations he wanted, he returned the journals to the desk and started for home. It was time to get to work on the final draft. Here is what Jerome handed in the next morning:

The Case Against the Legalization of Drugs

Our American cities have become war zones. You can't pick up a newspaper or turn on the television without hearing about murders and drive-by shootings. Night after night on the screen you see young people being hauled away in handcuffs or on stretchers covered by sheets. And behind every story, it seems, is another story—drugs. Cocaine and its derivative "crack" are brought into inner-city areas and sold for tremendous profits. This is what the gang warfare and the violence are all about: money. For whoever controls the turf also controls the profits. And innocent people are paying with their lives.

Some people have made the argument that the only way to put a stop to this violence is to legalize these drugs. Once crack and cocaine are controlled and distributed by responsible agencies, they say, the profit motive will disappear, and the gangs will disappear with it. Parts of this position are hard to dismiss. Proponents of legalization point to the disastrous condition of our legal system: prisons are overcrowded, dealers and users go free on easy plea-bargains; smart dealers are willing to take the risk of dealing for a chance at the profits. Prolegalization advocates ask: wouldn't it be better to spend the money on treatment centers? Others say that this is a free country and that adults ought to make their own choices about what they do with their bodies and lives.

Some of the arguments of the prolegalization advocates compare the present-day situation to Prohibition in the 1920s. There are certain similarities. The fact that the production, sale and consumption of liquor was against the law did not stop the activities of people who wanted to drink. It only made liquor harder to get and, therefore, more expensive. This played an important part in the emergence of syndicated crime. Whoever controlled the distribution and sales of bootleg liquor stood to make a great deal of money. Gangs formed and went to war to secure territory. Powerful gangsters like Al Capone terrorized the cities. Isn't this what is happening with drugs like crack and cocaine? Shouldn't the failure of Prohibition convince us that legalization is the best policy?

The comparison between the current drug crisis and Prohibition looks good on the surface. In both cases we find people undeterred by laws, risking imprisonment to buy their alcohol or their drugs. In both cases we also find a substantial increase in crime and gang warfare. If you don't pay close attention, you're apt to think the two situations are identical. They're not.

Alcohol and a drug like crack are not the same, and if these two substances cannot be seen as similar, the whole analogy fails. Alcohol, though it causes damage when it is abused, is a familiar thing. We know what it does and we have ways of dealing with the problems it causes. What's more, millions of people drink in social situations and never become alcoholics; most people use liquor in safe ways. Crack and cocaine are different: they are highly addicting and they cause violent changes in personality. We have not even begun to understand what kinds of damage they do to the body and mind. If we legalize these drugs, arguing that adults can make responsible choices, we are making a grave mistake. Maybe normal adults can make such choices, but is a person with a desperate craving for a high a "normal" adult?

Nor would adults be the only users. In the same way that alcohol is readily available to minors who want it, these drugs would be there for the taking. More than ever, in fact. They would be cheaper and young people would know just where to find them. It would be all but impossible for adults to educate them against use. Their legality would send the message that doing cocaine and crack was OK. We might get rid of the drug gangs, but we would have gangs of new drug takers. The trade-off is not worth it.

There are other arguments to consider. In their article entitled "Crackdown" *(The New Republic, July 10, 1989),* James Q. Wilson and John J. DiIulio, Jr., make the point that legalization would be an experiment the results of which we simply cannot predict. We don't know enough about the drugs or their users. Are we ready to rewrite the laws? Wilson and DiIulio also bring up the crucial issue of addicted mothers. What are a baby's rights? Shouldn't babies have the right to begin life without a life-threatening drug addiction?

Of course, arguing against legalization does not make our present problems go away. We have ineffective policing of neighborhoods, overcrowded prisons, plea-bargaining loopholes in our legal system. The crisis intensifies daily. What are we to do?

Wilson and DiIulio make a statement that needs to be heard. They write: "We believe that the moral and welfare costs of heavy drug use are so large that society should continue to enforce the laws against its use for the sake of keeping the number of users as small as possible. But we recognize that by adopting this position, we are placing a heavy burden on those poor communities where drug use is endemic. We are allowing these neighborhoods to be more violent than they would be if the drug were legal."

There are costs that must be understood. But the final fact is this: that a society has a moral and legal obligation to secure the safety and well-being of its citizens. We are having trouble right now in meeting the legal part of the obligation, but this is no reason for turning our backs on the moral considerations. The only answer is to keep working at every level—blocking the production, fighting the smugglers, locating the dealers, monitoring gang activities, increasing street protection, building necessary prisons, expanding the legal facilities, educating the young. . . . We should be doing everything we can to eradicate this tremendous problem.

EXERCISES

1. In an example given earlier in the chapter, two sentences expressing opposing views about smokers' rights were combined into one: "Although smokers claim the right to smoke in public places, they forget that nonsmokers have a right to breathe uncontaminated air." Look at the groups of sentences below. Can you combine the shorter sentences into a single sentence? Try putting one side of the argument in a dependent clause, as in the example given.

   a. The Olympic committee's rules governing drug use must be obeyed. Steroids have been shown to enhance stamina and improve athletic performance.

   b. Deep-fried foods taste delicious and are popular with restaurant goers. Medical tests have proved that diets high in cholesterol and saturated fats can lead to the onset of heart disease. Deep-fried foods are high in cholesterol and saturated fats.

   c. The livelihood of millions of Brazilians depends on the clearing of rain forests to make room for farmland. The earth's ozone layer is being depleted at an alarming rate. Trees are valuable because they convert carbon dioxide into oxygen and help to regulate atmospheric balance.

2. Working individually or in small groups, collect and analyze five opinion pieces from the op-ed pages of a newspaper. Find the writer's thesis. Make an outline that shows the structure of the argument. Does the writer attempt to convince? Can you identify any tactics of persuasion? Be prepared to present one op-ed piece to the rest of the class for discussion.

3. Pick a topic of controversy—gun control, sexism in the workplace, the rights of unwed mothers—and write two different openings for an op-ed piece. The paragraphs should reflect diametrically opposed positions.

4. Using the same issue you chose for Exercise 3, write two more paragraphs, both reflecting the view that you are most partial to. One paragraph should begin with a statement of the opposition's position and end with a statement rejecting that position; the other should begin with a statement of your thesis and then make time for the opposition. Look over Jerome Williams's different approaches to his topic.

5. Describe the flaws in these arguments.

a. You're stupid! That's why I'm right.
b. In 1989, Rupert Hudmill announced that he was no longer associated with the Virgin Vampires. When he decided to destroy the punk rock group, Hudmill gave no reasons.
c. When Luke hit the first pitch into the left-field stands, it was obvious that Mitchell could no longer pitch.
d. When we consider the question of aid to underdeveloped nations, we should always consider first that we, too, are an underdeveloped nation.
e. Since democracy died in Rome with the elevation of Caesar, one can no longer go to the Romans for lessons in the democratic process.
f. No one who dresses like that could possibly know Mozart from Mantovani.
g. Warmongers who masquerade as friends of Egypt or Israel attempt to deceive the gullible.
h. Everybody who votes for Cynthia is a racist.
i. You can't change human nature.
j. There will always be conventional warfare.

6. Write an application to a computer dating service for a friend. Present your friend's qualities (appearance, personality, special talents). Try writing different versions to appeal first to one imagined audience and then another. For instance, direct yourself to a service addressing populations in Boston, Salt Lake City, Atlanta, or any city or area that you know.

7. Pick one of these situations in which to practice the art of persuasion.

   a. The city announces plans to route a new highway directly through your residential neighborhood, which will require the demolition of well-maintained single-family houses and a park. You head a community action group trying to stop this proposal. Address the city's planning board.

   b. You are in the process of applying for your first job after college. Write a cover letter for your résumé to convince your prospective employer to hire you. Apply for the best job you can imagine getting.

8. Break up into groups of three or four for debating. Meet with one of the other groups to determine what issue you will debate and which side your group will take. Use thirty minutes to prepare for a ten-minute debate. Your teacher will set the rules and will moderate.

9. Here are two passages that argue a point of view. Examine them with these questions in mind: (a) Is the line of argument clear? (b) Is it reasonable? (c) Does it seem balanced, acknowledging the opposite point of view? (d) How is it organized? (e) Does the argument display any logical fallacies? If so, how do they affect the argument?

   a. In a society committed to sexual equality, single professional women would be applauded as pioneers. They are breaking down all sorts of ancient prejudices, from the sexual double standard to the connection between femininity and submissiveness, poverty, dependence, powerlessness and incompetence. In the current climate of antifeminist backlash, however, they are loose cannons on the deck. Clearly, the hope in many quarters is that they will give up this careers nonsense if it is made sufficiently arduous, and get back under male "protection" where they belong—even though that protection, in terms of a guarantee of lifelong support, no longer exists.
   This is the underlying message of a variety of seemingly disparate contributions to the public discourse. While Sylvia Ann Hewlett, in *A Lesser Life,* blames the women's movement for the absence of social supports for working mothers, as though the feminist goal of shared parenting were a piece of utopian lunacy, Deborah Fallows, in *A Mother's Work,* portrays women who use day care as shallow materialists, as though stay-at-home moms could waltz back into the workplace whenever they wished. While the Reagan Administration does its best to scuttle affirmative action and thwart comparable worth for pink-collar women, their white-collar sisters find themselves mysteriously "topping out," hitting the "glass ceiling" of covert discrimination. Abortion is under attack. Nonmarital sex is un-

der attack. Infertile women are selfish for having put careers before pregnancy, as though no man ever insisted on postponing fatherhood; but women who beat the clock by having babies without husbands are selfish, too.

Who would have thought that the modest demands of women for decent jobs, equal access to education, shared domestic responsibilities and all the rest would evoke such a torrent of censure? But then who would have thought that in 1986 women would have fewer methods of contraception to choose from then they had ten years ago?

The media coverage of the study, if not quite the study itself, is just another crack of the backlash. Women can't "have it all." Women must "choose": a career or a husband. By focusing on demographics, which cannot be changed and are no one's fault, commentators avoid asking hard questions about the social context that gives the demographics whatever limited significance they have—questions about the structure of work and marriage and child-rearing and society, and about the ways in which those work together to confront both single and married women with a dazzling array of Catch-22s.

Questions about—what a thought—men. It is curious that the study offers no figures on men. Ostensibly, that is because of the "poor quality" of the data, and perhaps that really is the reason. By its silence, however, the study appears to confirm the all too popular assumption that a college-educated heterosexual man's "chance" of marrying is a solid 100 percent right into the grave. Demographically, maybe so, but marriage does, after all, take two. Why assume that baby boom bachelors are God's gift to single women rather than those women's rejects, the men least able to deal with women's raised expectations of marriage?

If our magazine moralists applied themselves to those issues, they might discover that what keeps today's college-educated women unmarried isn't numbers. It's sexism.

> Katha Pollitt, "*That* Survey: Being Wedded
> Is Not Always Bliss" *(The Nation)*

b. You hear it asked, why are there no Martin Luther Kings around today? I think one reason is that there are no black leaders willing to resist the seductions of racial power, or to make the sacrifices moral power requires. King understood that racial power subverts moral power, and he pushed the principles of fairness and equality rather than black power because he believed those principles would bring blacks their most complete liberation. He sacrificed race for morality, and his innocence was made genuine by that sacrifice. What made King the most powerful and extraordinary black leader of this century was not his race but his morality.

Black power is a challenge. It grants whites no innocence; it denies their moral capacity and then demands that they be moral. No power can long insist on itself without evoking an opposite power. Doesn't an insistence on black power call up white power? (And could this have something to do with what many are now calling a resurgence of white racism?) I believe that what divided the races at the dinner party I attended, and what divides them in the nation, can only be bridged by an adherence to those moral principles that disallow race as a source of power, privilege, status, or entitlement of any kind. In our age, principles like fairness and equality are ill-defined and all but drowned in relativity. But this is the fault of people, not principles. We keep them muddied because they are the greatest threat to our presumed innocence and our selective innocence. Moral principles, even when somewhat ambiguous, have the power to assign responsibility and therefore to provide us with knowledge. At the dinner party we were afraid of so severe an accountability.

What both black and white Americans fear are the sacrifices and risks that true racial harmony demands. This fear is the measure of our racial chasm. And though fear always seeks a thousand justifications, none is ever good enough, and the problems we run from only remain to haunt us. It would be right to suggest courage as an antidote to fear, but the glory of the word might only intimidate us into more fear. I prefer the word *effort*—relentless effort, moral effort. What I like most about this word are its connotations of everydayness, earnestness, and practical sacrifice. No matter how badly it might have gone for us that warm summer night, we should have talked. We should have made the effort.

Shelby Steele, "I'm Black, You're White, Who's Innocent?"

8

Writing Research

Your college composition course probably requires that you complete a research project, usually with a formal, properly documented written report. You may be trying to prove a given theory or thesis, or you may be trying to find out information about a topic. Regardless of your purpose, research can provide you with the necessary background information to begin an essay, the necessary evidence and examples to support your arguments, or with guidance as you search for your own answers to questions.

Most research begins with a review of the literature already available on a topic. Browse through dictionaries, encyclopedias, books, magazines, newspapers, scholarly journals, on-line databases, or the World Wide Web (WWW). Public documents, including census reports, congressional records, and other government publications, may also be available in your university library, and many of these documents can be accessed on-line through information services or on the WWW.

The first and often the hardest part of any research project is getting started. To help you find a topic, review Getting Ideas for Essays in Chapter 3. Once you have a rough idea of what your topic will be, start searching through print and on-line sources. This preliminary research can help you clarify what the issues really are, what research and studies have already been done, and what your own position is. You already know how important it is to focus, narrowing your topic to something that can be dealt with adequately in the time and space allotted. Preliminary surveys of sources as a starting point can be essential.

Once you have narrowed your topic and decided how to approach it, you are ready to begin your research. Some of the sources you reviewed earlier in your preliminary research may have pointed the way to additional sources of information. For example, many books and scholarly journals include bibliographies (list of works cited or references); members of on-line discussion groups may have given you lists of print sources or of other on-line discussion groups, WWW addresses, or other electronic sites that house information; and these sources may have in turn pointed you to other sources. One student looking for information for a report on sexual abuse sent a message to an Internet discussion group on sexual abuse and was given the address of some WWW sites that provided additional information. The student was also able to bring her report to life with personal stories that members of the discussion group shared with her on-line.

Keep one caution in mind as you conduct your research: make certain that the sources you are using are reliable ones. Not everything that is in print is necessarily true or reliable, and on-line resources in particular must be carefully evaluated. (Any subscriber can post to most on-line discussion groups and pose as an "expert"; anyone with access and resources can create a Web page on a topic.) You must learn to read these sources critically, evaluating their reliability, and questioning those things that do not seem to be adequately documented or supported. (This may be a good time to review Chapter 2, "Reading, and Reading Well.")

Of course, research includes much more than searching libraries and electronic databases for information. Conducting your own research will often include not only searching through these sources but also conducting interviews, case studies, ethnographic studies, observation, and experimentation. Even watching television or reading advertisements can be forms of research, depending on your topic. Just as scientists conduct experiments to find out what happens if certain variables are changed, writers conduct studies and experiments, too. Students often stop at merely surveying the written work of others rather than conducting their own studies, but research means finding out. Of course, as students, it is important for you to learn where to look to find information, and to discover what information has yet to be discovered.

USING THE LIBRARY

Most library catalogues today are computerized, offering not only information about materials to be found in the library, but access to computerized databases and on-line information services. Large university libraries may be daunting at first sight, and the vast amounts of information now available through on-line sources have created an "information overload." But you can learn to manage these resources with a little practice. Many university libraries offer orientation sessions as well as printed handouts and pamphlets, which can help you find your way through what may at first seem like an impossible labyrinth. Finally, don't forget the reference librarians who are on hand to answer your questions and help you in your search.

The Library Catalogue

The search for information usually begins with the library catalogue. The catalogue lists all of the library's holdings—from books, newspapers,

Library of Congress Classification System	
A	General Works
B	Philosophy, Psychology, Religion
C-F	History
G	Geography, Anthropology
H	Social Sciences
J	Political Science
K	Law
L	Education
M	Music
N	Fine Arts
P	Language and Literature
Q	Science
S	Agriculture
T	Technology
U	Military Science
V	Naval Science
Z	Bibliography, Library Science

Figure 8.1:
The Library of Congress's breakdown of major subject areas.

magazines and journals to video and audio recording and government documents. Some libraries still use the traditional card catalogue—three-by-five-inch cards, organized by subject, author, and title. Most libraries, however, have installed computerized systems that make searching for sources faster and easier. Not only can you search the computerized library catalogue for subjects, authors, and titles, but you can often use keyword searches that will greatly increase your chances of finding useful information. The computer is able to search through a library's holdings in a matter of seconds, too, completing complicated searches that would have taken hours, or even days, using the old card catalogues.

Most libraries organize the books on their shelves according to the Library of Congress classification system. Figure 8.1 lists some of the major subject areas in this system. A basic knowledge of these categories can help you locate books and relevant works in your subject area. But don't overlook the value of simply browsing through the shelves themselves as you search for information, too—you can often find valuable sources overlooked during your searches through the library catalogue.

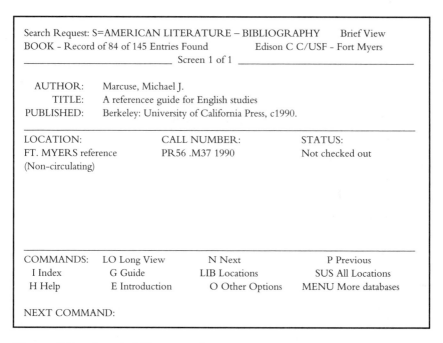

```
Search Request: S=AMERICAN LITERATURE – BIBLIOGRAPHY      Brief View
BOOK - Record of 84 of 145 Entries Found          Edison C C/USF - Fort Myers
_____ Screen 1 of 1 _____

     AUTHOR:      Marcuse, Michael J.
      TITLE:      A referencee guide for English studies
  PUBLISHED:      Berkeley: University of California Press, c1990.

LOCATION:                   CALL NUMBER:              STATUS:
FT. MYERS reference         PR56 .M37 1990            Not checked out
(Non-circulating)




COMMANDS:    LO Long View          N Next              P Previous
  I Index        G Guide           LIB Locations       SUS All Locations
  H Help         E Introduction    O Other Options     MENU More databases

NEXT COMMAND:
```

Figure 8.2: *A typical library catalogue screen entry*

Locating Information

If you are looking for a specific title or author, the library catalogue will give you the information you need to obtain the source. Most computerized catalogues will provide you with the Library of Congress classification numbers, publication information, including the name of the publisher and the year of publication, and whether or not the book has been already checked out.

Figure 8.2 shows a typical library catalog screen. At the top of the screen is an indication of the search request—in this example, s = AMERICAN LITERATURE—BIBLIOGRAPHY. The library catalog locates 145 entries on this subject, each of which can be looked at separately. The screen gives information on entry 84—including its author, title, publisher, location, call number, and circulation status. The commands along the bottom of the screen will lead to more information. "LO" (Long View) may give additional information about the work, such as the number of pages, and whether it contains illustrations or bibliographies. Other commands allow you to move around through the database, returning to look at other entries, beginning a new search, or moving to other databases.

Most computerized catalogues also allow for searches based on keywords—words or phrases linked to specific works and entered into the computerized database by the author, editor, or librarians. Subject searches will find only those sources whose entire subject matter is about the topic;

keyword searches will return sources that have substantial information on a given topic, even though this may not be clear from the title or description of the work. The search can be refined still further through Boolean operators—search terms that narrow or expand a keyword search as needed. These clever devices are usually indicated in uppercase letters and include words like "AND," "OR," and "NOT." To illustrate their usefulness, let's say you are confronted with a topic such as "literature." The computer database will probably flood you with more entries than you could ever wade through. Using a keyword search and Boolean operators, you can limit your work to something more manageable. Thus, if you are interested in finding literary criticism, you simply have to enter "literature AND criticism."

Specialized indexes and bibliographies may also be available through your library catalogue. Information services such as *ERIC* (Educational Resources Information Center) and *InfoTrac* allow you to download and print out full texts of articles. Or you may be able to search other libraries that participate in the interlibrary loan program, allowing you to request books that are not available in your own library. Check with a reference librarian for information on how to use these specialized services.

Perhaps the most obvious benefit of computerized databases is the speed with which they can be updated, thus providing users with the most current information on any topic. And instead of searching through several different volumes or file drawers, you can search the entire database with a few well-chosen keystrokes, limiting your search to certain years, publication types (books, journals, video recordings, etc.), or languages. Familiarizing yourself with your library catalogue can save you hours of frustration, wasted time, and effort, and leave you more time for writing your report.

Specialized References and Databases

Indexes and bibliographies are compilations of information about sources. They are valuable as guides to information available in specific subject areas. Some of these sources will summarize general knowledge about a topic, and many will also list bibliographies for further reference.

Dictionaries such as the *Oxford English Dictionary,* the *Random House Dictionary,* and *Webster's Third New International Dictionary of the English Language* are a rich source of information. In addition to defining terms, dictionaries can provide you with word origins, etymologies, and the evolution of meaning and usage. Dictionaries are available in print, on CD-ROM, through on-line services, and on the Internet (a searchable, hypertext version of *Webster's Dictionary* is located on the World Wide Web at http://c.gp.cs.cmu.edu:5103/prog/webster). Many word-processing programs have a dictionary or thesaurus built in as well. There are also many specialized references such as the *Dictionary of Cultural Literacy, Merriam Webster's Medical Dictionary,* and *Bartlett's Familiar Quotations* that can give you more in-depth coverage of specific topics.

Familiar encyclopedias such as *Encyclopedia Americana* and *The New Encyclopedia Britannica* are of course still standard references but many encyclopedias can also be accessed through your computer. For example, *The Software Toolworks Multimedia Encyclopedia* is available on CD-ROM, and America On-Line offers its subscribers on-line versions of *Compton's Living, Columbia Precise,* and the *Grolier Multimedia* encyclopedias. Specialized biographical sources such as *Who's Who in America* and *Current Biography,* which give biographical data on living persons, may contain information on many people not found in encyclopedias. The *Biography and Genealogy Master Index,* the *Biography Index,* and *Webster's New Biographical Dictionary* give information on both living and historical figures.

For contemporary topics, indexes to journal and newspaper articles provide the most current information. You are probably already familiar with the *Readers' Guide to Periodical Literature,* which indexes an array of non-specialized magazines. There are also specialized sources which index periodicals in specific subject areas, such as the *Applied Science and Technology Index, Biographical and Agricultural Index, Business Periodicals Index,* and *Engineering Index. ERIC* indexes journals and research in the field of education and can point you to valuable information on a wide variety of topics covered in this area. For locating newspaper articles, some of the better known indexes include the *New York Times Index, NewsBank, Wall Street Journal Index,* and *Washington Post Index.*

To locate government documents and information, you can look in the *Congressional Information Service Index,* the *Statistical Abstract of the United States,* or the *American Statistics Index.* The U.S. Government Printing Office publishes information on consumer, government, and citizen interests covering many areas of knowledge. These publications are listed in the *Monthly Catalog of United States Government Publications.* In addition, reports on legislation, hearings, public policies, treaties, and other government information are usually published and available to the public under the Freedom of Information Act. Many government documents are also available through on-line services and on the WWW.

Specialized bibliographies can help you to locate additional sources on most topics. The *MLA Bibliography* indexes books and journal articles on language and literature; *Books in Print* and *Paperback Books in Print* index currently available titles from publishers; and the *Book Review Digest* abstracts many published book reviews in addition to listing information to help you locate the original reviews. Almanacs and atlases can provide maps, statistical information such as population figures or economic statistics, and other pertinent information.

There are also overlooked sources that can be invaluable—among them the telephone book, the public relations offices of large firms and the public officials in your area. And your own university campus is home to specialists in many fields who can answer questions or point you in the right direction. Even friends and family members can be invaluable sources of historical, experiential, or expert knowledge.

ON-LINE RESEARCH

Besides helping you in your search for more traditional forms of print resources through computerized catalogues and search engines, on-line sources such as the Internet offer information that may not be available in print form, information that is being updated daily. In addition to published works, you can access sites such as MUDs (Multi-User Dimensions) and IRC (Internet Relay Chat), which allow multiple users to log on at the same time and talk to each other, and electronic discussion lists, which use electronic mail to send messages to multiple subscribers. Such sites would allow you to conduct interviews, case studies, and ethnographic research entirely on-line.

Many journals, magazines, and newspapers are now being published on-line. Some of these also appear in print, but many of them can only be accessed on-line. The Gutenberg Project has made the full texts of many short stories, novels, and other works of literature available on-line as well. Although these are primarily works in the public domain—old enough so that their copyrights have expired—some authors and publishers are now publishing new books entirely on-line. Many of these can be read or downloaded and printed out, usually at no extra cost or at substantially lower costs than traditional print copies. News services, magazines, and newspapers offer full-text articles, photographs, videos, and sound files for viewing or downloading. Information on businesses and products, government publications and information, and collections of student and scholarly research on a wide variety of topics can also be found on-line. Universities and libraries have compiled bibliographic sites that list important print sources as well as providing searchable databases and links to on-line sources. Newsgroups and listservs often include as members experts on a given topic. As noted, there are indexes to help you find groups discussing almost any topic imaginable.

The Internet

The Internet is a vast international network of interconnected computers sharing protocols that allow subscribers to access information remotely. Begun in the 1960s by the U.S. Department of Defense as a means of secure communication, the Internet has expanded to include millions of subscribers—from government, educational, commercial users to private individuals. The World Wide Web is not the same thing as the Internet. The Web is a way of organizing and viewing information on the Internet. New WWW "browsers" that use point-and-click graphical interfaces have made sifting through the layers of information much more user-friendly and greatly contributed to the rapid growth of the Internet in the last few years.

Figure 8.3 shows the home page for the Library of Congress on the WWW, viewed using a Netscape browser. The menu commands and buttons along the top of the screen allow you to move around through other

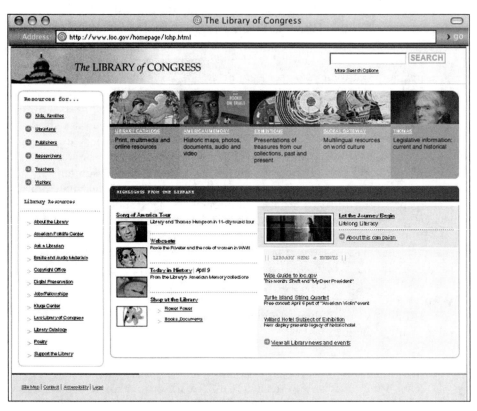

Figure 8.3: *WWW home page of the Library of Congress*

home pages on the WWW, and to perform functions such as saving, printing, or revising a document as well as obtaining additional information about the document. The Library of Congress page also has "buttons"—graphics that allow you to move through the pages on the Library of Congress site. For instance, by clicking on the SEARCH button on your screen, you can perform a keyword search of the WWW pages and gopher menus of the Library of Congress. Other text on the page is linked to specific information. Clicking on headings, such as AMERICAN MEMORY will take you to specific pages about that subject on the Library of Congress system.

Search engines can help you to locate information on the Web. Most popular search engines use plain English queries, keyword searches, and Boolean operators to locate information. Some popular search engines, such as Alta Vista, Lycos, and Infoseek—private providers—search through the myriad of sites on-line looking for the information you request; others, such as DejaNews and Tile.Net search through specific types of sources, such as newsgroups and listservs. Some large web sites, such as the Internet Public Library, offer their own searchable indexes as well.

Search engines work somewhat like the library catalogue—by searching for keywords you can obtain a list of possible sources on your topic. Many search engines include brief summaries of sites as well and will usually provide you with links—verbal cross-references—to the sites. However, like the library catalog, you must learn to narrow your searches to be productive. Spend some time browsing through the links and surveying the information you find. This can often help you focus your ideas and narrow your topic, as well as provide you with factual information. Make sure you keep a record of the sources you find in case you want to refer to them again or use them in your report.

WWW browsers are only one way to move through the Internet. Gopher and FTP protocols, which are older than the WWW, can be accessed with or without a WWW browser. Gopher is one of the earliest protocols for organizing information on the Internet, using a menu-driven system to find and retrieve documents stored on remote computers throughout the world. You can search through gopherspace using search protocols—procedures—with such whimsical names as Veronica, Jughead, and Archie.

FTP (File Transfer Protocol) is a system that provides storage of and access to files, documents, and programs on the Internet. Many of these sites offer anonymous FTP (using the login name "anonymous" and your E-mail address for a password) although some FTP sites limit access to authorized users only.

Telnet is another important way to access information on the Internet. Telnet protocols allow you to log on to remote computers and work in those computers just like you would on your own personal computer. Most Telnet sites require users to have an account on their server, but many allow guest accounts. You may already use the Telnet protocol to access your school's computer from home, and many libraries allow remote access to their library catalogue using Telnet protocols.

E-mail and electronic discussion lists are also valuable aids to the researcher. Many electronic discussion lists, such as Usenet newsgroups, are open to all subscribers. Most lists center on discussions of specific topics of interest to members, such as ACW-L, the listserv for the Alliance for Computers and Writing, or the alt.books.kurt-vonnegut newsgroup, which offers discussions of, you guessed it, books by Kurt Vonnegut. Of course, before using information from a discussion list, you should verify its reliability. Look carefully at the information on the posting: Is the Internet address of the sender a university address or a commercial site? Does the message include a signature file that gives information about the writer's affiliation? What makes the author an expert? You can find discussion lists on most topics using search engines such as DejaNews, which indexes archives of Usenet newsgroups, and Tile.Net, which indexes mailing lists and FTP sites as well as Usenet groups.

Other Electronic Sources

The term "on-line" is a rather nebulous term. You are on-line when you are connected to a local area network (LAN) or to a wide area network (WAN), to a local bulletin board service, or to the Internet. Bulletin board services (BBSs), like the Internet, are accessed using modems and phone lines and usually require an account on the host computer (the computer that houses the BBS software and files and to which other users may dial in and connect). BBSs come in a variety of configurations and sizes, from the local BBS organized entirely around a specific topic (such as computer user groups) to company BBSs where employees dial in and share information and files and can communicate with each other using electronic mail, to the one-size-fits-all mega-BBSs like America On-Line, CompuServ, and Prodigy. Some BBSs also offer a gateway to the Internet—or they may offer files, services, and information that cannot be found on the Internet and are available only to their subscribers.

For example, America On-Line offers reference sources such as encyclopedias, a thesaurus, and dictionaries. There are also countless "chat rooms" where students can "talk" to teachers in real time and get help with their assignments or subscribers can obtain technical support, ask questions of experts on various topics, communicate with celebrities, or just chat with on-line friends. Like the Internet, most BBSs also offer various message boards or forums, similar to Internet newsgroups, centered around topics of interest to subscribers, ranging from discussions of AIDs and politics to discussions of software and computers to discussions of books and films. Some of these discussion groups are limited to BBS subscribers, but others offer access to Internet newsgroups and electronic mail as well.

With the advent of CD-ROM technology—storage technology that allows for vast amounts of information to be contained on a small, round disk—more and more publishers are moving into the electronic realm. An entire set of encyclopedias can be obtained on a single CD-ROM, at a fraction of the cost of print, allowing for multimedia effects such as video and sound files and hypertextual—cross-referenced—linking that are not possible in print versions.

Many software programs now include information on a wide variety of topics as well—Intuit's *QuickBooks Deluxe* CD-ROM version includes information on how to set up a business. Specialized programs like *It's Legal* from Parson's Technology offer information on legal topics and *WordPerfect's* Grammatik checks documents for common grammatical errors and offers an on-line handbook that discusses the rules of grammar.

DOCUMENTATION

Writing is a conversation, between writers and their readers, of course, but also between writers and other writers. When you include information you have gathered from other sources, whether you quote it directly, summarize or paraphrase it, or when you use the ideas of other authors, you need to give credit. There are specific styles for citations in different disciplines. In the humanities, most writers follow the system of documentation outlined by the Modern Language Association in the *MLA Handbook for Writers of Research Papers* (4th ed., New York, 1995). For Internet resources, the Alliance for Computers and Writing has endorsed the Walker/ACW Style Sheet. Check with your teacher for the exact citation format you should follow.

The List of Works Cited

All properly credited research reports should include a list of works cited—a list of all the sources cited in the text. A report may also include a list of works consulted—a list of works that may not have been cited in the report but may have been helpful in formulating ideas. It is crucial to keep careful notes of the sources you consult as you do your research. Not only will this allow you to easily put together your works cited list, but it may also save you considerable time if you need to go back and consult a source again.

The information you need for your final list of works cited will include the author's name, exactly as shown on the title page of the work, and the complete title, including any subtitles, underlined if you are taking notes by hand or with a typewriter, italicized if you are using a computer or word processor. You will also need to note the publication information—the place of publication (the first one if there is more than one listed), the name of the publisher (see the *MLA Handbook* on how to list the names of publishers), and the year of publication for books. For journals and newspapers, you will want to note the volume and issue numbers, the exact date of publication, and the page numbers of the article.

The list of works cited begins immediately after the last page of a report. Entries must be alphabetized, usually by the author's last name or the first major word of the title if no author is listed. They should be double-spaced throughout. Book and journal titles should be italicized, if possible, or underlined. The second and subsequent lines of each entry are indented five spaces, or half an inch. If you are using a word processor, you can simply use the "hanging indent" feature of your word processing program to format each entry. The punctuation is an important part of the citation as well. Generally, a period is placed after each major item of information—after the author's name, after the title, and at the end of the entry. See specific examples below. For other types of works, see the *MLA Handbook*.

A Book with One Author:
Bolter, J. David. *Writing Space: The Computer, Hypertext, and the History of Writing.* Hillsdale, NJ: Lawrence Erlbaum, 1991.

A Book with Two or Three Authors:
Hairston, Maxine, and John. J. Ruszkiewicz. *The Scott, Foresman Handbook for Writers.* New York: HarperCollins, 1996.

A Book with More Than Three Authors:
Flower, Linda, et al., eds. *Making Thinking Visible: Writing, Collaborative Planning, and Classroom Inquiry.* Urbana, IL: NCTE, 1994.

A Book with an Editor:
Sutherland, James, ed. *The Oxford Book of Literary Anecdotes.* New York: Oxford UP, 1975.

An Article or Part of an Edited Collection:
Dyer, Richard. "Entertainment and Utopia." *The Cultural Studies Reader.* Ed. Simon During. London: Routledge, 1993. 271–83.

A Translation:
Martin, Henri Jean. *The History and Power of Writing.* Trans. Lydia G. Cochrane. Chicago: U of Chicago P, 1994.

A Book with More Than One Volume:
Gassner, John, ed. *A Treasury of the Theatre.* Rev. ed. 3 vols. New York: Simon, 1963.

A New Edition:
Williams, Joseph M. *Style: Ten Lessons in Clarity and Grace.* 5th ed. New York: Longman, 1997.

A Popular Magazine Article:
Paglia, Camille, and Neil Postman. "She Wants Her TV! He Wants His Book!" *Harper's Magazine* Mar. 1991: 44+.

A Journal Article:
Miller, Susan. "What Does It Mean to Be Able to Write? The Question of Writing in the Discourses of Literature and Composition." *College English* 45 (1983): 219–35.

A Newspaper Article:
Varma, Kavita. "Footnotes in Electronic Age." *USA Today* 7 Feb. 1996: 7D.

An Article with No Author Listed
"Demolition Derby." *Time* 3 Jul. 1995: 14–15.

A Lecture:
Haber, Chuck. "Juvenile Involvement in Gangs in Tampa and Nation-wide." Lecture. University of South Florida, 20 March 1996.

An Interview:
Ross, Theresa. Personal interview. 10 April 1996.

A Sound Recording:
Bream, Julian, perf. *A Celebration of Andres Segovia.* New York: BMG, 1984.

A Radio or Television Program:
"Treasure of the Andes." *Nature.* Narr. George Page. PBS. WEDU, Tampa. 1 Sep. 1996.

A Film:
Lucas, George, dir. *Star Wars.* Prod. Gary Kurtz. Perf. Mark Hamill, Harrison Ford, Carrie Fisher, Peter Cushing, Alec Guiness, and David Prowse. Videorecording. CBS Fox, 1992.

A Computer Software Program:
Site Builder Workshop. New York: Microsoft, 1996.

An Entry or Text From an Electronic Database:
Parras, John A. "Modern Poetic Prose: Lyricism, Narrative, and the Social Implications of Generic Form." *DAI* 57 (1996): 696A. Columbia University, 1996. 1 Sep. 1996.

A World Wide Web Page:
Hughes, Kevin. "Entering the World Wide Web: A Guide to Cyberspace." May 1994. http://www.eit.com/web/www.guide/ (28 Aug. 1996).

A Gopher Site:
Goodwin, John E. "Elements of E-Text Style." Vers. 1.0. 1993. gopher://caprica.com:70/00/use-guides/email/Elements-of-E-Text-Style (1 Sep. 1996).

An FTP Site:
Roush, Wade. "Have Computer, Won't Travel." 1993. ftp://ftp.media.mit.edu/pub/MediaMOO/Papers/Roush—Have-Computer-Won%27t-Travel (1 Sep. 1994).

A Telnet Site:
Internet Public Library MOO. telnet://ipl.sils.umich.edu:8888 (28 Aug. 1996).

An Electronic Mail Message:
Thomson, Barry. "MOO Project." Personal E-mail (10 Aug. 1996).

A Listserv or Newsgroup Message:
Kirkpatrick, Judi. "Computers and Writing '97 Call." rhetnt-1@ mizzoul.missouri.edu (26 Aug. 1996).

For more information on Internet sources, see the "Walker/ACW Style Sheet" at http://www.cas.usf.edu/english/walker/mla. html or the *MLA Handbook*.

In-Text References

Most plagiarism by students is unintentional; poor note taking and not fully understanding the difference between general knowledge and information that needs to be cited are often the culprits. Paraphrases and summaries as well as direct quotations need to be cited, no matter where the information was obtained. Even general information and ideas should be cited if they are new to you. For example, you would not need to cite a statement such as "Many young people today commit violent crimes." However, if you say "Violent crimes by young people have increased in the last thirty years," you should include your source. It is usually far better to document too much than too little.

In-text or parenthetical references are preferred to footnotes because they are less distracting to the reader. The purpose of the in-text reference is to point to the complete reference in the list of works cited. Generally, you will include the author's last name and the page number for the specific reference if it is listed by the author's last name. For example, if the entry in the works cited list is:

Bolter, J. David *Writing Space: The Computer, Hypertext, and the History of Writing*. Hillsdale, NJ: Lawrence Erlbaum, 1991.

A parenthethetic reference to this work would be:

Our notions of writing have changed many times throughout the years, from cave paintings to the printed word to electronic hypertext (Bolter 33).

If the author's name is listed in the text, however, you need give only the page number in the parenthetic reference:

J. David Bolter refers to our era as the "late age of print" (xv).

For entries in the list of works cited where no author is listed, the parenthetic reference would include the title, or a shortened version for long titles, and the page number:

One theory explains: "Western cultures tell young people to behave maturely; at the same time they are regarded as too young to enjoy the rights and privileges of adults" (*Grolier*).

Internet and electronic sources, and other sources that do not specify page numbers, will be cited using the author's last name or the title as appropriate. If more than one work by the same author is included in the list of works cited, give the title of the specific reference in addition to the author's name and the page number, if applicable. For example,

> Hemingway, Ernest. *A Farewell to Arms.* New York: Scribner, 1929.
>
> ———. *The Old Man and the Sea.* New York: Scribner, 1952.

References in your paper to one of these works would need to include the title as well as the author.

> The characterization of Catherine is at once both that of a strong woman and a woman who serves as merely a backdrop for the actions of the male character (Hemingway, *Farewell*).

Here are some specific examples from the citations on pages 262–264.

> A book with one author (Bolter 33).
> A book with two or three authors (Hairston and Ruszkiewicz 671).
> A book with more than three authors (Flower et al. 54–5).
> A book with an editor (Sutherland 176).
> An article or part of an edited collection (Dyer 277).
> A newspaper article (Varma 7D)
> An article with no author ("Demolition" 14)
> A computer software program (*Site Builder*).
> A World Wide Web page (Hughes).

See the *MLA Handbook* for more information on the use of parenthetic references and citations.

A SAMPLE RESEARCH PROJECT

Sharon Boyette, a freshman at the University of Maryland, was watching the evening news when her attention was caught by a report on violent crimes by juveniles. According to the statistics in the news report, violent crimes by young people were increasing at an alarming rate. She listened to a report about a young boy who drowned his four-year-old sister just because he was bored. The previous week Sharon had heard a lecture in her sociology class about teen gangs and the senseless violence sometimes committed by gang members. "Why?" she wondered. "What would make kids be like that?"

The next day in Sharon's freshman English class the teacher instructed students in how to use Internet search engines. Using keywords and Boolean operators, they were told to try and find information on a topic that they might want to use for their research papers. After class, Sharon logged on to the Internet and brought up the World Wide Web. Still thinking about the news broadcast, she decided to see if she could find anything on the Web about it. She went to the home page for the search

http://www.ncjrs.org/
tstfiles/fs-9408.txt
(4/4/96)

Cantelon, Sharon L.

"Family Strengthening for High Risk Youth"

U.S. Office of Juvenile Justice and Delinquency Prevention (OJJDP)
Fact Sheet #8
March 1994

Prevention of juvenile deliquency and influence of the family.

Figure 8.4: *A sample bibliographic card for a source on the Internet*

engine and typed in "Violent crimes." There were over 4,000 entries! Browsing through the summaries, however, she quickly realized that many of the entries had nothing to do with crimes by young people. She tried again, using the search engine and limiting her search with Boolean operators, she typed in "Violent crimes AND juveniles." This time, the search engine found over 2,700 entries.

Sharon realized her topic was still too broad, and she would have to narrow her focus for a paper. One of the entries the search engine had found caught her attention, however. It was entitled, "Teen Violence: The Myths and the Realities" by Randolph T. Holhut. According to the article, teen violence was not nearly as prevalent as the news broadcast had led her to believe. And, according to the author, the primary reason that teenagers commit violent crimes can be traced to poverty. But the little boy who had drowned his sister did not come from a poor family—his was an average, middle-income family, on vacation in Disney World.

She searched some more, finding a government site for the Office of Juvenile Justice and Delinquency Prevention that seemed to agree with the news broadcast that violent crimes by young people were increasing. One of the headings, "Delinquency Prevention," caught her eye and she searched through the fact sheets on-line, making careful notes of the URLs she found so she could return to the sites later. She wrote down the bibliographic information on three-by-five-inch cards, marking those sites that seemed to have the most valuable information and making sure she noted the date she visited the sites (see the sample bibliographic card in Figure 8.4). She realized she would need to do some more reading on her topic, but now she had a good idea of what she was looking for: why young people commit juvenile crimes and what can be done about the problem. She still did not have enough information, however, to formulate a thesis.

RC
555
.M27

Juvenile Delinquence -- Causes

Magid, Ken, and Carol A. McKelvey

High Risk: Children without Conscience

New York: Bantam, 1988

Possible causes of juvenile deliquency. Includes a bibliography.

Figure 8.5: *A sample bibliographic card for a book*

After class Sharon went to the library and searched through the online catalog. She typed in the subject "juvenile delinquency" and found that the library had nearly 1,300 entries. She tried again. Using a keyword search and Boolean operators, she entered "juvenile delinquency AND prevention." This time the catalog returned 612 sources. She brought up the list of results and noticed that they were sorted by date, with the most recent books listed first. Her teacher had said that for most topics she should try to find the most current information available. She noted the call numbers of several recent books that her library owned, making sure they were not checked out. She was able to locate them easily on the shelves by their Library of Congress call numbers. She carried the books to a table and began browsing through them. On three-by-five-inch note cards, she wrote down the author's name, the title of the book, and the publication information. In the upper left-hand corner of each card she noted the call numbers, and in the upper right-hand corner she listed the general category or subject covered by the book (see Figure 8.5). The card would help her if she needs to relocate the book later for her paper. It would also keep her from duplicating her efforts if she needed to search again.

The research librarian helped Sharon locate additional sources. He showed her how to use the *Readers' Guide,* and he helped her search through the newspaper indexes that her library subscribed to. He also showed her how to use the microfiche reader and print out a copy of an article she found in a back issue of the *Dallas Times Herald.*

Although Sharon realized that she would not use all of the information and sources she found in her final paper, the research helped her to formulate her own opinions. Many of the authors of the books and articles

---

Magid and McKelvey, *High Risk*   *Causes*
p. 3

    "What happens, right or wrong, in the critical first two years of a
    baby's life will imprint that child as an adult."

Figure 8.6: *A sample bibliographic card for a quotation*

she looked at presented conflicting opinions. She checked the statistical information carefully by looking at several different sources, and, remembering what her teacher had said about checking the validity of her sources,
she noted the authors' affiliations. She read critically, trying to discover the
author's purpose in writing the work—was any bias on the part of the author evident? How reliable was the information?

   Finally, Sharon began to feel confident that she was ready to begin
her paper. She had a good idea what her thesis would be: strengthening the
family can help prevent juvenile delinquency. She took notes carefully,
making sure she copied quotations exactly, enclosing them in quotation
marks on her note cards so she would not mistakenly present them as her
own words. She was also careful to note the page number and source on
her note cards so she could recheck the sources later if necessary and cite
them correctly in her final paper (see Figure 8.6). Most of her notes either
summarized or paraphrased the information in her articles. For instance,
the ACLU "Fact Sheet on Juvenile Crime" reported: "Contrary to public
perception, the percentage of violent crimes committed by juveniles is low.
According to one estimate, only 13 percent of violent crimes are committed by young people." In her notes, shown in Figure 8.7, she summarized
the information in her own words.

   At home, she sorted the note cards, jotting down key ideas on a piece
of paper in the same order as the cards. This would become the rough outline for her paper. She realized she would have to omit some of the infor-

---

ACLU, "Fact Sheet on Juvenile Crime"   *Statistics*
(4/4/96)

    The incidence of violent crimes actually committed by young people is
    much lower than most people believe -- only 13%.

Figure 8.7: *A sample bibliographic card showing a paraphrased summary*

mation she had found. She set these cards aside. Other points she decided needed more clarification or support, and she marked these for her next trip to the library.

Sharon was finally ready to begin. She stared at the blank computer screen for a few minutes and then typed, "Strengthening the family can help prevent juvenile delinquency." She continued writing, developing the major points from her outline into complete sentences. Then she went back and, using her note cards, added support. She used statistical information from her notes and summaries of important ideas as evidence. She included examples and definitions of key ideas. Using the story that had first caught her attention and prompted her interest in the problem of violent crimes by juveniles, she developed her introduction.

When she finished her first draft, she printed it out and read it over. Pen in hand, she noted where the logic seemed weak, where she had made statements that needed support or that seemed to be contradictory. She marked up the draft, changing the order of some of the paragraphs. Some of her sentences just did not seem to fit. For instance, she had included information on how much money was spent to incarcerate juvenile delinquents. She realized now that this did not belong in her paper, so she deleted it. Since she was using a word processor, revising the draft was easy. Once the logic and the order seemed clear, she read her paper again and rewrote sentences that seemed awkward or unclear. She checked the grammar carefully, making sure that subjects and verbs agreed, that verb tenses were consistent, that modifiers were in the right place. Using a grammar handbook, she noted the correct spacing and use of ellipses, checked her commas, and verified the format for her citations. Then she set the draft aside.

A few days later, she reread the draft. This time she was able to distance herself a little from the paper, reading it as she hoped her audience would. Several sentences still seemed unclear, but she was able to revise them and make the worlds flow much more smoothly. She added the final touches, the header with her last name and page numbers using the document header feature in her word processor, retyping her outline and adding a title page. Using her note cards, she prepared the list of works cited, carefully checking the information as well as the format and punctuation. Her final paper follows on the next page.

Juvenile Delinquency Begins at Home

by

Sharon D. Boyett

Expository Writing

Prof. D. Noonan

Spring, 1997

```
       Juvenile Delinquency
         Begins at Home


   Thesis: Strengthening the family
can help prevent juvenile delinquency.
    I. Introduction
       A. Michael kills his four-year-
          old sister.
       B. Michael shows no remorse for
          his crime.
          1. Children like Michael are
             unattached; they have
             never bonded with a pri-
             mary caregiver.
          2. The fault is not in the ju-
             venile justice system but
             in the home.
   II. Statistical Information
       A. The incidence of violent
          crimes committed by young
          people has increased, and the
          crimes are more serious.
          1. In the 1950s, most crimes
             by teenagers were rarely
             more than hubcap thefts and
             truancy.
          2. Since 1985, murder and non-
             negligent homicide, rob-
             bery, aggravated assault,
             motor vehicle theft, and
```

       drug abuse have increased
       alarmingly.

   B. Federal, state, and local gov-
      ernments have been taking mea-
      sures to alleviate the problem
      of juvenile delinquency.

      1. Governments have increased
        the security and size of
        juvenile detention centers.

      2. Governments have introduced
        new programs to help reha-
        bilitate offenders.

III. Causes

   A. One theory is that juvenile
      delinquency is caused by con-
      flicting messages, such as
      telling young people to act
      maturely but not giving them
      any of the rights and privi-
      leges of adults.

   B. Infants who fail to establish
      a close bond with a care-giv-
      ing adult are more likely to
      become juvenile criminals.

IV. Reasons

   A. Children fail to bond with a
      primary care-giver.

   B. Focus on punishment and reha-
      bilitation instead of preven-
      tion.

V. Conclusion

    A. A major cause of juvenile delinquency is the breakdown of the family.

    B. We need to take steps, such as instituting family leave policies and working to strengthen families, to prevent the problem of juvenile delinquency before it occurs.

Sharon D. Boyett

Expository Writing

Prof. D. Noonan

Spring, 1997

Juvenile Delinquency
Begins at Home

It is nine o'clock on Saturday morning in Orlando, Florida, a beautiful day for a family trip to Walt Disney World. Michael plays quietly by the hotel pool with his four-year-old sister waiting for his parents to get dressed. Michael becomes bored and begins to pace around the pool side. Suddenly, he grabs his sister and throws her into the swimming pool. She cannot swim. He smiles as he watches

Attention-getting introduction

Use of present tense to make the story more immediate

his sister sink to the bottom. In-
trigued, he pulls up a chair and
watches his sister's lifeless body in
the pool. He returns to the hotel room
and watches cartoons while he waits
for his parents to get ready. After a
few moments of silence, he asks his
mother, "What is the white stuff that
comes out of your mouth when you are
drowning?" His mother immediately
asks, "Where is your sister?" Michael
smiles and answers, "In the pool."

During police questioning, Michael   *Introduction of key*
shows no sign of remorse, but seems to   *ideas*
enjoy the attention. He is later diag-
nosed as an unattached child that
never bonded with his primary care
giver. One can go into any library and
find case study after case study of
children ranging in age from four to
eighteen years old who commit violent
crimes with no remorse or guilt of any
kind. Although thousands of professionals working to correct problems in
the juvenile justice system feel that
these children can be rehabilitated,
the problem is not only in our juvenile justice system, but in the home
as well. Strengthening the family can   *Thesis statement*
help prevent juvenile delinquency.

In the 1950s, the majority of crimes committed by youths under the age of eighteen were rarely more than hubcap thefts and truancy. By the 1980s, a new type of young criminal was emerging, however, literally from the house next door. Federal, state, and local governments have been taking measures to alleviate the problem of juvenile delinquency by increasing the security and size of juvenile detention centers and by introducing new programs to help rehabilitate offenders. Have these measures improved the situation? The answer, quite simply, is no. Crime and delinquency will be reduced only to the degree that we are willing to address the wider social problems, such as maintaining and supporting the family unit. "The hopes and dreams of juvenile delinquents are not much different from that of a normal teenager," says Andy Hjelmeland in *Kids in Jail.* "Some dream of becoming a famous movie star or athlete. However, the majority of them just want a good job, and . . . a functional family" (40). Society must be concerned with keeping children out of trouble, instead of attempting to rescue them af-

Author's name cited in text; parenthetic reference includes page number only

Use of ellipsis to indicate omitted material

ter they have crossed the line into the world of juvenile delinquency.

A juvenile delinquent is any child, an unmarried person under the age of eighteen, alleged to be dependent, who has committed a felony, misdemeanor, contempt of court, or violation of a local penal ordinance, and whose case has not been prosecuted as an adult. Since 1985, murder and nonnegligent homicide has risen 321%, robbery 87%, aggravated assault 98%, motor vehicle theft 175%, and drug abuse 1420% (Zelfden A1).

Statistics cited from a newspaper article

There are several theories that criminologists who study juvenile delinquency use to explain the causes of delinquent behavior. One theory explains: "Western cultures tell young people to behave maturely; at the same time they are regarded as too young to enjoy the rights and privileges of adults" (*Grolier*). Still another theory holds that infants who fail to establish a close bond with a care-giving adult are more likely to become juvenile criminals. Numerous frustrated and confused children who see no hope for the future simply do not know which direction to take. Most

Author's last name and page number in parenthetic reference

Electronic source with no author or page number; shortened version of title in parenthetic reference

need love and guidance but feel they have to find it on their own. Many of these children have never properly bonded or attached with a primary caregiver. They perceive that "adults don't have it together" and know nothing about life, parenting, or love. A child develops healthy social skills and excels if at least one of the parents has bonded with him or her. Loving parents provide children with a secure environment in which to perceive life as a series of challenges that build confidence, rather than as a progression of unsolvable problems that destroy self-worth. Many sociologists and counselors who deal with delinquents blame the rapidly escalating number and seriousness of juvenile crimes on the lack of parental bonding and attachment. A child's love for his or her parents provides a safe, secure, calming feeling that is imperative in proper social growth.

Other factors that could contribute to delinquency are high divorce rates, day care problems, lack of national parental leave policy, epidemic teenage pregnancies, too-late adoptions, the foster care system, ab-

sence of the mother and/or father during critical periods, post-partum depression, infant medical problems,
abuse, neglect, and infant unrespon-
siveness (Magid and McKelvey 4). Any
or all of these problems can lead to
juvenile delinquency. For example,
Michael was an adopted child caught up
in the foster care system until he was
about three years old. By the time
Michael was officially adopted and began living with his new parents, he
had been in the arms of various people, never bonding with any one certain individual. Michael never learned
how to trust and depend on a primary
figure in his young life.

Work by two
authors

Nearly one-hundred thousand children under the age of eighteen are
confined in juvenile institutions in
the United States, for crimes ranging
from theft to murder (Hjelmeland 69).
In a large number of the case studies
of juvenile delinquents, the children
were raised in an environment where
the parent or parents failed to bond
with the child at infancy. Socializa-
tion begins at birth: "What happens,
right or wrong, in the critical first
two years of a baby's life will im-

Citing a paraphrase

print that child as an adult" (Magid
and McKelvey 3). The existence of a
blood relationship between the child
and the caregiver doesn't seem to matter; what does matter is "the relationship this caregiver has to the
child" (60). However, recent studies
suggest that one of the primary causes
of today's rapidly increasing crime,
particularly by children, is unattach-
ment (63). This is partially due to
the demands of the mother working outside the home. Chuck Haber of the
Hillsborough County, Florida, Sher-
iff's Office Gang Suppression Unit
says that statistics gathered by his
office indicated that most gang-re-
lated crimes occurred between the
hours of 3:00 p.m. and 6:00 p.m. when
the parents of these children, in a
mostly upperclass suburb, were still
at work. Researching the history of
these juvenile delinquents revealed
that the majority of their mothers
worked full-time jobs during the
child's infancy. Young children need
their parents, not money. According to
the American Civil Liberties Union
(ACLU), "It is more a 'time bulge'"
than an epidemic. In their "Fact Sheet

First reference in the paragraph includes author's name and page number of reference; subsequent references omit the author's name

Citing information summarized from a lecture

Defining acronyms and abbreviations the first time they appear

on Juvenile Crime" they argue that the
incidence of violent crimes actually
committed by young people is much
lower than most people believe—only
thirteen percent. Although experts
disagree on the prevalence of violent
crimes by juveniles, many experts
agree that a major cause is the breakdown of the family. "In the past, we
looked to our neighborhoods, our
churches, our schools, and our families as parties in raising our children," says Steven Rossman, director
of the Dallas County Juvenile Department (Zelfden A1). John J. Wilson,
Acting Administrator of the Office of
Juvenile Justice and Delinquency Prevention, agrees that "'Healthy childhood development is crucial for a
child to become a well adapted and
productive member of society"' (qtd.   *Citing an indirect*
in Cantelon). And Sharon L. Cantelon   *source*
adds: "The influence of the family environment on the child's social development lasts a lifetime. Accordingly,
effective delinquency prevention efforts must involve the family, and
should incorporate family strengthening." Perhaps the availability of an
extended two-year maternity leave

would be a step in the right direction. Another option would be to encourage proper attachment of the newborn child by permitting the father to stay home. America's population is growing at an alarming rate, and it is true—mothers of today are going back to work within a few weeks after giving birth. Our nation's children are an important resource. Juvenile justice programs need to focus on prevention rather than punishment, however— "Crime prevention programs work," according to the ACLU. "They have been shown to reduce crime substantially when compared to imprisonment after crimes have been committed." Government officials, sociologists, and criminologists are all working toward finding a solution, and many of the solutions focus on prevention by focusing on strengthening the family. According to Theresa Ross, a teacher, "A child needs a framework within which to find himself [sic]; otherwise, he [sic] is an egg without a shell."

Noting gender bias or errors in the original source in brackets

Works Cited

American Civil Liberties Union (ACLU).   *Internet source with*
    "ACLU Fact Sheet on Juvenile   *corporate author*
    Crime. 14 May 1996.
    http://www.aclu.org/congress/juve-
    nile.htm (10 April 1996).

Cantelon, Sharon L. "Family Strength-   *Government publi-*
    ening for High-Risk Youth." U.S.   *cation on the Inter-*
    Office of Juvenile Justice and   *net*
    Delinquency Prevention (OJJDP)
    Fact Sheet #8. March 1994.
    http://www.ncjrs.org/txtfiles/fs-
    9408.txt (4 April 1996).

Grolier New Multimedia Encyclopedia.   *CD-ROM ency-*
    Vers. 6.03. On-Line Computer Sys-   *clopedia*
    tems, 1993.

Haber, Chuck. "Juvenile Involvement in   *Lecture*
    Gangs in Tampa and Nationwide."
    Lecture. University of South
    Florida, 20 March 1996.

Hjelmeland, Andy. *Kids in Jail.* Min-   *Book with one au-*
    nesota: Lerner, 1992.   *thor*

Magid, Ken, and Carol A. McKelvey.   *Book with two au-*
    High Risk: Children without Con-   *thors*
    science. New York: Bantam, 1988.

Ross, Theresa. Personal interview. 10   *Personal interview*
    April 1996.

Zelfden, Alan Van. "Life Cheaper to   *Newspaper article*
    Delinquents." *Dallas Times Herald*
    17 Oct. 1991: A1.

9

A Brief Review of Grammar, Punctuation, and Mechanics

This book is mostly about style and structure, about making writing lively, honest, energetic, and clear. As you move through the text, you find grammar when you need it. Here, we want to make a concentrated review of the most common errors in grammar, punctuation, and mechanics, so that the beginning writer who feels confused—What *is* a whole sentence? When *do* I use a colon?—will have a place to come for answers to questions. It may also serve the writer who, after a summer vacation or a year away from the classroom, needs a quick review of grammar and mechanics, concentrating on errors frequently made.

If our grammar is loose and shabby, our punctuation random, and our mechanics haphazard, we will lose our audience. We must put sentences together by rules because rules describe the readers' expectations. If our language ignores these rules—if we substitute commas for periods or neglect to match parts of sentences to each other—readers will be confused and bored; they will not follow where we want to lead them, even if our ideas are profound and our information fascinating.

When things go wrong in mechanics and grammar, for an inexperienced writer, they go wrong usually because of a few mistakes. If we can follow six general rules, we will avoid most of the errors beginners fall into.

1. Make whole, clear sentences.
2. Match the parts of sentences that need matching.
3. Connect modifiers with what they modify.
4. Keep the sentence consistent.

5. Keep punctuation clear.

6. Keep mechanics conventional.

These rules will become useful only if we do some explaining and give examples. Almost everything mentioned here is repeated from earlier chapters; this chapter is repetitious, but it ought to be useful. It differs from the text in the approach to writing. In the text we talk mostly about the choices a writer can make to express meaning with vigor and clarity. Here, we look at the swamps that writers can sink into, the traps that can keep all of us keep from reaching our goals.

Many inexperienced writers have trouble with only one or two of the problems we list and not with the rest. Students sitting next to each other in class may have opposite troubles in writing. Neighbor A writes sentence fragments, B uses commas for periods, C mixes up pronouns, and D dangles modifiers. None of them has the problem that the other has, and each is thoroughly confused by his own problem. With this chapter, each student can go directly to his particular problem; we hope it can help the whole alphabet of writers.

MAKE WHOLE, CLEAR SENTENCES

Sentence Fragments

Beginning writers commonly make sentences—groups of words beginning with a capital letter and ending with a period—that do not complete an action. In an essay a student wrote

The effects of World War II.

as if the phrase told us something. But the sentence is incomplete, a sentence fragment. What *about* World War II? Did he want to say

Hungary suffered the effects of World War II.

or

World War II brought prosperity.

or what? In his essay, the writer had said

The economy began picking up finally in 1939. The effects of World War II.

He needed to connect the sentence fragment to the sentence, making something like this:

The economy began picking up in 1939 because of World War II.

The best writers sometimes put sentence fragments to good use (see pages 131–134), but when you are inexperienced, you should avoid them entirely. Wait until you have developed a firm and exact feel for the whole sentence's shape. Do not write

He was a good teacher. Being sympathetic with students and fascinated by his subject.

Instead, write something like

He was a good teacher, sympathetic with students and fascinated by his subject.

Here are some inadvertent sentence fragments, indicated by italics.

After the sun finally sank behind the hills. It was dark and we were ready.
The principal of my high school was a nice person. *Believing that every kid was potentially all right.*
Seeing the Buick with all its tires flat and rusted out in the grass, with no license plates on it.
The people at the fair stared at the twins and began to talk about them. *Because they looked different, I guess.*
Teachers in my opinion do not have the right to strike and miss their classes. *When students have already paid their tuition.*

Inadvertent sentence fragments are mainly of two kinds. Many fragments are subordinate clauses treated as if they were whole sentences. In three of the examples, the sentence fragments begin with *because, after,* and *when.* These words—like *although, since,* and *while*—mean that the clauses they introduce depend on, or hang from, a main clause; they are dependent or subordinate clauses. In the preceding examples, the main clauses (not in italics) make whole sentences themselves. The sentence fragments could become subordinate clauses in complex sentences.

Teachers in my opinion do not have the right to strike and miss their classes, *when students have already paid their tuition.*

The other category, shown in the second and third examples, is the fragment that modifies a main clause and ought to be separated from it by a comma—not by a period and a capital letter.

The principal of my high school is a nice person, *believing that every kid is potentially all right.*

Watch out for sentence fragments that begin with an *-ing* word, just as you watch for fragments beginning with *when* or *because.*
You can correct sentence fragments in several ways. You can correct *many* sentence fragments simply by using a comma instead of a period. Or you can add a verb to the fragment and make it a whole sentence, equal to the other.
Here are some alternate repairs for some of the sentence fragments used earlier.

He was a good teacher. He was sympathetic with students and fascinated by his subject.

He was a good teacher because he was sympathetic with his students and fascinated by his subject.

We saw the Buick with all its tires flat, rusted out in the grass, no license plates on it.

The principal of my high school was a nice person. He believed that every kid was potentially all right.

The people at the fair stared at the twins and began to talk about them; they looked different, I guess.

Notice that frequently a sentence fragment can become a whole clear sentence if you remove the subordinating word, like *because,* or change the modifying participle into a subject and a verb—like *we saw* for *seeing.*

EXERCISES

1. Each of these three passages contains one or more sentence fragments. Identify each fragment, and revise it into a whole sentence in two ways.

  a. When the sun rose high in the sky. All of us gathered twigs and fallen branches to make a fire. Then making breakfast for the whole group.

  b. No-fault insurance helps all motorists. The good and the bad. Every state should pass no-fault automobile insurance.

  c. When the Ford Motor Company named a new car the Pinto, they did a lot of research into the power of names. Names on the final list were largely the names of animals. Based on the discovery of a market research firm.

2. Combine the sentence fragments in this paragraph into whole sentences.

When I rented my first apartment, I learned a lot. How to make spaghetti. By the potful. And to keep dirty shirts and socks from piling up on the floor of my closet. I'll never forget the first time I went to the laundromat. Pouring bleach straight on the clothes. Holes in everything. Even my favorite jeans.

Comma Splices

Comma splices (or comma faults) and run-on sentences are the opposite of sentence fragments. In the comma splice, a comma is forced into the work a period is meant for; in the sentence fragment, a period is pressed into the service a comma is designed for. Here is a typical comma splice, two whole sentences incorrectly joined by a comma:

The Union stands back from the street about a hundred feet, it was built when land was still cheap.

Substitute a period for the comma, capitalize the next word, and you have two real, whole sentences.

Often the same writer makes sentence fragments and comma splices because both errors depend on an insecure grasp of what makes a sentence. By reading your prose aloud, pausing according to the punctuation, you can sometimes discover these errors in time to revise them.

The comma splice is confusing to the reader because two whole ideas are connected (spliced) as if they were not each whole and separate. The writer gives a signal by the comma, but the sentence denies the message that the comma carries. The comma gives us the information that we are reading one continuous idea, which conflicts with the wholeness of each of the two spliced sentences. The best writers sometimes use the comma splice to good effect (see pages 286–289), but beginning writers should avoid the device entirely, until they have developed a firm sense of the sentence.

Writers often make comma splices when they use conjunctive adverbs like *however, moreover, consequently, therefore, besides, then,* and *otherwise.* When these words connect main clauses, use a semicolon between the clauses, before the adverb, and a comma after the adverb. Do not write

> She was intelligent, moreover she had a Ph.D. from Harvard.

but write

> She was intelligent; moreover, she had a Ph.D. from Harvard.

Here are comma splices taken from student essays.

> The port of New York has minimum safety requirements, some vessels have to dock in Hoboken.
> The inevitability of war became obvious to even the most casual observer, maneuvers were constantly being held.
> My father grew up on a potato farm in Idaho, he never saw a movie until he was twenty-two years old.
> She walked through the door into the dining room, she wore nothing but a bikini.
> When they were little, they liked to play in the empty warehouse down the block, it was a spooky and exciting place.
> The canoe started tipping as I approached the falls, I was terrified that I would lose all my gear.

When you correct a comma splice, you have four alternatives. Two of them require only a change in punctuation; two of them require another word.

1. You can substitute a semicolon for a comma to repair most comma splices. Making a comma splice often means you want to show a close connection between two whole sentences. You try to move quickly from one to the other, without the long

pause implied by a period and a capital letter. The semicolon was invented for just this purpose: to show that two whole sentences follow quickly upon each other and are closely related. Here are comma splices repaired by semicolons.

> The port of New York has minimum safety requirements; some vessels have to dock in Hoboken.
> The inevitability of war became obvious to even the most casual observer; maneuvers were constantly being held.

2. You can use a period and a capital letter; they will always be correct.

> My father grew up on a potato farm in Idaho. He never saw a movie until he was twenty-two years old.

3. You can make a complex sentence, if you find that one sentence can depend on the other, by using a subordinating conjunction.

> When the canoe started tipping as I approached the falls, I was terrified that I would lose all my gear.

4. You can connect the two sentences into one compound sentence with *and, but, or, not, yet,* or *so;* the two clauses will be equally strong, or coordinate.

> The port of New York has minimum safety requirements, and some vessels have to dock in Hoboken.
> She walked through the door into the dining room, but she wore nothing but a bikini.

Each of these four solutions makes a slight difference in tone or meaning. In your context, one of the four will be best. Compare these variations of one sentence:

> When they were little, they liked to play in the empty warehouse down the block; it was a spooky and exciting place.
> When they were little, they liked to play in the empty warehouse down the block. It was a spooky and exciting place.
> When they were little, they liked to play in the empty warehouse down the block because it was a spooky and exciting place.
> When they were little, they liked to play in the empty warehouse down the block, and it was a spooky and exciting place.

The writer's choice should depend on mood and rhythm appropriate to context. The semicolon makes a slight pause, and the period brings the thought to a full stop. The conjunction *because* makes the second part of the sentence depend on the first, implying cause and effect. The conjunction *and* connects two clauses in an equal partnership.

EXERCISES

1. Here are three passages from student essays. Identify the comma splices, and revise the passages into whole, single sentences. Use any of the four methods listed above. Then revise these passages again, using another of the four methods.

    a. Carbon monoxide filled the foggy air, we could breathe only with difficulty.
    b. Sunset fell rapidly, we had to hurry to set up our tent.
    c. When the waitress removed an empty platter, she was back with a full platter a moment later, I never ate so much in my life, I was so full I thought I would burst.

2. In this paragraph, make whole sentences from the comma splices.

> Behind my uncle's barn sat four old cars, they were in various stages of disintegration, most were rusting in the tall weeds. The grille on the '32 Chevy grinned like decayed teeth, I thought when I was little, the doors sagged open. Years of rain had soaked the velour upholstery, the windows were shattered in weblike patterns from kids throwing stones. I would get in on hot summer afternoons, put both hands on the steering wheel, pretend to drive.

MATCH THE PARTS OF SENTENCES THAT NEED MATCHING

Matching Subjects with Verbs

When the subject of a sentence is one thing (singular), the verb must be singular also. When the subject is more than one thing (plural), the verb must be plural also. In standard English, we say, "The newspaper covers the waterfront murders," not "The newspaper cover the waterfront murders"; or we say, "The newspapers, which share a reporter, cover the waterfront murders," not "The newspapers covers the waterfront murders."

Here are some frequent pitfalls and how to avoid them.

Sometimes we get into trouble because a phrase comes between the subject and the verb and confuses us. If we have a single subject followed by a prepositional phrase that ends with a plural, we may make the verb plural because the plural phrase rings in our ears. "The newspaper of the six northern suburbs" is a singular subject. We should say

> The newspaper of the six northern suburbs covers the waterfront murders.

not

> The newspaper of the six northern suburbs cover the waterfront murders.

With words like *anyone, each,* and *everybody* (called indefinite pronouns), use a singular verb. It is confusing: *everybody* refers to many people, but it is a single thing, a single "body"—as single as the *one* in *anyone* or *everyone.* Say, "Everybody hurts this morning"; "Anyone who goes out alone at night takes a chance of being mugged"; and "Each member of the orchestra pays annual dues."

None can be either singular or plural, agreeing with a singular or plural noun elsewhere in the sentence. Context decides.

> Many cows are happy, but none is so happy as a cow in spring.
> Many pigs are intelligent, but none are so intelligent as Wilbur and
>   Angeline.

Do not say

> Everybody in town are going to the circus.
> Each of the forty-seven students howl like wolves.

Always find the subject *(everybody, each)* and make sure that the verb agrees.

When you write a sentence that uses *either . . . or, neither . . . nor,* or *not . . . but,* use a singular verb if both subjects are singular.

> Either the red-haired witch or her broomstick was on fire.

If one subject is plural and the other singular, the rule says that the verb should agree with the subject closest to it. Thus the rule would allow

> Either her two broomsticks or the red-haired witch was on fire.

But such a sentence, technically correct, is stylistically ugly. For style's sake, when one subject is plural and the other is singular, put the plural subject nearer the verb and use a plural verb. Say

> Either the red-haired witch or her two broomsticks were on fire.

Do not say

> Either her two broomsticks or the red-haired witch were on fire.

or

> Either the red-haired witch or her two broomsticks was on fire.

Do not say

> Neither the father nor the son want to follow the witch's track.

It should be *wants,* a singular verb. Do not say

> Not the Prime Minister but the members of his cabinet believes in
>   amnesty.

It should be *believe,* a plural verb matching the plural *members.*

These sentences are incorrect:

Neither Hitler nor Genghis Khan were conspicuous for humanitarianism.

Not the first potato but the second and the fourth contains the microfilm.

Either the roof or the shingling over the sheds were giving off a putrescent odor.

When a sentence uses a verb like *is* or *are* (a linking verb, a form of *to be*), make sure that the verb matches the subject of the sentence, not a noun that comes afterward. Say

The best part of the team was its outfielders.

not

The best part of the team were its outfielders.

Say

The outfielders were the best part of the team.

not

The outfielders was the best part of the team.

These sentences are incorrect:

The middle chapters was the section of the book I liked best.
The best section of the book were the middle chapters.

Watch out for subject/verb agreement in sentences beginning with "There is." Sometimes we begin such a sentence expecting a singular subject, then alter the subject without remembering to alter the verb. It is correct to say

There is one table in the room.

It would be incorrect and disagreeable to say

There is one table and one chair in the room.

EXERCISES

1. Identify and correct the errors in these sentences.

a. Each of the colored pencils have a different shade.

b. The store with its aisles of groceries, hardware, soft goods, and paperbacks, rest back from the road.

c. The green part of Northern Spy apples always taste best.

d. Neither the horse nor the cows in the barn hears the siren.

e. Either Bozo or Emmett Kelly get the prize.

2. In this section on matching parts, on pages 289–290, are many incorrect sentences introduced by "Do not say." Correct the errors in these sentences.

3. Rewrite this paragraph, making subjects and verbs agree.

> Fifty workers, dressed in gray canvas coveralls and aluminum helmets, descends into the dark, damp caves. Each carry a pail and a small curved knife. They emerge from the elevator and scatters among the earth-filled frames. Slowly, rhythmically, they fan out in groups of five which moves along the frames. Their helmet lights fall into yellow cones on the mushrooms, pale faces clustering in the blackness. There is no sounds except the dull thud of mushrooms tumbling one by one into pails, like soft rain. No clocks, which would measure off the minutes left in a shift, but a siren to tell them when to break for lunch. None of them hurry.

Matching Pronouns with the Words They Refer To

Pronouns *(he, she, it, this, that, you, we)* take their identity from a noún that comes before them, and which they refer to, called their *antecedent.* The noun can come before them in the same sentence, or it can appear in a sentence close enough to have the reference clear. Pronouns must match their nouns both in number (singular or plural) and in gender (male or female).

Mostly, we match pronouns to their antecedents without trouble. But there are a few troublesome exceptions.

In formal writing, we use a singular pronoun *(he, she, it)* with an indefinite pronoun like *anybody, everybody, each, none,* and so forth. We say

> Everybody carried his tennis racket.
> None of the actresses received her paycheck.
> Each of the seals extended its flipper.

not

> Everybody carried their tennis racket.
> None of the actresses received their paycheck.
> Each of the seals extended their flipper.

This is a rule of formal writing although we often bend it in informal speech. To avoid *his* as sexist, or to avoid *his or her* as awkward, we sometimes use the incorrect *their* (see pages 147–152). If you do it, know that you are doing it. Perhaps it is best, if possible, to avoid gender entirely.

> Everyone carried a tennis racket.
> None of the actresses received a paycheck.
> Each of the seals extended a flipper.

Words like *team, committee, jury, class,* and *orchestra* are collective nouns. They are singular words that refer to plural collections of people. Use a singular pronoun when you describe the whole group; use a plural pronoun when you describe the many members. Say

The team climbed on its bus.
The team dispersed to their lockers.

Don't say

The jury went to its separate rooms.
The committee voted to disband themselves.
The team voted to distribute their winnings among twenty-four ballplayers.
The group destroyed their petition to remove the governor.

When a pronoun matches two or more nouns joined by *and,* it is always plural.

When the boy and his dog wanted supper, they went to the tavern.

When a pronoun matches nouns joined by *or, nor, either . . . or,* or *neither . . . nor* and one of the nouns is plural, the pronoun matches the nearer of the two. When you use such a pair of nouns, the sentence sounds better if the second of the two nouns is the plural. Say

Although neither Margaret nor the Hamiltons are late, they hurry to the concert hall.

Don't say

Although neither Margaret nor the Hamiltons are late, she hurries . . .

or

Although neither the Hamiltons nor Margaret are late, they hurry . . . .

Never use a pronoun when it could refer to either of two words before it. We must use pronouns so that the reader will always be *certain* which previous noun they refer to. Uncertainty is confusing and intolerable. Don't say

When Wilhelmina declared herself to Bertha, she was aghast.
Leaving his father's house and the dry valley, he was happy to see the last of it.

Both of these sentences lack a clear antecedent to the pronoun. They are ambiguous. Which of the women was aghast? Was he happy to see the last of the house or of the valley or of both? To be clear, we should say something like

Wilhelmina declared herself to Bertha, who was aghast.
He left the dry valley, happy to see the last of his father's house.

Don't use the pronoun *this* or *that* or *it* to refer to general ideas in a previous sentence or to an antecedent that is not there ("This is true . . ."). Watch out for *this* and *that* when you use them as pronouns. Don't say

> The street cleaners roared down the street, raising clouds of gritty dust, mowing down the lilac bushes on the corner of the lawn, and dumping gravel all over the grass. That made my mother furious.

That lacks a clear antecedent, and the sentence drowns in imprecision.

Here are more examples of pronoun error from student essays. Troublesome pronouns are in italics.

> The state legislature never got around to getting the bill out of committee until October, and *it* was the reason the scholarships were never funded.
>
> The next thing that happened was that the screen door got stuck open and the mosquitoes could get in and the dog would get out whenever he wanted. My mother started crying about *this.*
>
> Preferential voting is fair because it gives the voter a chance to give a graded opinion of the different candidates, and therefore opens the way to third parties. *That* is the real justification for preferential voting.
>
> Down the block from me there was a family that had three cats. One of them was a big red tom named Mio, the biggest cat I ever saw— 34 inches long not counting his tail, and 28 pounds. The kids in the neighborhood couldn't get over *this.*

We make another common error when we use a pronoun far removed from its antecedent. The result is more ambiguity, vagueness, and imprecision. Here are two examples.

> The partnership of Hudnut and Greenall was breaking up; business had declined, Hudnut's wife was ill, and Greenall's son had run off to Tibet. One Tuesday, *they* suddenly stopped speaking to each other.
>
> When Sharon looked across the classroom, Bill winked and Larry looked away. Outside the window the clouds gathered for rain, and students were beginning to drive off for lunch, many of them carrying no books at all. Suddenly two girls ran toward a car that had stopped to pick them up. *She* saw that *it* was Matt.

EXERCISES

1. In these sentences, underline the errors in pronouns and what they refer to.

> **a.** When the Senate and the House convene, on rare occasions, they do not know how to behave toward each other.

    b. Panthers feed on zebras when they can, and zebras feed on grass. As a result of this, panthers live near the grasslands.

    c. I was late for registration because my father had the flu and then our car broke down outside Tucson. That made me more nervous than ever.

    d. Uncle Bruce is a career man in the navy, stationed in San Diego now, and it makes me think about enlisting myself.

    e. The department decided to hold their annual picnic on Riverside Drive.

    f. The Boosters Club adjourned its meeting and went to its respective houses.

    g. Either Rita or Carole were tardy last Tuesday.

    h. Everybody had their ticket to the rock concert.

2. Rewrite the sentences in the first exercise to correct faulty pronouns.

3. Here is a paragraph from a student essay with several examples of pronoun-antecedent and pronoun-verb disagreement. Revise to correct mistakes.

> In their cowboy movies, John Wayne and Gary Cooper each represents the idealized western hero. Walking slowly down the dusty main street of any frontier town, he commands respect. Neither ever flinch in the heavy crossfire of bank robbers or cattle rustlers. The crowd of townsfolk who look on know their sheriff will win the day. None doubt their safety under his leadership. That's why they are examples of courage and social order in a reckless age.

CONNECT MODIFIERS WITH WHAT THEY MODIFY

In most sentences, we write phrases that describe (modify) other things in the sentence. We use prepositional phrases as modifiers (to define, to limit).

> the bar *with the lavender paint*
> the girl *in the straw hat*
> the chapter *about grammar*

For similar purposes, we use clauses beginning with words like *that, who, since,* and *because.*

> the worst storm *since the winter of 1978*
> Herbert, *who tipped his homburg*

And we use phrases beginning with *-ing* words (participles), which also modify.

> the chapter *containing the examples*
> *hanging from the skylight,* the plumber

Most of the time we have no trouble controlling these phrases or clauses. We will find no trouble at all if we avoid two common errors.

Make sure that modifiers beginning a sentence really modify what the sentence claims they modify. If we start a sentence "Hanging from the skylight," we tell the reader something; we guarantee that the noun that will begin the main clause is what is hanging.

> Hanging from the skylight, the plumber screamed that he had climbed up there to escape the terrorists.

Too often, we are careless and make a sentence like the next one—which seems to start like the sentence above and then changes its mind.

> Hanging from the skylight, the plumber looked at the huge spider's web.

Common sense can untangle the mess. The reader will eventually understand that the spider's web is hanging, not the plumber. In the meantime, the reader has been first confused and then annoyed by the misdirection.

Here are more examples of dangling modifiers, which are shown by italics.

> *Being a wreck with no gears at all,* she got the bicycle free.
> *Before making a reservation,* my roommate recommended a travel agent to me.
> *Humbled by circumstances,* the town looked better to him now than it had looked before.

Make sure that your word order says what you want it to say when you place modifiers in a sentence. This advice applies to adverbs and adjectives, as well as to phrases or clauses that modify. The wrong word order can alter your meaning.

> I told her I would gladly lend her my car.

means one thing.

> I told her gladly I would lend her my car.

means something else.

> She heard only the words that hurt.

means one thing.

> She only heard the words that hurt.

means something else.

> He said only that he loved her.

means one thing.

> He only said that he loved her.

means something else. It is the writer's job to know the meaning and to say it. Here are some examples from student papers in which mistakes in word order made ambiguous, misleading, or silly sentences.

> Hattie is the cousin who gave me the present in a housecoat.
> Joseph borrowed an egg from a neighbor that was rotten.
> The autobiography tells the exciting life of the man who lived it quickly and modestly.
> The lecturer told us about the problem of alcoholism in room A-14.

EXERCISES

1. Correct the mistakes in the four sentences that end the preceding section.

2. Correct the errors in the following sentences.

> **a.** Desperate, clinging to life, our teacher told us about the surrounded tribe.
> **b.** Igor attempted one last time to climb the hill lacking food and ammunition.
> **c.** Never certain of which side of the road to drive on, American roads drove the Englishman crazy.
> **d.** Full of conceit, the application form looked like a cinch to him.
> **e.** I walked the last 5 miles to the city tired and full of martinis.
> **f.** She said that animals only burp the way he did.
> **g.** Without his fortune or his youth or his good health, the old house looked warm and solid to him.

3. Correct the misplaced modifiers in this paragraph.

> Walking against rush-hour traffic, the worn green raincoat gave the old man a sinister air. He was trying only to find Flossie. He shuffled along the pavement carrying the little red dish calling her name. His bony feet were beginning to hurt him encased in broken leather boots, and the corn throbbed on his toe. Frightened and tired, the police station stood on 104th Street just ahead.

KEEP THE SENTENCE CONSISTENT

Once we start a sentence, we commit ourselves to continue it as we started it. In the second and third sections of this review, we discussed the commitments to match number and gender and to connect a modifier with what it modifies. We also commit ourselves to other consistencies.

When we write parallelisms, or parallel constructions, as in a series of clauses, we must keep the words grammatically parallel for the sake of consistency. Otherwise, we find our sentences beginning to come apart, to veer off the road into incoherence. We list adjectives or we list nouns, but we do not list three adjectives followed by one noun. Don't say

He was tall, rich, funny, and a bank robber.

Say something like

He was tall, rich, funny, and fond of robbing banks.

When one phrase is constructed by one grammatical formula, its parallel phrase must be constructed in the same way. Don't say

The dog had a long nose, a black tail, and barked loudly.

Instead say

The dog had a long nose, a black tail, and a loud bark.

Don't say

The cities are deserted, the countryside parched, the government paralyzed, and the economy not in a healthy condition.

Instead, say something like

The cities are deserted, the countryside parched, the government paralyzed, and the economy ruined.

Here, the sentence must continue with phrases ending in *-ed* words (past participles), or it will be inconsistent.

Consistency is the rule. If you start a sentence—or a linked group of sentences—with one subject or person, be consistent. Don't say

When you get a good grade, one should be proud.

Say either *you* or *one,* and stick to it.

Don't use the active voice in one part of a sentence and shift to the passive in another, when you could perfectly well keep the active and use the same subject.

We could hear raucous sounds from the party as the house was approached.

Be consistent in using the past or present of verbs. Don't say

He went into the room, closed the door, opened the window, and goes to bed.

Remember that we need consistency within related sentences, as well as within the sentence. Here is an inconsistent paragraph.

The median tax on houses in Centerville is $852 a year. You could appeal to the city assessor if you wanted to. But one is advised not to; he can always hit you for more tax, and you are punished for asking.

EXERCISES

1. Revise the paragraph at the end of the preceding section so that its sentences are consistent.

2. Locate, name, and correct the inconsistencies in these sentences.

    a. She walked like a princess, ate like an ape, and her hair was at least 5 feet long.

    b. If you write a page a day in your notebook, you will discover that one learns from practice.

    c. Harriet opened the window to get some fresh air, and we all breathe deeply.

    d. Geology is boring, chemistry fatiguing, history overwhelming, but English was a useful class.

    e. We lifted the rock, peered into the mud, and a thousand grubs were seen.

3. Rewrite the following paragraph to make the subject singular and the verb tense present.

> The banditos waited in the canyon rocks for the evening coach from Sagebrush. They knew it carried bags of gold for the Union army, and they intended to grab the gold and disappear into the hills. At last, a cloud of dust appeared on the horizon. The men tensed, crouched lower against the jagged rocks, and watched intently, guns readied. When they saw the driver cracking his whip over the screaming horses, they opened fire.

KEEP PUNCTUATION CLEAR

Learning to punctuate correctly, we learn the conventions that an experienced reader expects of us. No one can argue that the conventions of English punctuation are ideal. But they are clear, and for the most part they are sensible.

End Punctuation

At the end of a sentence, we use a period, an exclamation point, or a question mark.

Period. Periods end sentences. Periods also indicate abbreviations (*Mr., no., St., etc., i.e., Mass., U.S.A.*). (See pages 313–314.) And periods indicate omissions in quoted material. (See pages 309–310.)

Exclamation Point. Use exclamation points only for a proper exclamation:

Oh! Zap!

or for a remark almost shouted:

It's Godzilla!

Avoid using them frequently, or they diminish in effect, like a vague intensifier.

I could not make out the face! Then I saw. It was Algernon!

Question Mark. At the end of a sentence asking a direct question, use a question mark.

Did you ask Fernando?
Have you bought the paper, the pins, and the manila envelopes?

Do not use a question mark to end a sentence that includes a question but does not ask it (an indirect question). These sentences are incorrectly punctuated:

He asked what time it was?
I waited to find out where the carnival was?

They should end with periods.

Commas

The most common mark of punctuation—and the most commonly misused—is the comma. (We will not talk here about the comma splice because we discussed it on pages 286–288.) Here are some of the main uses of the comma.

To Separate Whole Clauses. In the compound sentence, where two or more whole clauses are connected by *and, or, nor, for,* or *but,* we use a comma just before the connective.

The faculty senate debated for three hours, but no one could resolve
the issue of the blind pig.

When the main clauses are short, the comma is optional. The pause is shorter, and therefore the rhythm different. We can say either

The wine was old, and we drank it slowly.

or

The wine was old and we drank it slowly.

We can also opt to use the semicolon, which creates a longer pause, instead of the comma. Sometimes we want this extra pause when the main clauses are especially long, when they themselves contain commas, or when we want strong contrast between the two parts of the sentence.

The cliff was red, solid, and perpendicular; and the car disappeared
into the face of it.

To Separate Items in a Series. We use commas to separate words in a series:

> The dress was black, green, and purple.

to separate phrases in a series:

> She wore it to parties, in the bathtub, and at work.

to separate subordinate clauses in a series:

> She explained that it was warm, that it needed washing, that it was comfortable, and that it was in good taste.

and to separate whole clauses in a series:

> She shook her head, she stood up, and she left the room.

When we use *and* with each item in a series, we do not use the comma.

> He touched first and second and third.

It is possible to omit the comma before the *and* in a series of words or short phrases:

> He touched first, second and third.

but it can seem ambiguous, as if the baserunner were able to straddle and touch second and third at the same time.

To Set Off Introductory Words and Groups of Words. Adverb clauses, transitional phrases, and phrases introduced by verbals or prepositions, when they come at the beginning of the sentence, usually require a comma to set them off from the main clause. These adverb clauses need a comma:

> *If a dunce applies himself thoroughly,* he can dream of becoming President.
> *When I turned to the left at the end of the lane,* I found the old house intact.

Omitting these commas would leave the sentence hopelessly awkward and confusing. If the order of clauses is reversed, a comma, though possible, is no longer necessary.

> A dunce can dream of becoming President *if he applies himself thoroughly.*
> I found the old house intact *when I turned to the left at the end of the lane.*

An introductory adverb clause, if it is short, need not always carry a comma. A comma is optional in

> *If I lead* he will follow.

Introductory phrases of transition, like *on the other hand,* usually need a comma.

> *On the other hand,* sometimes they don't.
> *In fact* they are optional.
> *In fact,* they are optional.

Retaining the comma is appropriate in formal writing and is acceptable in all writing. Omitting the comma is rhythmically more colloquial. Interjections like *oh* or *shucks,* however, almost always take the comma.

> *Gosh,* that's not what you said the last time.

We use a comma when the sentence begins with a long phrase governed by a preposition.

> *In the century after the Civil War,* progress in civil rights was almost nil.

When the introductory prepositional or verbal phrase is short, the comma is optional and may be omitted when omission does not cause ambiguity.

> *At twelve* she was full-grown.
> *Having won* they adjourned to a saloon.

> *To Avoid Ambiguity.*   Sometimes we need a comma to indicate a pause that the voice would make, in speech, for clarity but that is not otherwise necessary.

> *Outside* the fields spread to the river.

is clearer with a pause:

> *Outside,* the fields spread to the river.

To find such potential ambiguities in your prose, sometimes it is helpful to read it aloud, pronouncing it as it is written—which means pausing where there is a comma, and *not* pausing where there is *not* a comma.

> *To Set Off Nonrestrictive, or Parenthetical, Clauses.*   It is useful to know the difference between a restrictive and a nonrestrictive clause. A restrictive clause describes or limits its subject, providing essential information.

> The knight *who was dressed in black* won all the events in the tourney.

Here, "who was dressed in black" defines the knight, as if we were pointing a finger. The absence of commas lets us know that there were other knights besides the one "who was dressed in black."

> The building *that overlooked the river* was the most popular of all.

In restrictive clauses such as these, no comma separates the clause from the rest of the sentence.

> Nonrestrictive clauses, in contrast, do not define; they could become separate sentences or coordinate clauses, and unless they are very short, they take commas at both ends. We could also write sentences in which the clauses above become nonrestrictive.

> Sir Galahad, *who was dressed in black,* won all the events in the tourney.

This sentence, as opposed to the restrictive example above, could be broken into two sentences, with no violence done to the meaning.

Sir Galahad was dressed in black. He won all the events in the tourney.

Or, using the clause from the other example, we could have the sentence

The library building, *which overlooked the river,* was built in 1975.

To Enclose Words, Phrases, or Clauses That Are Like a Parenthesis. Quotations are common parenthetical elements. So too are phrases and words like *of course, naturally,* and *heavens to Betsy.* When asides or parenthetical expressions appear at the beginning of sentences, place a comma after them. When they appear at the end of sentences, put a comma just before them.

God knows, the situation is desperate.
The situation is desperate, *God knows.*
Fellow Americans, I speak to you as a concerned citizen.
I am a representative of the people, *of course.*

Omitting commas in these examples would make the sentence ambiguous or hard to read.

God knows the situation is desperate.

Does He?

At times the commas can be omitted with no awkwardness or confusion, and the omission becomes optional. Short sentences in which word order precludes ambiguity give us this option.

The situation was of course desperate.

On occasion one can take stylistic advantage of the rhythmic speed offered by this option.

Use a comma before and after parenthetical expressions within a sentence.

I think you're tired, *Fred,* and hungry.
The student worked, *in a manner of speaking,* for three whole days.
I heard him calling, *"There's my bubble gum,"* to the audience.

To Set Off Appositives. Appositives are nouns or noun substitutes placed next to another noun to explain or define that noun.

Peter, *the flying dwarf,* escorted Tarquina, *his good fairy.*

In many of our first drafts, we use too many commas or put them where they do not belong. Beginning writers often feel that something is going wrong if they haven't used a comma lately, and so they shake commas over their prose like salt. Here are some sentences, taken from student essays, which have some commas they should *not* have.

But, it was not too late.
Clarke came by, later.
When I left she, followed me.
The dimensions were, approximately 3 by 5.

I quickly saw Ed, and Sara.
He thought she was sickly, and studious.
The old barn was painted, red.
A runner, who likes to win, has to train, every day.
The agency sold, life, fire, and theft, insurance.

EXERCISES

1. Remove unnecessary commas from the last group of sentences above.

2. The following sentences omit commas necessary to clarity. Add commas where they belong.

   a. The indiscreet Martian insensitive to the feelings of Earthlings disintegrated the beagle.
   b. "Horrors" I said to the surrounding observers.
   c. Of course the narrative begins to become incoherent when Hermione reaches this part of the journey.
   d. Beyond the river widened.
   e. Deciding that cinnamon toast was preferable to fried sardines we looked in the bread box.
   f. In a million or two million years the human toenail may disappear.
   g. In truth the final dispensation of the profits available to the institution will not be accomplished until the end of the decade.
   h. He looked through his pockets and found a comb two matchbooks four paper clips six pennies and a piece of bubble gum.

3. Punctuate, capitalize, and lowercase this paragraph.

for forty years they had come to this house by the lake and for twenty of those Years they had been as they thought a happy family but after Herbie died and Mary Lou went away to school and Joe jr married and started a family of his own it was different they were Strangers to each other and spent whole days staring at the lake stopping only for silent meals and sleepless Naps

Semicolons

Semicolons Between Whole Clauses. Semicolons separate whole clauses, making a pause longer or more emphatic than a comma but shorter and less definite than a period. The semicolon shows that the clauses follow each other closely, are connected in idea or narrative. We may use the semicolon between two (or more) balanced and equal clauses.

> The sun rose; the sky lightened; day had come.

Or we may use it between clauses of unequal length and different construction.

> The sun rose; instantly, the air was alive with birds singing so happily that anyone who heard them could not help but smile.

These sentences are compound, the semicolon replacing a conjunction.

Semicolons with Series.   Sometimes, in a long sentence, semicolons separate series or divisions, making the divisions clearer than commas would, particularly if commas are already within the divisions.

> There were three sorts of students waiting on tables at the inn: fraternity boys who were dating expensive girls; girls from Detroit whose daddies cut off their allowances because they had moved in with their boyfriends; and street people, boys and girls, working for a week or two until they got tired of it.

Semicolons with Conjunctions.   A semicolon used with a conjunction shows more separation or pause between clauses than the comma would show.

> He flew to Denver that night; and we were glad he did.

Adverbs acting as conjunctions in compound sentences *(besides, nevertheless, also, however, indeed, furthermore, still, then)* take a semicolon, as do transitional phrases in the middle of compound sentences *(on the other hand, in fact, in other words, on the contrary.)*

> Let us take the matter in hand; however, we must not be foolhardy.
> The sun rose in a clear sky; in fact, the sky was painfully bright.

Semicolons with Incomplete Clauses.   Semicolons also separate incomplete clauses when a verb in one of the clauses is omitted but understood.

> Poetry is one thing; verse another.

Apostrophes

Possessives.   We form the possessive by adding 's to singular nouns and most plural nouns (if the additional *s* makes pronunciation difficult, we add only the apostrophe).

> The bag was Sara's.
> It was the weather's fault.
> The technician's car was parked outside.
> the hens' feed
> Mr. and Mrs. Jones's automobile
> the women's club
> the Perkins' puppets

An apostrophe does not form part of the possessive of a pronoun. Pronouns have separate possessive forms: *my; your; his, her, its; our; your; their.*

Contractions.   We also use the apostrophe to show contractions. We use an apostrophe to show that we have omitted one or more letters in a phrase, commonly a combination of a pronoun and a verb. *I'm, she's, he's, who's, we've, you've, they're,* and so on; *we'd, you'd, he'd, she'd; he'll, she'll, who'll.* Three contractions become problems. *They're* (a contraction of *they are*) sounds like *their* and *there,* and we may spell one when we mean another. "*Their* out working" is as incorrect as is "*there* work" and "working *their.*" (Correct: "*They're* out working"; "*their* work"; "working *there.*")

It's always means *it is.* It is *not* possessive, like "*its* shadow." Whenever you write or see the apostrophe with these letters—*it's*—remember that the *'s* must stand for *is.* Or memorize the phrase

It's afraid of *its* shadow.

Who's is another common contraction and once again there is confusion. *Whose* gets mixed up with *who's.* Again, the *'s* means *is,* and *who's* always stands for *who is,* whereas *whose* is a possessive pronoun.

Who's drinking *whose* soup?

Other common contractions involve a verb and the negative: *isn't, aren't, doesn't, don't, can't, haven't, won't,* which are contractions of *is not, are not, does not, do not, cannot, have not, will not.*

Possessive pronouns used without a noun have no apostrophe: *mine; yours; his, hers, its; ours; yours; theirs.*

Her book.
The book was *hers.*

Plural of Numbers.   We use the apostrophe to form the plurals of typographic symbols, words referred to as words, letters, and figures.

The *7*'s on the new office typewriter are black as *e*'s, *8*'s are unreadable, and half the time simple *the*'s are obscure.

EXERCISES

1. Cross out the incorrect apostrophes in these sentences. Add the missing ones.

    a. Poor dog! Its too late for it's supper.
    b. That morocco-bound volume of Tolkien was supposed to be her's.
    c. Whose for tennis?
    d. Is'nt English spelling irrational?

   e. It's true he didn't know who's tax he had paid, his wifes or his own.

Quotation Marks and Punctuating Quotations

The exact words of a speaker or writer, included in a paragraph, are set off by quotation marks. Put a comma at the end of the quotation before the quotation mark, or a period if the quotation ends the sentence. If the quotation ends with a question mark or an exclamation point, these marks of punctuation take the place of the comma and occur inside the quotation marks.

Al asked Wayne, "Didn't you?"

However, sometimes we quote in order to exclaim or inquire about the quotation. In such a sentence, the exclamation point or question mark occurs after the quotation mark.

What did he mean when he said, "Good morning"?
She had the nerve to say "Hello"!

Notice that the first word of a quoted remark is capitalized. When we quote a passage longer than fifty words, in a research paper for instance, we can use a colon to introduce the quotation and detach the quotation from the text by indenting it. The quotation is not enclosed by quotation marks. Ellipses can help writers avoid long, detached quotations.

We use quotation marks to indicate the exact repetition of words from speech or writing.

As Macbeth would say, "Tomorrow and tomorrow and tomorrow . . . ."

We use them when we cite words as words.

"Jazz" and "condo" are derogatory words.

In writing that uses many short quotations, as in this book, an author may use italics instead of quotation marks: *mine, yours, his, hers, its, ours, yours, theirs.* In writing essays, use the traditional quotation marks.

We also use quotation marks to indicate the titles of songs and short literary works, like essays and short stories and poems and chapters or other sections of a longer work. We speak of Tennyson's short poem "Tithonos"; when we refer to a book-length poem by the same author, we use italics instead: *In Memoriam.* We speak of Hemingway's story "A Clean Well-Lighted Place" and his novel *A Farewell to Arms.* "The Dead" is part of James Joyce's *Dubliners.* We use italics for the names of newspapers, magazines, and movies: *New Haven Register, Blair and Ketcham's Country Journal, Animal House.*

When we quote *within* a quotation, we use single quotation marks: Molly said, "I'd like to read you Wallace Stevens's poem 'The Emperor of Ice Cream.'"

Other Marks of Punctuation

Brackets. Brackets are useful in prose in three places especially, all within or close to quotations. We use them when we add to a quotation material that was not in the original but that is needed for clarity. Sometimes a bracketed word supplies information lacking in the quotation but available in the context. The brackets can contain the antecedent to a pronoun:

> "He [O'Toole] smashed his fist through the window of the bar."

or some important fact:

> "It was mid-June [1986] that the storm began."

Sometimes, in quoting the spoken word, we use brackets to enclose an indication of action, like a stage direction.

> ". . . and, finally, I want to ask you willingly and cheerfully to share the huge burden of responsibility which the age has thrust upon us all." [Boos.]

Sometimes we use brackets to correct a quotation.

> "It all happened in the early hours of September 20 [actually September 21] when the sun began [to] rise over the boardwalk."

Colons. Colons direct our attention to what comes after them. Usually they follow an introductory statement that leads us to expect a follow-up, though sometimes the introduction is implicit, or the colon itself reveals that the clause preceding it was introductory. We use a colon when the second sentence fulfills a kind of promise made by the first. Here are some explicit introductions.

- To a long quotation, either included in the text in quotation marks or indented as a block quotation without quotation marks:

  > E. B. White wrote of his old professor: "In the days when I was sitting in his class he omitted so many needless words, and omitted them so forcibly and with such eagerness and obvious relish, that . . . ."

- To an example:

  > The results of the study were as follows: the closer subjects stood to the hoop, the more frequently they were able to make a basket.

- To a list:

  > Mona asked me to get a few things at the market: potatoes, carrots, and peas.
  > When you pack your child's luggage for Camp Winnewaka, please include the following: towels, toiletries, and personal medications.

- Less elegantly, to an appositive at the end of a sentence:

> Chosby took off his boots and looked at his toe: a swollen knob of pain.

A comma here would be just as correct and perhaps less prone to melodrama.

Sometimes we put a colon instead of a semicolon between two main clauses; it implies that the second clause is a result of the first.

> The hands of the clock seemed never to move: she had never been late before.

Here the colon adds a meaning that the semicolon would lack. The semicolon would present the two statements as closely connected but without the implication that the second clause derived from the first.

Dashes. Use dashes with caution—but use them. Type them as two hyphens next to each other.

In the sentence above, the dash shows a hesitation in the voice, followed with a rush by something that seems almost an afterthought. Dashes are informal. For some careless writers, dashes become substitutes for all other forms of punctuation; they not only lose any special meaning dashes may contribute, they also rob other punctuation of its meaning. For instance:

> Yet many people use them too often—they become substitutes for all other forms of punctuation—and thus lose their special meaning—at the same time they rob other punctuation of its meaning—

Two legitimate uses for the dash are the implied afterthought, as in the first sentence of this section, and the informal parenthesis. Marks of parenthesis ( ) look more formal; dashes give a sense of speech. These two sentences illustrate a slight, characteristic difference:

> The myth of connotative and denotative meanings was destroyed by Carnap (the logician who taught at the University of Chicago) some twenty-five years ago.
> The myth of connotative and denotative meanings was destroyed by a logician and philosopher—I think it was Carnap—about twenty-five years ago.

Ellipses. Three dots in a row . . . indicate that you have omitted something from a quotation. Use four dots if the words left out were at the end of a sentence: three to indicate the omission, a fourth for the period.

Ellipses are useful in research papers or arguments using references. Much of a paragraph we want to quote may be irrelevant to our point. To include the whole paragraph in our text would slow the pace and violate the unity in our argument. Therefore we piece-cut the quotation and make it blend smoothly with our essay. Here is the long way to use a quotation:

> Marlowe was more direct than Shakespeare and more vigorous. As Professor William Wanger puts it:

> If the *Jew of Malta* is Marlowe's *Merchant of Venice,* it is at the same time better and worse than Shakespeare's famous comedy. The lesser-known play has fewer quotable passages, perhaps, and certainly fewer that are quoted; but we must acknowledge that Marlowe's play has more energy than Shakespeare's. What it lacks in finesse it makes up in vigor, and the character of the Jew is surely more complex, and more thoughtfully observed, than the character of the Merchant.
>
> What Professor Wanger says of two plays, we can say of all . . . .

Instead, we can use ellipses and build the necessary quotations into our text:

> Marlowe was more direct than Shakespeare and more vigorous.
> Comparing comedies by the two men, Professor William Wanger found Marlowe "better and worse than Shakespeare . . . ," lacking "in finesse" but superior in "vigor" and "energy." He found Marlowe's characterization, in one comparison, "more complex, and more thoughtfully observed," than Shakespeare's.

When we are obviously making excerpts, as with single words like *energy* and detached phrases like the last quotation, we do not need ellipses, because ellipses provide information: if we already know that quotations are excerpted, we do not need rows of dots to tell us so. But after *Shakespeare,* earlier in the paragraph, when we cut between a noun and an apostrophe indicating possession, we need the ellipses. However, we need not use ellipses if we omit words at the beginning of a quote:

> Pelham told the conference, "Every day motorists kill one million animals on American highways."

Hyphens.   We use hyphens to break a word at the right-hand margin. Dictionaries usually indicate the syllables that make up a word by placing a dot between them *(com · poun · ed).* Hyphenate only at the syllable break. Write *com-/pounded,* never *comp-/ounded.* When the syllable to be isolated is only one or two letters long, avoid division *(a-long, man-y, compound-ed).* Never hyphenate one-syllable words.

We use the hyphen on occasion to join two adjectives, or words serving as adjectives, modifying a noun. They make a temporary compound word.

blood-red hair
mile-long avenue

Avoid the temptation to multiply hyphenated phrases, which can become a virulent form of adjectivitis.

The *purple-green cloud-forms sweep-crawl* . . . .

We use hyphens with some temporary compounds. Before *wheel* and *barrow* became the compound word *wheelbarrow,* there may have been a stage at which we wrote *wheel-barrow.* Consult your dictionary when you are in doubt. Hyphens in compounds are a matter of spelling.

We use hyphens in compound numbers from twenty-one through ninety-nine.

We hyphenate fractions.

a two-thirds majority
three-quarters of the population

We use the hyphen to avoid ambiguity. We must spell the word *re-creation* to avoid confusing it with *recreation.*

We use the hyphen with some prefixes and suffixes.

governor-*elect*
ex-wife
self-determined

We use the hyphen as a typographic device to indicate a manner of speaking, when we indicate that someone is spelling a word by writing it *w-o-r-d,* or when we indicate a stammer, *w-w-word.*

Italics.   When we type, or write by hand, we show italics by under-lining the word: <u>Italics.</u> It comes out in type, *italics.*

Use italics for the names of ships: the *Niña;* for the titles of books, films, and plays: *War and Peace;* for the titles of newspapers or magazines: *Sports Illustrated;* and for foreign expressions: *faute de mieux, in medias res.*

Also, we use italics to indicate a special use of a word.

We might call the directory an *encyclopedia* of has-beens.

We use them, from time to time, to indicate emphasis.

Do you really *mean* that?

Using italics for emphasis is tricky, however. Italics are a vague gesture, an attempt to register a tone of voice that often fails because it cannot indicate a *specific* tone of voice. A writer who relies on emphatic italics often is be-ing lazy; a more careful choice of words, a more precise context, and the emphasis will be clear without italics.

Parentheses.   Use parentheses to enclose material that digresses from or interrupts the main idea of the writing or that explains something but remains a detachable unit.

The minister continued to pace up and down (though he normally slept through the night) and to stare out the window into the darkness.

De Marque points out (not only in the *Treatise,* but in the *Harmonics* as well) that Jolnay was ignorant of Graf.

Fred Papsdorf (Charles Laughton bought his paintings) lives on Jane Street, near East Detroit, in a small bungalow.

She complained that she weighed 10 stone (140 pounds; a stone, an English measure of avoirdupois, is 14 pounds) and had been 7 stone a year ago.

Also, use parentheses for numbers or letters that divide parts of a list.

There are three reasons: (1) . . . , (2) . . . , and (3). . . .

EXERCISES

1. In these sentences, marks of punctuation are used incorrectly or loosely. Discover errors or places where exact punctuation would improve precision or clarity.

   a. Two thirds of the population is semi-literate, and has read nothing more complex than "Readers Digest."
   b. The triumvirate, a ruling-group of three, resembling a contemporary troika, took over from the dying emperor.
   c. The pumpkin stuffing October sun, as the poet (Rarity) called it in his sonnet, *Goose,* pumped calories into the uncoiling sausage of the valley.
   d. "Whatever you do", the potato farmer told me, "remember one thing; eat starch four times a day."
   e. The monk, with the Gucci shoes wearing the new tonsure, spoke, at last with a sigh, "Yes I am Ludwig Babo."

2. Punctuate and capitalize the following paragraph.

your grandfather a good man but not well educated came to this country when he was twenty two he worked in a dry goods store and then because he was industrious took a job with the greenwood star as a cub reporter he had a motto as he always told us work hard and keep your nose clean

KEEP MECHANICS CONVENTIONAL

Like punctuation marks, the mechanics of English prose are conventions that make life easier. We can argue that the rules of spelling or manuscript form are irrational, and we can make a good case. But if we all agree to abide by the same mechanical conventions—irrational or not—we can more easily understand one another. Here are some remarks about abbreviations, capital letters, manuscript form, numerals, and spelling.

Abbreviations

In formal writing, we abbreviate only some words that go with names, like *Mr., Mrs., Ms., Dr., St.* (for *Saint,* not *street*), *Jr., Sr.;* degrees, like *Ph.D.* or *M.A.;* and indications of era or time, like A.D., B.C., A.M., and P.M.

(We use A.M. and P.M. only when a specific time is indicated; we speak of "4 P.M.." not "it was the P.M.") We do not abbreviate *Monday* or *August* or *street* or *road* or *volume* or *chemistry* in ordinary writing.

Some writers use *no.* as an abbreviation for *number,* but it looks out of place in formal prose. So too does *U.S.A.* instead of *United States* and *Pa.* instead of *Pennsylvania, lb.* instead of *pound,* and *oz.* instead of *ounce.*

Some institutions are so commonly called by their initials that it is overly formal to spell them out. On the one hand, the *Federal Bureau of Investigation* seems a pompous way to talk about the *FBI.* On the other hand, consider your audience; many people will need to be told the first time you mention *SEATO* that is the *Southeast Asia Treaty Organization.*

In conjunction with a numeral, *mph* and *rpm* are used in formal writing. We write *50 mph* and *1,000 rpm.* But if we write without figures, we spell them out.

> It is difficult to assess the speed of a space capsule when it is told in *miles per hour.*

Titles like *Governor* can be spelled out or shortened. Frequently, we shorten a title when we give a whole name:

> *Gov.* William Weld

and spell it out with a last name alone:

> *Governor* Weld

Any abbreviation of titles is inappropriate to formal prose.

For the use of abbreviations in notes and list of works cited, see pages 261–265.

Capital Letters

Capitalize the names of people, cities, and countries; the titles of people, books, and plays; the names of religious or national groups, languages, days of the week, months, holidays, and organizations and their abbreviations; the names of events or eras in history and important documents; and the names of specific structures, like buildings and airplanes and ships. In titles of books, plays, poems, songs, television shows, and movies, capitalize the first word and all subsequent words *except* articles and prepositions.

John Doe	June
Great Britain	Memorial Day
Berlin	General Motors or G.M.
Mayor David Dinkins	"Why Do Fools Fall in Love?"
Moby-Dick	Declaration of Independence
The Importance of Being Earnest	Empire State Building
Methodist	the *Winnie Mae*
Polish or European or Bostonian	the *Titanic*
Monday	*Play It Again Sam*

Do not capitalize the season or the names of college classes *(freshman, senior)* or general groups like *the lower classes* or *the jet set.* Do not capitalize school subjects or disciplines except languages:

> physics
> French

Adjectives are capitalized when they derive from proper nouns and still refer to them, like *Shakespearean.* Other nouns or adjectives that derive from names but no longer refer to the person lose their capitals:

> boycott
> quisling

The title that is capitalized before the proper noun, as

> *Mayor* Hermann Garsich

loses its capital when it is used outside of its titling function, as a descriptive word placed after the proper noun:

> Hermann Garsich, *mayor* of our town

Sections of a country may take capitals:

> the *West*
> the *South*

but the same words take lowercase when they are directions:

> Go *west,* young man.

Capitalize the first word of a quoted sentence:

> Mother said, "Come back soon."

Manuscript Form

Type or use a word-processor if you can. Double-space the entire paper, using one side of 8-½-by-11-inch 20-pound white bond paper. Never use erasable paper; it will not take inked corrections, it smudges, it sticks together, and it is altogether unpleasant to read. (If you must use it, hand in a photocopy of the finished paper.) Use Ko-Rec-Type, Liquid Paper, or a similar easy device for corrections.

Set margins of 1 inch to 1-½ inches at top, bottom, and sides. Number pages consecutively, including notes, appendixes, and list of works cited. Put your name in the upper left-hand corner of the first page. Type the title, capitalizing the first letter of the first word and of all other words except articles and prepositions, 2 or 3 inches down from the top of the first page. Do not underline or add a period to your title. If quoted material is short—up to fifty words of prose or two lines of poetry—place it within the paragraph, and use quotation marks. With lines of poetry, use a slash mark (/) to indicate line breaks, and follow the capitalization of the poem.

> Of man's first disobedience, and the fruit / Of that forbidden tree . . . .

If quoted material is longer than fifty words or two lines of poetry, detach it from the text. Indent the quotation half an inch to the right of the place where you begin paragraphs, and double-space the quotation. Do not use quotation marks.

Always make a photocopy. The most careful graders occasionally lose a paper. The corporations providing stolen papers for rich students make off with manuscripts when they can. Keep a copy to protect yourself.

Numerals

In dealing with decimal points and highly precise or technical figures, it is wise to use numerals.

> 69.7 decibels

Type dates in numerals also:

> June 14, 1971

The same goes for population figures and addresses:

> 104,000 inhabitants
> 1715 South University Avenue

Spell out figures, except when they are long to the point of being ridiculous. If you can write that a town has *one hundred four thousand inhabitants,* it is easy enough to write it out. If necessity requires precision, *104,627* will do; *one hundred four thousand, six hundred and twenty-seven* might look precious.

Never begin a sentence with a numeral.

> 97.6 mph showed on the speedometer.

Either spell out the number (*Ninety-seven and six-tenths*) or rewrite the sentence.

> The speedometer showed 97.6 mph.

The sentence

> 30 people stood up.

should certainly be written

> Thirty people stood up.

It is unnecessary, unless you are a lawyer, to include both spelled-out numbers and figures. Do not write,

> The building was at least twenty (20) stories tall.

Either will do—preferably the written-out word—but both together belong only to legal or business documents.

Spelling

English spelling is irregular and irrational. There are a few rules of thumb, but the rules always have exceptions. We memorize the spelling of words. We must remember when to write *their* and when to write *there.* And we must learn the spelling of countless inconsistencies: *plough, although, enough,* and *slough.*

All of us have problems of our own, and sometimes we make up our own ways to remember the correct spelling. Suppose we have trouble with the *ite/ate* ending: *definate* is a common mistake for *definite.* Maybe we can remember that it resembles the word *finite:* or maybe the third *i* in *infinity* will help us. Or maybe we write *infinate* by mistake. Remember the antonym *finite* and remember *separate,* as in "*separate* rooms," and not *separite.* (Not *seperate* either, for that matter.)

Here are some problems in spelling and some suggestions about overcoming them.

I/e, e/i. People mistakenly write *concieve* instead of *conceive,* and *beleive* instead of *believe.* The old mnemonic

I before *E*
Except after *C*
And when sounded like *ay*
As in *neighbor* and *weigh.*

is useful. Examples, both ways: *achieve, niece, piece, receipt, ceiling, receive.* Exceptions: *either, seize, weird, leisure, species, foreign.*

Variant Plurals. Some words change spelling in moving from singular to plural: *wife/wives* (like *knife, life, calf,* and *half*); *man/men* (like *woman, milkman,* etc.); *hero/heroes* (like *tomato, potato*).

Dropping a Final -e Before a Vowel. Most words ending with a silent -e drop it when we change them to a participle or other form that begins with a vowel. We spell the verb *move,* and we spell the participle *moving.* The silent -e usually remains when the added form begins with a consonant. Exceptions to both generalizations occur (*argue/argument; mile/mileage*), but they are infrequent and the rule is an unusually safe one.

The Final -y. When -y is a final vowel after a consonant (*dry*) it turns to -ie before -s, and -i before other letters, except when the ending is -ing, in which case the -y remains: *dries, drier, drying; beauty, beautiful.* When the -y follows another vowel, it generally remains -y, as in *joys* and *grayer,* with occasional exceptions, as in *lay/laid.*

Doubling Consonants. We double a final consonant before -ed, -ing, -er, or -est when the original verb or noun ends with a short vowel followed by a single consonant. *Hop* becomes *hopping.* When the vowel is long or a diphthong, we usually show it by a silent -e after the single consonant, and a single consonant with the suffix. *Hope* becomes *hoping.* Notice the difference between *plan/planning, plane/planing, slip/slipping, sleep/sleeping.*

Homonyms. Words that are pronounced alike but spelled differently present an irritating problem to writers. We have already mentioned *their/there/they're* and *its/it's.* Here are a few more:

affect/effect
accept/except
capital/capitol
principle/principal
gorilla/guerrilla
stationery/stationary
illusion/allusion

Here are some words frequently misspelled.

accept	embarrass	probably
accommodate	exaggerate	professor
acknowledgment	existence	proceed
advice	explanation	quantity
advise	friend	quite
all right	fulfillment	receive
allusion	grammar	referred
a lot	height	separate
annual	hypocrisy	shining
arrangement	its	succeed
beginning	it's	surprise
believe	library	than
business	loneliness	their
capital	lonely	then
capitol	necessary	there
coming	nuclear	they're
committee	obstacle	to, too, two
complement	occurred	villain
compliment	piece	who's
decide	possession	whose
definite	precede	writing
desert	principal	written
dessert	principle	
divide	privilege	

EXERCISES

1. In this paragraph, circle every mechanical error and correct it.

During the weeks that I have spent on campus I have learned to except the principal that definate explinations are often to exagerated to beleive in alot. 9 out of 10 students embarass their professors by not realising the mayor of there towns name, or not being alright in grammer, or not suceeding in reading books like "Moby Dick." Its a disgrase.

2. Correct, capitalize, and punctuate this paragraph:

look at that shot thats ridiculous Graebner tells himself he glances at Carole who has both fists in the air pull yourself together Clark this is a big point Graebner takes off his glasses and wipes them on his dental towel stalling Ashe mumbles while he is waiting he raises his left index finger and slowly pushes his glasses into place across the bridge of his nose just one point Arthur Graebner misses his first serve again Ashe moves in he hits sharply crosscourt Graebner dives for it catches it with a volley then springs up ready at the net Ashe lobs into the sun thinking that was a good get on that volley I didn't think hed get that Graebner punches the ball away with a forehand volley deuce Ashe is rattling the gates but Graebner will not let him in Carole has her hand on the top of her head unbelievable

John McPhee, "Ashe and Graebner"

A Glossary of Usage and Grammatical Terms

The glossary entries are of two kinds:

- Words frequently misused—clichés, commonly confused pairs of words, and words or phrases that should be avoided.
- Grammatical and rhetorical terms and the names of figures of speech.

Each of these entries includes general comments and references to the pages in the text where the subject is discussed.

A, an

> See **Article.**

Abbreviation

> See pages 312–313.

Absolute element

> An absolute element is a word or a group of words that is grammatically independent of the rest of the sentence and that is not joined to it by a relative pronoun or a conjunction. It modifies the whole clause or sentence. Absolute phrases are often made up of a noun followed by a participle.

> > *All things considered,* he recovered quickly from his injuries.
> > *Her youth gone,* the old woman passed her days in remembering.

> Many absolute constructions are common phrases.

> > *Come hell or high water,* I'll get to Dallas by Thursday.
> > Neither twin was there, *to tell the truth.*

Abstract, abstraction

> An abstraction is a noun referring to the idea or quality of a thing and not to a thing itself: *redness, courage.*

We use the word *abstract* relatively, referring to more general and less particular words. *Enclosure* is more general, say, than *room* or *cage* or *zoo*. For remarks on abstractions and prose style, see pages 319–320.

Accept, except

These words sound alike but mean different things. *Accept* means to receive something voluntarily.

I *accept* the compliment.

Except as a verb means to exclude.

I *excepted* Jones from the group I wished to congratulate.

Except as a preposition is more common.

I congratulated everyone *except* Jones.

Acronym

An acronym is an abbreviation, pronounced as a word, that is composed of the first letters of the words in the title or phrase abbreviated.

SAC (Strategic Air Command)
snafu (situation normal, all fouled up)

Use with caution.

Active voice

Verbs are in the active voice when the subject of the sentence does the action the verb describes.

Bob *hit* the spider.

When the subject is acted on, the verb is passive.

The spider was hit by Bob.

See **Passive voice.**

Adjective

Adjectives describe or limit a noun or a noun substitute. These adjectives describe:

green onions
happiest year
The man was *old*.

Other adjectives limit in a variety of ways.

Indefinite: *Some* men walked in the road.
Demonstrative: *Those* men walked in the road.
Possessive: *Their* men walked in the road.
Numerical: *Twelve* men walked in the road.
Interrogative: *Which* men walked in the road?
Relative: The *larger* men walked in the road.

Nouns can be used as adjectives.

university professor

But the writer should beware of using several nouns in a row as adjectives.

For the formation of comparatives, see **Comparison of adjectives and adverbs.** For a stylistic approach to adjectives, see pages 104–110.

Adjective clause

An adjective clause is a dependent clause used as an adjective.

The man *whose nose is purple* will stand out in a crowd.

Adjectives frequently misused

Try to avoid the adjective used vaguely. These words once meant specific things: *terror* once inhabited *terrific;* now *terrific* can mean "unusually pleasant."

What a *terrific* summer day!

Some other adjectives are frequently used as vague praise, vague blame, or vague intensives.

terrible	nice	cute	real	unbelievable
funny	unique	wonderful	fantastic	wicked
awful	interesting	incredible	great	obvious

That *terrible* man with the *cute* name was *awful* to the *nice* girl.

Adverb

Adverbs describe or limit any words except nouns, pronouns, prepositions, and articles. Adverbs work with verbs, adjectives, other adverbs, verbals, and entire clauses. Adverbs commonly give information:

Degree: *extremely* hungry
Manner: ran *slowly*
Place: hurried *here*
Time: She *then* left.

For stylistic advice on the adverb, see pages 104–110.

Adverb clause

An adverb clause is a dependent clause used as an adverb.

I'll be gone *before she starts spraying.*

The adverb clause, *before she starts spraying,* modifies the verb *will be gone.*

Adverbs frequently misused

Most of the adjectives frequently misused become misused adverbs, with an -*ly* added. *Terrible* becomes *terribly,* as in "*terribly* comfortable." Strictly adverbial adjectives are misused also.

terrifically	actually	wonderfully	literally	incredibly
certainly	very	rather	hopefully	totally
absolutely	virtually	practically	really	obviously

It *certainly* was a *very* hot day and I was *practically* done at the *absolutely* last minute when *actually* a *rather* large man *virtually* beheaded me.

Advice, advise

Advice is a noun; *advise* is a verb.

I was *advised* to ignore your *advice*.

Affect, effect

The two words are commonly confused. These examples illustrate proper uses of them:

Bob *affected* (influenced) the writing of Wright.
Sarah *affected* (assumed) the manner of a Greek tragedian.
The harder spray was *effected* (brought about) by an adjustment of the hose's nozzle
The *effect* (result) of the new style was unpleasant.

Agreement

Correspondence in form, or the matching of one word with another, means that sentence elements must correspond in number, person, and gender.

He is so evil.
They are so evil.
Tom took *his* crocodile down to the river.
Tom and *Maria* took *their* crocodiles down to the river.
The *car* and *its* trailer rounded the corner.

See pages 289–295.

Agree to, agree with

One *agrees to* a proposal or an action; one *agrees with* a person.

All ready, already

The words differ in meaning. To say that someone is *all ready* is to say that he is prepared; the word *already* means beforehand in time, as in

He was *already* there.

All right, alright

All right is the correct form. *Alright* means the same thing, but is a recent creation based on an analogy to the old word *already*. In formal writing, stay away from *alright*.

Allusion, illusion

An allusion is an indirect reference; an illusion is a false belief or perception or a deceptive appearance.

Barnhouse bored us with his *allusions* to his illustrious family.
Under the *illusion* that he was invited, Barnhouse appeared for dinner at seven o'clock.

Almost, most

Almost is an adverb meaning "nearly"; *most* is an adjective meaning "nearly all" or "the greater part of." Avoid using *most* as a shortened form of *almost*.

Almost all of us lead lives of quiet desperation.
Most men lead lives of quiet desperation.

Along with

Avoid this wordy and useless phrase, in sentences like

Along with tennis, big-game hunting is my favorite sport.
MacDowell is my candidate for the presidency, *along with* Vanderschmidt and Creelman-Carr.

Instead, say something like

Big-game hunting and tennis are my favorite sports.
For the presidency, I favor MacDowell, Vanderschmidt, or Creelman-Carr.

A lot

Many people have taken to spelling *a lot* as one word, *alot*. *A lot* is two words, like *all right.*
A lot of police officers showed up.

Although, though

Although is preferable in formal writing.

Altogether, all together

The two do not have the same meaning. *Altogether* means *wholly* or *entirely*. *All together* combines two commonly understood words.

Xavier, Abby, Frank, and Al were *all together* at the table.
Guy Woodhouse was *altogether* disgusting.

Ambiguity

Writing is ambiguous when it has more than one possible meaning or interpretation.

Amid, amidst

Avoid these words, which are not common in American usage and which sound stuffy and bookish.

Among, amongst

Among is preferable; *amongst* is bookish.

Among, between

Use *between* when you are dealing with two things, *among* for more than two.

between you and me
among the three of us

In highly informal writing, this distinction is often ignored.

Amoral, immoral, unmoral

Amoral means outside morality, neither moral nor immoral.

Beauty is *amoral*.

Immoral is contrary to codes of morality.

Benedict Arnold was *immoral*.

Unmoral is a near synonym for *amoral* and is seldom used.

Amoral is often used when the assertion is argumentative, *unmoral* when the statement is merely factual.

Dogs and cats are *unmoral*.

Amount, number

Amount refers to a quantity of things viewed as a whole or to the quantity of one item; *number* describes the separate units of a group.

The *amount* of money in his bank account was staggering.
The *number* of dollar bills on the floor was small.
He took a large *amount* of salt a *number* of times.

Analogy

An analogy is an extended comparison, used for illustration and argument. For examples and stylistic uses, see pages 117–120.

And/or

This legalism frequently occurs in nonlegal prose where *or* would do just as well.

Cooking with pots *and/or* skillets requires nothing more than a hotplate.

Omit the unnecessary *and*.

Antecedent

An antecedent is a word or group of words to which a pronoun refers.

As *Kevin* and *Quentin* ran in, *they* dropped the gas pellets.

Kevin and *Quentin* are the antecedents of the personal pronoun *they*.

Antonym

An antonym means the opposite of another word. *Bad* is the antonym of *good*. As there are no exact synonyms, so we must not expect antonyms to be precisely opposite.

Any, any other

Be careful to use these words properly. If you say

"*King Lear* is more moving than *any other* play in the English language."

you are probably saying what you intend. If you say, however, that

"*King Lear* is more moving than *any* play in the English language."

you imply that *Lear* is not in English—or that *Lear* is better than itself, which would be nonsensical. If you say

"Sophia is sexier than *any* woman in Italy."

you imply that she is not in Italy.

Anybody, anyone

The words are singular, not plural. They take singular pronouns, as do *every, everyone, everybody.*

Everyone charges *his* meal at Alice's.

is formally correct, not

Everyone charges *their* meal at Alice's.

But an exception to this rule could make the second example the preferable form of the sentence. When a pronoun has *anybody* as an antecedent, and the gender of the person being discussed is unknown, we may wish to use forms of the plural *they* to avoid deciding between *he* and *she* because *they* does not indicate gender.

Did *anybody* call? What did *they* say?

Anyways

This form of *anyway* belongs to informal speech, not to writing.

Apostrophe

See pages 305–306.

Appositive

An appositive is a noun, or a noun substitute, that is placed next to another noun and that explains or defines it.

Peter, *the flying dwarf,* escorted Tarquina, his *good fairy.*

Flying dwarf is the appositive of *Peter,* and *good fairy* is the appositive of *Tarquina.*

Apt, liable, likely

Apt to means "having a tendency to."

Sarah is *apt to* be discouraged if she doesn't win.

Liable to should be used only in situations that imply negative consequences.

That child is *liable to* fall if he leans too far out the window.

Likely to implies "probably going to." Do not say "We will *likely* arrive . . ." Say instead

We are *likely to* arrive in Cincinnati by early afternoon if the radiator doesn't overheat.

Argument

Argument is writing designed to convince or persuade.

Article

The definite article is *the;* the indefinites are *a* and *an*. They are adjectives, always indicating that a noun or a noun substitute will follow.
The names a particular:

> *the* table
> *the* abstraction

A and *an* name a member of a class:

> *a* table
> *an* abstraction

The difference in meaning is small but indispensable.

The article *a* is used before words beginning with a consonant sound (even if the letter is a vowel):

> *a* train
> *a* unit

An is used before words beginning with a vowel sound:

> *an* imaginative idea
> *an* herb

As, like

As is a conjunction; *like* is a preposition. In speech we often find *like* used as a conjunction:

> He smiles *like* he felt good.

But in writing, we should avoid using *like* as a conjunction. We should use *as* or *as if* instead. Instead of writing

> I write *like* I talk.

we say

> I write *as* I talk.
> I write *as if* I talked like a Frenchman.

Like works as a preposition, in language written or spoken:

> He talks *like* a Frenchman.

Aspect

This noun is commonly used as a blank. Avoid it.

> We listened to a lecture on various *aspects* of fishing.

Usually if we remove the word we improve our sentence.

> We listened to a lecture on fishing.

At

Don't use the redundancy "Where are you *at?*" *Where* means "at which place."

Auxiliaries

Auxiliaries in verb phrases indicate distinctions in tense and person. Common auxiliaries are *will, would, shall, should, be, have, do, can, could, may, might,* and *must.*

> We *are* eating the chocolate.
> You *would have* done the same.

Awful, awfully

Literally, if we were *awful,* we are "full of *awe.*" We no longer use the word to mean what it means. It is a vague intensive like *terrific, wonderful,* and *horrible.*

Bad, badly

When we use the adjective *bad* after sensory verbs, in an expression like "I felt *bad* yesterday," we sometimes confuse it with the adverb *badly.* If you claim that you "felt *badly,*" your words mean that your sensory apparatus did not function correctly. This use of *bad* holds true for sensory verbs like *feel, taste,* or *sound,* and also for verbs like *seem, appear,* and *look.* In grammatical terms, *bad* in these circumstances is a predicate adjective.

Using *badly* instead of *bad* as a predicate adjective affects gentility but reveals ignorance. It is correct to say

> She looked *bad* when she came up to bat.

and incorrect to say

> She looked *badly* when she came up to bat.

The latter sentence denigrates her vision. It is correct to say

> They seemed *bad* this morning, after the ocean voyage.

referring to the appearance of illness. Do not say

> They seemed *badly* this morning after the ocean voyage.

Other constructions require the adverb *badly.*

> She played *badly* the first seven innings.

In

> She played *bad* the first seven innings.

bad is incorrect.

Badly has another sense, which is "very much." This sense is colloquial or informal.

> They wanted *badly* to be elected.
> She was *badly* in need of a drink.

If you mean to employ this colloquialism, be careful of your word order. If you say, "She needed to sing very *badly,*" you say something quite different from "She needed very *badly* to sing." If in doubt, be more formal; say

>>> She needed *very much* to sing.

not

>>> She needed to sing *very much*.

Balanced sentences

See pages 153–162, where we discuss balance and parallelism.

Being as

This is a common illiteracy.

>>> *Being as* it was almost noon . . . .

Rewrite to eliminate. Usually we can substitute *because*.

>>> *Because* it was almost noon . . . .

Beside, besides

Each of these words has several meanings of its own.

>>> She stood *beside* (by the side of) the bureau.
>>> Matt was *beside* himself (almost overwhelmed) with anger.
>>> It's *beside* (not connected with) the point.
>>> No one was awake *besides* (other than) him.
>>> *Besides* (furthermore), it's in questionable taste.

Between

See **Among, between.**

Bibliography

See pages 261–265.

Big words

Never use a big word where a little word will do. Never say *domicile* if you can say *house*. Never say *individual* where you could say *person*. Never say *utilize* where you could say *use*.

See also **Genteel words** and **–ize verbs.**

Brackets

See page 308.

Bring, take

Bring (to) implies movement toward.

>>> *Bring* me a cup of coffee.

Take (from) implies movement away from.

>>> *Take* the memo to the secretary.

Can, may, could, might

Both words express possibility. *Can* (or *could*) expresses *physical* possibility.

>>> He *can* go to market because he has the car.
>>> She *could* eat the potato salad, but she doesn't want to.

May (or *might*) implies that something is a *chance,* and often implies *volition.*

> He *may* go to Alaska (or he may not).
> She *might* be the last of the clan (or she might not).

Often we can hesitate between the two, and choose the one over the other for the precise shade of meaning. "He *could* take the exam" and "He *might* take the exam" offer different possibilities.

In conversation, and in the most informal writing, *may* often disappears in favor of *can,* and a distinction disappears, which is a loss. Or instead of saying "She *may* read Shakespeare or Julia Child or *Young Lust,*" we substitute the wordier "She *can* read Shakespeare or Julia Child or *Young Lust,* depending on what she feels like." The final clause supplies the chanciness and the volition implied in *may.*

In asking or granting permission, genteel prose uses *may.*

> *May* I enter?
> Randolph, you *may* not.

But *may* in this usage almost invariably sounds like an effort to be refined.

Cannot, can not

The spellings are equally acceptable. *Can not* looks more formal.

Can't hardly

Because *hardly,* as Bergen Evans says, "has the force of a negation," *can't hardly* functions as a double negative, or at least as an ambiguity. Does "I *can't hardly* hear you" mean "I *can't* hear you" or "I *can* hear you well" or "I *can hardly* hear you"? Logically, the double negative should make it mean the second, but the speaker probably meant the last. We should increase the clarity of our language by saying simply, "I *can hardly* hear you." The same advice applies to *can't scarcely.*

See **Double negative.**

Capital letters

See pages 313–314.

Case

See **Inflection.**

Cf.

We often find this abbreviation in footnotes and sometimes in parentheses. It tells us to "compare," as in

> This decision was an exception (*cf. Toothe* v. *Carey*).

Circumlocution

Circumlocution is taking the long way to say something, using clichés, verbs combined with other parts of speech instead of simple verbs, and filler words and phrases. In

> *Notwithstanding the case of* the seamstress, it is *going to be* obvious that *in general, in a manner of speaking, we do well to*

> *remember the observation that a man who* is always in a hurry
> will lose *something or other in the long run.*

the circumlocution occurs throughout, and phrases typical in circumlocution are in italic. Notice that the last seventeen words might be
rendered

> *Haste makes waste.*

Cite, sight, site

Cite means to quote or to refer to.

> They *cited* the constructive things they had done.

A *sight* is a view:

> a moving *sight*

or vision itself.
A *site* is a location:

> a building *site*

Clause

A clause is a part of a sentence with a subject and a predicate. It
may be principal (or main or independent) or subordinate (dependent
on a main clause).

> *The year ended* and *the year began.*

In the sentence above, two whole clauses are made into a compound
sentence by *and.*

> The year ended *when it had just begun.*

In this sentence, the italic clause is subordinate.
See pages 128–129.

Cliché

A cliché is a much used combination of words. *Writing Well* uses
and defines this word several times. See pages 101–102 and 112–113
for instance.

Collective noun
See **Noun.**

Colon
See pages 308–309.

Comma
See pages 300–304.

Comma Splice
See pages 286–288.

Common nouns
See **Noun.**

Compare to, compare with

To *compare to* shows similarities between things that are obviously different.

He *compared* the sparrow *to* a 10-ton truck.

(Of course by showing similarity, it reveals difference as well.) To *compare with* shows differences between things that are obviously similar.

She *compared* lunch *with* dinner.

(Of course it reveals similarities at the same time.)

Comparison of adjectives and adverbs

The comparison of adjectives and adverbs indicates relative degree. The three degrees are positive, comparative, and superlative.

Positive	Comparative	Superlative
good	better	best
obnoxious	more obnoxious	most obnoxious
quick	quicker	quickest
quickly	more quickly	most quickly

Comparisons

For a discussion of simile, metaphor, and analogy, see pages 115–120.

Complement

As a grammatical term, a complement is one or more words that complete the meaning of a verb or an object. A subject complement:

Phyllis is a wicked *girl*.

The predicate noun—*girl*—completes the sense of *Phyllis,* which it refers to. An object complement:

The dog chewed the bone *raw*.

Raw modifies and completes *bone*.

Complement, compliment

A *complement* makes something whole or complete.

Work is the *complement* of play.

A *compliment* is praise.

I paid you a *compliment*.

There is also an archaic meaning in which *compliments* means something like formal politeness, and which survives in the phrase *compliments of the season.*

Complex sentence

A complex sentence contains a main clause and a subordinate clause. Here the subordinate (in italics) is a relative:

I whistled at the boy *who hung from the cliff.*

See pages 131–132, 137–140, and 174–177.

Compound-complex sentence

This sentence type combines, as you might expect, the complex and the compound sentence. It has two main clauses and at least one subordinate clause.

The snow stopped falling when the sun rose, but the temperature stayed below 10 degrees.

See page 132.

Compound sentence

A compound sentence includes two or more main clauses and no subordinate clauses.

The moon rose at 10:35 P.M. and the stars appeared to recede into the darkness.

See pages 130–131 and 140–143.

Compound word

A compound word contains two or more words that are commonly used together as a single word.

president-elect
brother-in-law
blackbird
wheelbarrow
handwriting

Consult a dictionary for current spelling.
See page 310.

Conjugation

See **Inflection.**

Conjunction

Conjunctions connect or coordinate (*and, but, for, or,* and occasionally *yet* or *so*) or they subordinate (*after, because, while, when, where, since*). With coordinate conjunctions be careful to preserve unity by keeping the coordinate phrases or clauses parallel (see pages 153–156). With subordinate conjunctions, remain aware of the habits of complex sentences (see pages 131–132, 137–140, and 174–177). Contrary to the old rule, even the best contemporary writing uses conjunctions at the beginnings of sentences.

Conjunctive adverb

A conjunctive adverb can be used to connect main clauses: *then, besides, however, therefore, otherwise.* Use a semicolon between the main clauses (before the adverb) and a comma after the adverb. See pages 142, 286–288, and 305.

Conscience, conscious

These words mean different things. *Conscience* is a noun meaning the human faculty that distinguishes right from wrong.

After he lied to his boss, his *conscience* would not let him sleep.

Conscious is an adjective describing a state of awareness or being awake.

Eleanor was *conscious* of a sharp pain behind her left eye.
The patient became *conscious* after spending a week in a coma.

Consider . . . as

Writers frequently misuse the verb *consider* by adding an unnecessary preposition, *as*. Say

She *considered* him handsome.

not

She *considered* him *as* handsome.

Another use of the verb takes *as* appropriately. In the preceding example, *consider* means "believe to be." In the following example, *consider* means "think about" or "talk about."

She *considered* him *as* an administrator and *as* a scholar.

Consist in, consist of

Consist of refers to the parts that make a whole.

The government *consists of* legislative, executive, and judicial divisions.

Consist in refers to inherent qualities:

The value of democracy *consists in* the responsibility with which it endows the citizen.

Continual, continuous

The two words have slightly different meanings. *Continual* describes an action that is repeated frequently.

He called her *continually* throughout the day.

Continuous describes an action done without stopping.

The bleeding was *continuous* for three hours.

Coordinate

Coordinate means equal in rank. Two infinitives are coordinate, for instance, or two main clauses, as in a compound sentence.
See pages 130–131, 137–138, 140–143.

Correlative conjunctions

Both . . . and, either . . . or, neither . . . nor, and *not only . . . but also* are coordinating conjunctions and require parallel forms in the phrases or clauses they coordinate.

Could have, could of

The correct phrase is *could have*. *Could of* is a mistake. Don't say

She *could of* been a great actress.

But say

She *could have* been a great actress.

Counsel, council, consul

Counsel is advice or a lawyer or someone acting as a lawyer. Though it would be a confusing sentence, one could say

The court-appointed *counsel* gave his client *counsel.*

A different spelling, with the same pronunciation, gives us the word *council,* which is a legislative group.

Harris for City *Council!*

A *consul* represents his government in another country where he keeps residence.

The vice-consul was out to lunch.

Couple

In the idiomatic sense of *a few,* the word is extremely informal; substitute *two* or *a few* or *several.*

Cutting words from quotations

See pages 309–310.

Dangling constructions

A phrase placed loosely in a sentence dangles. Modifiers dangle frequently and disastrously.
See pages 295–297.

Dashes

See page 309.

Data

In the most formal prose, we recognize the etymology of *data* as a Latin plural and therefore use the word with a plural verb form. It is correct—if highly formal or scientific—to say

These data *convince* us.

rather than

This data *convinces* us.

The singular, rarely used, is *datum.*

Declension

See **Inflection.**

Deductive reasoning

A form of thinking that applies a general truth to a specific instance. Thus, if it is true that going through a time warp causes pain, we may *deduce* that if Quasimodo goes through a time warp, he will feel pain.

Demonstratives

Demonstratives are adjectives, like *this, that, these,* and *those,* used for pointing:

> *This* is the man who took it; *that's* my basketball.

They can also be pronouns; when they are, they should have clear antecedents. Do not say

> You said that you couldn't read and that you had never learned how. I could not believe *that.*

See pages 292–294.

Diction

The choice and use of words.

Different from, different than

Different from is usually preferable, especially in formal prose. When a clause follows, *different than* is acceptable.

This place is *different than* I expected it to be.

Direct address

The use of a noun or pronoun to direct a remark to a specific person, set off by commas.

> I was thinking, *Ron,* that you'd like to go up in a balloon.
> *Irving,* close that closet.
> Hey, *you!*

Direct object

See **Object.**

Direct quotation

See page 307.

Discreet, discrete

The two words have different meanings. *Discreet* means prudent in one's conduct or speech.

> She would never reveal it; she was exceptionally *discreet.*

Discrete means distinct or separate.

> The words are different; they have *discrete* meanings.

Disinterested, uninterested

These words are frequently confused. To be *uninterested* is to lack fascination about something, even to be bored by it.

> I tried to arouse his enthusiasm for a game of golf, but he was *uninterested* in such a pastime.

Disinterested is the condition of being impartial or neutral, or of having no stake in an issue. Frequently the word is used positively as a precondition for fairness, as in the phrase "*disinterested* party."

The judge declared his *disinterest* in the matter.

This judge proclaims his ability to judge the case fairly.

Doesn't, don't

Don't goes with *I, you, we,* and *they,* but not with *it, he,* or *she.* It contracts *do not.* It does not contract *does not; doesn't* does.

Double negative

A double negative occurs in a sentence that uses two negative terms when only one is needed.

He *didn't* say *nothing.*
You *shouldn't never* do that to a bird.

In earlier English such doubling was thought to give emphasis, as in "I never treacherously slew no man" (Bergen Evans's example). But today double negatives are regarded as unacceptable and illogical. If I should *not* never do something, then by implication I should (positively) do it sometime.

See **Can't hardly.**

Doubt but

Omit *but.* Also omit *but* in *help but.*

They couldn't *doubt but* that the Racquet Club was best.

becomes

They couldn't *doubt* that the Racquet Club was best.

and

They couldn't *help but* know the worst.

becomes

They couldn't *help* knowing the worst.

And always avoid "They couldn't *doubt but* what . . . ."

Due to

Never use *due to* for *because of* in adverb phrases. "She won the race *due to* her long legs" sounds unnatural. It is probably best to reserve the word for finance. Sometimes people multiply error by writing, "due to the fact that . . . ."

Each, every

Each is a pronoun:

Each went his own way.

and an adjective:

Each package of bubble gum has five pieces.

Each means the individual units of a conglomerate:

Each of the Boy Scouts

but *every* means the conglomerate itself:

> *Every* Boy Scout

In the Boy Scout examples, *each* is a pronoun, *every* is an adjective.

When the adjective *each* modifies a singular noun, the following verb and pronouns are singular.

> *Each* player *lifts his* bat.

When *each* modifies a plural noun and comes before the verb, the verb is plural.

> They *each go their* own way.

When *each* works as a pronoun, it is usually singular.

> *Each goes his* own way.

There are exceptions. In the preceding example, if the pronoun referred to men and women, we might have written

> *Each go their* own way.

When *each* refers to two or more singular words, or when a plural word comes between *each* and the verb, the number of the verb is optional. We may say

> *Each* of the players *is*

or

> *Each* of the players *are*

We may say

> When *Mark and Linda* speak, *each* of them *says*

or

> When *Mark and Linda* speak, *each* of them *say*

The negative of *each* is *neither*. Do not write *each* with a negative:

> *Each* did not speak.

but write

> *Neither* spoke.

Effect, affect
See **Affect, effect.**

E.g.
This is the abbreviation for a Latin expression that means *for example*. It is usually best to use the English, but on occasion we will find these initials, often in scientific or legal prose.

> The review board overlooked significant evidence, *e.g., Baxter* v. *Baxter.*

Egoism, egotism

Egoism has the connotation of a philosophy, *egotism* of a neurosis. *Egoism* is the other side of *altruism* and is a belief in the value of self-interest. *Egotism* is the necessity to use the word *I* all the time.

Either

Either, like *each,* can be pronoun or adjective.

> *Either* path leads us home.
> *Either* of the twins . . . .

When *either* means one or the other, it takes the singular.

> *Either* Rick or Chris *is* lying.

When it means both, it still takes a singular verb.

> *Either* of you *is* qualified.

Sometimes *either/or* and *neither/nor* connect a singular and a plural subject. Then the verb agrees with the subject closest to it.

> *Either* Peggotty *or* the Steerforths *are* coming to dinner tonight.

As a correlative conjunction, *either* takes *or* and does not take *nor. Nor* belongs to *neither.*

Elicit, illicit

Elicit means "to bring out."

> We could *elicit* no further response from the members.

Illicit means "not permitted."

> They were having an *illicit* love affair.

Ellipses

See pages 309–310.

Eminent, immanent, imminent

Eminent means outstanding.

> The *eminent* philosopher . . .

Immanent means inherent.

> . . . will discuss *immanent* ideas . . .

Imminent means impending.

> . . . *imminently.*

Enormity, enormousness

An *enormity* is a moral outrage. *Enormousness* is hugeness.

Etc.

This abbreviation meaning "and so forth," from the Latin *et cetera,* is out of place in formal prose. In formal and informal prose, it often trails off the end of a sentence into vagueness and avoids extending the brain. Stay away from it in formal prose. Think before you use it in any context.

See **Foreign words and phrases.**

Etymology

Etymology is the study of the origins and histories of words.

Euphemism

Euphemisms are fancy or abstract substitutes for plain words. We use them for social elevation, as when the *undertaker* becomes a *mortician,* or to avoid facing something unwelcome, as when we say *the man passed away* instead of saying *the man died.*

See pages 82–83, 102, 168–169, 339, and 341.

Everybody, everyone

Everybody and *everyone* take a singular verb.

> *Everybody goes* to church.

The words can take a singular pronoun, especially in a formal context:

> *Everyone* finds *his* seat and waits for the minister.

or a plural pronoun, especially when it refers to men and women and we wish to avoid picking either *his* or *her* (and being accused of sexist writing).

> *Everybody* waited until *they* caught *their* breath.

See pages xxx–xxx.

Exclamation point

See pages 299–300.

Expletives

When *it* and *there* fill space in a sentence without contributing to its meaning, we call them expletives.

> *There are* thousands of people in the United States who cannot read.
> *It is* understood that the rain was falling.

These could be written:

> Thousands of people in the United States cannot read.
> Rain was falling.

Exposition

Exposition is writing designed to explain or analyze.

Fact

Avoid the phrase *the fact that,* which is wordy and unnecessary.

Famous, notorious, infamous

To be *famous* is to be well known or celebrated. To be *notorious* is to be well known for something shady. To be *infamous* is to be well known for something detestable.

He was a *famous* movie star, musician, and second baseman.
He was a *notorious* pirate, extortionist, and linguist.
Bluebeard was an *infamous* character.

Farther, further

As "distance to go" the two are interchangeable. Where *further* means "more," *farther* is not a possible alternative.

We have no *further* use for him.

Few

See **Less.**

Field

A field is a place for growing hay or daisies. Don't use it as a blank, or invisible noun, as in "the field of agriculture."

Fine

This adjective is vague and overused.

Finite verb

A finite verb is complete, a predicate in itself.

The house *collapses.*

Gerunds, infinitives, and participles are not finite verbs but *verbals.*

Footnote

See pages 264–265.

Foreign words and phrases

Foreign words and phrases often look pretentious in our writing. In dialogue, they can be useful to characterize someone as foreign or as pretentious. Occasionally nothing in English seems quite so apt as a foreign phrase. But look hard before you give up. If you must use one, italicize it.

Foreword, forward

The two have different meanings. A *foreword* is an introductory statement at the beginning of a book. *Forward* is usually a direction. On occasion, *forward* means "bold" or "presumptuous."

She leaned *forward* and stuck her tongue out at him; she was very *forward.*

Fused sentence

See **Run-on sentence.**

Gender

Gender is a grammatical indication of sex. English nouns lack gender except as their own sense indicates. That is, *sister* is feminine, *brother* is masculine, and *sibling* can be either. Some pronouns have gender *(he, she),* but most do not *(I, they, you, we).* In some languages, all nouns are assigned a gender. In French, the word for *grass (herbe)* is feminine, and the word for *time (temps)* is masculine. In English both words are neuter.

Genteel words

Some words act as euphemisms by seeming socially preferable to plainer alternatives. People who use them seem to be *trying* to be genteel. Avoid them unless you are making a genuine distinction.

Genteel	*Ordinary*
perspire	sweat
wealthy	rich
home	house
luncheon	lunch

Gerund

See **Verbal.**

Get

We multiply this little word in our speech; it has small place in our writing. "I went down to *get* some wallpaper" is passable but often imprecise. In writing, it would be better to *choose* or *buy* the wallpaper.

Good, well

It is common to use *good* as if it were an adverb, but it is incorrect.

He ran *good.*

When referring to an action, *well* is the right word.

He ran *well.*

Be careful with the word *feels;* to say that a person *feels good* is to say that she is in a pleasant frame of mind; to say that a person *feels well* is to say either that she feels healthy or that her sense of touch is functioning efficiently.

Grammar

Grammar describes how words function in a language.

Guerrilla, gorilla

A *guerrilla* is an irregular soldier. A *gorilla* is an animal. *Guerrilla* is also used as an adjective and has been used adjectivally to indicate activity in the service of revolution: *guerrilla* theater, *guerrilla* television.

Had ought

This combination is clumsy. Instead of writing.

We knew he *had ought* to come.

write

We knew he *ought* to come.

Hanged, hung

Hanged pertains to the execution of human beings, *hung* to the suspension of objects.

> Sam Hall was *hanged* in October.
> We *hung* the portraits in the hall.

He, him

> *He* is a subject, *him* an object.

Other pronoun pairs, subject and object, are *I/me, they/them, she/her, we/us,* and *who/whom.* (See **Who/whom.**)

> *He* walked to Joe's. *He* and Jane walked to Joe's.
> Joe saw *him.* Joe saw Jane and *him.*

A common error uses the subject when it ought to use the object.

> Joe saw Jane and *I.*

is wrong. You would not say "Joe saw *I*" and therefore you do not say "Joe saw Jane and *I.*" It is correct to say

> Joe saw Jane and *me.*

This error, like many errors, is a false correction. When we are children we may say

> *Me* and Jane went down to Joe's.

We learn to correct this to

> Jane and *I* went down to Joe's.

which is fine because *I* is a subject. Then by mistake we use *I* when we should use the objective *me,* as if we corrected the old error.

This error happens most often after a preposition like *across, at, behind, between, by, for, from, in, of, on, over, to, under,* and *with.* Prepositions take objects. Always say

> This happened to Jane and *me.*

Never say

> This happened to Jane and *I.*
> This happened to Jane and *he.*
> This happened to Jane and *we.*
> This happened to Jane and *they.*

All of these examples are incorrect.

The way to remember: if it sounds wrong when you use the preposition alone, as in

> This happened to *I/he/we/they* . . .

then it is wrong when a proper name comes between the preposition (or the verb) and the pronoun.

See also **Pronoun.**

He or she

> This locution is awkward and clumsy. Sometimes we use it to avoid sexism.

See page 149.

Help but
> See **Doubt but.**

Homonym
> Homonyms are words that, although pronounced the same, are spelled differently and mean different things.

to, too, two	bare, bear	their, there, they're
through, threw	blew, blue	heir, air

Hopefully
> *Hopefully* is an adverb meaning "full of hope" that frequently becomes a dangling modifier. We say

> > *Hopefully,* the plane will be on time.

> when we do not mean to imply that the plane is full of hope. We could say

> > *Hopefully,* I awaited her arrival.

> We come to use *hopefully* as if it meant "I hope." The first example is meant to say

> > *I hope* the plane will be on time.

Hyperbole
> Hyperbole is extreme exaggeration to make a point.

> > That cat *weighs a ton.*

> Use hyperbole with discretion; do not use it, like some writers, a thousand times on every page.

Hyphen
> See pages 310–311.

I, me
> See **He/him.**

I.e.
> *I.e.* abbreviates the Latin *id est,* meaning "that is." We use it sometimes to introduce an explanation or definition of a word or phrase.

> > She was nonessential; *i.e.,* they didn't need to employ her.

> Usually, the expression seems overprecise and too much like legal or scientific writing. The sentence above can omit the Latinism and use instead a colon or a semicolon.

> > She was nonessential: they didn't need to employ her.

Immigrant, emigrant
> An *immigrant* is someone who enters a country; an *emigrant* leaves one.

> Our ancestors had to emigrate before they could immigrate.

344 A Glossary of Usage and Grammatical Terms

Incredible, unbelievable

In theory, these words are synonymous. In practice, *unbelievable* holds up better.

> The charges were *unbelievable*.

states rather straightforwardly the disbelief.

> The charges were *incredible*.

suffers from the use of *incredible* as a vague intensive.

> Those hamburgers were *incredible*.

simply praises the hamburgers in hyperbole from which constant use has withdrawn the strength. *Unbelievable* undergoes some of the same diminishment:

> . . . *unbelievably* rare

and may also lose its utility in time.

Indefinite pronoun

See **Pronoun** and pages 292–294.

Independent clause

See **Clause.**

Indirect object

See **Object.**

Indirect quotation

We use indirect quotations when we attribute a remark without claiming to use exact words and without using quotation marks.

> The congressman from Ohio then claimed that he had heard enough.
> She said that Herbert was the nicest boy she had ever met.

When we indirectly quote information taken from a source, we should footnote it just as we would a direct quotation.

Inductive reasoning

This form of thought draws general conclusions from particular examples or evidence.

> As a result of these experiments we conclude that if water temperature falls below 32 degrees the water will freeze.

Infer, imply

We *infer* or understand from what a speaker or writer *implies* to us. *Infer* means "conclude"; *imply* means "suggest."

> From the tone of her voice on the telephone, I *inferred* her terror. She *implied* that she had seen a face at the window.

We cannot say that another person *inferred* something to us. He or she *implied* it, and we *inferred* a meaning in the implication.

Inferior to, inferior than

Inferior than is incorrect. Say either *inferior to* or *worse than.*

Infinitive

See **Verbal.**

Inflection

Inflection is the change in the form of a word to indicate a change in meaning or grammatical relationship. The inflection of nouns and pronouns is called *declension;* of verbs, *conjugation;* and of adjectives and adverbs, *comparison.*

Inflection of nouns indicates *number* and *case.*

> aardvark, aardvarks, aardvark's, aardvarks'; man, men, man's men's

Inflection of pronouns indicates *case, person,* and *number.*

> she, her, hers; who, whom, whose; they, them, their

Inflection of verbs indicates *tense, person,* and *mood.*

> laugh, laughing, laughs, laughed
> spring, springing, springs, sprung

Inflection of modifiers indicates *comparison* and *number.*

> thin, thinner, thinnest
> this dog, that dog, these dogs, those dogs

In regard to, in regards to

In regard to is preferable. The good stylist rewrites to avoid either. Instead of

> In regard to your letter of May 9 . . .

we might say

> Answering your letter of May 9 . . . .

Intensive pronoun

See **Pronoun.**

Intransitive verb

An intransitive verb neither has an object nor is passive in form.

> I *was* at Annette's house in Santa Fe at the time.
> Quaker *has been waiting* on the flagpole for hours.

Irony

Intentional irony is a conscious statement intended to convey the opposite of what it seems to say. It can be used humorously; it can be gentle or sarcastic and biting. We can say that the weather is marvelous when we are standing in a downpour. Our irony is obvious. When Jonathan Swift wrote "A Modest Proposal," he suggested that

Irish babies be slaughtered and eaten, as a convenience to the English. He did not intend the suggestion literally. Most of his readers perceived his irony.

Irregardless

Use *regardless*. *Irregardless* is a redundancy, made in error on the model of *irrespective*.

Italics

See pages 311–312.

Its, it's

It's always stands for *it is*. *Its* is a possessive.
It's eating *its* supper.
See pages 297–298.

-ize verbs

Avoid making new verbs ending in *-ize,* like *"tomato-ize* the spaghetti." Avoid using some recent coinages too: *utilize* (say "use"), *personalize, finalize, prioritize.*

Jargon

Jargon is the argot of a profession, or a peer group, like educators or astronauts or rock musicians. Businesspersons fall into a jargon frequently. Sometimes they *firm up* a deal before they *finalize* it. Sometimes two negotiators are not *in the same ballpark;* one of them, however, may *come out of left field.*

Slang makes jargon too, and every campus—every year, every term—invents a local dialect of student jargon.

Jargon is a language by which we attempt to prove that *we* are the initiated and to keep noninitiates in confusion and befuddlement. It is language not to communicate but to exclude.

Jargon has a real purpose when it is the precise shorthand of a science. But for most of us most of the time, jargon has a tendency to be considerably vaguer than the larger language we share.

Kind of

This phrase is misused, and even used properly is often not helpful. When we say *"kind of* big" we are qualifying *big,* as if we said *"rather* big." It is a misuse of the word *kind. Kind* means species.

It is a *kind of* pine tree.

This usage works, but we often slide into vague species-making

She is a *kind of* blonde I can't stand.

The sentence cannot be rewritten; it must be rethought. What exactly is it that you cannot stand? Name it.

I do not like a blonde who has red eyebrows.

The same remarks apply to *sort of.*

Lay, lie

Lay/laid/laid, meaning to put or place, applies to the following uses: "she *lays* an egg"; "you *laid* the book on the table"; "I *laid* my pen on this pad." *Lay* takes a direct object. The past tense of *lie* is *lay,* which is a source of confusion. *Lie/lay/lain,* meaning to rest or recline, applies to these uses: I *lie* on the grass; she *lay* on the bed all day; we *had lain* in the sun. *Lie* never takes a direct object.

Lead, led

Lead is present tense, *led* is past, and *lead*—when pronounced like *led*—is the metal.

> Yesterday I *led* the class.
> Today I *lead* the escape.

Leave, let

Leave means "to go away"; *let* means "to allow."

> *Leave* me. (Go away from me.)
> *Let* me. (Allow me to.)
> *Leave* me out. (Don't include me.)
> *Let* me out. (Allow me to go.)

Less

This word is frequently misused where *fewer* would be correct.

> There are *less* flowers in the vase today.

should be

> There are *fewer* flowers in the vase today.

Fewer refers to actual numbers; *less* refers to quantity in general.

> The powerful nations are *fewer* than they used to be.
> Nations have *less* power.

Lie, lay

See **Lay, lie.**

Like, as

See **As, like.**

Likewise

This expression is a clumsy transition, almost always a piece of bone in the hamburger.

Linking verb

A linking verb expresses the relationship between the subject and the predicate noun or predicate adjective. The principal linking verbs are *appear, be, become, seem,* and verbs used for sensations *(feel, smell, sound, taste, look).*

> Lorca *is* magnificent.
> Rose *became* a mother.

Joe *looks* sick.
The steak *smells* rotten.

Literally

We often say *literally* when we mean the opposite: *figuratively*. We use a metaphor, but we realize that it is dead and we play Dr. Frankenstein to the monster by applying the cathodes of *literally* (or *literal*).

She was *literally* as big as a house.
He was a *literal* man of straw.
He hit the ball *literally* a thousand miles.

The monster never walks. Use *literally* only to emphasize that you mean just what you say.

When the police broke into the warehouse, they found
the prime minister *literally* weeping tears of gratitude.

Literal means "according to the letter" or "as it actually appears." Never use it unless you mean it literally. When you find yourself misusing it for the purposes above, you can either omit it and settle for the corpse of your metaphor, or you can make a new metaphor, "She was as big as . . . ."

Litotes

Litotes is a figure of speech understating something by saying the negative of its opposite. Saying "It's not a beauty" may mean "It's ugly."

Little

Often we misuse this word—which is necessary to common speech in its literal meaning—as a vague qualifier.

He's a *little* late.

We misuse *pretty* in the same way, without considering its meaning. James Thurber tormented his editor on *The New Yorker* by writing that something was "a little big" and "pretty ugly."

Logic

See **Deductive reasoning** and **Inductive reasoning.** See also pages 220–250 for some remarks about persuasion and an account of some common errors in thinking.

For further reading, consult Manuel Bilsky's *Patterns of Argument.*

Loose, lose

Different spellings make different words.

The dog is *loose.*
I *lose* the dog.
The *loose* rope *loses* the dog.

Lot, lots

These are informal substitutes for other quantitative words: *a great many, a number of.* Avoid in formal writing.

Mad, angry

Mad means "crazy" or "insane," but popular speech has made it synonymous with *angry*: "I'm *mad* at you" means "I'm *angry* with you." Use *angry* in formal writing.

Main clause

A *main clause* can stand by itself. It can be a whole, simple sentence.

They built an armadillo.

Two *main clauses* can make a compound sentence.

They built an armadillo and they traded it for a VW.

In a complex sentence, the main clause (in italics) governs a subordinate clause.

When night fell, *they built an armadillo.*

Man who . . .

A common circumlocution uses a noun (like *man* or *woman* or *person* or *senator* or *typist*) in a relative clause when the extra words serve no function.

He was *a man who* drank half a bottle of scotch before breakfast.
She was *a woman who* knew better.
She was *a senator who* always filibustered.

If this last sentence gave us the information that she was a senator, it would be justified.

He was *a typist who* never typed more than twenty-seven words a minute.

These sentences can become

He drank half a bottle of scotch before breakfast.
She knew better.
She always filibustered.
He never typed more than twenty-seven words a minute.

Manuscript form

See pages 314–315.

May, can

See **Can, may.**

Metaphor

See pages 115–118.

Mixed constructions

Avoid sentences that begin as if they will follow one form, switch forms, and become mixed and confusing. Do not say

Because the annual snowfall reaches 80 inches causes everybody to keep a supply of food.

This example uses a dependent clause as a subject. It could be repaired into

> Because the annual snowfall reaches 80 inches, everyone keeps a supply of food.

Here is a mixed construction in which an adverb clause is used as a noun.

> A Fourth of July celebration is when you have fireworks and picnics.

This can be changed to

> At a Fourth of July celebration, you have fireworks and picnics.

Modifier

Any word or group of words that describes or qualifies another word or group of words is a modifier.

For a general account of adjectives, adverbs, and other modifiers, see pages 104–110. For attention to some problems common in the use of modifiers, see pages 295–297.

Momentary, momentous

Momentary has to do with time. It refers to something that lasts only a moment or happens at any moment. *Momentous* means of extraordinary importance, as in the cliché "a *momentous* occasion."

> The affliction was *momentous.*
> She looked west, awaiting his *momentary* arrival.

Mood

The mood (or mode) of the verb indicates an attitude on the part of the writer. The mood may be indicative, imperative, or subjunctive. The *indicative* mood states a fact or asks a question.

> Jim Rice *is* here.
> *Was* Bill Walton there?

The *imperative* mood gives a command, gives directions, or makes a request.

> *Beware* of the darkness.
> *Turn* right at Golgotha.
> *Mend* my parachute, please.

The *subjunctive* mood expresses uncertainty, contradiction, wishfulness, regret, or speculation. It is the most common in contrary-to-fact clauses beginning with *if* ("If it *were* possible, I would fly") and after certain verbs such as *move* ("I move that the meeting *be* postponed") and *demand* ("They demand that the bail *be* fixed").

Morale, moral

Moral is a matter of ethics, *morale* of high or low spirits.

> Their *morals* were low, but their *morale* was high.

Murder is not a *moral* act, usually.

Ms.

A recently invented title, on the analogy of *Mr., Mrs.,* and *Miss, Ms.* reveals female gender while it conceals marital status.

Myself

Do not use *myself* as a substitute for *I* or *me.* Do not say

Richard and *myself* went to the circus.
The elephant paused a few yards downwind from *myself.*

Do say

Richard and *I* went to the circus.
The elephant paused a few yards downwind from *me.*

Narration

Narration is writing that tells a story in a connected series of events.

N.B.

This common abbreviation from the Latin means "Notice well!" and draws our attention to something.

Neither

See **Either.**

Neologism

A neologism is a made-up word, often used out of laziness or affection when an old word would do. *Finalize* is a neologism; *end* or *finish* are the old words.

None

None can be either singular or plural, depending on context and intention.

None of the other guys *were* going to the game.
None of his fellow senators *was* likely to take so strong a stand on the war.

Nonrestrictive modifier

A nonrestrictive modifier is a parenthetical expression that does not limit the noun or pronoun modified. It can be a nonrestrictive clause:

The Buick, *which was a car new to my neighborhood,* was the object of fascination.

or a phrase:

The banana, *a fruit new to our taste,* was divided evenly.

No one, nobody

These words take a singular verb. Third-person pronouns, singular and plural, can refer to them: *he, his, him, she, hers, her, they, them.* We use *they* and *them* when we feel that the gender of the pronoun would be invidious.

Not un–

    Eschew the habit of writing *not un-'s.*

> A *not un*distinguished gentleman, in a *not un*elegant dinner jacket, *not un*gracefully strode past the *not un*chic lady.

Noun

    There are several types of nouns. *Common nouns* belong to one of a class of people, places, or things *(woman, country, table)*. *Proper* nouns are names of specific people, places, or things. *(Max von Sydow, Liv Ullmann, Casablanca, Ann Arbor, Statue of Liberty)*. *Concrete* nouns name something that can be perceived by the senses *(acid, trees, eggs, horses)*. *Abstract* nouns name a general idea or quality *(terror, love, harshness, agony)*. *Collective* nouns refer to a group as a unit *(band, team, council, league)*. These categories are not mutually exclusive; a word like *tree* is common and concrete.

    Nouns, whatever their functions in a sentence, retain their basic form, varying it only in forming the plural and the possessive. The plural of most nouns is formed by adding *-s* to the singular, the possessive by adding an apostrophe and an *-s* to the singular or an apostrophe after the *-s* of the plural: *hen, hens, hen's, hens'; house, houses, house's, houses'.* Some nouns add *-es* for the plural: *hero, heroes, hero's, heroes'.* A few nouns change their internal spelling for the plural: *man, men; woman, women;* here, the possessive is formed by an apostrophe and an *-s*, in singular and in plural *(man's, men's).* Other nouns with an irregular plural are listed on page 316.

    For stylistic advice about nouns, see pages 96–102.

Nouns commonly used as blanks

    Many nouns, which are perfectly useful when spoken with care, are frequently used imprecisely, wordily, and without utility—nouns used as blanks: *aspect, case, character, factor, fact, field, element, effect, experience, nature, manner, respect, situation,* and *feature.*

> Some *aspects* in the *case* of Rumpelstiltskin have the *character* of *elements* that seem sinister in *nature*. The *fact* that the enraged dwarf was a *factor* in the *nature* of the King's *manner* is a *feature* with *respect* to which we can not distinguish the *effect.*

This paragraph has the consistency of mud or an annual report.

Noun substitute

    A noun substitute, whether clause or phrase or pronoun, functions as a noun.

Number

    See **Inflection.**

Numeral

    See page 315.

Object

A complete sentence needs a subject and a verb; it need not have an object.

The cat screeched.

is a complete sentence.

The cat clawed *Herbert*.

includes an object. An object is something a verb acts upon.

Objects are direct and indirect. A *direct object* is any noun (or noun substitute) that answers the question "What?" or "Whom?" after a transitive verb. Direct objects are the objects of the verb's action.

She toppled *the giant*.
He knows *what she wants*.

An *indirect object* is a noun or noun substitute that is indirectly affected by the verb's action and that tells *to whom* or *for whom* the action is done.

She gave *him* a karate chop.

Him is the indirect object, *karate chop* the direct object.

Object complement

See **Complement.**

Of

We often use *of* when we don't have to.

outside *of* the house
off *of* the ground
inside *of* the room

The phrases read more stylishly as

outside the house
off the ground
inside the room

Keep the *of* when the extra preposition changes meaning. *Outside of* can mean "to the exclusion *of*," and we are correct to say "Outside *of* scientific speculation, there is no use for such calibration." *Inside of* can mean "in less than." "Inside *of* an hour, he had finished the work."

One of the most . . .

This cliché is drained of meaning.

She is *one of the most* lovable people in the world.
The rodeo was *one of the most* exciting experiences of my life.

If you use this phrase, cross it out and consider the particulars to which you refer. One example, showing the character *being* lovable, is worth ten thousand assertions. An exciting anecdote from the rodeo makes assertion unnecessary. Show, don't tell.

One, you

Be careful not to use *one* in place of *you* so much that it sounds awkward or pretentious.

Should *one* be careful to avoid the use of the word "one"
when *one* is speaking to a woman whom *one* loves?

As suggested by this example, context is important when you consider using *one*. It is useful at times, but it has a way of seeming affected. Never use it as an obvious disguise for *I.*

One took an amusing jaunt to Cedar Point last summer.

Finally, be careful not to mix *one* and *you* or *I* in the same sentence.

Parallelism

See pages 153–162.

Parentheses

See pages 311–312.

Participle

See **Verbal.**

Passive voice

A verb is in the passive voice when it *acts upon* the subject.

LeFlore *was hit* by the pitch.

See **Active voice.**

Period

See page 299.

Person

In grammar, the person of a verb or a pronoun shows that someone is speaking (in *first person*) or is spoken to *(second person)* or is spoken about *(third person)*. In *I see, you see, he sees,* the person of the pronoun changes each time; the verb form of the first person and the second person happens to be the same, but the verb form changes to indicate the third person. With a few verbs, the form changes with each change of person (I *am,* you *are,* he *is*).

Phrase

Phrases function as a part of speech and do not have a subject and a predicate.

Infinitive phrase: I studied *to learn Greek.*
Prepositional phrase: The flower grows *in the mountain.*
Verb phrase: The zebra *is catching up.*
Participial phrase: Sliding into second, Zarido tore a ligament.

Plagiarism

Plagiarism is stealing another person's work, whether it is a published source used without acknowledgment or a friend's old paper or a term paper bought from a pirate.

Possessive

For the possessive of nouns, see **Noun.** For the possessive of pronouns, see **Pronoun.**

Precede, proceed

To *precede* is to "go before" or "in front of."

The Pirates *preceded* the Reds onto the field.

To *proceed* is to "continue" or to "begin again."

After the game, they *proceeded* to the airport.

Predicate

A predicate is the part of the sentence *about* the subject. It includes verbs and, on occasion, adverbs, direct objects, indirect objects, and clauses attached to the predicate. See pages 126–127.

Predicate adjective

See **Complement.**

Predicate noun

See **Complement.**

Preposition

Prepositions show the relationship between a noun or noun equivalent and another word in the sentence. Some of the most commonly used prepositions are *across, after, at, behind, between, by, for, from, of, on, over, to, under,* and *with.*

Tom hid *in* the attic.

The preposition *in* relates the noun *attic* to the verb *hid.*

Presently

This word means "in a little while," not "now" or "currently." Say

He is *at present* a milkman.

not

He is *presently* a milkman.

But say

He will come back to Chicago *presently.*

Pretty

See **Little.**

Principal, principle

Principle is a noun meaning a general truth (the *principles* of physics) or moral ideas (she had the highest *principles*). The adjective *principal* means "the foremost." One could speak of the *principal principle* of a science or a philosophy. The noun *principal* means the chief officer.

Alex Emerson is the *principal* of Bob's school.

Pronoun

A pronoun is a word used in place of a noun

Personal pronouns: I, you, he, she, we, etc.
Relative pronouns: who, which, that
Demonstrative pronouns: this, that, these, those
Indefinite pronouns: each, either, any, some, someone, all, etc.
Reciprocal pronouns: each other, one another
Reflexive, or intensive, pronouns: myself, yourself, etc.

For pronoun usage, subject and object, see **He, him.**

Proper noun

See **Noun.**

Prophesy, prophecy

The word with the *s* is the verb, the word with the *c* the noun.

The priest *prophesied* doom.
It was an accurate *prophecy.*

Proved, proven

Proved is the regular past participle form of *prove* and is preferred in American usage. *Proven* is a Scottish version of the participle, sometimes found in current usage.

Punctuation

See pages 299–312.

Quotation marks

See page 307.

Rational, rationale

Rational means "reasonable and sensible." It is an adjective. *Rationale* is a noun meaning "the whole system of reasons behind an idea, a position, or an action."

His arguments were *rational.*
Her *rationale* for the program was easy to discern.

Real, really

Conversational usage accepts *real* as an adverb, but it will not do in writing. Write

The boat was *really* handsome!
Josephine seemed to be a *really* happy girl.

Don't write

The boat was *real* handsome.
Josephine seemed to be a *real* happy girl.

Real as an adjective survives.

It was a *real* boat.

Frequently, we use *real* and *really* as weak intensifiers, but our sentences will be stronger without them.

Reason is because, reason why

Don't use these constructions. If you must use *reason is,* have it be *"reason is that . . ."*

Relative clause

See **Subordinate clause.**

Relative pronoun

See **Pronoun.**

Respectfully, respectively

Respectfully is an adverb that modifies an action full of respect.

I remain, yours *respectfully*

Respectively pertains to each of a number, in an order.

He swore that he saw Ted and Joan wearing a flower and a bowler, *respectively.*

Therefore to end a letter "Yours *respectively*" makes no sense.

Restrictive modifier

A restrictive modifier is a clause or a phrase essential to the identity of what is modified.

Everybody *who wants* can get to the top.

See **Nonrestrictive modifier** for contrast.

Rhetoric

Rhetoric is the art of discourse, either spoken or written. The use of *rhetoric* to mean "inflated or exaggerated speech" is recent.

The politician's promises were mere *rhetoric.*

Rhetorical question

The rhetorical question is a frequent device of argument or persuasion. We ask a question, not to be answered but to affect the listener or reader.

Are we born, to suffer and to die, only to satisfy the whims of rich warmongers?
Must we write themes forever?

Run-on sentence

A run-on sentence fuses two sentences.

I was eight my brother was ten.

is a run-on or fused sentence. It should read

I was eight. My brother was ten.

Satire

Satire is a form of literature, either prose or poetry, that uses ridicule to expose and to judge behavior or ideas that the satirist finds foolish or wicked or both.

Seldom ever

This phrase is redundant. *Seldom* will do. Instead of

He *seldom ever* brushed his hair.

say

He *seldom* brushed his hair.

Semantics

Semantics is the study of the meanings and associations of words. A good book on semantics is S. I. Hayakawa, *Language in Thought and Action.*

Semicolon

See pages 304–305.

Sensual, sensuous

The two words have different meanings. *Sensual* has unfavorable connotations and means "preoccupied with or inclined to the gratification of the senses or appetites."

He was wholly *sensual* in his priorities; his gluttony came first.

Sensuous has complimentary connotations and describes things that give pleasure to the senses.

The passage is one of the most *sensuous* in all literature.

Sentence fragment

See pages 132–134 and 284–286.

Sentence types

See **Compound-complex sentence, Compound sentence, Complex sentence,** and **Simple sentence.**

Shall, will

In common speech and most writing, we make small distinction between *shall* and *will.* Formally, *I shall* expresses a person's belief about his future.

I shall be twenty-one in December.

I will expresses his will power, his wish.

I will get to Japan before I die!

She/her

See **He, him.**

Should have, should of

The words are *should have,* which can be pronounced *should've. Should of* does not make sense.

Should, would

Should expresses obligation.

You *should* be ashamed.

It is confused with *would* when it is used in other senses.

I *should* not have reached Chicago without your loan.

When we use the past of *shall* in an indirect quotation, formal prose requires *should* instead of *would*.

I said that you *should* be ready before eight.

Would commonly expresses habitual activities.

He *would* visit the lake and fish from dawn to dusk.

When another phrase (like "every summer," if it were added to the last sentence) expresses habit, we can drop the *would* and use the past tense alone.

He visited the lake every summer and fished from dawn to dusk.

Sic

Pronounced "sick," this Latin word appears in quotations, enclosed in brackets, to signify that an error was made in the source material, not by the writer copying the quotation.

Studebaker writes, "I would rather be Thoreu [*sic*] unhappy than a contented pig."

Simile

Simile is a figure of speech in which comparison is openly made, usually by *like* or *as*.

He walks *like* a turkey.
The fabric was soft *as* a baby's bottom.

Simple sentence

A simple sentence has one main clause and no subordinate clauses.

She barked at the full moon.

See pages 129–130.

Slang

Slang is the special, idiosyncratic vocabulary or jargon associated with a culture or subculture. Slang words have been absorbed into English from various ethnic groups ("Fred is such a *klutz*, his career is *kaput*"), from sports ("It's your *ballgame*"), and most recently from technology ("I asked him to give me some *input* on that"). Most slang is short-lived. Avoid using it in formal prose.

So

This word is a stylistic pitfall for many beginning writers. As a coordinating conjunction, *so* is often boring and repetitious, leading the writer into dull compound sentences.

> She was tall *so* he asked her how she liked the weather up there.
> She was tired of hearing that question *so* she knocked him flat.

As a vague intensive, *so* is as useless as *wonderful* and *terrible* though it occupies less space.

> The building was *so* tall.
> I am *so* glad to see you!

Sort of

> See **Kind of.**

Spelling

> See pages 316–317.

Split infinitive

> An infinitive is the form of the verb that uses *to,* as in *to run, to think, to scratch.* When we place another word (commonly an adverb) in the middle of an infinitive, we are splitting the infinitive.

> to *quickly* run
> to *occasionally* think
> to *from time to time* scratch

Grammarians used to insist that the infinitive never be split.
People split them anyway.

> Remember *to never split* the infinitive!

Now, most grammarians consider a prohibition against split infinitives fussy. But careful writers rarely split them.

Stationary, stationery

> *Stationary* is an adjective that means "standing still." *Stationery* means "writing materials."

Style

> See especially Chapters 4–6. See also William Strunk and E. B. White, *The Elements of Style;* Bergen Evans, *A Dictionary of Contemporary American Usage;* and *A Dictionary of Modern English Usage* by H. W. Fowler, rev. and ed. by Sir Ernest Gowers. See also *The Modern Stylists,* ed. by Donald Hall, a collection of essays and excerpts by George Orwell, Ernest Hemingway, Ezra Pound, Edmund Wilson, James Thurber, and others.

Subject

> A subject is a noun, or a noun substitute, about which something is stated or questioned. The subject usually comes before the predicate. The complete subject is the subject and all the words (modifiers, etc.) that belong to it.

> *The grinning barbarian, his teeth clenched,* looked into the barnyard.

Barbarian is the simple subject; the first six words make the complete subject.

Subjunctive

    See

Subordinate clause

    A subordinate (or dependent) clause cannot stand by itself and make a whole sentence. It depends on a main clause.

> I cannot see *who it is.*
> The claws are not lethal *because he was declawed.*

Substantive

    A *substantive* is a word or group of words used as a noun; it may be a noun, pronoun, phrase, or noun clause.

Suppose, supposed

    The past tense often disappears, and meaning disappears with it. See **Used to, use to.**

Syntax

    Syntax is the way in which words are put together to form larger units, phrases, clauses, or sentences. It is also the part of grammar that describes this putting together.

Tense

    The tense of a verb shows the time in which an action takes place. In the preceding sentence, *shows* is in the present tense. In

> I *showed* you.

showed is in the past tense.

> I *will show* you.

uses the future tense.

That, which, who

    We use the word *that* in a number of ways. It is a demonstrative, as in "*that* cat." Many writers are confused about when to use *that* and when to use *which* in introducing clauses. Nonrestrictive (nondefining) clauses take *which.*

> The old car, *which* was struggling through the winter, seemed younger when spring arrived.

When the clause is restrictive or defining, we use *that* when it is possible, which is most of the time.

> The old car *that* Mr. Hornback owned was struggling up the hill.

Which is possible in this last sentence, but it seems overprecise or rigid and is stylistically inferior. However, when a sentence requires several restrictive clauses in a row, *that* can become confusing, and we had better revert to *which.*

> The old car *which* Mr. Hornback owned, *which* had one headlight dangling loose, and *which* smelled perpetually of gasoline chugged struggling up the hill.

Remember that *who* applies to people, whether the clause is restrictive or nonrestrictive, and *which* never applies to people.

The folks *which* lived next door.

is incorrect. Some writers, informally, substitute *that* for *who* on occasions when the person is seen as if from a distance.

The man *that* stood outside the door was tall and fortyish.

Their, there, they're
See pages 305–306.

Then
In a familiar balance, within a sentence, we use *then* after *if.*

If statistics imply the opposite, *then* the statistics are incorrect.

Then, than
These words are different in spelling, meaning, and function. *Then* refers to time, and *than* makes a comparison.

We were nice *then.*
She was taller *than* he was.

They, them
See **He, him.**

Through, thru
Thru is incorrect, merely a labor-saving device, adopted by sign painters, advertisers, and the fabricators of headlines.

To, too, two
These homonyms are sometimes confused. *Two* is only a number. *Too* is only an excess (*too* much is *too* much). *To* is a preposition (I handed the book *to* Geronimo) or part of an infinitive (*to* be or not *to* be ...).

Toward, towards
Either is possible. *Toward* is more American, *towards* more British.

Transitive verb
A transitive verb *must* have a direct object to fill out its meaning.

He *put the book* down.

Book is the direct object of the transitive verb *put.*

Try and
Try and see if she's home.

is a long way to say

See if she's home.

Type
Type is another word to stay away from. Even used grammatically, it is usually filler.

It was a strange *type* of animal.

boils down nicely to

It was a strange animal.

Occasionally, as with *sort* or *kind,* we actually mean something by the word.

Never use it next to a noun, without the preposition *of* coming between. It is useless to say:

a new *type* soft drink	their *type* business
a long *type* Buick	that *type* handsomeness

In all these examples, an *of* would make the phrases more acceptable; but in the first three, omission of *type* would be the better solution. We save a word. In the fourth example, the idea of *type* (or *sort* or *kind*) has more meaning, but could benefit from greater specificity.

Unthinkable, inconceivable

Something that is literally *unthinkable* is probably literally unmentionable. We use *unthinkable* as hyperbole, usually to describe something that we deplore.

His conduct was *unthinkable.*

Inconceivable means "impossible to imagine or explain."

Her absence was *inconceivable.*

Until, till

We say *till,* but we write *until. Till* looks stilted and literary on the page.

Used to, use to

The correct form is *used to.*

I *used to* see her every morning at nine o'clock.

Probably because of our slovenly pronunciation, we sometimes drift into

I *use to* see her every morning at nine o'clock.

when we write it down. We should use the correct form to make temporal sense. The same is true of *supposed to.*

Verb

For advice on style and the verb, see pages 89–94. Also see **Active voice, Intransitive verb, Mood, Object, Passive voice, Predicate,** and **Transitive verb.**

Verbal

Verbals are words derived from verbs but used as nouns or adjectives and sometimes as adverbs. Verbals are *gerunds, participles,* and *infinitives. Gerunds* always end in *-ing* and are used as nouns.

Flying is fun.

> *Running* is good exercise.
> Neal and Liz have benefited from their *running*.

Participles (past and present) are used as adjectives.

> This *flying* manual is essential.
> His *shattered* hip was mending slowly.
> "The *rising* cost of living" is a common phrase.

Infinitives are used primarily as nouns, but sometimes as adjectives or adverbs. They are composed of *to* and a verb.

> We started *to run* from Godzilla.
> *To fail* is a pleasure he can't afford.
> He dropped out *to begin* his career as a clown.

Vocative
> See **Direct address.**

We, us
> See **He, him.**

When
> Don't use *when* as an introduction to definitions.

> Loneliness is *when* you play the radio just to hear the announcer's voice.

You could say instead

> You are lonely *when* you play the radio just to hear the announcer's voice.

or

> It is a definition of loneliness to play the radio just to hear the announcer's voice.

Where
> See **When.** The same injunction applies.

Which, that
> See **That, which, who.**

While
> The word means "at the same time" or "during the time that." Sometimes writers use it in place of *although,* and it can work.

> *While* John is large, his stomach is not excessive.

But this usage is prone to ambiguity.

> Winter is warm in the southern hemisphere, *while* summer is cold.

Think about this sentence for a moment; it is absurd.

Who, whom
> *Who* is a subject, *whom* an object.

Who is on first?
To whom should I deliver the testimony?

In the last sentence, *whom* is the object of the preposition *to*. In formal writing, always say *whom* when it is an object—of a verb or of a preposition.

Sometimes position leads us into error. When a pronoun precedes a verb, it sounds as if it were a subject; it isn't always. We may be tempted to write

From *who* is the noise coming?

but the phrase is *from whom,* and *the noise* (not *who*) is the subject of *is.* We should write

From *whom* is the noise coming?

Sometimes a clause separates the subject *who* from its verb, and we misuse *whom* for *who.* We write

Herbert, *whom* she said would be here at 6:30, strolled in at 8:00.

In this sentence the three noun-verb combinations make a box within a box within a box. "Herbert . . . strolled" is the outside box, "who . . . would be here" is the middle box, and "she said" the inside box.

When *whom* comes before a preposition of which it is the object, it is correct but highly formal.

Whom am I looking at?

Here, we always write *who* in informal writing. Frequently, *whom* will sound too formal even in an essay that is mostly formal. Use your judgment. The position of the pronoun makes the problem, which comes up when it is the object of a verb as well as when it is the object of a preposition.

Whom do I see?
Who do I see?

The first is correct and the second incorrect—technically—but it would take a highly formal context to accept the "correct" form without creating a moment of stuffiness.

Whose, who's

See pages 305–306.

-wise

Stylewise, avoid this syllable in combination with words with which it has not been combined before. *Clockwise* and *otherwise* are parts of the language. Avoid *literarywise, poetrywise, intelligence quotientwise, Septemberwise, costwise, Sallywise, ecologywise*—and anything similar.

Woman, women

People sometimes forget that the two spellings show a difference in number. *Woman* is singular, *women* plural.

Acknowledgments

Martin Amis From *Visiting Mrs. Nabokov and other Excursions* by Martin Amis. Copyright © 1993 by Martin Amis. Reprinted by permission of Harmony Books, a division of Crown Publishers, Inc. *James Baldwin* From *Notes of a Native Son* by James Baldwin. Copyright © 1995, renewed 1983, by James Baldwin. Reprinted by permission of Beacon Press, Boston. *Robert Benchley* From "My Face" by Robert Benchley from *The Benchley Roundup, A Selection* by Nathaniel Benchley. Copyright 1938 by Robert C. Benchley. Copyright renewed. Reprinted by permission of HarperCollins Publishers, Inc. *Annie Dillard* From *Pilgrim at Tinker Creek*. New York: HarperCollins, 1974. *George Gilder* From "But What About Welfare's Grim Side?" by George Gilder from *The New York Times,* April 22, 1984. Copyright © 1984 by The New York Times Company. Reprinted by permission. *Elizabeth Hardwick* Quotation from "Boston: The Lost Ideal" in *The Penguin Book of Contemporary American Essays* (New York: Viking Penguin, 1959). *Edward Hoagland* From "Walking the Dog" by Edward Hoagland from *The New York Times,* April 17, 1979. Copyright © 1979 by The New York Times Company. Reprinted by permission; quotation from "The Courage of Turtles," from *The Courage of Turtles.* New York: Random House, 1970. *James D. Houston* Houston, James D., *The Men in My Life.* St. Paul MN: Graywolf Press, 1987, p. 178. *John G. Ives* From "Questionable Role of Law Review in Evaluating Young Lawyers" by John G. Ives, a letter to the editor of *The New York Times,* March 11, 1981. Copyright © 1981 by The New York Times Company. Reprinted by permission. *Randall Jarrell* Quotation from *A Sad Heart at the Supermarket: Essays and Fables* by Randall Jarrell. Copyright © 1962 by Randall Jarrell. Reprinted by permission. *Oliver Jensen* "The Gettysburg Address in Eisenhowese" by Oliver Jensen. Copyright © 1957 Oliver Jensen. Reprinted by permission of the author. *Andrew Kopkind* Excerpted from "U.S. To Critics: Keep Out!" by Andrew Kopkin, *The Nation,* April 28, 1984. Reprinted with permission from The Nation Magazine. Copyright © 1984 The Nation Company, L.P. *Phillip Lopate* Reprinted with the permission of Simon & Schuster from *Against Joie de Vivre* by Phillip Lopate. Copyright © 1989 by Phillip Lopate. *Mary McCarthy* Quotations excerpted from "America the Beautiful" in *On the Contrary.* Copyright © 1957, 1961 by Mary McCarthy. Reprinted by permission. *Antonio Machado* Quotation from *The Sea and the Honeycomb* by Antonio Machado, translated by Robert Bly. Copyright © 1971 by Robert Bly. Reprinted by permission. **Alberto Manguel** From *The History of Reading* by Alberto Manguel. Copyright © 1996 by Alberto Manguel. Used by permission of Penguin, a division of Penguin Books USA Inc. **Al Martinez** "Bad Luck Bob and His Dog" by Al Martinez from *Los Angeles Times.* Copyright © 1985 Los Angeles Times. Reprinted by permission. **Margaret Mead** From "Needed: Full Partnership for Women" by Margaret Mead. Courtesy of the Institute of Intercultural Studies, Inc., New York. **H. L. Mencken** From *The American Language.* New York: Alfred A. Knopf, Inc., 1936. **Mark Crispin Miller** From "The Lives of the Stars" from *Boxed In: The Culture of TV* by Mark Crispin Miller. Reprinted by permission of Northwestern University Press. **Susan Mitchell** Quotation from "Dreaming in Public: A Provincetown Memoir." Copyright © 1987 by Susan Mitchell. Reprinted by permission of the author. **V. S. Naipaul** From *The Return of Eva Perón with the Killings in Trinidad* by V. S. Naipaul. Copyright © 1980 by V. S. Naipaul. Reprinted by permission of Alfred A. Knopf, Inc., and Aitken & Stone Limited. **Michael Novak** Quotation from *Solzhenitsyn at Harvard: The Address, Twelve Early Responses, and Six Later Reflections,* edited by Ronald Berman, Ethics and Public Policy Center (1211 Connecticut Avenue, N.W., Washington, D.C. 20036), 1980. Reprinted by permission. **G. V. Perkins, Jr.** From "What's New in Agriculture?" by G. V. Perkins, Jr., *The New York Times,* March 25, 1984. Copyright © 1984 by The New York Times Company. Reprinted by permission. **Robert Pirsig** From *Zen and the Art of Motorcycle Maintenance* by Robert M. Pirsig. Copyright © 1974 by Robert Pirsig. Reprinted by permission of William Morrow & Co., Inc. **Katha Pollit** From *Reasonable Creatures* by Katha Pollitt. Copyright © 1994 by Katha Pollitt. Reprinted by permission of Alfred A. Knopf, Inc. **William Raspberry** ". . . and Men, Too" by William Raspberry from *The Washington Post.* Copyright © 1989 Washington Post Writers Group. Reprinted with permission. **Readers' Guide** Example of an entry in *Readers' Guide to Periodical Literature,* 1980. Copyright © 1980 by the H. W. Wilson Company. Reprinted by permission of H. W. Wilson Company. **Phyllis Rose** From "Shopping and Other Spiritual Adventures" by Phyllis Rose as appeared in *The New York Times,* April 12, 1984. Copyright © by The New York Times Company. Copyright © 1984 by Phyllis Rose, reprinted with the permission of The Wylie Agency, Inc. **Antoine de Saint-Exupéry** Excerpt from "Barcelona and Madrid" in *Wind, Sand and Stars,* copyright 1939 by Antoine de Saint-Exupéry and renewed 1967 by Lewis Galantière, reprinted by permission of Harcourt Brace & Company. **Scott Russell Sanders** "Under the Influence" by Scott Russell Sanders. Copyright © 1989 by Harper's Magazine. All rights reserved. Reproduced from the November issue by special permission. **Richard Selzer** From "The Knife" by Richard Selzer. Copyright © 1974 by Richard Selzer. Reprinted by permission of John Hawkins & Associates, Inc. **Shelby Steele** From *The Content of our Character: A New Vision of Race in America* by Shelby Steele. Copyright © 1990 by Shelby Steele. Reprinted by permission of St. Martin's Press Incorporated. **James Thurber** Copyright © 1959 by James Thurber. Copyright © 1987 by Rosemary A. Thurber. From *The Years with Ross* by James Thurber, published by Atlantic-Little, Brown. **Diane White** From "The Noble Asparagus" by Diane White from *The Boston Globe,* May 26, 1977. Reprinted courtesy of *The Boston Globe.* **James Q. Wilson and John J. DiIulio, Jr.** Quotation from "Crackdown" in *The New Republic,* July 10, 1989, pp. 21–25. Copyright © 1989 by The New Republic, Inc. Reprinted by permission.

Author and Title Index

Subject Index

big, 328, 346
as blanks, 85
collecting, 83–84
compound, 310–311, 332
foreign, 340
genteel, 341. *See also* Euphemism
histories of, 84, 339
insides of, 75–89
insides of; literalness and, 79–80
insides of; misusing, 81–83
insides of; sense words, 80–81
insides of; synonyms and, 77–79
loaded, 30, 82, 222, 234
order of, 296
original. *See* Originality
parallel construction and, 153–156
repetition of, 192–193
revising, 86–87
as smallest unit in writing, 75
sound and rhythm of, 36, 42–43
thinking with, 1–2

transitional, 194–195, 301
World Wide Web, 55, 256, 257–259, 265–266
Would, should, 358–359
Writing, 1–24. *See also* Essay writing
contact as reason for, 1–3
dishonest. *See* Cliché; Dishonest
expression
disorganized, 14–15
examples from print, 12–14
idea of audience in, 3, 47, 167
methods of learning, 15–19
pompous, 14–15, 168–169
purpose in, 46, 210–211
and reading, 12, 15–16, 25–26, 28–30
reasons for, 1
revisions in, 7–12
and rewriting. *See* Revision
sincerity in, 5–6

Yearbooks, 256
You, one, 354